"A BRILLIANT, RIVETING CONTRIBUTION TO THE ANNALS OF TRUE CRIME . . . A STORY SO CHILLING THAT YOU'LL WISH IT WERE FICTION."

—Professors Jack Levin and James Alan Fox,
Northeastern University, coauthors of
Mass Murder: America's Growing Menace

"FOR THOSE OF YOU WHO STILL IMAGINE THAT THERE IS NO SUCH THING AS UNDILUTED EVIL, READ *THE MISBEGOTTEN SON* AND HAVE YOUR DELUSIONS SURGICALLY CORRECTED. OLSEN'S WRITING GETS STRONGER AND MORE COMPELLING WITH EVERY BOOK."

—Carsten Stroud, author of *Lizard Skin* and *Close Pursuit*

"Arthur J. Shawcross is no smooth charmer of a sociopath, the sort of figure that's become almost comfortably familiar to us. This is a nightmare man, and his creepy story is spellbinding, enlightening, and—how does Jack Olsen do it?—hypnotically entertaining."

—Aaron Elkins, Edgar winner

"Jack Olsen has hammered home with a reality check on what serial murderers and serial murder investigations are really all about! Shawcross is absolutely the classic serial killer, and Olsen's in-depth and precise chronicle is superb!"

—Captain T. Michael Nault, Green River Serial Homicide
Investigation, King County Police, Washington

Also by Jack Olsen:

Predator: Rape, Madness, and Injustice in Seattle

"Doc": The Rape of the Town of Lovell

Cold Kill

Give a Boy a Gun

"Son": A Psychopath and His Victims

Have You Seen My Son?

Missing Persons

Night Watch

The Secret of Fire Five

Massy's Game

Alphabet Jackson

The Man with the Candy

The Girls in the Office

Slaughter the Animals, Poison the Earth

The Bridge at Chappaquiddick

Night of the Grizzlies

Silence on Monte Sole

"THE MISBEGOTTEN SON IS JACK OLSEN'S FINEST WORK TO DATE, NO SMALL ACHIEVEMENT FOR THE ACKNOWLEDGED DEAN OF AMERICAN TRUE-CRIME WRITERS."

—Michael Newton, author of *Silent Rage*

Praise for

*"The master of true crime"**

JACK OLSEN

And his spectacular best seller

THE MISBEGOTTEN SON

"THE MISBEGOTTEN SON is a terrifying, compelling exploration of the dark side of one man's mind. Olsen just gets better and better as a storyteller and chronicler of the evil aspects of man's nature."

—Harry N. MacLean, best-selling author of *In Broad Daylight*

"Without use of any clichés or labels, Olsen triumphs through vivid physical details and brilliant narrative organization. An important and enthralling book that conveys the misery without false pity for a human monster."

—Darcy O'Brien

"Jack Olsen's particular gift is his ability to illuminate the souls of his characters—both monsters and victims. *The Misbegotten Son* may very well be his finest book."

—Jonathan Kellerman

**Detroit Free Press*

Please turn the page for more extraordinary acclaim . . .

"JACK OLSEN TOOK ME SOMEPLACE I DEFINITELY DID NOT WANT TO BE: INSIDE THE MIND OF ARTHUR J. SHAWCROSS. THE TROUBLE WAS, I COULD NOT PUT OLSEN'S BOOK DOWN AND WHEN I FINALLY DID, THE STORY STAYED WITH ME. *THE MISBEGOTTEN SON* IS QUITE SIMPLY THE BEST BOOK ON THE MIND OF A SERIAL KILLER I HAVE EVER READ."

—Michael Weissberg, best-selling author of *The First Sin of Ross Michael Carlson*

"A DISTURBING, EXPERTLY DRAWN PORTRAIT of the face of horror that breathes beneath the mask of the commonplace."

—Nick Tosches, best-selling author of *Dino*

"*THE MISBEGOTTEN SON* is more than a typical case study. Victims and their families loom large in this true story, and the fascinating clinical report is a thorough and comprehensive analysis."

—Marvin E. Wolfgang, Professor of Criminology and of Law, University of Pennsylvania

"A WELL-CONSTRUCTED AND THOROUGHLY CONVINCING PSYCHOLOGICAL PORTRAIT."

—Philip Jenkins, Professor of Criminal Justice, Pennsylvania State University

THE MISBEGOTTEN SON

A SERIAL KILLER AND HIS VICTIMS

the True Story of Arthur J. Shawcross

JACK OLSEN

ISLAND BOOKS
Published by
Dell Publishing
a division of
Bantam Doubleday Dell Publishing Group, Inc.
1540 Broadway
New York, New York 10036

ISBN 0-440-21646-X

Reprinted by arrangement with Delacorte Press

Printed in the United States of America

Published simultaneously in Canada

October 1993

10 9 8 7 6 5 4 3 2 1

OPM

In memory of
Jack Owen Blake, Karen Ann Hill, Dorothy Blackburn,
Anna Steffen, Dorothy Keeler, Patricia Ives,
Frances M. Brown, June Stott, Elizabeth A. Gibson,
June Cicero, Maria Welch, Felicia Stephens,
and Darlene Trippi.

There is too much torment bottled up inside of me, too much anger that needs to be rid of! I should be castrated or have an electrode placed in my head to stop my stupidness or whatever. I just a lost soul looking for release of my maddness.

Please God, let someone help me.

—Arthur John Shawcross,
handwritten account, March 1990

I

MURDER IN THE NORTH COUNTRY

One of many quiet and pleasant towns in this area is Watertown, with a population of 33,000. Serious crime is virtually unheard of. The county jail rarely houses any prisoners charged with an offense more serious than being drunk and disorderly.

—*U.S. News & World Report,* 1967

1.

Mary Agnes Blake ran a salon of the poor: her own nine children, runaways, distant relatives, her alcoholic husband and his shiftless friends, anyone who dropped into the old frame house in the hollow. The percolator rattled all day, recharged with shoplifted coffee. She'd been called "Ma" since her early twenties.

"Long as I can remember," she explained, "I been lookin' after people. When I was five years old, I took care of the neighborhood kids so they wouldn't get hurt. That's why the Lord put me on earth, roit?"

Mary spoke unpretentious English, short on terminal *g*'s and long on the "North Country bray" heard from Albany to the St. Lawrence River. She spat her consonants and tortured her vowels: "brad" for bread, "cap" for cop, "mawney" for money, "coultn't," "fonny," "ten o'clack," "salad" for solid, "yaird" for yard. She preferred weak verbs: "runned," "borned," "buyed." She said "awright" and "ain't."

Sometimes her dead parents spoke through her mouth: "I'll be jiggered." "Shake a leg." "The bum's rush." "The cat's meow." Her everyday tone was brassy and nasal, not oppressively loud, but in heated discussions her voice became an industrial cutting tool. She refocused wandering attention by snapping "Roit?" and peering intently through her dark blue eyes. She seldom lost arguments or backed down.

In her mid-fifties, the matriarch stood an inch over five feet and weighed ninety-eight pounds, and since she seldom ate a full meal, she maintained a compact figure. Her disarming smile and sly Irish look suggested she was amused but not fooled. Her nose turned up; her skin was clear and her face unlined except for crinkles around her eyes. Through the years her hair had darkened to brown with streaks of gray. She wore it almost to her shoulders and didn't worry much about style. There was too much else to worry about.

2. MARY BLAKE

I was borned at home by a midwife on Thanksgiving Day of 1934 in Watertown, New York, thirty-five miles from the Canadian border. My mother said I was the biggest turkey she ever had. I was the thirteenth of fourteen kids: seven boys and seven girls.

My father's people, the Lawtons, were German, Irish, Indian, and French, and my mother's people, name of Litz, were mostly German; so us kids were mongrels. Folks called us "the black Lawtons"; I don't know if it was because we always lived around the Black River or it had somethin' to do with the Black Irish. Or maybe it was 'cause of the way we lived. Lots of times we had to steal to eat.

My dad started as a farmer in Lafargeville, a little place just north of Watertown toward Lake Ontario, but the land was too poor and he turned to bootlegging. They used to call this area "Little Chicago" when the whiskey come in from Canada. Even after Prohibition, people went to my dad's place to beat the taxes on booze. My father's grandfather was a English earl, and most of the Lawtons are well off and respectable today. They're the ones that never drop around.

I was my father's baby, but some of the other kids belonged to my mother's boyfriend Fred Burnham, even though my ma woultn't admit it. My dad drank and ran with other women and beat my mother. He finally moved into his own place on Factory Street and drank himself to death. I had plenty experience with alcoholism—it was on both sides of my family and in my own kids, too. If it ain't a disease, it'll do.

My ma raised the fourteen kids by herself in our wood house on Water Street. She let Fred Burnham move in; he wasn't even our stepfather, but he used to get drunk and hurt us. And when he wasn't drunk he stood us in the corner or made us kneel on rice. He comes in one night, lifts me up and slams me down on the woodstove. It's a good thing there was no fire.

When he got drunk my mother would herd us kids in the bedroom and wedge butter knives in the crack so he coultn't open the door. Soon as she come out, he'd beat her up, and if he spotted one of us kids, he'd go after us, too.

I never knew why my ma din't report him. In those days the caps were our friends; the chief of police used to visit. Caps patroled our street; they came into the house for coffee or just to warm their hands and feet on nights when the wind came from Lake Ontario to the north and your spit froze before it hit the ground. In the thirties, the law din't ride around in warm cars, roit?

Pollution from the factories finally killed my ma in 1970. Black Clawson made equipment for paper mills, and New York Air Brake made brakes for trains, and both of 'em sent out smoke and sparks. Clawson's foundry sounded like a rocket exhaust and lit up our neighborhood. We lived right under the stacks of those factories, and when I was a girl the noise never stapped—switch engines on the siding, heavy machinery, motors humming and buzzing, trucks in and out. Our house was set behind another house, as though the builder din't want folks to see our place from the street. The wet river air collected in my ma's lungs. Puffs of soot came off the maple leaves. The rain stained our clothes: we called it black rain. The smell was terrible. Oh, my Gad, a gray cloud hung over our neighborhood.

The Black River's no wider than a kid can throw a tennis ball, except where it's been dammed for water power, and it always stunk. Years after the last steam train come through, the river still ran with soot and coal dust from the paper mills that used to line both banks—thirty or forty of 'em all the way up to the Adirondacks, and only a handful left today. That's why there's never been enough work for the young people in Watertown—there's always another mill damping its boilers for good. You can see the ruined mills up and down the river—empty windows, walls falling against each other, piles of brick and wood. The Grand Hotel for rats and mice! Most folks moved away years ago. Me, I was borned here and I'll die here. My kids feel the same way. It stinks, it's noisy, it's unhealthy, it's home.

We always scratched for mawney, never had enough, still don't. When I was little, my mother used to fill a jug with water and hike through the woods to the dump on Bootjack Hill. Wore a bandana over her head so she woultn't get stroke. The dump stank from the slag brass, iron, capper, plate glass, paper, and wood—all fused together. Trucks from the Air Brake dumped hot loads, and six or eight people would start diggin' while it was still smokin'. My mother clawed her way into the bank till all we could see was the soles of her shoes—if the hole caved in she woulda been buried alive. She come out coughin' and sneezin', scorched her hair, burnt her hands, but she din't stop. My brothers filled barrels and rolled 'em to Abe Cooper, the junkman. His yard was down by the New York Central tracks that ran down Factory Street. My sister Nancy found a piece of slag brass that was so big it took a baby carriage to carry it. That was our biggest haul.

We seldom went hungry. If Ma had a bad day at the dump, she'd dig a kettle of dandelion greens for us, cook 'em with salt pork and splash some vinegar to perk up the taste. Or she'd pick wild strawberries for shortcake. My brothers snuck into farms and dug potatoes at night—the midnight harvest. They's worse-tasting things on earth than potatoes with salt pork grease. The farmers had millions of turkeys runnin' around, but they woultn't give you one if you was starvin' to death. Roland was one of the first turkey rustlers; sometimes he'd get more than we could eat and he'd sell 'em down at the restaurant on the corner and spend the mawney at the pool hall. He always had a story about how he got the turkeys, 'cause our mother was strict against stealing.

When I was ten, Roland come home with a hog and we butchered it in our kitchen. He told our ma he chased it down in the woods. Roland quit rustling after the State Police caught him and he was fined fifty bucks. That was more mawney than we'd ever seen, but he had to pay it or go to jail.

Rustling was in our blood, I guess. My favorite uncle, Earl Lawton, got himself runned out of Watertown for rustling cows. That was before my time. They had a warrant that if he ever set foot in Jefferson County they'd jail him on the spot.

Us younger kids din't steal much, but some of my brothers made up for us. Roland and Frederick grabbed any metal they could lay their hands on. They'd steal from tractor-trailers parked up on the boulevard—big boxes full of coffee, shampoo, hair oil, canned vegetables, sardines. My brother Junior was caught stealing a big mess of capper wire. He'd been a Ranger in World War Two, shot in the leg, had a Purple Heart, but he went to jail anyway.

Myself and my sisters, we robbed tomatoes from neighborhood gardens. Nothin' went to waste, not even the cores, roit? I was caught shaking an apple tree for my sister. The lady put a spotlight on me and I coultn't shinny down fast enough. My ma spanked hell out of me.

We din't get toys on Christmas, but we always had a good holiday meal. Before my dad died in the sanitarium, he would send mawney for me to go to a movie. Most of the time we managed to enjoy ourselfs. We were poor but we din't know no better. My mother hugged us and kissed us every day. All my life I worked hard and never minded a bit of it. The only way to live.

• • •

When I was seventeen, a girlfriend escorted me to The Question Mark, because Ma woultn't allow me to go anyplace without a chaperone. There were a lot of soldiers from Camp Drum, just north of town. After a while one of the sergeants come up and asked me to dance—a good-looking guy with blue eyes and brown hair and ribbons on his chest. His nose was crooked and it gave him a kind of offbeat look. He wasn't a six-footer but he had a nice compact body like a boxer or a construction worker. He told me his name was Allen Blake but to call him Pete. For an instructor with the ski troops, he was sure heavy on his feet. I coultn't wait for the dance to end.

Later that night my girlfriend said, "You know what he asked me about you? He said, 'What do you do when you fall in love at first sight?' "

My girlfriend said she warned him not to get fresh with me or nothin'. See, I was never touched. My mother always told me, "You let a boy mess with you, you'll get babies." And I went by what my mother told me, 'cause she spanked hard, roit?

Pete came to our house the next night and we talked. He told me he come from a rich family in Michigan. A piece of shrapnel broke his nose in Korea when he was with the Lost Regiment of the 190th Engineers and he got a Purple Heart and three battle stars. He was finishing out his hitch at Camp Drum, training a buncha tenderfeet that come into town and partied every night. Pete was proud of his looks, used to lay out in the sun and get a tan. Folks turned their heads when we walked in the public square.

I liked him, but I kept him at a distance. I said, "You're nat the only pebble on the beach, ya know." My girlfriends were doing things with boys and they told me how much fun it was. I let Pete kiss me but nothin' more.

Well, he wanted me bad. One night he drove right through the gates to visit me. The MPs took and shot at him, and he was busted to private. He told me that he din't care about nothin' in the world except me. He always had pocket mawney—whenever he was broke, he'd write his mother in Michigan and she'd send him a check. And if the mail was a little slow, he'd go out and rob something. He learnt how to steal from one of my brothers.

I finally let him do it to me after he promised it wouldn't hurt. But it hurt real bad. It wasn't nothing like what my girlfriends had described. I never enjoyed sex after that, not once. It was just something you did for the man.

By the time Pete finished his hitch, we'd been goin' out for two years. I was nineteen years old and six months pregnant. The night he was discharged he came to take me to the movies, and he had all his mustering-out pay, three hundred dollars. If ever there was a night he din't have to steal, it was that night. He'd gone shopping in the afternoon, and he was real proud of himself in civilian clothes.

We drove a few miles down the road and somethin' told me to get outta that car, so out of a clear blue sky I says, "Stap right here!" Gad has always been with me, right?

Pete said, "What for?"

"I just want out," I says.

He said, "Well, I'll give you a ride back home."

I said, "I ain't ridin' in that car for nothin'." He asked me why and I din't know. I swear, it was like the hand of the Lord reached down. Seven-thirty at night. Dark as the inside of a cow.

So Pete drove to town and I headed home. After a while I heard the ambulance. I thought, Oh, my Gad, Pete's got in a wreck!

It was dark and I was scared, so I ran home. I sat up all night worrying.

The next morning me and my mother heard some ladies talking up to Newberry's store. They said, "Oh, we seen a bad accident last night. This man was walkin' around with his arm hanging in shreds. They put a tourniquet on his arm."

My mother said, "Was he all by hisself?"

The woman says, "Yeah."

"What kind of car was it?"

"A coupe. With a rumble seat."

Me and Ma rushed to the haspital. They asked if I was his wife and I lied and said yes.

He was laying on the bed. "Oh, rub my arm," he says. "It hurts."

I seen he had no arm. I fainted.

What happened was, Pete ditn't go to the movies after I got out of his car. He drove straight to the Black River waterworks and grabbed some big heavy pipes. My brothers Fred and Roland used to steal water pipes and railroad tracks all the time, sell 'em for junk. Pete come from a 'vironment where he din't have to steal and fell into a 'vironment of thieves.

After he sold the stuff, he was drivin' back toward my house with his left arm restin' on the open window and he was sideswiped by a drunk driver.

Pete was charged with theft, but the judge said, "You paid enough for what you did." The state troopers coultn't believe one man lifted those pipes, but he was still in good shape from the army.

When my mother found out I was pregnant, she made him marry me. Pete coultn't get a decent job, so him and me hired on at Bob Gardner's farm, digging potatoes. When I was eight months pregnant with Richie, I was picking up fifty-pound pails. A workhorse like my mam!

Say what you want against my husband, he worked hard. For twenty-five years, he dug potatoes, drove the tractor, handled every jab that Bob Gardner give him. But Pete never wanted to be a husband. And when our baby was born, I found out he never wanted to be a father, neither. He was always runnin' with his crowd, gettin' drunk and leavin' me with no food, nothin' for the baby. He lied about what time the sun come up. He wasn't loving, wasn't even friendly. He *never* sat at the table with the rest of us and had a meal. He'd tell me what to get at the store, usually apple pie, chicken and biscuits and gravy.

I'd spend the whole day cooking it. "Come on, Pete," I'd say. "Supper's ready."

He'd say, "I don't want none of that gaddamn garbage." I knew what was eatin' him. One day he was a ski trooper, laying out in the sun, and the next day he was an amputee, roit? He coultn't handle it. He had a natural-looking arm made in Syracuse, a hand and hair and everything, but he never wore it. He wore the one with the hook.

When he wanted sex, he took down his pants. He gave me kids but he din't want no part of 'em. Dr. Rossen told him, "I oughta take a shotgun and blow that thing right offa you and tie it up on the wall with a ribbon. Your family'd be better off."

When I was six months pregnant with our third kid, Dawn, Pete come home drunk and kicked me in the stomach. Then he took off his artificial arm and attacted me with it. I grabbed the arm and split his kneecap with the hook. I runned up Burlington Street to a friend's house and she told me to have him arrested 'cause I was afraid to go back to the house. I begged the drunken old judge to drop the charges, but he woultn't, and Pete served six months.

We went out to Michigan to visit his parents and they looked down on me 'cause I came from poor stock. Pete forged a two-hundred-dollar check in his stepfather's name to get us back to Watertown, and his stepfather called the caps. He finally drapped the charges on condition we leave Michigan for good. Pete never got over his losses—first his arm, then his family. When we got home, he stole worse'n ever. He was sentenced to twenty-five days and twenty-five dollars for stealin' a box of day-old brad over in West Carthage—"pig brad," they called it. It was always petty stuff like that—enough to buy him a whiskey battle so he could lay up and drink, or run across the Canada border to party with his friends.

As a kid I only went to church on Christmas, but I made up my mind to raise a God-fearin' law-abidin' family, and I saw to it that my own kids all made their first Communion at Holy Family Church. Just because you come from one generation of thieves don't mean you have to raise another. I was the mam, the discipliner; Pete never raised a hand. When our son Allen Jr., "Little Pete," killed a kitten under the trestle, I let him have it good. When my kids stole from parking meters, I reported 'em to the police and made 'em return the mawney. If they stole from a store, I marched 'em right back with the stuff.

I was my kids' defender, too, and that got me in trouble with the caps. My oldest son Richie got into a fight across the street when he was twelve or thirteen and beat this punk fair and square. The mother come runnin' up as the two boys were makin' up and shakin' hands. This big six-foot woman, she took my son's arms and pinned 'em behind his back and told her kid to hit him. I'm small, but I spun her ass around and dumped her into an empty garbage can and broke her arm.

The judge gave me ten days suspended and warned me not to fight no more. I says, "Your honor, I'm sorry, but anybody that lays a hand on my child, I'll fight."

He just laughed and let me go.

I lost one baby, then another, but I kept on getting pregnant. After Richie I had Deborah, Dawn, Susan, Rosie. When Robin was born, I told Dr. Rossen, "Another gaddamn girl. I don't want no more girls. I want a boy."

Well, I knew this man, Bob. He was a businessman, a good joe, earned a nice living. He listened to me, paid attention to me, told me about his problems, his feelings. Pete never mentioned feelings. Maybe he din't have none, roit? Bob bought us food; he kept oil in our stove in the winter while Pete was running off to Canada with his friends. I'd meet Bob up around the corner when the kids were in school. Then we started meeting in a house that he owned. I put him off for a long time, and then I felt guilty, 'cause I din't get no sexual pleasure from Bob, either. It was always what *he* wanted, not what *I* wanted. And I was still lettin' Pete do whatever he wanted with my body, 'cause he was my husband.

One night we conceived Jack alongside the Black River Road, near the drive-in. As a baby, Jack looked exactly like Bob. When I brought him home from the haspital, I decided I couldn't go on lying no more. I took my husband aside and said, "Pete, you're not Jack's father. If you do not want to accept that, then leave. If you're gonna stay, you're gonna be a father to all our kids and you're gonna treat Jack as your own."

Pete grabbed his shatgun to kill Bob. I din't know what to do, so I decided to take the baby and stick our head in the gas oven. But first I called Dr. Rossen and told him how I was feeling. He said it was just the after-baby blues and sent me over some yellow pills.

Pete din't kill Bob; he killed a bottle instead. Later I had my eighth and ninth kids, Little Pete and Pam. I think they were my husband's.

Jack grew up fast. He was always moving, always into something. His asthma made him wheeze but never slowed him down. One day he was putting in a light bulb, bracing himself on the top of the door. My youngest child Pam was five, and she runned upstairs and slammed the door and took off the tip of his finger. I wrapped a towel around his hand. We went and found Bob and he drove us to the haspital. The doctor sent back to find the end of Jack's finger and they sewed it on like new.

Jack always took care of his younger brother. When Little Pete fell in the river, Jack grabbed his arm and pulled him out just when he was going under for the third time. I had a niece that drowned in the river near there. There's times when the Black isn't much more than a trickle and times when it's so powerful that anyone who falls in drowns. If you try to jump in and save 'em, you're dead, too. The Black was never much use except for killin' people. Runs north, too, *up* the map. Who ever heard of a river flowin' north?

One winter Jack shoved Little Pete off a runaway toboggan just before it hit a tree. He was always doin' things like that. Cared more about other people than he did about hisself.

He wasn't the kinda kid to get in trouble. He took a loaf of day-old brad from the SPCA around the corner, but I forgave him 'cause his father drank up his paycheck and we weren't eating at the time. I've taken a few things when I was hungry—everybody has, roit? If my kids were starving, I'd break a store window to feed 'em. But I raised 'em honest and they stayed out of trouble. Oh, Jack put his foot through the roof of a convertible, and the owner griped to the caps, but that was just being a boy. And sometimes he played hooky.

He had blond hair, freckles, big ears and a pug nose like mine and a turned-in foot that made him limp. My other kids called him "mama's boy" and I guess he was. When he was seven years old and I was having a miscarriage in Mercy Haspital, I heard a yell outside my window and it was Jack: "Mommy, are you coming home? I miss you." My own husband never came to visit me, too tired from luggin' potatoes.

Whenever Jack left the house, he hugged me and said he loved me. Never forgat. He was different from my other children that way. Maybe it was because he had a different father, even though he din't know the truth till he was ten. I had to tell him after he come to me in tears and wanted to know why his sisters din't like him.

I said, "They *do* like you."

"No they don't, Mommy. They call me jackass, donkey's ass. They're always picking on me."

"Kids do that, Jack. It's not that they don't like you. They *love* you, son."

He looked like he still din't believe me, so I says, "Jack, you're a special little boy. *Everybody* loves you."

He asked what was special about him.

I said, "Remember the man that took you to the haspital after you cut off your fingertip? The man that bought you cake and candy bars?" I took a deep breath and said,

"Well, that's your real father. That's who I was with when I had you."

He just stood there blinking his blue eyes. Maybe he had an inkling. Kids are smart that way, roit?

I said, "That doesn't mean you shouldn't respect Pete. He's treated you like his own flesh and blood for ten years —*better* than his own flesh and blood."

It was true. Pete was mean, but never to Jack. I remember one day when Richie went out in the snow and changed a flat on our car, and Pete yelled, "I din't tell you to do that, you son of a bitch. I woulda did that myself." And the girls could never do nothin' right. But he was good to Jack. Maybe it was Jack's bad foot—one cripple to another. Or just the nice way Jack talked to him.

Jack never said a word when I told him who his father was. Just lowered his head and walked away. When he had something on his mind, he'd go up to his haven by the railroad tracks and work it out.

I din't tell him the part about Big Pete threatening to kill Bob and how I started to stick our head in the oven. He din't need stuff like that. I just said, "Well, I wanted you to know about your bloodline. Always remember, you have a father that's gat some class."

A coupla minutes later I seen him curled up with his white cat. I din't know who was comforting who. I went out and bought him a new pair of sneakers.

It was that same spring of '72 when Jack come home and told me that a stranger took him and Little Pete fishing. Without asking my permission! I says, "Don't you never go near that man again. My Gad, he could take you somewhere and I'd never know what happened."

A few days later I opened the door and there was Jack with a dark-complected white man with close-set hazel eyes that slanted from the inside down. There wasn't much to his chin. He had long heavy sideburns that were so dark it looked like he used mascara on 'em. He wore glasses with black frames and talked in a low, rumbly voice and wore a navy blue jacket. Jack was four-foot-seven then, and this guy looked about a foot and a half taller. He was wiry-looking, twenty-four, twenty-five years old. He had muscular arms and his shoulders sloped.

Jack says, "Ma, I just sold Art a dollar's worth of worms. Can I go fishin' with him?"

I said, "What'd I tell ya the other day?"

Big Pete comes shufflin' over to the door and this guy Art said, "I took your boys fishin' the other day. I hope you don't mind."

Pete said, "Yes, we *do* mind!" It wasn't noon yet, and he was already half drunk. "We never laid eyes on you before. Don't take my boys anywhere!"

Jack says, "Oh, Mommy, Art won't hurt me. He's my friend."

I said, "Your father and I don't want you anywheres near this man."

The guy took a step backward and I'll never forget what he told Jack: "If your mother don't want you to go fishin' with me, I'm not gonna take ya. Always abide by your mother's wishes. She don't want you with me." Then he smiled and left.

I thought, That's good advice. But I was surprised to hear it from a creepy-looking guy like him.

The next Sunday, Pete promised to take the boys fishing as soon as he had his eye-opener. Jack liked to go with his dad, but he never got to do much fishing. All day long he'd put worms on the hook for Pete and then he'd have to stand back and watch. Time was, the Black River was full of trout, bass, walleye, but the pollution put an end to that. Now it was mostly catfish.

Around noon Pete was still pouring hisself one last drink and the boys were waiting in the yard. I said, "Why do you keep lyin' to these kids and tell 'em you're gonna take 'em fishin'? Heavens above, you're just gonna get so drunk you can't get outta the house. I don't like you lyin' to the boys."

He told me to shut up. So I went outside and said, "You kids may as well go play 'cause your father's too drunk to take you fishin'."

Little Pete cried, but Jack just shrugged. He went through this before. I give him a dollar to buy food for his white cat at Ruthie's store up on Grant Street. He says, "Mommy, can I go over to play at Maywood Terrace?"

I said, "Go wherever you want. Just be home for dinner. It's your turn for bingo." I knew he woultn't miss that treat.

3.

A few hours after Mary Blake said good-bye to her son, William "Corky" Murrock was working at his motel and gas station on State Route 12E when a wiry-looking man in his early twenties stumbled onto the premises from the rear. His leather engineer boots were spattered with mud.

"Where'd *you* come from?" Murrock asked, puzzled. His home was only a hundred feet away and he didn't like the idea of strangers emerging from the swampy woods without warning.

Breathing hard, the man pointed in an easterly direction and said he'd hiked through the woods. He said his name was Art Shawcross and he lived at the Cloverdale Apartments. He held up a battered fishing rod and said he'd found the two sections at different places along Kelsey Creek. Funny thing, he went on, they fit together. This was his lucky day.

The intruder hung around for about fifteen minutes, scraping off mud and washing up. As he walked away, Murrock asked him where he was headed.

The man said he was on his way to visit relatives up the road. Murrock relaxed. A harmless fisherman, he said to himself. He put the incident out of his mind.

4.

Mary Blake fingered her cards at Immaculate Heart Academy and tried not to think about Jack. Bingo took her mind off things. She got a kick out of the bumper sticker she'd seen recently: "THIS CAR STOPS AT ALL BINGO GAMES." The other Watertown favorites were "INSURED BY SMITH & WESSON" and ".357 MAGNUM ON BOARD." She thought they were neat. She came from a family that had owned a weapon or two.

Jack enjoyed bingo almost as much as his mother, and she couldn't imagine what had made him so late that he'd missed his dinner and the game. It was unlike him. The family always took meals together, except of course for Big Pete, nursing his booze in the other room.

Mary tried to concentrate on the numbers. She'd intended to check around the neighborhood before leaving the house, but recent surgery had left her too weak to do much walking. She told herself that Jack was probably just playing somewhere. He would give her a big hug when she looked in on him and Little Pete at bedtime. She'd have to discipline him, of course. Ten-year-olds couldn't come home for dinner whenever they damn well pleased. She'd give him a few whacks and a good-night kiss.

Mary needed the distraction of a winning card, but the numbers wouldn't come. Just before 10:00 P.M. her friend Josephine offered to drive her home. For thirty-five years, as child and adult, Mary had lived in the same two-story wooden house across Water Street from the railroad spur along the Black River. Every spring the dirty old river overflowed its banks in the upstream lowlands and came through town like a herd of wild animals. The runoff was already building.

If the water's too rough to fish, Mary thought, Jack'll be disappointed. He'd been selling worms for a penny apiece to buy a new bike. At night, he poured water under the lilacs to force the nightcrawlers to the surface, then picked up the slithering strings while Mary watched from a window to make sure he wasn't bothered by neighborhood derelicts. He'd also earned thirty dollars shoveling snow for old Agnes Thomas, but his dad spent the money on whiskey. Jack didn't complain. He was easy with his money. Once he found twenty dollars in a snowbank and gave most of it to a friend. He wasn't stingy like some of the other Blake children.

The ramshackle little house was dark when Mary stepped from her friend's car a few minutes after 10:00 P.M. Her husband's snores blasted through an open window. Mary wondered what the neighbors thought. She climbed the wooden steps and went inside. Twelve-year-old Rosie was rocking in the big chair in the living room. The child looked pale. My poor baby, Mary thought. It's been a month since she was raped and she still can't eat, can't sleep, can't do nothing but sit and brood. The son of a bitch tore her wide open. A married man with kids, claimed he thought she was eighteen.

Mary winced as she recalled how Pete had refused to drive his own daughter to the hospital after the rape. "Call a fuckin' cab," he'd ordered when she woke him in the middle of the night. "I ain't going nowhere." Now Rosie was under the care of a therapist, and Social Services talked about having her committed to straighten out her head.

"Ma," the child said as Mary snapped on the light, "Jack ain't home."

Mary gulped. "Oh, my Gad," she said, "I wonder where he can be."

She was thinking, Jack never stays out this late. *Never.* He's scared of the dark. Did he run away? No—impossible. Not my Jack. Of all her kids, he had the least reason to leave. She wondered if she'd made a mistake telling him about Bob. It was only a week ago. The boy hadn't seemed upset at the time.

"Is he staying with a friend?" Rosie asked.

"No, no," Mary said, trying not to show her anxiety. Jack was too young for overnight visits. Some mothers permitted their ten-year-olds to stay out, but Mary wouldn't think of it. Jack belonged under this roof where they could keep an eye on him—she and Pete were firm about that.

She went into the boys' room and looked at the empty bed. She shook Little Pete and asked, "What happened to your brother?"

5.

The eight-year-old boy hadn't slept. Little Pete was an epileptic, a sweet-faced boy, small for his age, with dark brown eyes and light hair parted in the middle. He shoplifted and stole from parked cars and was on his way to a life of petty crime, but he tried to keep his rage under control so the other children wouldn't dislike him. Sometimes he set off the fire alarm near the Black Clawson plant, then ran home and hid under the covers. He tried to get Jack to join in the game, but Jack was two years older and treated him like a baby. They'd had to give away their German shepherd Queenie because of Little Pete's allergies, and Jack was still grieving. Sometimes Little Pete wondered how a person became allergic. Was it nervousness from stealing? He idolized Jack and tried to hang out with him. Richard, the oldest of the three brothers, had gone off on his own a lot, and was in the Army now.

Little Pete sat up in the lower half of the bunk bed and tried to answer his mother's questions without getting in trouble. No, he insisted, he hadn't seen Jack since early afternoon. He knew why his mom was so upset. Jack was missing. It gave him an empty feeling in his stomach. He thought, What'll I do without him? It felt as though an ice cube was stuck in his throat.

His mother wanted to know every last detail of the boys' afternoon activities. Little Pete told how they'd gone to Burlington Street to try out Bugs LaRosa's new bike. Halfway down the hill, Jack had crashed and broken the gearshift lever. "I'm calling the cops!" Bugs yelled.

"No cop's gonna get me," Jack muttered, and the two boys fled toward East Main. Then Jack split off to visit his girlfriend in the Cloverdale Apartments, a low-rent public housing facility a few blocks away. Little Pete hadn't seen his brother since.

"My Gad," his mom said, shaking his thin shoulders, "why din't you tell me this before?"

"Ma, you din't ask me," the eight-year-old replied.

There was something else the boy didn't tell his mother.

Both parents had warned him and Jack to stay away from the fisherman, but they hadn't obeyed.

They'd first encountered the man a month earlier, standing on the riverbank across from their house, still-fishing with a sinker and a worm. "Smell that water?" Jack told him. "You can't eat fish outta there."

"I just like to catch 'em," the man said. The boys hung around, watching. Some fishermen hated company, but this one seemed friendly. He was dressed neatly and looked clean. He introduced himself as "Art." He cast his worm into a pool and propped his rod against a rock. His line started to tighten but then went slack.

"Missed him," the man said as he reeled in. The worm looked untouched. The boys exchanged glances. There was nothing in this hole but stunted bass and sunnies the size of their hands.

After forty-five minutes or so, the boys walked across the railroad tracks to their home. They didn't mention this first encounter with the man; their mom would only get mad. Bums slept along the river when the weather was warm, and when it was cold they huddled inside boxcars on the siding. Mary Blake always made them out to be fiends who did bad things to boys.

A few days after the man named Art had been rebuffed at their door by their parents, Jack and Little Pete had noticed him walking across the old iron bridge by the Black Clawson plant and glancing toward their house. Once again he seemed pleased to see them. "Would you guys like to go trout fishin'?" he asked.

Jack said, "Our mom and dad told us not to go fishin' with you. And they don't like us near the river when it's high." Every spring, someone drowned in the Black. Sometimes the remains weren't found.

The man said he was headed upstream to a stretch of flat water above a dam. "Come on," he said. "I'll fix it with your parents when we get back." The brothers figured it would be okay. Their mom was out and their dad was drunk.

At the Eastern Boulevard Bridge, two miles upriver from their home, they watched while Art fished a set line. Nothing bit, but he didn't seem to care. He was too busy talking his head off. He said he drove a truck at the city dump. Little Pete thought, Didn't he tell us he had some other kind of job? He decided he must have heard wrong. He was only eight, and his brain didn't always work right.

Art advised them never to go near the river alone. He said he liked kids and wouldn't mind taking them whenever they wanted to go. He explained that he had a couple of sons but his wife wouldn't let them fish with him. "Why not?" Jack asked.

"I dunno," the man said. He acted as though it was the most natural thing in the world for a father to take strange kids fishing and leave his own at home. He said he lived in an apartment in the Cloverdale housing complex and they were welcome to visit. He seemed to take a special interest in Jack, directing his words toward him and reaching out to muss his blond hair.

After an hour or so Art announced that he was hungry and led them to a market on nearby State Street. Then they trooped along the Burrville Road to Marzano's Gravel Pit, where he wrapped some bacon in foil and heated it over a small fire. As they nibbled away, he explained that he'd learned to cook in Vietnam. He told how he'd killed a couple of Vietcong infiltrators and then found out they were little girls. "I was just confused," he explained. He acted as though he felt bad about it. "I still have blackout spells from Nam," he said. "I got hit by shrapnel."

He pulled a magazine from his pocket and showed pictures of naked women. "Nice tits, huh?" he said, and pointed to some other parts. He told the boys how he "got" his wife and made her moan. It sounded dumb to Little Pete. Jack just laughed.

They'd been together about three hours when the man suggested that they try for trout in a brook near the stone quarry. He led the little boy by the hand while Jack ambled ahead. "Hey," the man yelled, "come back here with us!"

Jack walked faster. When he was about thirty feet in front, Art squeezed Little Pete's arm so hard that it hurt. "Make your brother come back," he ordered. His voice sounded mean.

"Why?" the child asked, trying to pull free.

Art grabbed him by his shirt and pants and dangled him over the edge of the quarry wall. "I'm gonna drop him!" he yelled to Jack. "Come back right now!"

Little Pete looked twenty feet straight down. *"Jack!"* he yelped.

When his big brother scurried back, Art set Pete on his feet and laughed as though he'd been kidding. Without a word, the two boys ran. Little Pete was so scared that he ran in front of a car on State Street. "That guy up there," he yelled at the driver, "he—"

The car slowed, then sped off.

The boys were careful not to breathe a word to their mother, but they confided to their father that they'd fled from the weird guy named Art at the stone quarry. Pete Blake reddened and said, "That asshole again? My little girl in the closet'll take care of him." His "little girl" was his shotgun.

"Oh, Dad," Jack said, "he's really okay. He was in the Army like you."

After his mother left the little bedroom, Little Pete tried to put the fisherman out of his mind and get to sleep. He told himself that Jack would be back soon. He *had* to be. They weren't only brothers; they were best friends.

6.

At 10:30 P.M. on that bingo night, Mary began phoning neighbors, relatives, Jack's playmates. She tried waking her husband again, but he didn't stir. She grabbed Rosie by the arm and walked the darkened streets, softly calling, "Jack. *Jack!*"

When there was no response, she returned home and phoned the police. "My son hasn't come home," she said. She was told that they couldn't take an official missing persons report until the individual had been gone for twenty-four hours, but they would send an officer.

It was after midnight when the patrol car pulled into the driveway. A uniformed cop advised her through his open window to check with Jack's friends.

"I did," she said.

"Was he in the habit of staying out at night?"

"No. Never. He's ascared of the dark. He's either hurt or there's something wrong."

Then she remembered the man who'd come to the door —Art somebody. She wondered why she hadn't thought of him earlier. She told the cop how he'd seemed overly interested in her boys, especially Jack.

The cop asked, "What's the guy's name? Where's he live?"

She asked him to wait. Little Pete was sitting on the side of the bed. "The fisherman," she said. "What's his name?"

"Art," the boy said.

"Art who?"

"Just . . . Art."

"Where's he live?"

"I think maybe Cloverdale."

Mary passed the information to the cop and handed him a photograph of Jack. After the patrol car drove off, she made more coffee and lit another cigarette. She didn't know what else to do. The more she thought about "Art," the more she wondered if he was involved. She paced the living room while poor frazzled Rosie tried to comfort her. Everyone else was in bed. She thought, Jack didn't run away. He's a happy kid. Not one of my kids has run away. . . .

Jack's white cat rubbed against her leg. The stray had wandered into his life like all his other pets—turtles, snakes, birds. They seemed to comfort him. She thought, Jack would never leave his cat.

She checked the boys' room again. Little Pete lay on the lower bunk, his eyes closed. Nothing seemed missing or out of place. Jack's baseball cap hung from a nail.

"Let's go," she told Rosie.

"Where?" the child asked.

"Cloverdale."

Most of Watertown lay uphill from their house in the river bottom. They trudged up Pearl Street to Starbuck Avenue, then six blocks along the New York Air Brake property line next to two huge smokestacks marked with "NYABC" in fading letters. Mary felt woozy; she wasn't completely recovered from female surgery two weeks earlier. Rain dripped from her nose to her shoes, but she hardly noticed. She hadn't even put on a raincoat, nor had Rosie. The poor child cried the whole way; being raped had made her fearful. But Mary needed company.

The two-story brick apartment house lay in stark profile against the big playground to its rear. A police car jerked to a stop just as they arrived, and Mary recognized the officer who'd come to the house. He didn't seem to object as they followed him across the wet lawn and into the office, where he searched the tenant list. With Mary and Rose standing behind, he knocked on the door of apartment 233.

The man named Art answered so quickly that Mary was sure he'd been peeking. The apartment was dark behind him, but he was fully dressed. A woman in a bathrobe stood alongside.

At first Mary couldn't hear the conversation, but the man seemed to be talking normally. "Where's Jack?" she cried out. "Where's my son?"

Art said, "Jack Blake? The last I seen him, he was on the cement blocks in the park."

"When was that?" she asked.

"This afternoon. He was playing with a boy named Jimmy."

Out of Mary's earshot, the policeman resumed his questioning. Then the apartment door swung shut and he headed toward his car.

Mary hurried to keep up. "What else did he tell ya?" she asked the cop.

"Nothin'."

"But . . . that guy's been hangin' around Jack."

"Lady, we can't arrest a guy for hanging around."

Mary and Rosie trudged back to Water Street. The cop didn't offer them a ride and Mary didn't ask. It was all downhill.

Back home, she poured hot water through the coffee grounds and ripped open another pack of cigarettes. The doctor had ordered her to stop smoking till she was fully recovered from her surgery, but she had to keep her hands occupied.

She ordered Rosie to bed, and the child said, "Ma, I can't sleep." Her face glistened with rainwater and tears.

Mary said, "There's nothin' more we can do." As she slumped into a chair, she thought. Maybe I should've kept my mouth shut about his real father. Every Wednesday Jack went to church school at Sacred Heart Academy; it was his own idea. He was a sensitive, religious boy, and maybe it hurt him too much to learn how he'd been conceived.

She decided to clear the air as soon as he came home, tell him how Big Pete had run around on her and left her with no food in the house and nine kids to feed and never talked to her or showed her any kindness or love. Then Jack would understand and never leave again.

She sat up all night rehearsing her lines.

7.

The Watertown police department took no special notice of Jack Blake's disappearance. Incoming watches weren't briefed; the mother's phone call wasn't logged, and the beat man in the patrol car filed no report. The Blakes were easy to ignore. When they came to police attention, it was usually as drunks, thieves, or scavengers. Every cop in town knew what Allen "Big Pete" Blake had been up to the night his arm was ripped off. It was the wages of sin.

Mary seemed honest enough, a survivor, but some of her clan would steal the chrome off a casket. Her oldest son Richie had been the prime suspect in four burglaries before he escaped into the Army and went overseas, and when the boy known as Little Pete was six, he'd stolen a transistor radio from the police chief's car. Mary had made him return it with an apology, but the cops suspected that he went right back to his thieving ways and his brother Jack right along with him.

Besides, it was the spring of 1972, and swarms of kids were hitting the road. Who could keep track? Years ago, Watertown had been an important papermaking town, but for most of the twentieth century there'd been little to keep its young people at home. Along the Black River, abandoned mills dropped into the water brick by brick. The Depression of the thirties never really ended in the North Country; Watertown wasn't even prosperous during World War II. It was a hardscrabble place, insular, unwelcoming, its social fabric worn thin by the cruel weather, the corrosive fight for jobs, political cronyism, the shortage of resources, alcoholism, inbreeding. Incest rates were high. The permanent hard times had made many of the citizens bitter, clannish, xenophobic. They tended to distrust anyone from "away." At a public meeting, a woman who proudly pointed out that she was born in the next county was told scornfully, "That's still away."

A former city official described Watertown as "a college town without the college—all townies." The cultural level was generally low, public services minimal, the most popular activities drinking and sex. Young people moved away by the carload. In such a dispiriting place, what cop could get excited about one more missing child?

8.

At daylight, Mary Blake arose from her rocking chair and trudged into the files of saplings that ran up the slope behind the house. Jack played there often. Sometimes poachers sifted through the stunted maples, jacklighting deer, snaring rabbits. Poaching was a cottage industry in depressed Watertown and the Blakes had done a little themselves.

Mary wondered if Jack lay unconscious somewhere. There was epilepsy in the family; maybe he'd had an attack. She followed a narrow footpath up Bootjack Hill and came to a clearing not far from the dump where her mother had picked slag. Someone had scratched out a circle in the dirt, perhaps for a game of marbles. In the middle of the circle were the footprints of a dog and a barefoot child. She took a closer look and saw that the middle toe was elongated, like Jack's. Behind it was the distinct impression of an adult shoeprint.

She doubled back to Jack's hideout along the railroad tracks and found it empty. When she returned home an hour after she'd left, her husband was talking to her older brother Roland. Big Pete told her that the guy named Art had shown up at the door a few minutes before and asked if he could join in the search for Jack.

"I've seen that asshole around," Roland said. "He works at the city dump."

"What'd you tell him, Pete?" Mary asked, bristling.

"I told him we didn't need his kind of help."

Big Pete had to go to work, leaving Mary with her brother. When no more policemen showed up, Roland cursed the cops and began his own search in the brush and debris that had collected for a hundred years behind the Black Clawson plant across the narrow river. Mary monitored the phone and kept thinking about the man named Art. He looked calm enough the night before, she said to herself, but how come he was wide awake and waiting for the police at 3:00 A.M. if he didn't do nothing wrong?

At noon she left Rosie in charge of the other children

and retraced her steps to the Cloverdale Apartments. Her mouth was dry and her eyes burned as she sloshed through puddles of overnight rain.

This time a small woman with dark brown eyes cracked open the door of apartment 233. A man was faintly visible behind her.

"That boy Jimmy," Mary said. "Did you remember his last name?"

"Yeah," the man's voice said. "Jimmy Knight. Lives around here somewhere. I seen him playing."

He sounded so matter-of-fact that Mary had the sinking feeling that she'd made a mistake, that this shadowy figure couldn't be the same guy who'd taken her boys fishing. But then he turned sideways to the light. It was him: *Art.* She was sure. For all she knew, he was the only one who could lead her to Jack. Maybe he'd hurt the boy. Maybe there were bloodstains. . . .

"I want to see your jacket," she blurted out. "That navy blue jacket you wore the day you come to our house."

The woman stepped in and said something to the effect that she'd washed the jacket and was wearing it herself.

Mary said, "You can't be wearing it. He's twice as big as you are."

The man stepped backward and the door slammed shut. Mary banged her fists against the wooden slab, but there was no response.

She went around back to the playground and found a boy who told her that he'd played with Jack and some other children the day before. "Then Art came over and started talking to Jack," the boy recalled.

"Art who?" Mary asked.

"The only Art I know." The boy pointed to the corner apartment. "Jack asked him if they could go fishing, and Art said he didn't have no worms. Jack said he had night-crawlers at home. Then he left."

"With Art?"

"I dunno. I wasn't paying attention."

Mary's heart pounded as she hurried down Starbuck Avenue toward home. She threw open Jack's big worm-box. It was empty.

She called the police number and announced that a man named Arthur Shawcross had taken her son fishing and hadn't returned him. The voice on the other end didn't seem to comprehend.

"Shawcross," she repeated. "Art Shawcross! He lives in the Cloverdale Apartments. He's gat my son."

The conversation was like a bad dream. She wanted Shawcross arrested and the cop refused. When she tried to explain, he told her to hold the phone and then came back to say that no Jack Owen Blake was listed as missing.

"Of course he's listed," Mary said. "I listed him myself."

"When?"

"Last night. Ten-thirty, eleven o'clack."

The cop told her to wait another hour or so and call back; maybe he could take a report.

9.

By Tuesday morning, two days after she'd said good-bye to her son, Mary Blake still hadn't been to bed. She was running on coffee, cigarettes, diet pills and nerves. As far as she could tell, the police still weren't searching. She phoned the *Watertown Daily Times* to ask for assistance, and a reporter promised to write an article about Jack. He asked what he'd been wearing, and she said, "A light green jacket, black pants, new black sneakers. And a T-shirt that said, 'I act different because I *am* different.' His favorite."

When she called police to ask if they'd arrested Shawcross yet, a friendly voice told her that officers were checking out a report that a man had been seen leading a boy into Pool's Woods the day before.

"That's him and Jack!" Mary said. "Cloverdale Apartments is right near there." Pool's Woods was a spooky place, the scene of two suicides by hanging.

The headquarters cop said he would see what he could do for her. "See what you can *do*?" Mary mocked him.

"Why, you can go out and look for my son. You can arrest that Shawcross!"

"Lady," the cop said, "we gotta have probable cause. This isn't TV."

She stewed for a few more minutes and then started phoning public officials. Her state senator promised to help. Mayor Ted Rand ordered an immediate search. Jefferson County sheriff Irving Angel assigned a deputy to the case. At last, Mary said to herself, I got their attention.

Around noon a city juvenile officer knocked on her door. Less than an hour had passed since she'd made her last call. "I've just searched Pool's Woods," the cop reported. "Your son's not there."

Mary was confused. "Nobody can search Pool's Woods that quick," she insisted. "It's fulla swamps."

The officer informed her that he'd been brought up nearby and knew the area, and no kid was in Pool's Woods, dead or alive. When she asked how he'd managed to emerge clean and dry, he turned and left. Mary shrieked, "You're a gaddamn liar!"

When headquarters informed her that nothing further was planned, she hurried to Pool's Woods herself. A few patches of sooty snow lay under insulating leaves. The earth was softening in the spring thaw. She'd just started to push through the underbrush when a sharp pain lanced her abdomen. She barely made it home in time to throw up.

That afternoon she read the headline in the *Times*.

Boy, 10,
Missing
In City

The reporter had kept his promise. The short article began, "City police continued their investigation today into the disappearance of Jack O. Blake, 10, of 525 Water St., who has been missing since Sunday afternoon."

Mary thought, Continued *what* investigation? Was a skimpy search by one juvenile cop an "investigation"? Farther down, the article quoted the newly appointed Watertown police chief, Joseph C. Loftus, as saying that he was "limited by manpower."

Mary was glad to see Jack's description in print. Now the whole town would be on the lookout. And she was also pleased that the paper had printed her criticism of the cops: "The mother, Mrs. Mary Blake, charged today that police have not put forth enough effort in the search."

She thought, Maybe that'll get 'em off their fat ass. She called headquarters to prod. To her surprise, a detective confirmed that Art Shawcross was almost certainly the man who'd led Jack into the woods on Sunday afternoon. And a records check showed that a man named Arthur John Shawcross had served two years in Attica and Auburn state prisons for burglary and arson and was now on parole. He lived in the Cloverdale Apartments. This Shawcross, the detective went on, wasn't known as a child molester, but he'd given contradictory versions of his contacts with Jack on Sunday.

"Well, why'n hell don't you pick him up?" Mary asked. She knew about parole procedures. "Can't you put a forty-eight-hour hold on him?"

The detective asked her to be patient. "Before we can do anything, we need evidence of a crime. Shawcross said that the last time he saw your son, he was playing on the blocks behind Cloverdale. We talked to him again and he said he dropped Jack off at North Junior swimming pool. So he's telling two different stories."

"Arrest him!" Mary demanded. "Shake him up." She was remembering times when the cops had picked up her son Richie and other members of her family and roughed them up.

"I *told* you, Mrs. Blake," the detective said, "we have no evidence of a crime." There was an edge of impatience in his voice. "We don't even have a body."

"A body?" Mary said. "That's what you're waiting for? A gaddamn *body*? Does Jack have to be dead?"

The cop insisted that his hands were tied.

"Then you're no gaddamn good," Mary said, and slammed down the phone.

Once again she churned up to the Cloverdale Apartments. Shawcross was on the front lawn when she shoved her nose in his face. "Now you just told the caps you were with Jack," she yelled in her piercing voice, "and I want to know where my son is right now!"

Shawcross quick-stepped toward his door. He muttered, "I dropped your fuckin' son off at Starbuck School."

Mary thought, ya rotten thing ya. That's the third different story you've told. *What did you do with my Jack?*

10.

On Thursday, May 11, news of the three-day disappearance reached Oswego, fifty miles southwest on Lake Ontario, and the town's renowned rescue team volunteered to bring infrared equipment and begin a professional search. Just the day before, Watertown Chief Loftus had complained publicly that he didn't have enough men to do the job, but in a burst of local pride he declined the offer. Oswego was "away."

To Mary Blake, it was clear that the police department considered Jack a runaway and his mother a pest. A volunteer searcher confirmed her conclusion by reporting the offhand comment of a town detective: "That boy don't want to be found."

That afternoon, Mary read in the *Times*.

> Commenting on a report that Mrs. Mary Blake, the boy's mother, said a man was seen leading the child into the woods, Chief Loftus called it "unfounded.
>
> "We have questioned the man, and there is nothing to the story. We've been doing everything we can, and have checked every possibility. We talked to friends of the boy, and have been told he left the area."

Mary cursed to herself. *Left the area?* If the police chief was giving that sicko Shawcross a clean bill of health, then who the hell *was* he investigating? She knew that the cops hadn't looked everywhere and that her son hadn't "left the area," at least not voluntarily. Jack had asthma and needed his medication. He was with somebody or he was hurt. Mary agreed with her daughter Rosie: the cops just couldn't be bothered to help the poor.

She phoned Camp Drum, her husband's last post, and asked if soldiers could be dispatched to help search for her son. Colonel Frank W. Frazier replied that he would need an official request from the city. At Mary's insistence, he offered to send volunteers.

Encouraged, she contacted fire departments, the New York State Police substation and other agencies, and by the time the sun went down unofficial search parties thrashed through the underbrush in Pool's Woods, looked into outbuildings behind the Seaway Shopping Center, and walked furrow by furrow through the truck farms just northeast of the Cloverdale Apartments. Salvation Army workers rigged a portable canteen, and Mary poured coffee all night.

11.

At dawn Thursday, a company of sweaty National Guardsmen dragged out of Pool's Woods. A sergeant reported that they'd found no sign of Jack. Mary begged him to keep searching. The men ate doughnuts and sipped coffee, then filtered back through the tree line.

She was still at the canteen late that night when she learned of the Watertown P.D.'s latest decision. Chief Loftus had declared, "We've checked every place in the city we think the boy could or would have been." The case was closed.

By daybreak Friday, the volunteers had dwindled to a handful, including an off-duty Watertown patrolman and two sheriff's deputies. Mary hadn't slept in five days. Her small hands shook as she served coffee, and she constantly spattered herself.

Her friend Henrietta Thomas was shocked at Mary's condition. She phoned the Blakes' family doctor and advised him that his patient was ready to drop. Dr. Rossen ordered Mary to bed and sent over an emergency supply of Thorazine.

She swallowed three and began a new round of phone calls, trying to enlist more searchers. In the middle of a call to a cousin, she slumped to the living room floor. Faint pictures appeared before her eyes; she felt as though she were floating above her body looking down. She saw the circle and footprints that she'd observed on Bootjack Hill the morning after Jack disappeared. A black cloak fluttered over a face in the middle of the circle. But no matter how hard she tried, she couldn't make out the features. Oh, God, she thought, is it Jack? *Why can't I see his face?* . . .

She pulled herself to her feet when Big Pete arrived home from work and tweaked her shoulder with his hook. She figured she'd slept for an hour. It was time to start dinner.

12.

By the first weekend after the disappearance, Mary hadn't given up on finding her son alive and neither had other Watertown citizens. Local clannishness produced a distrust of outsiders, but it also produced hometown loyalty. Whipped up by Mary Blake, the townspeople distributed posters with the missing child's picture and a written description—"blond hair, blue eyes, a chipped tooth in front." A citizens' band radio group coordinated efforts from Syracuse all the way north to Quebec City.

A Watertown woman named Jean McEvoy told the *Times* that her son and other teenagers had been searching till 1:00 and 2:00 A.M. every night. "The kids formed arm chains and walked a creek for the boy," she reported.

Others dragged the brooks and ponds around Huntingtonville, where Art Shawcross had taken the Blake boys fishing. A search of Kelsey Creek, just north of town, went on by lanternlight. Inspectors from Niagara Mohawk, the electric company, checked canal locks where bodies had fetched up in the past. A man from Evans Mills lent his bloodhound. The abandoned railroad trestle across the road from the Blake house was checked, and other trackage was walked by teams of Boy Scouts. Searchers fought for purchase along the rocky banks of the Black River, its waters now topped with yellow froth from Adirondack freshets, and did brisk little sidesteps as bursts of sewage from riverside shacks and oddly canted boardinghouses anointed their heads. The attitude of the townspeople had always been that it was only shit and would soon flow to Lake Ontario.

Volunteers went door to door on Water Street, checking empty houses and basements. Men with flashlights followed the trails of water rats. Searchers picked through closets and back rooms in disused stores and buildings and tried not to fall through the rotting floors of empty mills and factories.

Mary pumped up the searchers and checked out tips. A friend of a friend called and said that a woman named Madeleine had seen something suspicious on the Sunday afternoon when Jack disappeared. Mary called police and repeated the information: "She says she seen a man crouched down in back of North Junior swimming pool by the sewer pipe. He was wearing dark clothing and it looked like he was dragging something."

A detective drove Mary to the scene. The heavy cover to the sewer lay off to one side. She asked herself what she hoped to find. Jack's . . . body? Surely no. They were just looking for clues. His wallet or something. Anything but a body . . .

A piece of scrap metal was propped against the open sewer hole. It looked like part of a refrigerator. The plainclothesman tried to crawl inside the pipe, but he was too big. He asked if there was any chance that Jack had fallen in the river.

"He's lived on the river all his life," Mary replied. "When his little brother fell in, Jack saved him."

"A lot of drowning victims," the detective said, "we never find 'em."

Mary was irked. "Why don't you quit your goofy ideas and just lock up that Shawcross?" she asked. "Don't you know he was buggin' Jack for a month?"

"Shawcross is an arsonist," the detective reminded her.

"Can't an arsonist molest kids?" Mary snapped back. "Can't an arsonist be a pervert?"

"We talked to the guy again. These ex-cons are hard to crack."

"Just do your gaddamn job," Mary said. She was glad when his unmarked car passed from sight.

She enlisted the help of a skinny boy who poked into the sewer. The gas almost overwhelmed the child. There was no sign of Jack.

Early that evening two cops marched a bedraggled boy of about seventeen up the Blakes' front steps. They told Mary he was a runaway and they'd caught him in the woods above the house. Was this her missing son?

Mary shook her head in disgust. Jack was blond and fair, and this kid looked like an Indian. He was six feet tall and had black hair. She wondered if the cops had even bothered to read Jack's description.

Despite the apparent lack of police interest, the *Daily Times* ran frequent updates on the human-interest story:

City Boy, 10
Still Missing

Boy's Mother
Believes Son
Is Near City

Missing Boy's Parents
Unhappy Over Search

Local TV and radio stations joined in the campaign, and their coverage produced a few leads. A man with a distant look in his eyes came to the Blake home on Water Street and reported that he'd seen Jack and three boys hanging a dog from a tree on Starbuck Avenue the very day he'd disappeared. The man said he'd cut the dog down and arranged to have it spayed. When he identified himself as Matt Dillon, "I gave him the bum's rush," Mary explained later.

Other sightings had to be taken more seriously. An out-of-towner said he recognized a picture of Jack in the *Times* as a boy he'd seen in Theresa, miles north of Watertown, on that same Sunday afternoon. He said the Blake boy had been a passenger in a banged-up old junker driven by a redheaded teenager in a purple jacket.

Then a Watertown boy returned from a visit to Theresa and told the Blakes that he'd observed Jack and a red-headed boy chasing each other on a grassy slope. He said he'd called Jack by name and asked what he was doing, and Jack had answered, "Playing." Someone else phoned with a report that Jack and the red-haired boy were squatting in an empty house near the Theresa village park.

After a police official told her that he couldn't authorize another futile search, Mary talked a friend into driving her to Theresa. She located the empty house, ripped the boards off one of the windows and climbed inside. She found a pair of socks that looked like Jack's. A thick Bible lay under dust atop a foot-pumped organ. The creaky old bed had been slept in. In the kitchen Mary found opened cans of pork and beans.

She thought, Jack's been here! He's alive!

A local storekeeper told her that two young strangers had just bought candy with handfuls of pennies. Mary thought, That's exactly what Jack would do. "What'd they look like?" she asked excitedly.

The clerk described a red-haired boy and a younger boy with blond hair and a limp.

At Mary's insistence, a sheriff's deputy spent twenty-four hours in Theresa looking for Jack, and the State Police sent in a two-man unit to assist. They reported a cold trail.

• • •

A psychic phoned from Hoboken, New Jersey, and told Mary that he'd received newspaper clippings about the case. "Your son is alive," the man said. She frowned when he asked, "How far is the town of Theresa?"

"About eighteen miles," she said. She wondered, How the hell does a guy from New Jersey know about a little burg like Theresa?

"He's not *in* Theresa," the psychic advised her in an upbeat voice, "but he's not far from there. And he's alive, alive, alive!"

Once again, Mary was encouraged. The psychic offered to help in the search but needed a hundred dollars in travel money. She promised to get off a money order. Encouraged, she made several more trips to Theresa before giving up on the lead.

Every few hours she checked Jack's bed. It remained empty.

13.

On the second Monday of her son's absence, Mary took a call from a woman who identified herself as a fireman's wife from Black River. "Mrs. Blake," she asked in a screechy voice, "did your son get home yet?"

"No," Mary answered.

"Well, my husband and I were driving to work at seven this morning and we seen a boy walking in a ditch. We're sure it was your son. . . ."

As the woman rambled on, something in her voice made Mary realize that the call was a hoax. There'd been other mean calls. She wondered about cruelty, both human and divine. Why would God take Jack so early? Sometimes she would flop in the living room chair, squeeze her eyes shut and concentrate on making him appear at the front door, smiling, his chipped tooth catching the light. When he didn't arrive, she offered deals: "Please, God, tell me where

Jack is and I'll never miss Mass again. Lord, send him home right now, Lord. Give me a sign! . . ."

She began to distrust the God who refused to answer. Out of all the women in Watertown, why had He singled her out? Was she being punished for her affair with Bob? Plenty of women had affairs, didn't they? Or was she being punished for telling Jack the truth? Was that why he'd left?

When her son had been missing for nine days, she picked up a copy of the *Watertown Daily Times* and started to read an article about a City Council meeting. Twelfth Ward supervisor John H. Kriesick, her own ward leader, was quoted as saying, "I would like to commend City Police Chief Joseph C. Loftus and all the officers on the finding of young Jack O. Blake." Kriesick added that he was certain that Jack "is all right."

Mayor Rand was quoted as responding, "Thank you, Supervisor Kriesick. . . . There has been a lot of criticism, and a little bit of malice."

Mary's fingers shook as she dialed the newspaper's number. "My son!" she blurted out to the first voice on the line. "Where's he at?"

She was told that nothing had changed; Supervisor Kriesick had simply misspoken.

With public interest waning and official interest dead, Mary continued the search alone. She haunted the streets around the Cloverdale Apartments, asking people to look in their sheds, their cellars, anyplace where a boy could hide. Sometimes she found herself stopping strangers on the street and begging for help. She heard that people were laughing at her, saying she was nuts, that she was wasting her time. She kept on searching.

Her firstborn child Richie arrived from Germany on compassionate leave and was placed under arrest. Mary rushed to City Hall and demanded, "Why'd you take my boy?"

She was told that Richie was wanted for burglary. She bailed him out and promised to prove to the cops that he'd been overseas when the crimes were committed. "That's typical," she complained to Big Pete when he came home from the farm. "Whenever something's stolen, they grab Richie." Pete made a disbelieving face and poured himself a drink. He'd always been hardest on his oldest son.

Over the radio, Mary heard that the authorities were still getting tips; people who saw little blond boys kept reporting them as Jack. Some of the sightings were forty and fifty miles away. She tried to check out every lead. She didn't know how to drive and couldn't always find a friend with a car. When her husband was sober enough, he chauffeured her to nearby places like Lowville and Huntingtonville, but he seldom got out of the car. At home, he sank in his chair and drank till his eyes glazed. Mary understood. He'd given up on himself the day he'd lost his arm. The absence of Jack was finishing him off. Big Pete just wanted to die.

She thought about her lover Bob, his kindnesses, the way he listened to her and treated her like a real person. In a moment of unreason, she made the long walk to the drive-in on Black River Road. A ring of white stones circled the parking place where Jack had been conceived. Mary stepped into the middle and babbled, "This circle can't be broken." Then she went home and considered the possibility that she was losing her mind.

The urge to contact Bob diminished in her grief. She'd halfway expected him to offer his assistance—wasn't Jack his own flesh and blood?—but weeks went by without a word. Mary promised God unconditionally that she would never see Bob again.

14.

In her neat two-story apartment at Cloverdale, Penny Nichol Sherbino Shawcross was wishing the Watertown P.D. would get off her husband's case. Art was moody enough already, and this hassling wasn't improving his disposition.

She'd never been fond of cops. The Sherbino clan had been around the North Country for a century and the cops took delight in rousting certain of her friends and relatives. She was sick of it.

Penny was a short woman, an inch over five feet, with lively brown eyes, tawny hair, a good figure, and a rural vivacity that took the form of a ready laugh and giggle. She was proud that Sacajawea, heroine of the Lewis and Clark expedition, was her father's fourth great-grandmother. "Sherbino," she insisted, was *not* Italian in origin. It was a corruption of the original "Charbonneau" and pronounced French-style, with the accent on the first syllable.

She'd met Art in the late 1950s when they attended General Brown Central School, but she hadn't paid him much mind even though she was tight with his sister, Jean. In later years, Penny vaguely recalled being warned by another high schooler to stay away from the Shawcross boy; she couldn't remember why. At the time he'd seemed a loner but otherwise unnoteworthy. After the ninth grade, he hadn't reappeared at school.

In January 1972, four months before the disappearance of Jack Blake, the twenty-three-year-old Penny had bumped into her old classmate in front of the JCPenney store in the public square. Art seemed excited to see her again. He was twenty-six now and told her that he'd left the Army six months earlier after combat service in Vietnam. She saw that he'd grown into a good-looking six-footer with narrow hips and barrel chest. He seemed pleasant, straightforward, a good talker with a sly sense of humor that she hadn't noticed in school. The cleft on his chin put her in mind of an economy-size dimple. She recognized the twinkle in his eye; she'd never had a problem attracting males and didn't let it bother her.

When he asked where she was living, she explained that she and her two children had moved in with her parents. "I'm not married," she hastened to explain. "I don't believe in it. I *hate* marriage."

Art told her that they hadn't made the mule big enough to drag him down the aisle. He nodded pleasantly when she explained that her children's father had begged her to marry him but she'd refused. Now the boyfriend was out of the picture and she was attending Jefferson Community College as a single parent.

Penny ended up taking Art to her parents' home for dinner. They went out again the next night and the next. He seemed as randy as other males but didn't force things. He had plenty of time for listening, a trait she hadn't noticed in many other Jefferson County men. And he seemed fascinated by her four-year-old son and two-year-old daughter.

After their fifth date she discovered that she was pregnant. Art promised to stick by her and the baby. He told her he worked for the Watertown Department of Public Works. When summer came, he said, he would be assigned to the city's "grass gang," cutting and trimming public lawns, but right now he worked at the city dump at the far end of Water Street.

They moved into subsidized housing in the Cloverdale Apartments, corner accommodations with two bedrooms upstairs and a living room and dining room downstairs. For Penny's children, there were acres of grassy playground, and the municipal swimming pool was a short walk. Sometimes Art brought home discarded dolls and toys and surprised Penny by playing enthusiastically with her kids, almost like a kid himself. His job paid one hundred dollars a week, but he told her he was looking for something better.

He proved quieter as a live-in companion than as a suitor. If he had feelings for her and the children, he kept them concealed. She told friends that he was "a neat freak," carping when she failed to meet his standards. He demanded a freshly ironed white shirt every morning, even on days when he was assigned to the dump, and he refused wash-and-wear. He also refused to drive, said it made him nervous. He thought nothing of walking six or eight miles in his rolling gait or pedaling his bike twenty miles to the St. Lawrence River and twenty miles back.

He had a curious hobby: he would lay a pane of glass atop a picture and trace a copy in bright-colored paint. To Penny, some of his glass-paintings looked salable, but he didn't seem interested in turning a profit. When she asked where he'd learned the technique, he changed the subject. One day he found a crack in one of his paintings and yelled, "Those fuckin' kids!"

"I broke it accidentally," Penny confessed.

His face softened. "Oh," he said. "It's okay then."

After a few weeks in their apartment, his moods and actions began to vary sharply and Penny wished she could figure out what was wrong. He would disappear after dinner and stay out till long after midnight. He left a bouquet of wildflowers on a female neighbor's doorstep with a note, "These are for your grave," then refused to explain. He flirted with barmaids and waitresses. And although he claimed that Penny's kids got on his nerves, there seemed to be a special magnetism between him and children. He seemed to favor blond-haired boys and enjoyed roughhousing with them. On a typical day, he would come home from work around 4:00 P.M. and go outside to wrestle or play catch, kickball, tag, hide-and-seek. Sometimes she would hear loud voices and find him in the middle of a yelling match. Sometimes he turned mean. He'd been a wrestler in high school and his outdoor job kept him in good physical condition; he didn't always realize how much stronger he was than his small playmates. More than once she saw children fleeing from him in fright. A woman named Lutz complained to the cops that he grabbed her son by the neck, but it blew over. Penny's two-year-old cried and complained whenever she was left in Art's care. It crossed Penny's mind to ask if he was abusing her, but she didn't want to alarm the child.

Most of the family's household activities were conducted in stony silence. He left for work before daybreak and barely said hello when he returned. The loudest sound at dinner was the clink of silverware. Sometimes he seemed to retreat into himself, mute and immobile for hours, totally ignoring her and the kids. She was a quiet person from a quiet family and tried not to take offense. Few of the housing project's marital relationships were graced by sophisticated conversation.

After his afternoon romps and an early dinner, he often went fishing, returning after dark. She kidded him that he couldn't catch a cold. Even when she asked him to bring home some fish to stretch their budget, he didn't produce. Nor did she ever smell fish on his hands or his clothing. She figured that the neat freak must be washing up at the river.

Neither of them drank or used drugs. He smoked cigarettes, but not to excess. When they went out, it was usually to stroll around the sprawling playground. He liked to sip coffee in an all-night diner and chat with policemen and sheriff's deputies. Sometimes Penny wondered what he found in common with cops, and it crossed her mind that maybe he'd been in trouble. But she wasn't a nosy person and didn't ask.

He was undemanding about sex and seemed satisfied with their partnership. The subject of love never came up. Conventional sexual positions suited them both. He was slow to reach a climax and seemed to prefer to lie in her arms and be comforted. He moaned with pleasure when she rubbed his back or tickled his ribs. She told him he was "like a little kid."

She wondered if his need for comforting had anything to do with his mother. Betty Shawcross was barely five feet tall, but she had the vocal style of an Adirondack lumber boss. She made her house shine and ruled the home at Shawcross Corners like an empress. She was a plain-looking woman with a Mediterranean cast to her features; Art explained that her swarthy complexion and dark hair came from Italian and Greek ancestry.

To Penny, he seemed thoroughly cowed and confused by the tiny matriarch. He swore that he loved her deeply and sang her praises, but he seemed nervous in her presence. On visits to the family home, he couldn't seem to sit down. The father, Arthur Roy Shawcross, a county roadworker and heavy-equipment operator like his father before him, was as subdued as the mother was brash. Sometimes Art spoke favorably of his father and sometimes he put him down for allowing the mother to take command.

Penny had to admit that she'd never met a more intimidating woman, but she developed a grudging admiration. "Betty's a domineering type," she explained to a friend. "But she's the best thing going in that family. If she wants something, she's gonna get it. And if she doesn't like what people are saying about her or her kids, she'll tell 'em off in plain English."

After the apartmentmates had lived together for several months, Penny's parents began pressing for a marriage. Penny liked Art but doubted that she could ever learn to love a man who could block her out so thoroughly, without reason or explanation. But her pregnancy was beginning to show and she agreed not to sully the Sherbino name by flaunting another illegitimate birth. Art's mother and his sister Jeannie, Penny's old friend from school, opposed the marriage but refused to say why. Penny wondered if they knew something bad about Art, but she couldn't imagine what it might be. A medical problem? Something in his past? She decided to take her chances. For all his eccentricities, Art was a decent, honest, hardworking man. She prided herself on understanding males, and by all indications he was a good catch from a good family. Love would come later. And if it didn't—well, she could always get a divorce. At least the child would bear his name.

They were married on April 22, 1972, four months after their chance meeting in front of JCPenney. They had a small reception at her brother's house and returned to their apartment. Art changed clothes and went outside to play with the children.

Two weeks later the first cop arrived in the middle of the night with questions about some damned runaway kid. Penny knew where her husband had been that day and wasn't concerned. He'd fished for a while, then hiked up the hill to her parents' house and spent four hours chatting with her father. He'd come home looking the same as he looked on any other day: neat and clean, cool and calm.

His navy blue jacket had a few stains and she washed it at his request. He seemed even quieter than usual, but there was nothing incriminating about that.

So why had the cop questioned him? And why had a detective backed him against a wall the next day and then a few days later? It was about a kid named Blake. She'd never seen the kid before and neither had Art.

Eleven days after the police had begun bothering Art, Penny was discouraged to learn that he was in more trouble involving children. Instead of going fishing after dinner, he'd played behind the apartment with his young friends. Just before the sun went down, he dumped a small child into a burning barrel of trash, then grabbed six-year-old Michael Norfolk and stuffed handfuls of grass in his shirt and pants. When the boy resisted, he pushed him down and spanked him.

Art explained to Penny that they were just horsing around. But young Norfolk's mother didn't understand and lodged a complaint.

The judge fined Art ten dollars for harassment. On the court papers, Penny read: "Works for city—parole to Lyle Sylver." *Parole?* She couldn't imagine why a parole officer was involved. They were only for ex-convicts, weren't they?

The incident wasn't mentioned on the radio or TV or in the *Daily Times*. And Penny was relieved that the cops finally stopped getting in Art's face about the runaway Blake kid. He seemed chastened for a while, hung around the house and kept to himself. But after a few days, he returned to his carefree ways, working all day at the dump, frolicking on the playground, then fishing till dark or later. His luck didn't seem to improve. After four months of living together and dozens of fishing trips, Penny realized that he'd never brought home a fish.

15.

Mary Blake refused to let up on the cops and the politicians. If Jack had been some ward heeler's brat, she told her husband, the piggy-wiggies wouldn't be sitting on their fat asses making up theories about how he runned away or was visiting a pal somewhere. *Jack came home every night before dark, gaddamn it! Why won't anybody believe us?*

By the third week of May, two weeks after the disappearance, Mary's insides were fairly well healed and every few days she would clomp across the short iron bridge over the Black River and up Factory Street to harangue the police and the city fathers. Sometimes she dropped in on newsmen to demand more coverage. The *Syracuse Post Herald*'s bureau chief, Bob Strom, talked with her often and wrote more stories about Jack than he'd intended. The *Watertown Daily Times* lightened its coverage when there was nothing new to report, but then ran a few more pieces at her insistence.

Her relations with the Watertown P.D. weren't enhanced when the cops showed her some clothes they'd found in an abandoned car and asked if they were Jack's. She held the waist of the pants up to her chin, and the legs dangled to her ankles. "Jack's four-foot-nine," she said contemptuously. "Nat nine-foot-four."

She was encouraged when a detective called and asked in a friendly voice if she would lend some articles of Jack's clothing to a woman in Tonka Falls.

"For what?" Mary asked.

"Well, this gal's a psychic," the cop said, "but she's good." Mary didn't refuse any assistance, supernatural or otherwise. A seer had come to the door and asked for articles of Jack's clothing, and Mary had turned over socks, underwear, and a shirt from the dirty laundry bag. Her husband had handed over a pair of Jack's pants to another psychic, who examined them and announced that the boy was "absolutely, positively alive." Other items had been given to the police and a few pieces to a man with a bloodhound. Now Mary looked in the boys' room and found Jack's rubber boots.

The Tonka Falls psychic said she preferred working with cloth, but promised to do her best. While awaiting results, Mary received a call from still another psychic, who said she'd been recommended by the same Watertown detective. "Can you lend me some clothes that your son actually wore?" the woman asked.

"No," Mary said. "I've given all his dirty clothes away."

Mary flushed with anger as she told a friend what happened an hour later:

"There was a knack on my door and when I opened it this detective barged into the house like King Kong. He says, 'Mary, where the hell's Jack's clothes?'

"I said, 'Whattaya mean?'

" 'Didja bury 'em?'

" 'Did I *bury* 'em? What are ya, nuts or sumpin'?'

" 'Mary, didn't you just tell somebody on the phone you didn't have no more of Jack's clothes?'

" 'I told her I din't have no more *dirty* clothes. I got bushels of clean ones. Why? You wanna try 'em on?'

" 'Don't get smart with me.' "

Mary warned herself to cool down. It seemed obvious that the cop had some odd ideas and the call from the psychic was a setup. When he had the nerve to ask if Mary and Big Pete would be willing to go downtown for lie detector tests, she said, "You're damn right. I'll do anything that'll help find Jack. But after I take the test, mister, I want *you* to take one, see what makes your ass tick. 'Cause you're *nuts*!"

An hour later a police work crew arrived with shovels, and a plainclothesman said, "We have to search the house, Mrs. Blake. We have information and we gotta check it out. It's for your good as well as ours."

Mary didn't understand.

"We don't have a body," the plainclothesman went on. "We're not even sure your kid's dead."

"Well, he's *nat* dead!" Mary exclaimed.

"Then where is he? Mary, we got a tip you and the mister buried Jack and his clothes in your basement."

"The beds ain't made," she said, opening the door wide, "but come right in. Dig till ya drap."

The crew left after an hour, leaving the cellar a mess. "Sorry to disappoint ya," Mary cracked.

When the detective called later to set up the lie detector test, Mary said, "Why don't you test Shawcross?"

"The lie box don't work on nut cases," he answered.

A date was set, then canceled. Mary waited but heard nothing further on the subject. When she saw one of the detectives in the public square, she ran up and said, "Now that we're in the clear, does that mean you'll start lookin' for Jack?"

The cop hurried off.

As the weeks passed, Mary tried to maintain a semblance of normalcy in the little house on Water Street, but her eight remaining children were taking Jack's absence hard. Twelve-year-old Rosie raged about the case, how the bad man had stolen her brother and the cops hated poor people and somebody better bring Jack home pretty soon or she'd get even. Sometimes Mary suspected that the child was on pills—LSD, maybe, or uppers. It wouldn't be the first time that her children had dabbled in drugs.

On a warm spring day, a police car deposited the distraught Rosie in the Blake yard. She was slobbering and clawing at her face. A cop said, "We found this crazy thing up at the public square."

Mary's sister Kitty said, "Don't you call her crazy! She's been through a lot."

Rosie rolled on the grass. There was a whitish outline around her mouth.

By the next morning the child was still raving, and Mary took her to the Mental Health unit at Mercy Hospital. The doctors reported that she was suffering a nervous breakdown and committed her to the State Hospital at Ogdensburg for three months. When Big Pete heard the news, he sighed and opened another bottle. Mary cried and asked herself, What did we do to God that God done this to us?

A religious program appeared on the TV screen and she watched without thinking. She seldom attended church and was turned off by the Bible with all its begats and verilies. But as the TV preacher recited the Twenty-third Psalm she found herself following with her lips.

When it was over a couple of the verses lingered in her mind. *The house of the Lord . . .* Was that where Jack was? She thought of the churchpeople who'd brought money and groceries and the preachers who'd led prayers for her son. From now on, she said to herself, I better pay more attention to religion. It can't hurt. But I'm still plenty pissed at God.

II

LINDA RUTH NEARY: A MARRIAGE

1.

Linda Neary held the newspaper as though it were one of the snakes that sometimes frightened her horses. The blaring headline only added to her unease:

SEARCH FOR BOY CONTINUES

It was the latest in a series of news items that were destroying her sleep. The minute she'd learned that the police were searching Pool's Woods for a missing boy, she had an eerie feeling that the child was dead and her ex-husband Art was involved. He'd been married before, right out of high school, to a woman named Sarah Chatterton; Linda had been his second wife and Penny Sherbino was his current and third. Linda hadn't laid eyes on him in years, but she'd heard that he was living in the Cloverdale Apartments with Penny, not far from the spot where the boy was last seen. She didn't know exactly why she was so sure that Art was the killer, and she didn't know where to go with the information. If she told the cops, they would demand the whole story back to day one. But some parts were too hurtful to recall. Maybe too dangerous, too.

Linda was a stocky woman but well proportioned, with deep blue eyes and pleasantly chiseled Nordic features. Her golden hair hung to her thighs; she joked that it took her three days to shampoo. Despite her Brunhilde shape and look, she rode with an equestrienne's grace, and she was robust enough to control the rankest horse. She'd seldom been far from horses, even while studying for a teaching degree. Her favorite was an Appaloosa-Arabian mixture she'd owned as a child, when the family first moved from Bergen County, New Jersey, to Clayton, New York, northwest of Watertown.

She was born Phyllis Lee Brown but adopted by the Nearys and renamed. After graduation from high school in Clayton, she accepted the engagement ring of a gentle, soft-spoken man who'd dated her for months without ever mentioning sex. Three days before the wedding he explained that he was gay. Linda implored him to go through with the marriage, but he told her that he couldn't involve the woman he loved in his sexual confusion. Then he left for a new life in Rochester—and eventual death from AIDS.

With her fiancé gone, Linda had felt adrift, rootless. She wanted to be surrounded by people, make new friends, stay ahead of her grief. In 1966, she landed a daytime job as bartender at a square-dance hall called McFarland's Loft. She soon found herself breaking up fights and fending off the advances of amorous soldiers and salesmen and millhands who stared over the tops of their drinks at her modest décolletage. She was sturdy enough to take care of herself and didn't mind the attention. Her voice was soft and her English devoid of the harsh North Country accent by reason of her early years in New Jersey, but she found that she could yell loud enough to summon the cops or the bouncer. She felt wanted and needed; her life was righting itself. Then she met Art Shawcross.

2. LINDA NEARY

He looked like a gentleman, nicely dressed, shoes shined. He had brownish wavy hair, neatly combed. I didn't know it then, but he never left the house unless he looked perfect. If his work clothes weren't pressed just so, he threw a fit.

My shift ended at 7:00 P.M. and I was sitting at the bar sipping a ginger brandy with some friends. He said "Hi" from two seats down. Up to then, I hadn't seen him talk to anybody, men *or* women. He just seemed to want to be by himself. I'd served him a rum and Coke earlier; you could see he wasn't much of a drinker. Neither was I.

He surprised me by asking for a dance. I didn't understand because there were lots of prettier girls there. He was shy and so was I, but after a few dances and another drink we opened up and realized we were both on the rebound. He told me he was twenty-two and separated from his wife. He said he'd been married for three years to a woman named Sarah Chatterton from Sandy Creek, about twenty miles south of Watertown. He said they hadn't wanted kids but one came along anyway, and after that she refused to have sex. That's what he claimed, anyway. Then she took the baby and walked out. He said it hurt him to lose his son. It seemed so much like my situation, losing the love of your life and trying to recover.

I asked what he did for a living, and he said he packed cottage cheese. He said it was a miserable job, standing in a cold damp dairy stuffing boxes, snapping the tops on and sealing 'em. He said he had a line on a better job. He certainly didn't look like a cheese packer in his neat shirt and tie.

We went on a few dates. He was very quiet, didn't swear. He hated crowds and didn't like to be confined. He never let me or anybody else buy him a drink; he seemed to resent favors. There was nothing fancy about him; he'd been brought up in Brownville, a little paper-mill town on the Black River, and he had the North Country way of talking. He said he wasn't a good student—"I didn't like being in the damn school." But he was a long way from being stupid. He told me to call him "Art" or "Artie," never "Arthur." I got the impression that "Arthur" was also his father's name and they didn't get along.

After a while we started going steady. I lived with my folks in Clayton and he lived with his parents. My dad had a boat and took him fishing in the St. Lawrence for perch, northern pike, bass, muskies. Art was crazy about fishing. He'd hitchhike the twenty miles from Watertown or ride up on his bike. Most of the men I'd known were into cars and motorcycles and pickups, but he hated to drive. It seemed odd for a grown man. He mentioned something about a schoolmate being killed in a car accident; then later he said he got nauseated and felt anxious in a car. I didn't press him. He didn't like being pressed.

His mother and father seemed like good people. A little distant, but nice. They lived at a crossroads called Shawcross Corners, just outside of Brownville, about five miles northwest of Watertown. The house was on a little country road, two-lane, a bumpy lumpy road with a high crown. Art said his grandfather had bought the land and split it up for his two sons after World War II, and Art's father built a little wooden house on his parcel. The countryside was what they call "broken"—low rocky hills, marginal farmland, dairies, patches of wheat and corn, a narrow creek with no name, swampland, patches of limestone, woods full of scrub maples, oaks, beech trees, hickory. Art told me he spent most of his childhood in those woods.

He talked constantly about his mother, how much he loved her and she *didn't* love him, how he wanted her approval and couldn't get it. He'd always say, "No matter what I do, it ain't right."

One day he showed up in a bad mood. He said he told his mother how well he was doing at work and she said, "Well, if you had a real education you wouldn't have to take every menial job that comes along." He said he never had a job or a girlfriend good enough for his mom.

I asked him about his childhood and he said she used a belt on him, but not all that much. His father never raised a hand. That struck me as odd. His mom was barely five feet tall and his dad was an ex-Marine. Why was she handling the discipline?

You could see she had Art thoroughly intimidated. His father was such a nice man, a quiet man, but Betty had him intimidated, too. I noticed a couple of odd things about Art, but I was an inexperienced kid and it only made him seem more interesting. Lots of people have one-track minds, but his was extreme. If we were going to a movie, that's where we went—we didn't stop off and have a drink, we didn't change our minds and go bowling, we didn't alter our plans in any way. If I said, "Let's get a cup of coffee," he'd say, "Nope. We went to the movies. Now we're going home." He never improvised; he acted like the sky would fall if he showed any flexibility. And he was super-strict about being on time and expected the same of everybody else. If you were two minutes late, he flared up.

Sex wasn't a problem because we didn't have any. He said he didn't believe in sex unless I wanted it, and I said, No, not outside of marriage. He always tried to please me.

After he was drafted in April 1967, his first wife Sarah agreed to give him a divorce, provided he signed off on their eighteen-month-old son. It hurt him bad to give up his baby for good, but he wanted to be free to marry me. Later Sarah remarried and her new husband adopted the boy. Art never saw his son again.

My mother and father kept asking us not to talk marriage till Art finished his hitch in the Army, but we couldn't wait. I was working at the Coffee Pot restaurant in Watertown when he came home on a thirty-day furlough in September. The day before his leave was up, we got in my car and looked for a preacher. We finally got married at nine o'clock one night in a little church down the Interstate. I was twenty and Art was twenty-two.

It was three in the morning when I dropped my husband off at his parents' house. My mom was waiting up when I got back to Clayton. She said, "You're married, aren't ya?"

I said, "Yep."

"You know how I feel about it."

"Yeah, Mom."

The next morning Art phoned and said, "Do you remember we're married?" He sounded excited.

I said, "Yeah." It felt nice, being Mrs. Arthur John Shawcross.

Later that morning he hitched back out to see me in Clayton, and for six hours I sat on the stones next to McCormick's Restaurant while he fished. I guess fishing was more important to him than consummating our marriage. I asked about his parents' reaction and he said he'd been afraid to tell them at first, but when he got up his nerve, all his mom said was, "You shoulda been man enough to tell us right away." As usual, it got him upset, but I told him he was overreacting. His mother and him, they just aggravated each other.

While he fished, he made a few confessions. He said he'd been arrested when he was eighteen. He broke a window in the Sears store and set off a burglar alarm. A few years later a kid hit him with a snowball and Art chased him into his house and got arrested for assault. Both times he was put on probation, so it didn't amount to much. I just figured he was still young and wild at the time. And I respected him for telling me. It showed he wanted our marriage to start on an honest basis.

At five o'clock that afternoon, he packed up his fishing gear and left for the airport. A week later he was in Vietnam.

The *Watertown Daily Times* reported our marriage, and Art's ex-wife Sarah phoned me from Sandy Creek and said, "I can tell you an awful lot about your husband if you want to know."

She said he was violent and she'd always been afraid of what he might do to the baby. I flat didn't believe her. I'd seen him with his son a couple of times and he was very gentle. Art loved children, got along great. I couldn't imagine what Sarah was talking about. She gave the impression that he beat her, but she didn't give details. I figured, It's just sour grapes.

After a while I wanted to feel closer to my husband, so I went to Shawcross Corners to visit his folks. The first time I set foot in that house as Art's wife, I gave his father a big hug. He kinda looked surprised and stepped back. I said, "I'm used to it. My dad hugs me all the time." So Mr. Shawcross smiled and hugged me back. A nice man!

I went through the same thing with Mrs. Shawcross. Later I noticed that both of them were kind of distant with their kids—no touching, no hugging. That's just the way they were. I'm sure they loved their children, but they showed it in other ways. Betty did the childraising. It seemed like Mr. Shawcross spent most of his time running the snowplow or working at the county barns. I figured that was why Art always had to be carefully dressed, every crease in place and his tie knotted just right. He was more influenced by his mother's tastes because his father was gone so much.

At first Betty didn't take to me, but when we started exchanging information from Art's letters she turned real nice. She told me he'd always been the "bane" of her life—that's the word she used. And she said, "You know, he was in trouble when he was younger."

I said, "Yeah, he told me."

"Well, it just seems that no matter what he does, he can't seem to get along with people."

Betty thought there was something wrong with his brain. She said he'd been knocked unconscious a few times and it distorted his thinking. I thought, Well, his thinking seems all right to me. But I didn't say anything. Betty was such a strong personality, it was better just to listen.

At first, Art's letters confused everybody. He wrote me that he'd seen Vietnamese women and children killed and it upset him to be "made to kill." He said he'd been ordered to assist in body-bagging and some of his buddies' bodies were mutilated. I wrote back and tried to console him. He never mentioned things like that again.

One day Betty got a letter saying that he'd been hit by shrapnel, and she sounded shook. But he didn't mention the wound to me—he didn't want to upset me. Then Betty got a letter about a big battle scene, and she was *really* upset. He was very thoughtful to both of us, sent cards on birthdays and holidays. He didn't miss a single chance to be recognized or loved.

3. ARTHUR SHAWCROSS (PSYCHIATRIC INTERVIEW)

I went on a search-and-destroy mission. . . . They told us over the radio, Surround that one area and kill everything there right down to the chickens and pigs. We surrounded that area, we just filled that place full of bullets and grenades, whatever we had. We went in and killed off all the animals and stuff. We did some things to the women that were there that didn't die outright. We just put them all in a big pile and burned it. . . . Everything, the bodies, the building, you know, we burned everything. Then we just dug a hole, a big dish and put everything in it, all the ashes in there, covered it over, went and got sod and grass and dug up small trees and stuff and planted it over that area just like there wasn't nobody there. . . .

One time we . . . came across three Green Berets tied to trees by their hands behind the tree. They were skinned from their necks to their ankles. Do you understand that? You can see everything in the stomach, muscle, you know, the gut. It's like looking in a plastic bubble. These guys are covered with mosquitoes. One guy was still alive. He had his eyelids cut off so his eyes were open all the time. He couldn't see, but he could hear. His lips were cut off. He was begging us to kill him. We got all the information on who they were, then the lieutenant shot the guy in the head and got their dog tags. When you see something like that, you get told to kill somebody or shoot the enemy or whatever, you do the same thing they've done to you. . . .

I didn't get no sexual satisfaction out of it. I was just satisfied probably to the point where, I don't know, like I did something right.

4. LINDA RUTH NEARY

After Art had been overseas for six months, I joined him for two weeks of R&R in Hawaii. He'd made pfc. by then. It was a delayed honeymoon and he was gentle when we first made love. We went out in a glass-bottomed boat and saw the sunken ships at Pearl Harbor, drove to Diamond Head and the Dole pineapple place, and went to a cherry blossom festival. He was nice, a good husband, but he was also a little moody. I figured it was just the war. He told me a lot of funny stories about Army life, but he never said a word about combat.

I was surprised that most of his friends were black. I'd hardly ever known a black person, and I enjoyed their company. They had a lot of life, a lot of humor, common sense. I could understand it when Art said he got along better with the black officers than the whites. They were outcasts together.

His overseas tour ended in September 1968, and we spent his leave in a cottage behind my parents' house in Clayton. The second night he was home, I touched him while he was asleep and he nearly broke my jaw. He felt awful afterward, said he dreamed he was back in Vietnam. He cried and said over and over, "I didn't mean to hit you." From then on I kept my distance when I woke him up. Flashbacks, he called it.

After the leave, he was assigned to Fort Sill as an armorer, repairing weapons, and we drove all the way to Oklahoma with our cat Smoky and a bunch of clothes and canned goods. Art wouldn't drive my little English Ford with the right-hand drive unless I was with him. Something about driving scared him. After the Ford broke down and we bought a used Cutlass, he refused to drive at all.

We found a small apartment in Lawton, and every day I drove him to and from Fort Sill. By this time he had a couple of stripes and was fixing rifles and other weapons. For a few months, our life was normal. He read a lot—war stories, history, sports, but mostly science fiction. We visited an Indian village together. He complained about the local fishing, but he enjoyed rattlesnake hunts and other outdoor things. I did some volunteer teaching in a literacy program and kept busy.

We'd had okay sex before, but now he began having problems. He would be too fast or have trouble getting an erection. It bothered him because he felt he wasn't pleasing me. I just told him to relax: "Slow down. You're not only supposed to please me, you're supposed to please yourself."

After that, things improved a little. If I talked to him, calmed him, he could perform. But he still had trouble getting an orgasm. I didn't know what to do.

He began going off by himself, brooding, sullen. He couldn't sleep. He'd take long walks, around and around, no destination. I tried to figure him out. I knew he'd seen some terrible things. He'd gone to Vietnam with no sense of self-worth, and I realized that he still saw himself that way. All that blood and gore overseas made him feel worse about himself—trash, scum, a crazy killer. I couldn't seem to change his mind. He felt beaten down; he was no good; he could never please. He told me he'd never had friends. Sometimes he'd get depressed, and I'd say, "Go ahead and cry. It's a natural feeling. It's not gonna hurt anything if you cry a little."

He said, "I wasn't allowed to cry when I was growing up, even when I was spanked." I never understood that. He said his mother told him, "You're not much of a man if you cry." It seemed like whenever he talked about something bad in his life, he blamed it on his mother.

He was affectionate enough, but he never could say "I love you." The "L" word made him highly nervous. I would say it but he wouldn't. He wanted me to hold him *all* the time. He was cuddly and easy to love, but he had no idea how to give it back. He wanted someone to be close to him, make him feel he belonged. He'd get in this quiet mood where he just wanted to be close. He'd *absorb* my love. I asked him once, "What did your parents consider love?"

He said, "Giving me the things I wanted."

I guess they never realized that what he really wanted was to be held and loved. He was very possessive about me. I was *his* woman, and he didn't want the other GI's to talk to me. He even resented my parents. Or maybe he realized what they thought of him. My father and mother never liked him, told me right from the beginning that he was no good. My mom said, "I just have that feeling. There's gonna be nothing but trouble for you." But being twenty years old, you don't listen. You're in love and that's all you can see.

I kept trying to find out what was eating him. I knew it wouldn't be wise to push him for answers, but things seeped out. He hated authority, and he was always in trouble for acting disrespectful. He'd come home steaming about the sergeant or the lieutenant, and I'd say, "Well, that's part of the Army. You've gotta do what they say."

He said he wanted to be treated with respect. I told him he better find a different occupation, and he just mumbled and walked away.

For months he seemed totally depressed. I'd ask about his day and he'd say, "Don't wanna talk about it." He'd eat supper and take off on a three-hour walk. He told me he blacked out a couple of times on his walks, once for a few minutes and once for an hour or so. He said he couldn't remember where he was or what he'd done.

One night he came back shaking and sweating, and I hugged him and asked what was wrong. He told me he'd been thinking about Vietnam. It took a long time to get it out of him. "I had to kill her," he said, and he started to cry.

I said, "Kill who?"

He said, "A kid. She was carrying bombs for the Vietcong. It was kill or be killed." He told me that the My Lai incident was nothing compared to what he'd seen. It tore him up. I figured he identified with kids because he'd been a hurt kid himself.

One night he came home and told me he'd set a big brush fire near the barracks. "I flipped a match into the weeds," he said. "I didn't mean to start a fire. It just caught —*whoosh*!" There was a glint in his eyes. I'd noticed that he always took himself off the hook when he did something wrong, as though things happened accidentally and he always got the blame.

He was like a little kid about fire, fascinated. He'd light book matches one by one and flip them in the ashtray. I figured it was just nerves. He was having terrific changes of mood—he'd be hyper one minute and the next minute his head would be on his knees. I would talk to him and he wouldn't even acknowledge me. He'd always been moody, but it seemed deeper now. I could speak to him for three or four minutes before he snapped out of it. I gave him lots of love and attention, but I guess that wasn't enough.

One afternoon he called from the post and told me not to pick him up after work; the sergeant would be driving him home. He said, "You better have dinner ready," and hung up. He was getting bossier, but I figured he was under pressure.

He walked in at nine o'clock, four hours late for dinner, and he was so depressed he could hardly talk. I asked him where he'd been and he said, "Walking." He sounded so lethargic that I asked if he'd been taking drugs or something. He said, "No. I want to see a psychiatrist."

It didn't click in my mind, but later I wondered what happened that night. Did he have another flashback? Or did he do something else . . . hurt somebody? It makes me shudder to think what he might have done on his walks.

All together, I drove him to four different appointments with the Army psychiatrist. Each time I waited on the dispensary steps. On the fourth visit the doctor told me Art had run out the back door.

When he got home late that night, I asked him what happened and he said, "They're not helping me. I don't wanna talk about it."

I said, "What upset you so much? What were you and the doctor talking about?"

He said, "That's between me and him."

In the morning the psychiatrist told me that Art wouldn't cooperate and gave me commitment papers to sign.

I said, "What's the matter with him?" The doctor told me it was confidential, but Art was mentally ill. I asked if it was something new or if it went back to childhood, and he just shrugged. He did tell me that Art had to kill some people in Vietnam, but no details.

When I was leaving, he said, "Keep him away from fire, Mrs. Shawcross. I don't want to discourage you, but this is the way he gets his sexual enjoyment."

That night, Art asked if I thought he belonged in a psycho ward. I said, "You've changed so much from the time you went overseas. You're just not the same person. I don't want to see you hurt anybody."

I wasn't worried about myself. He'd never given me any reason to be afraid of him, except the time I woke him up abruptly.

I asked him if he felt he needed mental help and he said yes. I said, "Do you want me to stay home with you?" I was working part-time at a fast-food place so we could make ends meet.

He said, "No, Linda. You're always here when I need you."

I just couldn't make the decision about committing him. I wasn't even twenty-one. I called his mother and father and told them, "I don't think I have the right to have him committed. You're his parents. I'll mail the papers up to you."

Art's father seemed to think it was a good idea, but Betty said, "There's nothing wrong with my son!"

I gave her the name of the Army psychiatrist and said, "At least call and ask why they want to do this."

Betty said, "Well, they can send all the papers they want, but there's *nothing* wrong with my son." She sounded annoyed.

That was the last I heard about the mental hospital. The doctor gave Art a couple bottles of pills, but they didn't seem to do much good. Our blue tick hound, six months old, gave him a little nip, didn't even break the skin, and Art threw the dog against the wall and snapped his neck. Then he burst into tears. He kept repeating, "Oh, Linda, I didn't mean to hurt him. . . ." He wrapped the dog up and cried. I helped with the burial, and the rest of the night I cuddled Art and calmed him down.

I kept thinking how quick it happened: *instantly.* What would he do the next time he lost his temper? He seemed to be losing control. He'd go from quiet to violent in a split second, *and there didn't need to be a reason.* I was afraid of him. I still loved him, but I kept hearing the dog's neck snap.

A few days later I phoned our house around 3:00 P.M. and the line was busy. I tried two or three more times and the operator said there was no conversation on the line. It didn't make sense; when I'd left for work, Art seemed okay.

I told my boss, "There's something wrong," and he let me go home.

Art was stretched on the bathroom floor in full uniform, ribbons and tie and all. I shook him and he didn't move. There were two empty pill bottles on the sink and a Baggie with a white powder residue. I couldn't find a note.

The medics took him away. The way he looked on the gurney, I was sure I'd never see him again.

After a while the hospital called. They'd pumped his stomach. If I'd found him fifteen minutes later, he'd have been dead. Maybe it would've been better.

When he came home, I asked him why he tried to take his life. He said he felt that I didn't love him anymore. I was surprised. I loved him and I'd always gone out of my way to show it.

He said, "I've done so much to hurt you."

I was surprised at that, too. He'd never pushed me around or threatened me. He was having mental problems and acting weird, yeah, but I never took it personally. I figured it was just something he'd brought home from combat and we'd work things out together. Don't all young couples have problems?

I asked him, "What have you ever done to hurt me, Art?"

He looked at the floor. I knew that mood. There was no use talking to him when he was like that. He would just block you out.

A few mornings later his sergeant called me at home. He said, "Where the hell's Art? He's two hours late."

I said, "I don't know. I dropped him off on time."

When he came home that night I asked where he'd been.

He said, "None of your business."

I said, "Well, I don't care, Art, but the sergeant's gonna ask you when you go in tomorrow."

He said, "I was out walking." From the look on his face I

knew not to press him. That was another time when I wondered what he'd been up to, but he never explained.

In the spring of '69 he got his honorable discharge after two years service. We drove the Cutlass back home to Clayton and rented the cottage behind our family house for fifty dollars a month. Things were tough, but I wasn't about to give up on our marriage. I was three months pregnant and I thought a baby might help, especially if it was a son.

All Art wanted to do was fish from my dad's boat. He refused to look for a job. He couldn't stop talking about friends he'd lost in Vietnam, and he chattered constantly about death and dying and body bags. I got the idea that he was afraid of death, but at the same time he was attracted to death himself. It was always on his mind.

His whole personality had changed from when we first met in the dance hall. He had to have things exactly his own way and he threw temper tantrums like a two-year-old. I couldn't get him to go to church. And he lied about everything. No subject was too small for him to lie about.

I drove him to job interviews and he always came away mad. It infuriated him that there was no veteran's preference. People seemed to resent that he'd served in Vietnam. It struck me that he'd never gotten much credit in his life, and now he'd done something brave and wasn't getting any credit.

I tried to buck him up. "You fought as hard as anybody. It's just that this wasn't an accepted war."

He said, "I did my time and they treat me like dirt."

For the first time in our marriage, he began to drink heavily. Johnnie Walker, Cutty Sark, J&B—he went from almost a teetotaler to a heavy drinker. He'd sit on the end of the dock and drink from the bottle. Then he'd go on a long walk, three or four hours. When he came home, he jumped on me: "You're not keeping the house neat. . . . You're getting too fat. . . ."

The doctor said my weight was fine. I'm just a stout

woman, that's all. And I kept that little cottage the same as I always had—gleaming.

He began saying things like, "How the hell are we gonna support a baby?" He had these black moods. And when he drank, any little thing would set him off. *Anything.* I would say, "Aren't you gonna eat your dinner?" and he'd blow up.

Early in April he got a laborer's job with Knowlton Brothers paper mill on Factory Street in Watertown. He fed paper into a machine and cut it off the line, then helped put it on big rolls and stack them with a forklift. He was still afraid to drive so I shuttled him back and forth in our old Cutlass. Most nights he'd open a bottle as soon as we got home, then start right in on me.

After he'd been on the job three weeks, he earned a commendation. There'd been a big fire and he discovered it in time to save the plant. The plant was down for a month while they made repairs. Dumb me—I never suspected Art. I trust people.

In June my brother came to visit. I put Art's dinner in the oven and told him I'd be at my parents' house next door for a little while. He didn't seem to mind, but when I came back to serve his dinner I saw the empty bottle of Scotch and I knew what was coming.

He said, "How come you were so long?" He was jealous; he never wanted me to be close to anybody else, not even my own family.

I said, "Art, I was only gone an hour. I haven't seen my brother in eleven years."

He said, "Well, you could spend some time with me."

I said, "I'm *always* here with you."

I shouldn't have talked back. When I asked if he was ready for dinner, he got the same look on his face that he'd had the night he killed our dog. I was four months pregnant and I tried to put my hands over my stomach, but I couldn't block his fists. He beat me till I blacked out.

It was early evening when I woke up on the floor, so I

hadn't been unconscious long. Art was gone. I dragged myself next door and my folks drove me to the hospital. I was bloody, my eyes were black, my face swollen, but nothing was broken. I miscarried a little boy. He would have been my parents' first grandchild and it was very hard on them. I cried, too, but maybe it was for the best.

My brother went to our cottage that night and punched Art out. My brother told him that if he ever laid hands on me again, he was dead meat. Art was a big, powerful man, but I don't think he even defended himself.

The second day I was in the hospital I asked my father to get word to Art that I didn't hate him. How could you hate such a tormented man? I figured it was the bad moods and the drinks that made him hit me.

My father went over and found Art on the floor. He'd slit his wrists in two places. They had to take him to the hospital to be stitched up.

A social worker asked me if I wanted Art arrested, and I said I just wanted out of the marriage. I heard that he asked permission to visit me, but my father warned him away.

I stayed in the hospital for two weeks, and when I came home Art refused to leave our cottage. Dad and I waited till he went to work and packed his stuff. We put it on the front steps of the cottage and locked the place up.

A few days later he called. I said, "I'm so afraid of you now. I don't want to see you or have anything to do with you. I want a divorce."

He said, "I'll contest the divorce. I want to make things right."

I told him that things would never be right. I couldn't stand to hear him cry, so I hung up.

He moved in with a friend in LaFargeville, about six miles southeast of Clayton, and went on a rampage. He helped a couple of guys break into Hammond's gas station in Clayton and steal $407. He burned down a barn at Delafarge Corners, then set fire to the Crowley milk plant. When he was questioned, he admitted the Knowlton arson, too. He told the cops that he was upset about losing me and didn't know what he was doing. He said that on the night of the barn fire, he'd gone for a long walk in a thunderstorm, wandered off the road and sat down outside the barn, crying. A voice told him to set the place on fire. Three thousand bales of hay went up. You have to wonder how his mind worked.

I filed for divorce, and in the middle of October they brought him from the Jefferson County jail on Coffeen Street for a hearing downtown. Before it started, they asked me if I wanted to talk to him. I knew it wouldn't take much for me to take him back. He was a smooth talker and I still had feelings. So I said, "No, I don't want to see him. I'm afraid of him."

He was led into the courtroom in his jail clothes. The first thing he told the judge was that he contested the divorce. He said he was sorry he'd hit me and we lost our child and he wanted to make things right. You could see he was trying not to cry.

The judge turned to me and said, "Mrs. Shawcross, I'll give the two of you some time alone."

I said, "No! I don't want to talk to him. I want a divorce."

After the hearing, the deputies led him away in handcuffs. On the way out the door, he yelled, "Don't do this! Linda, don't leave me! *I love you!*" I could hear him all the way down the hall. It was the only time he ever said he loved me.

5.

Now, two and a half years later, Linda stared at the headline:

SEARCH FOR BOY CONTINUES

In October 1971, two years after the sentencing, Linda had heard that Art was back with his parents at Shawcross Corners. Then he'd married Penny Sherbino and moved into the Cloverdale Apartments. The Blake boy vanished from the same neighborhood. To Linda, the connection was apparent.

She wondered if the Watertown police were aware that her ex-husband had already killed a child in Vietnam. She decided to tell the whole story to a detective—Art's confessions about Vietnam, his sessions with the Fort Sill psychiatrist, the night prowlings, the killing of the dog, all his irrational acts. But something restrained her. She was convinced that the missing boy was dead and there was nothing she could do or say to bring him back. How would Art react if she went to the police? She still remembered his fist crashing into her swollen belly.

She started to call headquarters several times, but she couldn't lift the phone.

III

"I DIDN'T KILL NO GIRL"

My life is a tiny civilization. And a very frail one.

—*Pascal Quignard,* The Salon in Württemberg

1.

On a warm summer night, Mary Blake learned that the loss of one child doesn't prepare a mother for the loss of another. It was July 15, 1972, and Jack had been missing for seventy days. Daughter Rosie was in the mental hospital in Ogdensburg. Mary's husband, Big Pete, was drinking more heavily than ever. Not a word had been heard from Bob, her former lover and Jack's real father, and Mary no longer gave a damn. But she hadn't given up on her missing son. Jack was alive somewhere. He was too good a boy to die at age ten. The Lord wouldn't let things like that happen. Then eight-year-old "Little Pete" went fishing and didn't come home.

Of all her children, he'd been the closest to Jack. He'd idolized his big brother and missed him beyond a child's ability to express. For weeks after the disappearance, he'd wandered in a daze, lifting Jack's pillow, looking under bushes on the slope behind the house, peering into caves and under rocks on the riverbank. The little brother's big brown eyes stayed wet, bloodshot. Mary would see him sitting at the window staring at the empty street. Sometimes she draped her arm across his shoulders and helped him watch.

For a long time, Little Pete had refused to do anything that reminded him of Jack—fishing, bike-riding, exploring. He shut down the nightcrawler business and avoided mutual friends. But lately Mary was glad to see that he was fishing again. She warned him not to go to the river by himself, but he'd never been obedient like Jack and she wasn't overly disturbed when she returned from an errand on a Saturday afternoon to learn from the other children that he'd spaded up a few garden worms, grabbed his K mart rod, and pedaled away on his red bike. Mary was sure he'd be home for dinner in an hour, no more than an hour and a half.

By seven o'clock dinner was over and there was no sign of Little Pete. Three months earlier she wouldn't have worried. Her children had always come home . . . until Jack.

She couldn't wait. She distrusted the Watertown police, so she went to the Jefferson County sheriff's office. It was an old house with a jail grafted onto the back. Sheriff Irving Angel lived in front, and his wife was the matron.

A deskman listened to her complaint. "Now start over and slow down, missus," he told her when she was finished. "I can't help you if I can't understand what you're talking about."

"I'm talking about my son," Mary said, trying to catch her breath. "Allen Blake Jr. We call him Little Pete. He's an epileptic."

"Yeah," the deputy said, "I know about you Blakes. I helped look for your other boy." He promised to see what he could find out. She was glad she didn't have to wait the customary twenty-four hours.

By the time Mary got home, a patrol unit had reported seeing a boy near Seven Bridges. He was riding a red bike and carrying a couple of fish on a stringer.

Mary sat at the front window of her house and watched the daylight fade. It was eight-thirty and Little Pete was two hours overdue. The red bike still hadn't appeared.

She remembered that Dr. Rossen had told her to breathe deeply when she felt woozy. She went out into the front yard so she could see Little Pete when he rode up. She heard the water burbling; the river wasn't as high as when Jack disappeared but it was high enough to carry off a boy who barely weighed fifty pounds. She crossed the street and the railroad spur and looked down the steep embankment. The river was as black as its name and she realized she was wasting her time. If he'd slipped into those churning rapids, it was already too late.

She walked back to the house. It was 9:30 P.M. Her mouth was dry; she went into the kitchen for a drink of water.

Little Pete was leaning over the kitchen sink. "Mom!" he said. "Look what I got ya!"

Mary ripped the string of bullheads from his hands and flung them out the back door. She cut a maple switch and went to work on his backside. He started to cry, and a slurred voice came from the living room: "Hey, what's goin' on?"

"I'm blisterin' your kid's ass!" Mary answered.

Big Pete didn't comment. He didn't comment on much of anything these days.

In the morning, Mary was sick with guilt. Richie was away in the Army, Jack was missing. Little Pete was the last boy in her house and she'd sent him to bed in tears. He'd suffered so much over Jack. What kind of mother would add to a little boy's hardships?

She felt relieved when he returned her hug. She'd always drummed into her kids that their feelings for one another made them as rich as anyone up on Washington Street. Mother and son huddled together in love and grief.

2.

In that same summer of 1972, Arthur Shawcross complained to Parole authorities that he was having problems in his marriage with Penny. He seemed willing to accept the blame and expressed doubts that he understood "the true meaning of love." He used the interview to take a swipe at his mother, describing her as "a domineering person" who downgraded her husband and son.

His parole officer, Lyle Sylver, ordered him to a Watertown mental health clinic for an evaluation. He was found to be functioning at "borderline level of intelligence" and exhibiting "defective moral and social development."

Shawcross insisted that his past crimes were the result of

financial and marital problems, a statement the psychiatric social worker interpreted as an indication that he was unwilling to take responsibility for his actions, typical of the sociopathic personality.

"When he becomes upset," the psychotherapist reported, "he acts impulsively. . . . He describes himself as always having felt that rules are to be broken and did everything in his power to break rules at home as a child and in school. . . . His mother had a very bad temper."

Shawcross described his childhood as unhappy and said his parents were always bickering. The social worker's report concluded with a diagnosis of "dissocial behavior" and a note that the parolee "did not seem interested in any of our services."

3.

By the Labor Day weekend, Jack Blake had been missing for almost four months, but the case had been unpublicized in Helene Hill's hometown of Rochester, and when a friend suggested a holiday visit to Watertown, she had to stop and think before she could position the place in her mind. She'd never visited any of the deep-freeze towns near the Canadian border, but she'd heard their names on weather reports: "The coldest spot in the nation today was Watertown . . . Massena . . . Ogdensburg. . . ." They seemed so forbidding—blank, impersonal, as interchangeable as ice cubes. What kind of people lived there? Even the place names sounded cold.

Helene was a petite and pretty woman with shoulder-length wavy reddish-brown hair, large brown eyes, and delicate features—unlikely looks for the family clown. Friends said she looked like Arlene Dahl and acted like Soupy Sales. Nieces and nephews couldn't get enough of her: "We want Aunt Eenie to come over. She's so *funny*."

The family clown liked to amuse her captive audience. When she was asked how she'd become so funny, she explained that being poor had helped. Her mother had raised the family with little help from an alcoholic husband; she'd washed their sheets in the bathtub because they couldn't afford a washing machine, held two jobs, and never lost her good humor. Helene and her eight brothers and sisters grew up as a tight-knit unit of survivors. Even as adults, they barged into one another's homes, baby-sat the nieces and nephews, exchanged gifts and favors. Any excuse was good for a family party. Telephone conversations ran for hours. In the end, Helene figured that the family closeness was what kept her from going crazy.

A year had passed since her divorce from an Eastman Kodak machinist with a drinking problem, and her lighthearted approach to life was being put to the test. Just when she'd been growing accustomed to raising four kids alone, her mobile home burned to the ground and the whole brood had to move in with her mother. Helene wasn't dating, but she met Stan Fisher at an impromptu party and enjoyed his company. He was a warm, likable man and a hit with her children. It wasn't love, but it beat loneliness.

Now Helene decided to accept Stan's offer of a weekend visit to Watertown to visit his half sister and other relatives. She thought it was a little early to be meeting each other's relatives, but if he didn't mind being chaperoned by her daughter, Chrissie, not yet three years old, it might be an enjoyable Labor Day outing. Helene's sister Wallis, named for the duchess of Windsor, agreed to baby-sit the other three Hill children: Bob, twelve, Tom, ten, and Karen Ann, eight.

4. HELENE HILL

At the last minute Karen begged us to take her along. It was hard to turn her down. She had a mind of her own. She was always telling me, I can do this, Mommy. I can do this *by myself*! How could I say no? She looked so forlorn with her big chocolate eyes and her honey-blond bangs. She'd been in a growth spurt and she was all legs. She said,

"Mommy, don't leave me. Please, please, Mommy, take me to Watertown with you."

Stan said, "Let's take 'em all," but I didn't want to inflict four kids on people I hadn't met. So we left my two boys with my sister Wally, and Karen climbed in the backseat with baby Chrissie. They laughed and giggled all the way to Watertown, two little blond girls rolling on top of each other. I told Stan how Karen was born on Father's Day and weighed seven pounds, six ounces. I told him how I complained to the nurse, "That's not my baby," and the nurse said, "Helene, this *is* your daughter," and I said, "No, it isn't. Look at that pitch-black hair!" I'd thought, God, what a homely baby. I took her home and four weeks later she was as blond as the others. I'm French and Norwegian; we figured the black hair was French but the Norwegian hair shoved it all out. Now she was eight and a gorgeous child.

Watertown was a surprise. It was a sunny September day and not a snowbank in sight. We passed big houses and old trees—Washington Street, the main drag. We saw buildings with Grecian columns and a big statue that looked carved from white marble. The public square was kind of oblong. Traffic flowed one way around it and nobody seemed in a hurry. At the lower end there was a church with a big clock on the steeple and at the upper end Stan pointed out the plaque on a small Woolworth's: "Birthplace of 5&10 cent business." Karen got excited when we passed a statue of a nymph in a fountain. Stan said you could throw pennies for luck.

We drove down a narrow street between buildings that looked like they hadn't been used in years. I was nervous about meeting Stan's relatives and I didn't notice that we passed over a narrow river. It was still afternoon, but the sun doesn't shine much between the brick walls and it's easy to miss things, even in daylight, especially when you're thinking about meeting strangers. And the Black River is only fifty or sixty feet wide and the low bridge doesn't look much like a bridge when you're driving across; it just looks like part of the road.

Stan's half sister Linda Miles and her husband Dick lived

in a little wooden house at 503 Pearl Street, across from the Black Clawson plant where they made heavy machinery for paper mills. The house was right around the corner from Mary Blake's house on Water Street, although I didn't know about the Blakes at the time. There was a rundown bar on the corner. It was the kind of neighborhood where housemaids and factory workers live. The air smelled like the steam locomotives that used to run through Rochester when I was a kid. When we got out of the car, I noticed a haze. The whole place looked like a stage set, only bigger. The air smelled heavy, smoggy, with a trace of oil or wet cinders to it.

I liked Linda and Dick from the start. They had kids of their own and they were nice to my girls. My daughter Karen kept bugging me about throwing a penny in the fountain and making a wish, so after we got settled in, I took her hand and walked her back up to the square, about a fifteen-minute walk. She didn't have to tell me her secret wish; I already knew. She wanted to grow up and be a movie star and marry Tom Jones. She'd always been a music and dancing nut, like everybody in my family. One day I heard her telling the baby, "C'mon now, I'm gonna show you how to do the jitterbug." That was a sight. When she told me that her favorite song was "Joy to the World," I said it was one of my favorite carols, too, and she said, "Not *that* one, Mom, I mean the one by Three Dog Night." She loved that line, "Fishies in the deep blue sea."

By the time we were finished throwing pennies in the fountain, it was late afternoon, so I bought her a sundae at a little restaurant named Enrico's. The waitress sat us in front so Karen could watch the fountain through the plate glass.

When we got back home to Pearl Street, it was turning dark. A priest named Benoit Doste was visiting. He grabbed Karen and put her on his knee, and I heard her ask, "Why do you wear that collar?" Before I could apologize he was answering her in a funny French-Canadian accent. He didn't seem offended. After a while, he put her down and left, and I said good night to him, never knowing the part he would play in my life.

I woke up the next morning and pulled back the curtains. It was a nice Saturday, sunny and bright. I opened the window and the warm air smelled like fresh laundry. I figured the factories were shut down for the holiday weekend. I dressed Karen in matching red, white, and blue top and shorts because it was Labor Day.

A little before two o'clock she said she wanted to play outside and I told her to stay close. I didn't warn her about the river because I didn't really know it was there. Then, too, I was still a little nervous at meeting Stan's people, a little distracted and apprehensive.

I wanted to look extra nice so I decided to wash my hair. But first I went to the screen door and checked on Karen. She was holding a white bunny that belonged to one of Linda's kids. I said, "Honey, Mommy's gonna wash her hair. You stay in the yard, okay?"

She said, "I will, Mom." She gave me her impish look. That meant maybe she would and maybe she wouldn't. But I wasn't worried. We lived a long way from school in Rochester and my kids walked it every day. They knew their way around cities. What could happen to a little girl in a peaceful place like Watertown?

5.

Around 2:00 P.M. a college student named David McGrath was driving over the Pearl Street bridge on his way to a gas station when he observed a blond girl climbing the yellow fence that ran from the corner of the Black Clawson plant to the end of the bridge. A new-looking ten-speed bike was propped against the latticed iron fencing.

As he watched, the child began picking her way down the stony embankment below the factory wall. She seemed to be searching for something.

McGrath thought, A kid her age shouldn't be going down there alone. But he believed in minding his own business and didn't slow down. By September, this branch of the river looked more like an oversized creek. Most of the drownings occurred in the spring runoff, when the water ran bank to bank.

Ten minutes later McGrath returned from refueling his 1966 Corvair and noticed that the bike was still in place. The child was nowhere to be seen. He continued on home.

A few minutes later, four teenage girls, on their way to visit a relative on Stuart Street, reached the same iron bridge as a man was climbing up the bank and over the fence. He wore dark shorts, sandals, and a white shirt, and his bike was white with brown fenders.

As the girls fell into single file to pass, the man began tying a creel to a flat carrier on the back of the bike. Two fishing rods were propped against the railing. He glanced at them and smiled. His clothes were stained and his bare legs were wet. The girls giggled and hurried along.

At 2:45 P.M., sixteen-year-old Terry Roy Tenney walked past Gateway Electronics on Factory Street near the railroad tracks. He was on his way home from the public square and carried a shopping bag full of clothes. Near the Black Clawson plant and the iron bridge, he saw a man on a bike. The boy recognized Art Shawcross, his weird neighbor in the Cloverdale Apartments, and gave him a wave. Art's return gesture seemed a little hesitant as he continued pedaling toward the square.

A few minutes later Terry heard a noise behind him. "Hey," Art asked, skidding to a stop on his bike, "you want an ice cream cone?"

The boy accepted but wondered what the crazy guy was up to. They hardly knew each other, and he'd never acted friendly before. He was out of uniform, too. He was usually neatly dressed, but today he was in soiled dark blue shorts and a dirty T-shirt.

Art smiled and said, "I have trouble remembering people lately. I been fishin'. You want me to ride that stuff home for ya?"

"I don't care," Terry said. "Just don't lose 'em. They're school clothes."

Art took the shopping bag and rode unsteadily in front of the boy. When they reached the sidewalk grating at the approach to the iron bridge, he stopped and peered at the riverbank below. Terry had to detour around him on the sidewalk.

Then Art yelled "Gotta make the light!" and rode furiously across the intersection of Pearl and Water. He turned left at Starbuck Avenue and disappeared.

Ten minutes later Terry arrived at the Cloverdale Apartments and retrieved his shopping bag from his neighbor. What an oddball he was! He did favors for people but made little kids cry. Well, Terry said to himself, what can you expect from a thirty-year-old guy that still gets around on a bike?

6. HELENE HILL

After I washed my hair and got dressed, I went to the back door and called Karen. I went out in front of the house but couldn't see her. I walked past the bar and around the corner, then doubled back and checked in the other direction.

I wasn't worried. She did things her own way and it wouldn't have surprised me if she'd walked all the way to the public square. She was crazy about the nymph statue and the fountain.

At four o'clock Stan and Dick came back in the car, and I mentioned that I couldn't find Karen. By this time she'd been gone for a couple of hours, but I still wasn't upset. It was a sunny Labor Day, lots of traffic, plenty of people walking around. Watertown seemed like such a harmless little place after living in Rochester all my life. I figured Karen was seeing the sights.

After a while I said to Linda, "Let's walk uptown and take a look."

Stan offered to drive us, but I said we'd walk. That way we could check out yards and alleys. We passed a junkyard and I asked two women, "Did you see a little girl? Honey-blond hair, brown eyes? She was wearing saddle shoes, all brown. Like Buster Browns?"

The women said no.

I explained, "Well, maybe she's lost, 'cause we're just visiting."

We walked up to the square and asked a couple of kids if they'd seen her. A little boy said, "Do you want me to help ya look, lady?"

I said, "No, but if you see her, would you tell her to please come back to the house?"

He nodded. Then he said, "Didja look around the river?"

I said no. Talking to Linda, I'd walked over that iron bridge without even looking down.

We went to Enrico's restaurant and found the same waitress. I said, "Do you remember I was in yesterday with my little girl? Have you seen her today?"

She nodded and said, "She hasn't been in."

Right then is when I started to worry. It was like somebody dumped a bucket of ice on my head.

I said, "Linda, we gotta go home and call the police." I was afraid Karen was wandering around lost and it was only a few hours till dark and she'd be scared to death.

We just about ran home. Stan was waiting in front. I told him I wanted to call the police. He said, "Let me go look in the woods first."

We ran up the slope and into the woods behind the house, calling her name. Then we went door to door. I thought maybe she'd found a little playmate and lost track of time. Everybody was very nice. I was worried, but I still didn't think anything horrible had happened.

At a quarter after six I called the police. Karen had been

gone for over four hours. I said, "I think my little girl walked away and got lost and can't find her way back."

The officer asked her age and I told him.

Five minutes later a police car pulled up with its lights flashing. I described Karen and gave the officer a picture from my wallet. He said, "Okay, Mrs. Hill, we're gonna start looking right now."

7.

Around the corner on Water Street, Mary Blake was up to her elbows in soapy water and wondering how other folks celebrated the Labor Day weekend. It was business as usual in her household—Pete sucking on his evening bottle, the kids in and out, Mary scrubbing dinner pots and missing Jack. She knew he was still alive. Just the week before, she'd hiked to the dump where her mother used to dig and picked around the edges for clues—footprints, scraps of clothing, another mysterious circle. She found nothing and wondered how to get her hands on a bulldozer to turn over the whole dump.

She heard a noise and turned to see her neighbor Linda Miles striding into the kitchen. Mary wasn't annoyed; folks in the river bottom often entered homes without knocking, and Linda was always welcome. Her face was red and she was sweating.

"Mary!" she blurted out. "Have you seen the blondheaded girl that was playing in our yard?"

"No," Mary said. "Why?"

"Well, she's been gone since two o'clock."

Mary's eyes widened. "How old is she?"

Linda said, "Eight," and rushed out the door. Mary caught a glimpse of a pretty redheaded woman standing on the front lawn with her hands pressed to her cheeks. You poor soul, Mary thought. You must be the mom.

She yanked her husband out of his favorite chair. "Another kid's gone," she said. "We gatta go look."

Even half drunk, Pete knew where to start. The

Cloverdale Apartments lay in early-evening shadow. A dim light shone from 233. The playground behind the complex was deserted.

They drove twice around the public square. Hippies were smoking in front of the old Crystal restaurant, but the youngest looked sixteen or eighteen. They spotted a child being dragged past JCPenney by a woman, but they were black. Mary figured they were Camp Drum dependents, just about the only nonwhites in town.

"Let's go home," Pete said after they passed Grant's and the Rexall. "We can't do no more."

Mary didn't want to quit, but she had kids of her own to watch over and she couldn't search the whole town. When they returned to Water Street, she saw a cop walking along the railroad spur and two more poking their flashlights around Agnes Thomas's backyard.

Mary had just started rinsing the dinner dishes when there was a loud knock. A cop introduced himself as Augustine Capone. "Mrs. Blake," he said, "can I borrow one of your kids to help search the woods?"

"Take Little Pete," Mary said. "He's got hideouts up there." The boy was eager to go. "Where else have you looked?" she asked.

Capone told her they'd checked every house on Pearl up to Starbuck, East Main to the dead end, the ball lot, the riverbanks in both directions, and most of the sprawling New York Air Brake property. Mary stifled an impulse to say, Did you check the Cloverdale Apartments? That no-good Shawcross? But she'd been singing the same tune for nearly four months and she knew the cops didn't want to hear it.

Just before the searchers headed into the woods behind their flashlight beams, Mary couldn't resist saying, "Maybe you'll find Jack up there." She yelled her final instructions through cupped hands: "And while you're at it, don't let nothin' happen to Little Pete!"

The cops returned her son in thirty minutes and thanked Mary for the loan. They'd found no sign of the missing girl but said they intended to make a sweep through the woods in the morning.

Mary was sure that whatever was going on, Shawcross was involved. That son of a bitch, she said to herself. I wouldn't put nothing past him.

8.

A half hour after the first policeman had arrived at the Miles home, Helene Hill phoned the station again. An officer said, "Nothing yet, Mrs. Hill. We're still looking."

She started to cry. She was convinced that Karen was hurt; she'd been hit by a car; she'd fallen down a well; she was lying in a ditch, calling for help, and no one could hear. A lost little girl in a strange town. Helene's stomach tightened.

Headquarters called back twice. There was still no trace. Helene looked out the window and saw a light bobbing up and down in the yard across the street. The police were on the job; it made her feel a little better. Her daughter might be hurt, but soon she'd be home.

As she watched, the flashlight snapped off. It was the darkest night she'd ever seen. She hated to imagine Karen trying to find her way in all that black.

9.

At 9:30 P.M., David McGrath was waiting on customers at the Dairyland store on State Street when he heard a radio report that police were looking for an eight-year-old girl with blond hair and bangs. WOTT seldom broke into its format with news flashes, but the community had been sensitized to missing children by the Blake case.

The college student phoned headquarters and a police car pulled up within minutes. He told the two officers about the blond girl he'd seen climbing the rail of the

Pearl Street bridge. The cops thanked him and took his name and address.

10.

Mary Blake had just put Little Pete to bed when the front door banged open and two of her daughters ran inside. "Mom!" Dawn shouted. "They found the little girl!"

Debbie was crying, biting at her knuckles. "Under the iron bridge," she said.

11. HELENE HILL

Linda answered the phone, said a few words, and hung up. "Helene," she said, "we've got to go to the police station." Her face was stone white.

I said, "Did they find Karen?"

She said, "I don't know."

I said, "They must've found her." I figured she probably had a broken arm or leg; she'd been in a hospital or a doctor's office all this time and that's why we hadn't heard anything.

Linda drove us across the iron bridge. A policeman was leaning against the rail. Linda pulled over and I said, "Hello, I'm Mrs. Hill. I called earlier. About my daughter missing? Do you know if they found her?"

He hesitated, then said, "No, ma'am."

The police station was crowded with officers, against both walls, behind the counter, at least a dozen men in uniform and others in civilian clothes. I thought, Now we're getting somewhere.

I told the man behind the counter, "Hi, I'm Mrs. Hill. Did you find my daughter?"

He said, "Yes, we did, Mrs. Hill."

I said, "Did she break her arm? Did she fall and break her leg or something?"

When he didn't answer, I turned and glanced at the others. They were quiet, just looking down. A sergeant took my arm and said, "Mrs. Hill, could you step in the back, please?"

I noticed two empty rooms leading off the front area. I said, "Where's Karen? I don't see her."

The sergeant led me to a private room. A priest was talking to some policemen. He turned toward me and I said, "Oh, hi, Father Doste." I remembered him from the night before, when he'd played with Karen. His face looked like it was whitewashed.

Somebody told me to sit down. I said, "I don't *want* to sit down! Where's Karen?"

The sergeant said, "Mrs. Hill, we found your daughter." I could hardly hear him, he talked so low. He said, "Mrs. Hill, she's dead."

I didn't believe him. I couldn't understand what made him say such a thing. I said, "No, she isn't! Now I want to know! *Where's my daughter?*"

Father Doste put his arms around me. I said, "What do they mean she's dead? Did a car hit her? What happened?"

He said, "Helene, the poor dear was murdered."

12.

Detective Charles Kubinski of the Watertown P.D. was getting ready for bed when headquarters ordered him to the Pearl Street bridge. Two city policemen and two state troopers had checked out a tip from a telephone informant named David McGrath and found a girl's body.

Kubinski was forty-six, just under six feet tall, barrel-chested and sturdy, a career cop who was often called out on breaking cases and considered it an honor. He'd pounded beats in blizzards, ridden bikes in ice storms, and won a reputation as a willing workhorse. No law enforcement duties could be more rigorous than a childhood spent milking fifty cows twice a day on the family's farm in Lowville, up the Black River.

As the detective picked his way down the slippery, rocky

slope, he almost bumped into a uniformed officer. "It's bad, Charley," the patrolman moaned. "It's awful. Oh, God, it's terrible."

Chief Joseph Loftus scrambled up the bank as though being chased. "I can't take it, Charley," he said, wiping his eyes. Kubinski knew Loftus as a fireman's son, a good man, but regarded him as a little excitable for his new job as chief. Once he'd dispatched a team of officers to search for his own "missing" son, sound asleep in his room.

A huddled group of lawmen made room for the lead detective. Kubinski recognized Assistant District Attorney Hugh Gilbert and five or six policemen and troopers. The river gurgled softly; in other seasons, this part of the embankment would be under three or four feet of water.

Next to a cast-iron sewage pipe lined with algae and muck, he spotted a bare foot. He leaned closer and saw a tousled head of blond hair. The body lay facedown and was covered with flat paving slabs that apparently had been dumped over the rail a long time before. The child's head was uncovered.

Kubinski dropped to his hands and knees and touched a partially closed finger. It was cold and hard. A livid reddish ring circled the child's neck, and there were bruises on her face. Under the paving blocks, the body was naked from the waist down. Off to one side he saw a pair of red, white, and blue shorts. A pair of blue children's panties with the trademark "DOBB" were stuffed into a crevice. Both appeared bloodstained.

Kubinski was working his sixth homicide investigation and ordered the others to back off till the evidence technicians arrived. From the roadway above, he heard his chief's broken voice. "I'm goin', Charley," Loftus said. "Please, Charley, *get this guy*!"

At ten minutes before midnight, the assistant county medical examiner, an émigré from Bombay, appeared at the railing above. "Come down, Doc," Kubinski called out.

The pathologist looked upset. He was in his ninth month on the job. He said, "I can see quite well from up here."

"No you can't," Kubinski insisted.

"It's such a pathetic situation," the doctor said in his clipped accent. "I've seen quite enough."

Kubinski raised his voice: "You gotta come down! We don't want any questions later."

As the medical examiner negotiated the slimy rock, Kubinski asked his fellow officers, "Anybody seen Shawcross today?" Ever since the Blake disappearance, the dump worker had been a person of interest to the local law. A few months back, he'd been suspected of setting a fire at the Cloverdale Apartments, but as with most arsons there wasn't enough evidence to justify a charge.

A patrolman said, "Somebody saw him on a brown-and-white bike. I'm not sure where."

"I heard he bought a new bike," another officer said.

Kubinski said, "Let's grab him."

When the last photo had been snapped and the body removed to Mercy Hospital at the assistant ME's instruction, Kubinski asked one of the state troopers to arrange for a tracking dog. He thought about dusting the latticework railing for fingerprints, but so many gawkers had arrived and so many lawmen had climbed over the rail that prints would have been smudged beyond recognition. He took a final look at the murder scene; the technicians seemed to be doing their jobs. Then he drove to headquarters to talk to Shawcross.

Waiting for the ex-convict's arrival, Kubinski scanned the day's reports and noted that a citizen had seen a white female, blond, age about nine, climbing the bridge's fence at a point just next to a new-looking brown-and-white bike. My God, he thought, we got the son of a bitch. It's Shawcross! That rotten bastard killed this little girl. He's sure as hell good for the Blake case, too, if we ever find the body.

In his mind he could still hear Mary Blake snapping at him—"That gaddamn Shawcross kidnapped my Jack and you caps're all sittin' on your ass." He'd heard that she'd been having problems with her other children lately—dope, shoplifting, misdemeanor stuff. Kubinski wasn't surprised. Mary kept the whole family stirred up. Every time a cop came near her home, she yelled, "You're pickin' on us. Get outa here!" No matter how reasonably she was treated, she wanted to fight. But Kubinski had to admit that she'd had Shawcross pegged from the beginning. Not that he'd ever doubted her. He'd wanted to charge the guy at the time, but the evidence wasn't there.

The hospital called with a preliminary report. Karen Ann had been dead for eight to twelve hours. Kubinski was surprised the doctors didn't pinpoint the time better; four hours was a hell of a spread. The child had been punched in the face and stomach, strangled with her own shirt strings, and raped so viciously that her skin was split. Semen was present in the vaginal and rectal cavities. Her mouth and throat were plugged with mud and soot.

Kubinski recalled that Shawcross had been fined a while back for spanking a six-year-old boy and stuffing grass down his pants. He wondered, Is the guy a lunatic or what?

The suspect arrived in a patrol car and was asked to wait in a small interview room. For someone who'd been rousted at midnight, he looked cool. Kubinski thought of the child's bloody body and wished the law would let him pound out a quick confession. How simple this case would have been in the old days! But instead he read the Miranda warning in a soft voice and asked if Shawcross understood.

The man answered, "No problem."

"At this point we're just talking to you, Art," Kubinski said, as though they were old friends. "You're not under arrest. You're welcome to ask for a lawyer or leave anytime you want."

The suspect said he was glad to help, and asked, "What's this about?"

"A little girl was assaulted at the iron bridge." The detective watched for a reaction, but Shawcross didn't twitch. "We need to know where you were today."

Shawcross nodded. "No problem," he repeated.

Kubinski remembered how cool he'd been when he was

questioned in the Blake case. The guy seemed to follow a pattern: smiling, agreeing, sympathizing, but pulling your chain when it suited his purpose. On tough questions, he would hang his head and act as though he was deaf, dumb, and blind.

His story sounded rehearsed. He said he left his apartment at 7:00 A.M. to go fishing, rode his new bike on Starbuck Avenue to Pearl Street, down Pearl to Factory Square, then out Huntington to the river. He said he tried several spots, but the bass weren't biting, so he pedaled to Gifford Street to fish for trout in the brook. After a late-morning break at home, he rode to the Bargain Center and bought a Coke at a tent in the parking lot. He dropped in on a friend in East Hills, stayed a few minutes, then rode back to Factory Square. He wasn't sure exactly when he'd crossed the iron bridge, but he remembered that he ran into a neighbor from the Cloverdale Apartments, bought him an ice cream cone, and carried the kid's shopping bag home on the bike, arriving at Cloverdale at about 3:15 P.M. The cops could check with the kid; his name was Terry.

Kubinski thought, What a snaky son of a bitch! He knew he was seen at the bridge with his bike, so he went out of his way to establish that he wasn't there till an hour after the murder and he wasn't doing anything unusual except eating ice cream. Mr. Nice Guy! He was like other ex-cons the detective had interviewed. They could be slobbering idiots, too stupid to come in from a Lake Ontario ice storm, but when it came to creating alibis they were artists, supersalesmen, craftsmen of the dubious and false. It was as though every ounce of their limited brainpower went into weaseling out of their crimes.

Kubinski asked what he'd done after he got home, and Shawcross told of two more cycling trips in the late afternoon, both to Seaway shopping plaza. He'd bought several items for himself and returned to the plaza to buy sneakers for his four-year-old stepson. He'd spent the rest of the evening at home; his wife Penny would back him up.

The door opened and District Attorney William McClusky took a seat in the corner. Kubinski thought, All the heavy hitters are turning up. I hope McClusky has a stronger stomach than Chief Loftus. The detective preferred one-on-one interviews, but in this case he didn't mind the intrusion. Where murder was concerned, there was no room for error by the cops or the prosecutor or anyone else.

He led Shawcross through his story again and noticed that some of the details varied, especially in the midday time frame. The DA put in a few questions of his own, but mostly he listened attentively. Kubinski tried not to show his annoyance at the way the killer shucked and jived. Not only was the guy lying in general, but he was playing games about the time the child had died. The detective wanted to bear down but didn't dare. Shawcross wasn't under arrest; he could walk out the door anytime. If he demanded a lawyer, the interview would be over.

At 2:00 A.M. he was taken home in a squad car.

Later Kubinski learned that Shawcross had omitted something from his timetable. In between his two trips to the Seaway shopping plaza, he'd pedaled three miles to his childhood home near Brownville to bring a bouquet of flowers to his mother. The detective asked himself, What the hell does *that* mean?

13. HELENE HILL

When they told me my daughter was dead, I accused them of making it up. I didn't want to believe. Even when I realized they were telling the truth, I tried not to believe. There *had* to be a mistake.

After I cried myself hoarse, one of the officers tried to tell me the details. I told him to stop. I didn't know how Karen was killed and I didn't *want* to know, ever. I said, "Please, I've gotta make some calls."

I tried to reach my ex-husband in Rochester, but there was no answer, or maybe I just dialed wrong. My fingers were shaking. I couldn't remember my sister Wally's number even though I knew it as well as my name. The operator looked it up for me and my brother-in-law answered the phone. I said, "Gary, Karen's dead. Please, get up here right away."

A woman from Mercy Hospital called and asked me to identify Karen's body. I told her I couldn't do it.

She said, "Well, somebody's gotta."

I told her my brother-in-law was on the way from Rochester and hung up.

Then a man called from the hospital and said, "Listen, missus, we gotta have somebody down here right away."

I told him I couldn't go. I just . . . couldn't. I didn't want to see Karen because I didn't want to know how she'd died. She was gone, that was the most I could grasp. All I wanted to do was get home to my mom and my family.

I took some Valium, but I couldn't sleep. I would drift off for a few minutes and then wake up; I still couldn't believe that it happened. Once I dozed and said to myself, "This is just a nightmare. I've been dreaming."

My brother-in-law drove a hundred and fifty miles in two hours. Then my ex-husband Bob arrived and the two of them went over to Mercy Hospital to identify Karen's body. I started packing, cramming stuff into my suitcase, forgetting things, trying to keep my control. I had to get away from this town.

14.

After cutting Shawcross loose in the small hours of Sunday morning, Charley Kubinski learned that a high school girl had phoned in to report that she and three friends saw a man climb over the Pearl Street bridge at about the time of the murder. He'd been tying something on a new-looking white bike with brown fenders and he'd worn dark shorts, a T-shirt, and sandals. It had to be Shawcross.

"Art," Kubinski asked over the phone, "where's your bike?"

Shawcross said that his new ten-speed was at home. He sounded wide awake.

"Would you mind if we came over and took a look?"

"No problem."

Kubinski asked what had happened to the clothes from his fishing trip, and Shawcross said that they were in a hamper. His wife Penny intended to launder them in the morning. "You want to see 'em?" he volunteered.

"Yeah," Kubinski answered. "We'll send a car. Maybe you can come back here and answer a couple more questions."

"No problem."

Kubinski thought, This guy is guilty as sin and daring us to prove it. It's a game. He did the same thing in the Blake case, even offered to help look for the boy.

But we're coming, he said to himself. We're getting there. I'll have his ass by sunrise. He looked at the clock: it was a few minutes after 4:00 A.M.

The dirty clothes seemed to match the description given by the four girls: soiled blue cutoff pants labeled "Hondo," a dirty white Fruit of the Loom T-shirt, cheap brown sandals marked "Made in Italy." There were a few dark smears on the shirt, but they didn't look like blood. A pair of tattletale gray Jockey shorts, labeled "Body-bits," completed the Shawcross ensemble.

After Kubinski logged in the clothing, he walked to the evidence room to see the bike. A basket was strapped to the front and a child carrier bolted to the back. Something was wrong. He parked Shawcross in an interrogation room while he confirmed that none of the witnesses had seen anything resembling a child carrier.

Goddamn, Kubinski said to himself, I *know* Shawcross killed that child and I *know* his bike was at the bridge, but how the hell could five or six sharp kids miss something as conspicuous as a child carrier? The detective had been awake for nearly twenty-four hours and was beginning to doubt his own perceptions. Damn, he asked himself, where did I screw up?

He decided to try a few more questions. It was 5:00 A.M., but if Shawcross could stay awake, so could he. And as long as the guy was willing to talk, the interview remained legal. Just to be on the safe side, he repeated the Miranda. Then he asked, "Art, how long have you had that child carrier?"

Shawcross didn't answer. For the first time all night, he went into the deep funk that Kubinski remembered from the Blake interrogations almost four months earlier.

"Art, *Art,*" the detective insisted, "answer me! That black thing on the back of your bike. It looks new. When did you buy it?"

Shawcross looked up with a querulous expression. "Oh," he said. "I don't know. Uh—recently."

"When 'recently'?" Kubinski said, leaning forward.

Shawcross delayed for another few minutes before saying that he'd bought the carrier at Grant's.

"When, Art?" the detective demanded. "Not where. *When?*"

Shawcross said it wasn't too long ago.

"You know we can check, don't you?" Kubinski challenged. "We'll go through the store receipts. Do you wanna make us do that, Art?"

Shawcross studied his lap again, then admitted that the carrier might have been one of the items he'd purchased the evening before.

Kubinski bore down. "Why were you changing the look of your bike?" he asked. "Was it because you were spotted after you killed the girl?"

Shawcross said, "I didn't kill no girl."

"Fine," the detective said. "You didn't kill no girl. Then you won't mind if we take it from the top one more time."

The killer didn't seem to mind. He said that his day had started at 8:00 A.M. when he'd left home to go fishing. Keep talking, Kubinski said to himself. Earlier tonight, you told me you left at seven.

The suspect contradicted himself on other points. We're

coming, the detective thought. We're coming. He grabbed a yellow legal-size pad and began to take notes.

Shawcross turned vague, especially about his activities from noon till he'd run into his neighbor Terry Tenney. He seemed uncomfortable about the time period. Kubinski pressed for an exact sequence. More contradictions followed, and soon the yellow pad was filled.

All at once Shawcross lowered his chin and stopped talking. He didn't blink. He looked as though he'd turned to stone. Kubinski wondered, What's with this guy? It's like he jumps back and forth between here and Mars. "Art," he said. "Art?" There was no response.

He tried everything—reasoning, cajoling, insulting, using words that hadn't passed his lips since the kamikazes had attacked his LST in World War II.

After a half hour it was plain that Shawcross didn't intend to respond. But there was a pattern to his quirkiness. The detective dismissed the idea that the guy was crazy. Was lunacy so one-way? So self-serving? If he's a lunatic on the tough questions, how come he's not a lunatic on the easy ones?

Kubinski seldom wasted time trying to read minds; that was somebody else's job. He'd been described by a reporter from the *Syracuse Post-Standard* as "an old-style cop—he'd arrest his own mother." He had no time for psychology, didn't comprehend it or try. But he prided himself on understanding criminals. There's a word for this guy Shawcross, he said to himself. The word was "rotten." Rotten to the bone. Born rotten or turned rotten, what's the difference? Rotten is rotten.

Out in the hall, he told Assistant District Attorney Hugh Gilbert, "He blocks me right out, like we're not even in the same room. Same thing he did in the Blake case."

It was six o'clock on Sunday morning. The ADA concluded that there still wasn't enough evidence to make an arrest. Kubinski frowned as he summoned a squad car and installed Shawcross in the backseat. Look at that rotten SOB, he said to himself as the car left for the Cloverdale Apartments. I won't sleep till I got his ass good. . . .

• • •

Just after 8:00 A.M. a station wagon pulled into the police parking area and "Corporal of Redstone" waddled out. The dog was a purebred bloodhound with a loose pelt, twitchy nostrils, and ears that touched the ground. The troopers had been showing him at the State Fair in Syracuse, seventy miles south, when the request for a tracker arrived.

Kubinski, Chief Loftus, and other officers stood at one end of the Pearl Street bridge and watched Troop D's star canine go into action. The detective suggested that they start him at the spot of the crime, but the dog's handler took note of the steep slope and the sharp rocks and announced that Corporal of Redstone was too valuable to risk injury. The dog sniffed Shawcross's Italian-made sandal, meandered alongside the iron railing, slowed at the grating in the sidewalk, and stopped at the point where the bike had been parked. Then he led his handler and several police cars up Pearl Street at a half trot.

On a loose leash, he turned left at Starbuck Avenue and followed his nose to the rear of the Cloverdale Apartments, six blocks north along the New York Air Brake fence. He stopped at several doors, then pawed at the rear entrance to 233. It was the Shawcross apartment.

15.

Arthur Shawcross's third wife was hotter than ever at the Watertown cops. Penny Nichol Sherbino Shawcross wondered when the harassment would end. Every time somebody turned up missing, would they roust poor Art? Why? Because he shoved grass down a kid's pants? That was horseplay, harmless. *Who gave a shit?*

Now it was Sunday morning and they were dragging him back to headquarters for the third time since midnight.

"I've gotta warn ya, you're a suspect," she'd heard one of the cops say. Penny knew that Art was incapable of such a crime. He got upset when a goldfish died. Yeah, he was a little different. But he *loved* kids, played with her two-year-old girl and her four-year-old boy, carried them on his back, bought them candy and presents. He'd wanted a child of his own, but Penny had miscarried three months earlier. She remembered how upset he'd been. "I'm sorry, Penny," he'd said, looking away so she couldn't see his eyes. "I'm so sorry." It was the closest she'd seen him to tears. It still hurt that the hospital hadn't told them the stillborn's sex.

On this third trip to the police station, Penny insisted on coming along. She had plenty to tell the cops, mostly about themselves. She and Art had discussed the Karen Hill murder while rounding up his clothing and his bike, and he'd assured her that he wasn't involved. Then he'd retreated to the bedroom, sitting in the dark, staring into space. It wasn't the first time she'd seen him withdraw. Well, who could blame him? He was fighting the whole goddamn P.D.

A mean-looking detective escorted the two of them past the front counter and down a hall in the Municipal Building. A grumpy guy followed along; he turned out to be an assistant district attorney.

"Art," the cop began, "I'd like to ask you a few more questions." When Penny heard what followed, she started to cry.

16.

Kubinski had decided to press for a confession before the strangler pressed for a lawyer. Since Miranda, it was elemental police procedure. You gave the guy his rights and hoped to Christ he ignored them.

While Penny Shawcross and ADA Gilbert listened quietly, the two antagonists faced off. Room A in police headquarters was a boxy cubicle reserved for hardball interrogations—no paintings or gewgaws, just a few chairs and a window overlooking Sterling Street. Kubinski yanked down the shade—one less distraction. He wanted total attention.

He ran Shawcross through his timetable for the fourth or fifth time and once again took note of the soft spot between noon and 2:30 P.M. With each recounting of his story, Shawcross seemed to revise his facts, but still not enough to justify an arrest.

Fifteen minutes after the interview began, a uniformed cop beckoned Shawcross's wife and the ADA outside. There was talk about getting a search warrant and Penny was needed back at the Cloverdale Apartments.

Alone with his quarry, Kubinski bore down. "Art," he said, "look at me."

Shawcross stared at the wall.

"Goddamn it, Art, *look at me!*"

Shawcross continued to look away.

"I'm talking to *you,*" the detective insisted. "Now you talk to *me*! Don't go looking off."

There was no response. Kubinski returned to a gentler approach. "C'mon, Art, let's be reasonable." He'd been a cop for eighteen years and a detective for eight, and he'd never encountered such a flake. The guy seemed to be counting the floorboards, his lips in a hard straight line.

"Hello?" Kubinski spat out. "You hear me?" Shawcross didn't blink. The detective raised his voice: "You know what you are, man? You're a rotten son of a bitch! You killed that girl. You know it and I know it."

To himself, Kubinski said, Listen to me. I'm being the good cop and the bad cop at the same time. A terrific new technique. And where's it getting me? *Nowhere* . . .

He wagged his finger under the man's nose. "You no-good son of a bitch," he said, lowering his voice so he couldn't be heard in the hall. "I ought to shoot you right now, you bastard! Think what you done to this girl."

Shawcross's face was a mask. Kubinski thought, How the hell does he block me out like that? The possibility of failing in such a horrifying murder case made him so agitated that he stepped outside to compose himself. No one was in sight. When he reentered the interview room Shawcross was mumbling. Kubinski wasn't certain, but he thought he heard the dreaded word "lawyer."

"Wait a minute, Art," he said. "I'll be right back."

He found the ADA talking to a patrolman. Penny Shawcross had left for Cloverdale. He hoped she never came back. Criminals seldom confessed in front of relatives.

"The guy's getting restless," he told Hugh Gilbert. "I think he's gonna ask for a lawyer." The ADA advised him to do nothing to jeopardize the case. That meant following Miranda to the letter.

When the detective reentered Room A, Shawcross was getting up. "Wait a minute, Art," he said quickly, patting him on the shoulder. "Sit. Let's talk some more."

The strangler frowned and sat. Kubinski reminded himself that a cop with a badge had an unfair advantage over an ex-con who worked in a dump, but he also thought, No matter how I handle this joker, I got a clear conscience. I *know* he's a killer. What am I supposed to do, worry about *his* welfare? How about the little girl? How about the parents that'll live with this for the rest of their lives?

"All right, Art," he said. "Let's talk about what you were doing from twelve till three."

The sparring resumed, slow, tedious, with frequent heavy silences. Sometimes Shawcross would ask what would happen to him if he confessed. Presented with his contradictions, he would shrug.

Every time Kubinski felt like quitting, he refocused his thoughts on the scene at the bridge ten hours earlier. When the cement slabs had been lifted off the child's body, splotchy bloodstains appeared in the light of a half-dozen flashlights. The pathologist said there was a chance she'd been murdered before she'd been raped. Or maybe the two acts were simultaneous. Kubinski shuddered. If there's a God in heaven, he said to himself, she was already dead.

By 9:00 A.M., both men were flagging. Kubinski kept waiting for Shawcross to call off the questioning, but he seemed strangely reluctant to quit. There were criminals like this, "tough" guys who hated to give in, hated to ask for a break or demand their rights. The detective figured it had something to do with saving face, machismo, some kind of stupid pride. Or maybe it was because they were afraid of looking like pussies, the criminal world's second lowest form of life after snitches. They convinced themselves that they could outlie and outmanipulate the smartest questioner. And some could. But not this one, Kubinski said to himself. Not if we have to sit here and talk for a month. We'll see who folds first. . . .

The mental duel continued for another half hour before Shawcross looked up from one of his funks and said, "Well, I musta done it."

Kubinski tried not to show his excitement. Now we're coming, he said to himself. Now we're *really* coming!

But he couldn't accept the mealymouth phrasing. "Bullshit!" he said. "Don't gimme 'I musta done it.' You did it. You *know* you did it!"

Shawcross said, "I *probably* did it. But I don't actually remember." Then he dummied up again.

Kubinski stepped into an adjoining room where ADA Gilbert and a State Police investigator were standing by. "I think he's ready," he told them. "Why don'tcha come in and witness?"

In front of the others, he asked Shawcross a formal question for the record: "Do you want to tell us about what happened underneath the iron bridge located on Pearl Street between 2:00 and 2:30 P.M. on the second of September 1972?"

Shawcross hesitated, then said in a voice just above a whisper, "I musta done it. But I don't actually recall doing it."

Kubinski pressed, but the killer wouldn't budge. A huddled conference was held in the hall, and District Attorney McClusky complained, "That's a pretty weak confession."

Kubinski said it was a beginning.

On the DA's instructions, Shawcross was booked on a charge of murder and held in the city lockup. A few hours later, the four teenagers who'd seen him on the bridge picked him out of a lineup. Kubinski hoped the ID's would be enough for a conviction. The girls couldn't place him with Karen Ann, but they put him pretty damn close.

The detective gulped more coffee and set about cleaning up odds and ends—arranging for background reports on Shawcross, logging evidence, ordering more photographs of the bridge and the murder scene, reaching out for more potential witnesses. It was afternoon before he started to compose his preliminary report.

"Our theory," he typed with his strong milker's fingers, "is that Arthur Shawcross after leaving East Hills rode directly down Huntington Street to the area of the iron bridge, left his bike leaning against the rail of the iron fence, and went down to the riverbank and went fishing. Apparently as Karen Hill was walking on the bridge in this area Arthur Shawcross lured her over the fence to where he was, sexually molested her, murdered her by strangulation, and then covered her body by placing stones on top of her and leaving the scene at approximately 2:30 or 3:00 P.M. when he was observed by the four girls who happened to be walking in the area at the time. He used Terry Tenney, who he happened to run across on Factory Street immediately after leaving at about 2:30 or 2:35 P.M., as an alibi. . . . As he looked through the gratings of the sidewalk with Tenney it was to see if the body could be seen. . . ."

It took the detective an hour to prepare the preliminary report. When the draft was finished, his thoughts turned to Jack O. Blake. A belated bit of evidence had arrived—not enough to guarantee an indictment in the Blake case, but a start. William "Corky" Murrock had phoned headquarters to report that a few months back he'd intercepted a man hiking out of the woods behind his motel and gas station near the North Watertown Cemetery on State Route 12E. He couldn't be sure of the date, but it was around the time of the Blake disappearance. The man's boots had been muddy and he'd carried two sections of an old fishing rod that he claimed he found alongside Kelsey Creek. Murrock said the man had identified himself as Art Shawcross and explained that he'd crossed the four-lane Interstate 81 on foot. Murrock told police that he'd nearly forgotten about the incident, but he'd been reminded of Shawcross when he heard the name on the radio.

Kubinski pulled out a Watertown map and followed his fingernail to Murrock's place of business on the city's northwest border. It was adjacent to a small triangular wooded area that was drained by Kelsey Creek and isolated by three surrounding roads and a spur of the Penn Central. He was willing to bet that Jack Blake lay square in the middle.

At eight o'clock that night, the detective leaned back in his office chair and tried to think his way through a few hard realities. He still had nothing on Shawcross in the Blake case except the certainty that the crazy son of a bitch was involved. But grand juries didn't indict on police intuition. A lot more evidence was needed, preferably a body and/or a confession. And even then, Kubinski reminded himself, the case could be a loser. Watertown was an inbred little community where influence could be brought to bear in the courts and where the current district attorney was a man he regarded as a wishy-washy pol. If the bad guys didn't slip off the hook one way, they slipped off another.

He decided to move fast. He hadn't slept in two days, but it didn't occur to him to drive home or catnap in a back room. He had to make Shawcross confess before the courts assigned him a lawyer. Sleep could wait.

Just before 9:00 P.M. he went to the killer's cell and engaged him in a few minutes of chatter, trying to strengthen the fragile bond that had developed during the talks about Karen Hill. Kubinski said softly, "Art, I'm telling you this for your own good. You killed the little girl and I know you killed the little boy, too. You can tell me about it, Art. You're being charged with Karen's murder anyway. So clear your mind for once. Get it all off your chest."

Shawcross didn't respond.

"Think about it, Art," Kubinski said. "I'll be back."

The detective briefed Chief Loftus, then revisited the

killer just after 10:00 P.M. He was sprawled on his bunk. "Hey, Art," the detective said. "How ya doin'?"

The killer smiled.

Kubinski managed to smile back and asked, "You got anything to tell me?"

"I might," the killer replied.

"Well, let's talk."

Shawcross said, "No problem." His favorite expression. It could mean anything.

The detective said, "Art, somebody told us they saw you leading Jack Blake into Pool's Woods."

"Not Pool's Woods," Shawcross said.

"Well, what woods was it?"

Shawcross stared at the floor.

"Was it near Corky Murrock's gas station?"

Kubinski looked for a reaction, but the man's expression didn't change. The silence lengthened. Then Shawcross mumbled, "It mighta been near the tracks."

"What tracks?"

"The railroad tracks."

"The Penn Central?" the detective asked.

"Did I say that?" Shawcross said, a wiseass look on his face.

"Art, is the body north or south of the tracks?"

Shawcross folded his hands and looked down. The detective said, "C'mon, man, don't cut me out again. I hate that bullshit. *Look at me!* I need your help." He paused and lowered his voice. "You'll feel better if you tell the truth."

The killer slowly raised his head. "Okay, Charley," he said softly. "I'll help ya. And maybe you can help me. But . . . lemme sleep on it."

The detective knew he couldn't force the issue. This type of criminal could dance on the brink forever. You had to work slow, act friendly, convince him that there was something in it for him if he came clean. It also didn't hurt to hint that you had a little influence with the judge and the DA. The trick was to seem to promise something while not giving away the store. It was probably unfair, the detective admitted to himself, but it was also unfair that an innocent little girl had been beaten and suffocated and raped and abused and covered with blocks. He wasn't dealing with an Eagle Scout.

The Municipal Building was almost deserted when he drained his last cup of cold coffee and headed home. His pretty wife Frances kissed him good night and left him alone. She'd learned that there were times when he didn't want to hear about her day or talk about his.

Seated in his darkened living room, he kept seeing Karen Hill in his mind. He reminded himself that horror was part of his job and it was unprofessional to take it personally. He couldn't imagine a crueler crime, a worse sin. There weren't enough fires in hell for a man like this.

When he tiptoed into the bedroom at 2:00 A.M., he was still flashing back to the child's matchstick legs, her hurts and bruises, the mud stuffed all the way down her throat. By an effort of will he turned his thoughts to the case of Jack Owen Blake. It would be solved in the morning or it would never be solved. He was absolutely convinced.

17. LINDA NEARY

The day after Art was arrested, one of his friends came to me with a confidential message from the jail. "Linda," he said, "Art just wanted you to know that he didn't mean to do it." He said that Art had had another flashback from Vietnam and that's how he came to kill the little girl. It was like the time I woke him up and he smacked me.

It gave me a lot to think about. He'd gone through so much in Vietnam—it tore him up, changed him completely. If he was a monster, it was because of that.

I wondered if Karen Hill was the first person he killed. Maybe that's what he was so upset about in Oklahoma. Maybe he killed somebody on one of those nights when he didn't come home from Fort Sill. Maybe that's why he attempted suicide down there. A man can only handle so much guilt.

But I kept my ideas to myself.

18.

After a few hours of sleep, Charley Kubinski walked into Joe Loftus's office to bring his chief up to date. He didn't intend to pass along the fuzzy information about Jack Blake's body. It was too soon. The last thing he wanted was a premature search by cops and cadaver dogs. Let the killer make a full confession and lead them to the scene of the crime himself; then there could never be any doubt of his guilt, no matter how he weaseled and waffled later. The detective still lived in dread that another confirmed criminal would beat the North Country system of justice. He'd seen it happen too many times.

He was halfway through his verbal report to Loftus when he reconsidered his decision. This was the biggest case in Watertown history, and his superiors needed to know exactly what was going on. "Chief," Kubinski said, "I think I know where Jack Blake's body is."

On a wall map he pointed out the triangle of woodland drained by Kelsey Creek and bordered by Interstate Highway 81 and State routes 37 and 12E, about a mile from the Cloverdale Apartments. "Somewhere in there," he said. The area had been lightly searched at the time of the disappearance.

"If you're so sure, why don't we send a search party?" Loftus asked.

"I'm *not* sure, Chief. I want Shawcross to show us the body. That way we got a lock on a conviction."

Loftus seemed reluctant to wait. "There's a lotta pressure, Charley," he said. "The mother's givin' us fits."

"We waited this long," Kubinski said. "Let's do it right."

Outside the chief's office, a TV reporter told him that a judge had appointed lawyer Paul Dierdorf to represent the accused murderer. Kubinski wished the judge had selected one of the weatherworn old hacks who hung around the courtrooms trying to pick up a few hours of work. Dierdorf was young and green, but he had a reputation as an infighter. He quickly talked the judge into ordering a "730" psychiatric evaluation to see if Shawcross was competent to stand trial. And he threatened to file more motions. Kubinski realized that he had to finish his business with the killer before he was shut down by a court order. Upstart lawyers like Dierdorf understood Miranda rights and police techniques a lot better than their clients did.

Early in the afternoon a jailer informed Kubinski that the prisoner was attracting comment by the staff—"Nobody can put their finger on it, but there's something off about the guy." His parents had paid a visit and Shawcross had hung his head and talked baby talk. The parents hadn't stayed long.

The detective summoned the prisoner to his office for another interview. By now the talks had started and stopped so many times that one of the sergeants dubbed them "The Art and Charley Show."

Kubinski motioned the killer to a straightback chair across from his desk. Shawcross looked rested and relaxed; Kubinski wondered if he was faking or just didn't understand the danger he was in. He'd heard that the guy had phoned his probation officer at 2:00 A.M. the first night to complain that the cops had dented his new bicycle, but he hadn't mentioned that the bike was evidence in a murder case.

This time Shawcross was the first to talk. "I been thinkin', Charley," he said. "If I help, what can ya do for me?"

"Let's wait and see," Kubinski said, choosing his words carefully. "I'll do what I can." Which won't be much, he reminded himself. In this Republican county, us Democrats are piss-ants. There's not much I can do for this animal, and thank God for small favors.

Shawcross seemed satisfied. "I'll help ya, Charley," he

said. "Did you know I was in the woods behind the gas station the day the kid come up missing?"

"With Jack Blake?"

Kubinski took the silence as a "yes." But it still wasn't evidence.

"You wanna take me to the place?" he pressed.

Shawcross didn't answer. When the detective repeated the question, the killer mumbled, "Yeah. Maybe I'll take ya down there."

"Okay," Kubinski said, standing up. "I'll get a car."

"Wait! I need some time."

Kubinski sat. "Do you wanna talk to somebody else?" he asked.

"No," the man said. "When I talk, I'll talk to you. But . . . keep your pants on."

The detective could see that the slow way was still the only way. "You got it, Art," he said. "Take all the time you need." Sometimes this ex-con seemed dense, but there was a flicker of intelligent treachery behind his close-set green eyes. "I'll work with ya," Kubinski said, and thought, Sure I will. I'll even drive you to Attica. . . .

As Shawcross was being led away, the detective said, "Remember one thing, Art. We both know what happened. That kid deserves a decent burial."

The prisoner frowned. "*You* might know what I done," he said, "but I don't remember a thing."

"Art, be reasonable. Don't you think it'll help your memory if you took us to the body?"

The killer paused, then said, "No problem, Charley. Just gimme a little more time." The detective had a strong feeling that the Blake case was about to be cleared.

19.

The next morning, Wednesday, September 6, 1972, Kubinski was at home when he learned that Watertown policemen and Jefferson county deputies were forming a search party. It was his worst fear. Less than four days had passed since the murder of Karen Ann Hill, less than four months since the Blake disappearance—what difference, he asked himself, would another day or two make? Shawcross was on the verge of leading police to the body, an absolute guarantee of a conviction. But what if they found the body without his help and he went back into that tough ex-con's shell of his—for good? How could the DA connect him to the crime except with a bunch of suspicions, hearsay and intuitions that would be inadmissible in court?

Chief Loftus wasn't available. Kubinski rushed to Deputy Chief Clarence Killorin's office and pleaded with him to back off. The detective's boss refused.

"The Art and Charley Show" resumed on a crash basis, and by late morning the two antagonists seemed closer. Kubinski didn't deceive himself that the killer liked his looks or enjoyed his company. The guy was looking for an edge, a friendly word to the judge or the DA, a confirmation that he'd earned a break. In other words, Kubinski said to himself, he's running a con game. And so am I. Several times he hinted to Shawcross that he might be able to help lighten his sentence, but only if there was reciprocation. "You don't seem like a bad guy, Art," he said. "If you'd just give us a little help . . ."

By lunchtime, the killer was clearly bending. For about the tenth time, he asked what was in it for him if he cooperated. Kubinski tried to sound upbeat and encouraging but made no promises. Shawcross asked for a little more time in his cell.

20.

The first sweep of the wetland woods took four hours and turned up nothing more exciting than the whitened bones of small animals and birds. At three-thirty in the afternoon, during a second pass, Watertown detective Gordon Spinner and county undersheriff John Griffith noticed that long strips of bark had been peeled from a tree and neatly aligned atop a bulge in the spongy earth.

Spinner moved one of the strips with his poking strip. Bluebottle flies rose from a rotting lump of flesh. The slight skeleton was unclothed. A wisp of blond hair grew from the middle of the skull. Animals had moved some of the bones out of position. A few teeth appeared to be missing. There were no apparent fractures or bullet holes.

The searchers secured the scene with tape and examined the surrounding underbrush on hands and knees. Thirty-five feet from the skeleton a deputy found a gray T-shirt bearing a faded message across the front: "I act different because I *am* different." On the back of the shirt, "BLAKE" appeared in faded block letters. Scattered nearby was a green jacket, its arms tied together in a knot, plus two black sneakers and a pair of socks.

A hundred and twenty-six feet from the skeleton, a pair of blue dungarees lay in a trough of blackened leaves. An expended yellow shotgun shell bulged in a front pocket of the pants, evidently a final souvenir of a stroll in the woods. When the jeans were lifted, a pair of boy's underpants fell to the ground.

To the officers, the scattered clothing showed that the child had been stripped before death. A knocked-out tooth, found after a search with screens and forks, confirmed that there'd been violence. It appeared that Jack Blake had been chased through the thorny brush in a murderous game of cat-and-mouse. Cinders under the foot bones indicated that he'd reached the railroad tracks before being caught and dragged back to the woods. Every man in the search team recognized the telltale signs of a sadistic murder.

21.

Around 4:00 P.M., Charles Kubinski was informed that his new friend wanted to talk. A jailer escorted Shawcross to the detective's office. "Charley," the prisoner said, "I decided to help ya."

Kubinski didn't jump up and grab a confession form, nor did he offer congratulatory comments. In seven interviews over three days, he'd learned to let the man act as though he were in control. If you didn't, he could be as stubborn as a heifer.

After another typical silence, the killer said that a judge had assigned him a lawyer named Dierdorf "and I can't show ya the kid's body without clearing it with him." But he assured Kubinski that the attorney's permission was only a technicality. "I thought this out by myself," Shawcross said. "You been good to me and I'm gonna cooperate."

Kubinski showed a measure of patience that he didn't feel. After a few more minutes of small talk, he heard a yell from the hall: "We found Blake!"

Kubinski pretended he hadn't heard. Shawcross looked stricken and began babbling under his breath.

"Huh?" the detective asked. "What'd ya say, Art?"

"I said you can all go to hell."

Kubinski knew exactly what he was thinking: *Charley can't help me now. It's out of his hands.*

"You got the body," Shawcross said. "Do what you want." He glared at the floor.

For another hour, Kubinski argued, promised and threatened. When he saw that nothing would work, he stormed into his chief's office. A victory party was just getting started.

"Siddown, Charley," said Sheriff Irving Angel. "I ordered some beer."

Kubinski recognized reporters from the *Watertown Daily Times* and the broadcast media. He winced as Loftus smacked him on the back and told him what a great job he'd done—"The body was right where you said."

"Where's that leave us, Chief?" Kubinski asked coldly.

"Charley," said Deputy Chief Killorin, "didn't you hear? *We found the kid!*"

"You found a body," Kubinski said. "Now tell me how you're gonna connect it to Shawcross."

Loftus and the others kept acting as though the case was solved, but Kubinski remained dubious. "How the hell are we gonna prosecute?" he asked. "Where's the hard evidence?"

Killorin advised him to leave the worrying to the DA's office. Kubinski wished he felt more confident. Bill McClusky had been a popular prosecutor for six years, but to some of the detectives he seemed hesitant to take a case to trial unless the evidence was overwhelming. Old-time cops wanted all cases tried, weak or not. They wanted a DA with the killer instinct. Bill McClusky was just too nice a guy. Kubinski decided to leave before he ruined the party.

In the hall he encountered a detective who'd just returned from the sheriff's office on Court Street. He reported that Mary Blake and her husband had identified their dead son's clothing. Allen "Big Pete" Blake was too drunk to comprehend, but his wife burst into tears when she saw the T-shirt. Afterward, the one-armed man almost lost his balance and had to be helped down the hall by his wife.

Kubinski hadn't seen the Blakes for a few months and asked how they looked. The other detective said that the husband had put on weight. He'd worn a soiled white T-shirt and stained work pants and needed a shave. "But the missus," he said, "she's still the same. Mean, loud." He made them sound like good qualities. "I think she still hates our ass."

Kubinski said he wouldn't be surprised.

22. MARY BLAKE

Yeah, I went in and identified a body for 'em. I din't know no better.

I was watching TV in my living room when it come on that they found a kid's skeleton in the woods. The picture showed them carrying a garbage bag and some other stuff. Big Pete and me waited for a phone call, but nothing happened. Damn piggy-wiggies! I guess they thought, Why call those river rats?

Ended up, a friend drove us to the sheriff's office. The clothes were Jack's, all right—the black sneakers I bought him just before he come up missing, the shirt, everything. There was a mend in the jacket where I fixed a little rip the day he wandered off. I hated to cry in front of the caps, but I coultn't help myself.

Later that night somebody called from the medical examiner's office and asked if they could keep Jack's body till they finished some tests. He said, "You can bury the empty casket and we'll dig it up later and put in the remains."

I said, "No damn way, mister!" I thought, What mother should be put through a canversation like this? I said, "If there's gonna be a funeral, my son's gonna be in that bax. He's no different than anybody else. He's a little boy human being."

The guy said he'd call us back.

IV

JUSTICE

1.

Two physicians interviewed Arthur Shawcross in his cell and reported that his IQ was slightly subnormal and he was mentally disturbed, probably from battlefront service in Vietnam. Charley Kubinski was ordered to escort his prisoner to Mercy Hospital for a skull echogram, X rays, and a neurological examination. All tests were negative. The doctors pronounced the defendant competent to stand trial for the murder of Karen Ann Hill.

The court-appointed defense attorney, Paul J. Dierdorf, immediately moved for dismissal of the charges on the grounds that Shawcross was "of low-grade mentality and unable to freely and intelligently waive his right to remain silent and to have aid of counsel." The only evidence, the lawyer argued, was "inadmissible and illegal admissions" made to Kubinski in marathon sessions that went far beyond reasonable limits. On top of all the other holes in the state's case, said Dierdorf, not one witness had come forward to place Shawcross and the murdered Karen Ann Hill together.

When the motion was denied, the lawyer filed several more. Among other preliminary triumphs, he succeeded in convincing a judge to ring down the curtain on "The Art and Charley Show," forbidding Kubinski or anyone else from interviewing Shawcross out of the lawyer's presence.

At the arraignment, the defense lawyer instructed his client to plead innocent and argued unsuccessfully for release on bail. In a convincing plea for strengthened security, Dierdorf reminded the judge that there'd been threatening phone calls and noted the courtroom presence of a buzzing knot of spectators. He also cited a rarely used New York State statute about pretrial publicity, laying the groundwork for excluding press and public from the preliminary hearing. Again and again the tenacious young lawyer battled for his client's interests, sometimes at the expense of his personal popularity with angry citizens of Watertown.

Charley Kubinski tried to strengthen the state's case but made little headway. His prime source of information, the defendant himself, no longer returned his hellos. Chief Loftus was still betting on a conviction and a life sentence, but the lead detective had his doubts. Strange things happened in the courts of Jefferson County. He redoubled his efforts. He didn't want to live in a town where a man could kill and go free.

2. PENNY SHERBINO

When I went to visit Art in jail, a deputy grabbed me by the arm and said, "The sheriff wants to see you upstairs."

I said, "I got nothing to say."

"Well, you can't see your husband till you talk to the sheriff."

"Okay, fine, no big deal."

Sheriff Angel and a couple of deputies talked to me for an hour and a half. He wanted to wire me up in case Art said anything incriminating. He told me that the cops weren't allowed to interview Art anymore, but maybe I could get him to confess.

I wouldn't do it; my husband was innocent.

Angel kept insisting. He told me about Art's police record and the two years he'd spent in Attica and Auburn for arson and burglary. I totally disbelieved him. I thought, These people must be nuts. I didn't marry an ex-con; I couldn't be that bad a judge of character.

The sheriff and his sucks didn't like my attitude. They were rude and arrogant, overbearing—total bastards. They were determined to make me help them. I thought, You people are assholes. I got pissed and started yelling and crying, and they finally backed off.

Art was tense. He kept saying, "I didn't do it, I didn't do it." He claimed they framed him because he had some trouble with police when he was a kid, stuff like that. He even cried. He said they put him in an isolated cell and he didn't understand what the other prisoners had against him.

God, he made me feel sad! I couldn't get out of that jail fast enough.

3.

Copies of the protocol on the Blake autopsy were delivered to both sides. Working with whitened old weatherbeaten bones and a few ounces of maggoty flesh, pathologist Richard S. Lee had been unable to pinpoint a specific cause of death. His report noted:

"Because of the attempt to conceal the body of the deceased by strips of bark, and because of the scattering of clothing which are not stained by decomposed body products, such as fat and degenerative products of soapy nature, it is highly probable that the deceased was disrobed prior to death. The absence of staining of the clothes by decomposed body products, and its scattering in the vicinity, suggests that deceased was disrobed either forcibly or was forced to disrobe in that area. In view of these findings, a ruling of homicide is issued by this Office, although the cause of death is undetermined."

Unofficially, the medical examiner's office theorized that the boy's death had been caused by asphyxiation and/or strangulation. But with the preliminary hearing on the Karen Ann Hill murder approaching, no charges were brought in the Blake case. As Kubinski had warned, the evidence was too weak.

4. HELENE HILL

I took Karen home to Rochester and laid her to rest. After that, I kind of lost track of things. Then I heard on the radio that the police had made an arrest.

I tried to figure out where this Shawcross grabbed my baby. Karen would never climb an iron fence to go to a strange man. Never, never, never, *never.* In Rochester, she walked seven or eight blocks to school every day; she knew how to handle herself, who to trust, who not. I would stake my life she didn't climb that fence voluntarily. She might lean over and peek at the river, she might wave her hand or say "hi," but she'd never climb down that bank unless there was a very good reason.

I figured the guy must have lured her. The boy who watched her climb the rail said he was pretty sure her hands were empty. What happened to the white rabbit? She would never have put it down, never have risked letting it run away. She just . . . wouldn't. But why would she carry a bunny down to the riverbank? It made no sense. I understand Shawcross liked to taunt kids, tease them, make them cry. Maybe he grabbed the rabbit and ran. *Then* she'd have followed him down the bank for sure. You couldn't have stopped her.

After a few weeks at home in Rochester, I went back to Watertown. Something compelled me. I felt no hatred or anger—just numbness. I felt as though it was up to me to see that the murderer didn't get away. Yes, I know. It was irrational.

I went to Linda Miles's house and the first thing she showed me was the rabbit's empty cage. We wondered if maybe Shawcross threw it in the river—or threatened to—and Karen ran down the embankment to save it. She had all the guts in the world, and she was crazy about animals.

I went to court to get a look at the killer. My knees were shaking. I didn't tell anybody who I was because I didn't want any attention.

I'd barely sat down when the judge cleared the courtroom. I thought, Wait a minute! I'm her mother! *I've got a right*. . . . I was proud that I didn't cry.

5.

Arthur Shawcross sat stiffly at the defense table, staring straight ahead. In previous courtroom appearances he'd worn casual pants and an open-necked shirt, but Paul Dierdorf had dressed him for this preliminary hearing in a neat blue shirt, pressed blue slacks, and a dark blue sports jacket. He looked more like a young businessman than an ex-con.

Detective Charles Kubinski told his story under questioning by Assistant District Attorney Hugh Gilbert, then spent almost an hour answering combative questions by the defense. Dierdorf took the detective over the exact times of each Shawcross interrogation in an effort to convince the judge that the all-night questioning had exceeded legal limits and that the suspect should have been assigned counsel. The feisty young lawyer also established that Shawcross's clothes and bike had been collected without benefit of search warrant. Then he opened an attack on the investigative work at the scene of the crime.

"Did you check the bridge for fingerprints?" he asked Kubinski.

The detective said, "We were unable to by the time we were prepared to do this because of the [public] activity around this area."

Dierdorf repeated, "The bridge was *not* checked for fingerprints?"

"It was not."

The lawyer seemed obsessed about the activities of "Corporal of Redstone," the State Police bloodhound. "Was he taken under the bridge?" he asked.

"No, sir," Kubinski testified.

"Not under the bridge? On *top* of the bridge?"

"On top of the bridge," the detective answered.

A few minutes later Dierdorf returned to the subject: "The dog was not taken to where the body was found?"

"Not actually to where it was found."

The lawyer hammered his point one more time. "[The dog] was on top of the bridge?" he repeated. "Never below the bridge?"

"No, sir."

After Kubinski stepped down, Dierdorf drew surprising admissions from the assistant medical examiner who'd been summoned to the bridge the night of the murder.

Q. Doctor, could you list for me the tests you performed, if any, on the body?

A. I performed an autopsy and smear examination of the vagina.

Q. Did you take the girl's blood type?

A. No.

Q. Were you able to establish the cause of death?

A. Yes.

Q. It was asphyxiation?

A. Asphyxiation and suffocation, right.

Q. Did you make any tests in relation to the time of death?

A. I didn't. Correct. I didn't do those steps.

Q. Are you able to estimate what the time of death was?

A. There was livor mortis and rigor mortis present, so it is difficult to pinpoint the time. I would say eight to twelve hours.

Q. Did you take the body temperature?

A. No, I didn't.

Q. Is that the usual test taken to determine the time of death?

A. That is one of the tests.

Q. There are other tests?

A. Yes. There was rigor mortis and livor mortis. It depends on the temperature outside.

Q. You estimate the time of death was eight to twelve hours?

A. Yes.

Q. From when?

A. From when I examined the body, about, say, eleven-fifty. I examined the body at that time. I am not one hundred percent positive of the time, but I estimate the time between eight and twelve hours.

Q. In your testing, did you find semen in the girl's vagina?

A. Yes.

Q. Did you do any tests on the semen?

A. We didn't pick up the semen. There was semen and spermatozoa.

Q. Did you attempt to type that or classify it?

A. No.

Q. . . . You did not perform any chemical tests of any sort with any microscope or anything like that at the time?

A. No.

Q. Have you reviewed any results of state examinations from state laboratories?

A. No. We just examined the smears at the hospital—Mercy Hospital. We didn't get anything from the state testing, no.

The imprecision of the medical testimony severely diminished the impact of the rest of the state's evidence. In a rape-murder case, nothing could be more significant than a comparison of the defendant's blood type with the type found in the semen. And the use of body temperature to determine time of death was a standard procedure.

With each subsequent witness, Dierdorf drove home another point: there'd been a steady flow of holiday traffic over the iron bridge during the four-hour span in which death might have occurred. Shawcross and his bike might have been on the bridge and he might have had ample opportunity to murder the child, but the same could be said for dozens of other citizens.

When the last witness stepped down, City Court judge George Inglehart asked Dierdorf if his client wanted to take the stand.

"No, Your Honor," the lawyer answered. He demanded that the charges be dropped on the spot. "There is nothing to link my client to the death of this girl," he argued. "It is at most circumstantial evidence: a bicycle which resembles his in the area. Specifically, in view of the doctor's testimony, they are unable to pinpoint the time of death. He was seen on that bridge for a few minutes in the afternoon. I do not think that is sufficient grounds for the court to be holding him on a murder charge."

Courtroom insiders knew how the judge would rule. Already there'd been shouts in the hall by citizens who wanted to escort Shawcross to the nearest tree. If the judge dismissed the charges, he would be run out of office.

"The motion is denied," Inglehart said crisply. "The evidence is mostly circumstantial, but there are factual questions raised which in the court's opinion require they be decided by a jury. I find reasonable cause defendant committed the felony and am therefore going to hold the case over for the grand jury without bail."

6.

Charley Kubinski felt as though he were watching the last scene of one of those artsy-fartsy movies where the cops are crooks and the bad guys win. Under the American system of justice, it was part of the agony of every dedicated police officer to watch while an occasional criminal beat the system. At the preliminary hearing, the defense lawyer had torn one hole after another in the Karen Hill case—and Jack Blake hadn't even been mentioned. Kubinski shuddered at the thought of Art Shawcross's return to the playground behind the Cloverdale Apartments: taking kids fishing, spanking them, wrestling on the lawn, stuffing grass down their pants, faking playfulness when what he really wanted to do was to rip off their clothes and rape them dead.

The grand jury proceedings did little to dispel his forebodings. The twenty-three members indicted the killer on two counts: intending to commit the murder of Karen Ann Hill and causing the child's death while engaged in the act of rape. But the Blake murder wasn't even presented.

As chief investigator on both cases, Kubinski asked the DA for an explanation. McClusky advised him not to worry —"We're working something out."

"You don't mean . . . a plea bargain?" Kubinski asked.

McClusky asked him to be patient.

7.

The prisoner was examined by psychiatrists at the St. Lawrence Psychiatric Center and again found competent to stand trial. A psychologist reported that Shawcross acknowledged "that he was in need of psychiatric help. He stated that not only does he hear voices commanding him to do certain things, he also experiences a premonition of what is about to happen. He asserted that he does not want to be turned loose on society under any circumstances until such time as he obtains psychiatric help over a sustained period of time."

DA McClusky perused the medical evaluations and then laid the groundwork for his own political demise by arranging an interview session in an anteroom of the Jefferson County jail. The unstated purpose was to provide the basis for a plea bargain.

"Today is October 16, 1972," he noted for the record. ". . . I am William J. McClusky, district attorney of Jefferson County, and you are Arthur Shawcross. Also here is attorney Paul Dierdorf . . . and Sheriff Irving P. Angel is also in the room. Art, the purpose of this conversation today is to talk about Jack Blake and the goings on, on or about May 7, 1972. The purposes are, in itself, [not] to discuss Karen Hill other than to state for the tape recorder that based partly on this conversation we are having here now, that I will in County Court amend the charge pending against you to that of manslaughter, first degree, to take into consideration both the death of Karen Hill and Jack Blake. Do you understand, Art?"

Shawcross said yes, and the polite questioning began:

Q. Now, first, if you would want to tell us about May seventh, on a Sunday?

A. Yes.

Q. Did you go fishing on that day?

A. No.

Q. What did you do that day?

A. I left my house about twelve in the afternoon and had one fishing pole with no fishing line on it. And I went out Hoard Street and out Bradley Street and Jack Blake was following me about a couple hundred yards. . . . I walked down the railroad track to see if I could lose him and got down there almost down to Longway's and he was still coming down the track and I ducked into the woods. He followed me and he got up there, too, and I told him to go home and he said, "No." I got mad and belted him one with the back of my hand and hit him in the face and he hit a tree and fell down. I got scairt then and I laid him down on the ground . . . stretched him out on the ground and put some bark on top of him, ran away from him.

Q. He still had his clothes on him?

A. No.

Q. Did he take it off?

A. No, sir.

Q. You never tied his jacket arms in knots?

A. No, sir.

Q. Then, had you been fishing at all on that day?

A. No, sir.

Q. Did there come a time after that that you met a person in a gas station named Bill Murrock? . . .

A. When I left the woods I went cross-lots and walked, climbed along a fence across a crick without getting wet and then come up behind there, crossed 81 and come up behind Motel 47 and a gas station.

Q. The gas station is right there with the motel?

A. Yes.

Q. Did you go in there and sit down a while?

A. Yes. I was in there about twenty minutes.

Q. And you talked to a man in there who ran or worked in the gas station? Did you know him then?

A. I didn't know him, but I knew the place was there before. He had a restaurant-type self-service, coin-operated machines in there. . . .

Q. He has told the sheriff's department, as far as this investigation is concerned, that when you came in, you had quite a lot of mud on your legs and trousers. Is that right?

A. No mud on my pants. The only thing that was dirty was my shoes.

Q. Were they muddy?

A. Yes, sir.

Q. Your pants—you weren't going through any marshes or anything during this period of time?

A. No, sir.

Q. And then did you go home after that?

A. No. I went from there up to my father-in-law's. . . .

About one-fourth mile, about one hundred yards this side of 342, out Bradley Street.

Q. And how long did you stay there?

A. About quarter after ten that night.

Q. And how did you then get home?

A. My father-in-law brought us home.

Q. And who was "us"? Was your wife there also?

A. Uh-huh.

Q. Did you at any time go back to the scene where Jack Blake was?

A. No, sir. I went by there, but I never stopped there.

Q. You said his head hit a tree when you swatted him down. Did it hit it hard? Did you know he was dead at the time? Did you think he was?

A. No, sir. I thought he was.

Q. Irv, can you think of anything?

Q. (by Sheriff Angel)—What did Jack Blake say to you when he finally caught up with you? Did he indicate that he wanted to go with you?

A. Yeah. He said he wanted to go fishing. He thought I was going fishing.

Q. Had you ever gone fishing with Jack Blake before?

A. Yes, sir. I went fishing with him. He followed me fishing on April first on opening day of trout season. Him and his brother.

Q. Did you have an altercation with him at that time?

A. No, sir.

Q. Did you check to see if he was breathing before you left him?

A. No, sir. I got scairt and left.

Q. Did you make any attempt to help him in any way?

A. No, sir.

Q. To carry him in any way?

A. No, sir.

Q. Did you tell your wife when you got to your in-laws? When you got home? Did you tell them what happened?

A. No, sir.

Q. Have you ever told anyone what you are telling us now?

A. No, sir.

A. (by Dierdorf)—Except me.

Q. Except your attorney? Were you aware that almost within a reasonable period of time—say within a couple of days—there was an intensive search on for this boy?

A. Yes.

Q. Were you aware of it? How were you made aware of it?

A. By everybody that come to my house.

Q. At one time you were picked up by members of the Watertown Police Department and questioned?

A. Yes, sir.

Q. And denied any knowledge of his whereabouts?

A. Yes, sir.

Q. And you were also picked up by detectives of this department and questioned? Right?

A. Yes, sir.

Q. Just a few days after his disappearance?

A. Yes, sir.

Q. And you again denied any knowledge of his whereabouts?

A. Yes.

Q. Did you assume at that particular time that he probably was dead?

A. Yes, sir, I did.

Q. Did you ever at any time sexually molest this boy?

A. No.

Q. Did you ever on prior contacts sexually molest this boy?

A. No, sir.

Q. Did he ever ask you to?

A. No, sir.

Q. And he refused?

A. No, sir.

Q. I think that is all.

Q. (by McClusky) Would you have anything to add, Paul? Okay, thank you.

8.

When Charley Kubinski read a transcript of the questions and answers, he blew up. As far as he was concerned, McClusky and the sheriff had let the killer get away with one lie after another.

The detective shook his head as he read Shawcross's flat denials that he'd molested the boy. My God, he thought, if only I could've asked a few questions. Hey, Art, who scattered the kid's clothes? *Chipmunks?* Why was he found stripped? What were a kid and a grown man doing in that woods in the first place? Sunbathing? Bird-watching? *Naked?*

To the tough cop, this was a simple case of child-rape and murder and it belonged in court. Admittedly the investigation hadn't been perfect—but what case ever was? He despised the way lawyers made their deals. Reading the transcript, he could just imagine Dierdorf's demands in the bargaining session: *You can ask my client this but you can't ask him that. You can dig into this but you can't dig into that. . . .*

Okay, Kubinski said to himself, it's a defense lawyer's job

to protect his client, but what's McClusky's excuse? Why did he roll over? He went to the iron bridge that night, didn't he? He saw the blood, the mud, those thin bare legs. Didn't that show him what kind of goddamn maniac we're dealing with? Doesn't he know that Shawcross beat and stomped and buggered Jack Blake to death?

He voiced his complaints to Chief Loftus and was advised to butt out. He put in a gripe to his immediate boss, Deputy Chief Killorin, and was patted on the back for making the case.

Walking off his anger in the public square, Kubinski ran into the affable McClusky near the statue of the nymph. The two men were business friends; McClusky had represented Kubinski in a real-estate transaction and had done a good job.

"Bill," the detective said, "I wish you'd give the Blake case to the grand jury."

The DA said he was nervous about the lack of evidence. There was heavy pressure by lawmen, jailers, and others to clear both cases and pack Shawcross off to the penitentiary. Every time he was transported to court, crowds threatened a lynching. The DA's switchboard was clogged with outraged calls. The situation was becoming explosive.

"We'll get more evidence," Kubinski protested. "Chrisakes, Bill, don't hand it to the guy."

McClusky confided, "We've got a deal where he gets twenty-five years for manslaughter in the Hill case. In return, he admits killing the boy. I think the public needs to know about that. We'd never be able to prove it in court."

Kubinski thought of the killers who'd served their time and killed again. "Shawcross won't change," he said. "He should be sent away for life."

The prosecutor agreed. "Give me the evidence, Charley," he said, still speaking pleasantly. "I've always said that a DA who's worth a damn can get anybody indicted on a ham sandwich. But . . . not in this case." He said he doubted if he could win a conviction in the murder of Karen Hill; there just weren't enough witnesses.

Kubinski was astonished. "What about the girls that saw him on the bridge?" he asked.

"Lots of people were on that bridge," said McClusky. "I can't charge 'em all with murder."

"But Terry Tenney saw him acting weird, looking through the grate. And how about the people that spotted his bike?"

McClusky pointed out that he couldn't indict a bike.

The two men argued for a few minutes before Kubinski returned to the sore subject of the Blake case. "How about the report that he led the kid into the woods?" he asked.

"Who made that report, Charley? Nobody ever came forward. It's unsubstantiated."

"Well, what about Bill Murrock?"

"He saw Shawcross walk out of the woods with muddy boots. Not bloody hands, Charley—muddy *boots.* And he's not sure of the date."

"A kid saw Karen climb the iron bridge rail."

"He didn't see her with Shawcross. *Nobody* saw her with Shawcross."

The DA mentioned one more weakness in the state's case: the pathologist's imprecision about the time of death. "Think how many people crossed the bridge in that four-hour time span," he told the detective. "And on a holiday, too."

Kubinski brought up the killer's record of child abuse and the way he'd harassed the Blake boy and his suspicious activities on the playground and the fact that every law officer in the North Country knew in his heart that the man was a stone killer.

Once again the DA agreed, but he said he couldn't put police opinions on the witness stand no matter how expert they were and he couldn't introduce the ex-convict's record unless the defendant took the stand, which he certainly wouldn't. And in the Blake case, no one had even established a cause of death, a time, or a solid Shawcross connection.

"Can't you just get him indicted and see what happens?" the detective pleaded.

"It's too big a risk, Charley. If we go to trial and lose, he walks. We can never try him again."

Kubinski thought, That damned double jeopardy law does a hell of a job protecting the rights of the criminals. Who the hell's protecting the rights of the people?

9. MARY BLAKE

Now that we finally had Jack's remains, we arranged services up at the Hart Funeral Home. We expected our priest, Father Doste, but he sent his assistant. I guess something come up.

The funeral parlor was cold, and the priest didn't know Jack or what to say about him. What do you say about a little boy you never saw, a little boy human being that got murdered and the caps din't even bring charges?

There was us family members and a few of Jack's classmates from the fifth grade at the Wiley School. Of course, the caffin was closed. For all we knew, Jack was still in some plastic bags in an icebox at the municipal building. Later on, me and my friend Josephine talked about digging up his remains to see if they really did bury him.

I tried to keep calm, but when I heard my other kids crying I cried, too. We missed Jack. He'd've been eleven years old a month later, on October 18, 1972.

My brother Irvin, he was the caretaker at the North Watertown Cemetery, not far from where Jack's body was found. Irvin put a cement block over the grave, and some people started to raise mawney for a regular stone, but Chief Loftus put a stap to it—that's what I heard, anyway. All's I know for sure is we never saw a cent of that mawney. Me and the piggy-wigs weren't speakin' at the time.

Jack had a rock collection, and I found a nice one to mark his grave. But Irvin never put it on. I don't know if he forgot about it or what.

Then a family friend come over to the house and said, "Hey, Mary, I wanna take you for a ride."

I said, "Where?"

He said, "Don't ask no questions. Just come along."

I said, "I don't wanna ride with you. You been sniffin' glue again."

"Please, Mary," he says, "I'll be careful this time."

I go out to his car and my drunken husband was sittin' in the backseat, so I knew they'd schemed something up. They drove me to Jack's grave, and there was a lovely statue of Jesus and the Virgin Mary! They said they took it from a cemetery in Pennsylvania.

A few weeks later, somebody stole it. I never heard of such a ratten thing in my life.

10.

At 8:00 A.M. on Tuesday, October 17, two weeks after Arthur Shawcross's arrest, an unpublicized hearing was held in County Judge Milton Wiltse's chambers. Technically, the proceedings were open to the public, but so many lawmen crowded inside the small room that reporters had to stand in the hallway, craning their necks.

Security was tight at the Jefferson County Courthouse. For days, the sheriff's office and police department had taken calls from citizens who threatened everything from simple execution to displaying the killer's testicles in the public square. Shawcross had already been attacked by a kitchen trusty at the jail and was confined to his cell for his own safety.

In a smooth proceeding, DA McClusky informed the judge that he'd reduced the murder charges to first-degree manslaughter in the Karen Hill killing. He cited a section of the New York criminal law calling for a finding of manslaughter in cases involving "extreme emotional disturbance." He noted the two main weaknesses in the state's murder case: Shawcross's confession had been vague ("I musta done it, but I don't actually recall doing it"), and the few available witnesses were unable to place defendant and victim together. No jury would convict on such skimpy evidence.

Then the district attorney turned to the second element of the plea bargain: an admission by Shawcross that he'd killed Jack Blake. McClusky observed that there'd been no other way to clear the Blake case except by the voluntary statement, and the anxious parents of Jefferson County deserved to know that the man who'd committed the killing was off the streets.

Judge Wiltse asked Shawcross, "Do you fully understand what you are doing?"

"Yes, Your Honor," the killer replied in a voice just above a whisper. He was wearing the same neat sports outfit that had replaced his jail coveralls for court appearances. Asked to plead, he said, "Guilty, Your Honor."

Defense attorney Dierdorf requested that his client be committed to a treatment program "rather than a long jail term," arguing that no amount of incarceration would bring back the dead children.

While Shawcross looked at the floor in his usual meek courtroom pose, Judge Wiltse pronounced an indeterminate sentence of up to twenty-five years. Under a technicality of New York law, he could be released in ten months, when the State Board of Parole would meet to set his minimum term, but everyone in the courtroom expected the child-killer to serve his full sentence.

At 8:48 A.M., eighteen minutes after the hearing began, Shawcross was handcuffed to a bailiff and rushed out the side door in the middle of a phalanx consisting of Sheriff Angel, an undersheriff, three deputies and three detective sergeants. The lead detective had stayed home. Charley Kubinski was still convinced that the prosecutor, as he put it later, "gave away the store."

A *Daily Times* photographer snapped a picture of the prisoner as he was reentering the Jefferson County jail. His shoelaces had been removed out of respect for his talents as a strangler and also as a routine suicide precaution. The picture also revealed that Shawcross, still in his sports coat and slacks, had pulled his white socks up over the cuffs of his pants, biker-style. For someone who wouldn't see a bicycle for years, it seemed an odd sartorial note.

• • •

Alerted by a courtesy call from Sheriff Angel, Penny Shawcross was allowed a last-minute visit to her husband. Nothing memorable was said and there were no lavish signs of affection. Penny was followed by her in-laws, Arthur Guy Shawcross and Bessie Yerakes "Betty" Shawcross, who reported later that Art seemed depressed, hung his head and again used baby talk. "I don't know why," the mother observed.

All three were surprised to find Art packed for travel. The standard procedure was to transport prisoners the day after sentencing.

The visitors had hardly been ushered out before the convicted man was led to a patrol car. Less than two hours after the sentencing, the most notorious criminal in North Country history was looking at the low green hills around the correctional facility known as Attica, thirty-six miles southwest of Rochester. One day less than a year had passed since he'd been paroled after serving his sentence for burglary and arson. He was admitted at 12:45 P.M.

Later that afternoon, Sheriff Angel's office took an anonymous call. "I'm gonna get that sumbeetch," a male voice said in a foreign accent. "I blow his fokkin' head off."

The deputy advised the caller that he would have to break into a maximum-security prison to do it.

11.

From her noxious hollow in the river bottom, Mary Blake wasted no time in rising up to smite the hated Watertown police—"the piggy-wigs and them other crooks in bow ties," as she described them. Expressions of official sympathy were rejected; Mary meant business. She even found something to complain about when a city councilman issued an invitation for her to air her grievances in a closed-door meeting. Her angry reaction made page one of the *Watertown Daily Times:*

"What's wrong with them up there? Don't they know Jack has a father, too? I'm not a widow. My husband's pretty mad about this."

She neglected to mention that her one-armed husband was seldom in condition for public appearances. "I don't have no faith in the police anymore," Mary was quoted as saying, "and I can't trust the council anymore, either. If they don't have nothing to hide, why shouldn't it be open to the public?"

From the beginning, the townspeople had been on her side. Irate citizens marched on the municipal building, held boisterous protest meetings, and filled the airwaves and newspapers with complaints and second-guesses. A hot-line radio show devoted a week to the case. Mary phoned and said, "If Bill McClusky knew his onions, Shawcross would rot in hell." Several of her other remarks were beeped out.

Charley Kubinski had predicted a public outcry over the plea bargain, but he hadn't expected the abuse that was heaped on him and some of his colleagues in the Watertown Police Department. Mary Blake set them up by going out of her way to praise state troopers, the sheriff's department, and especially Deputy Chief Killorin. She lambasted Chief Loftus for calling her original suspicions about Shawcross "unfounded" and jumped on Kubinski and other detectives for "screwin' up." If Loftus and his men had shown the skills of the Keystone Kops, she charged, Shawcross would have been arrested in May and "little Karen would be alive today."

City Manager Ronald Forbes countered by asking reporters, "Don't you know she was complaining all along?" He defended the officers as "good family men."

Mary's policy was to respond to all comments. In the next edition of the *Daily Times,* she was quoted as saying that it didn't matter whether those useless detectives were family men or not—"I don't want to hear about the personal history of all these men. So what?"

Convinced that there was no justice in Jefferson County, she wrote Governor Nelson Rockefeller:

> I am the mother of Jack Owen Blake, 10 yrs, who was murdered by Arthur Shawcross. The people of Watertown N,Y and my family are bitter and outraged at the lack of help by our police department.
>
> On the day of my son's disaperance we called the police to help us find Jack, Instead of help we have been living a nightmare ever since. Arthur Shawcross admitted he was the last person to be with Jack. He was a convict out on parole from Attica prison. The police wouldn't take him in for questioning. Instead, they ask my husband and myself to take a lie detector test after 4 months of being called a complainer by the police.
>
> A little girl 8 yrs old was murdered by the same man. Karen Ann Hill was raped and murdered and God only knows what Jack had to suffer at the hands of Arthur Shawcross. We think a Grand Jury Investigation should be made and the treatment given us by the police department of Watertown NY.

When he heard about the letter, DA McClusky hastily released a statement of his own:

> More than eight hours after the boy first left home, two members of the Watertown city police spent the night searching for him. On May 8, the following day, city policemen spent many hours searching for him and again on the 9th and 10th. Sheriff's detectives and the New York State Police entered on a search on the 9th and 10th of May. Shawcross was interviewed on May 7, 8, 11, and at various times thereafter by the city police department. However, as there was no evidence of any crime and he didn't admit anything, the police were stymied.

McClusky's response was ignored by the public and the media. It wasn't what they wanted to hear; the earth mother from Water Street made better copy. Mary was viewed as a heroic symbol of the weak and oppressed, and she set about making the city fathers pay for every indignity she and the Lawtons and the Blakes had suffered in her thirty-seven years of life. Her claims and counterclaims, some real, some exaggerated, were trumpeted by the media to a populace that couldn't get enough of the North Country passion play.

In the middle of the firestorm, another mourning mother tried to calm the public in an open letter to a Watertown newscaster. "There isn't anything anybody can do for Mrs. Blake or me," Helene Hill wrote from her home in Rochester, "except to give us your understanding and friendship."

The bereaved woman recalled her shock on the night of the murder: "I couldn't believe this had happened to my Karen—it was a mistake—God wouldn't do this to her—not my Karen who loved life so much, who wanted to grow up and be a movie star and marry Tom Jones."

Now, she wrote, it was time to "stop all this vicious talk and gossip. Have we not had enough heartbreak? . . . Common sense tells me that if the police department had had more to go on, Mr. Shawcross would have been held and questioned [when Jack Blake disappeared]. Let it be understood that in no way am I dissatisfied with Mr. McClusky or the police department. . . . Stop all this vicious talk and gossip!"

The noise level only increased. At a special City Council meeting, aired live over local station WNCQ-FM, Mary Blake was besieged with questions from her admirers. Her replies were so inflammatory that City Manager Ronald Forbes took the microphone to quiet the crowd. He proclaimed his belief that the police department had done everything possible in the Blake case and added, "I have no reason to believe the search was not careful or proper."

In the sandblasting voice that she usually reserved for family arguments, Mary begged to differ. "How come there was only one man assigned to search for my Jack?" she asked as a *Daily Times* reporter took down her words.

She waved a finger at Mayor Theodore Rand and yelled, "I talked to you on the phone! You told me you would send the police to Pool's Woods to look for my son. You sent one officer—Mr. Mooney."

Spectators shouted approval while Mary waited for quiet like an old trouper. Then she said, "Now, I don't think there's only one officer in City Hall, because about twenty was in my front yaird looking for Karen Hill when she disappeared, and she sure wasn't in my yaird, because I'd already searched it."

"Ma'am," the mayor replied patiently, "when you called me I called the police department. From that day on I personally am convinced all the officers in the Watertown police department did their utmost."

"I never seen a *one*," Mary responded. "I was in the woods myself. I only seen Mr. Mooney, and he went through the woods in less than an hour! And he just can't do it."

Before the session ended, she leveled one last blow at the hated piggy-wiggies. With an innocent look on her round face, she said sweetly, "I'd like to know if you, as councilmen, could get my son's picture from the police department, which I give them on the seventh of May."

Mayor Rand looked embarrassed. "That will be done," he promised.

The *Daily Times* demanded "a full dress inquiry" into the case, a rare pressure by one entrenched Republican institution on another. Petitions bearing 758 signatures arrived in the offices of New York Attorney General Louis Lefkowitz and U.S. Attorney General Richard Kleindienst, but both agencies politely declined jurisdiction.

City Manager Forbes arranged for additional sworn statements, including one from the angry Kubinski, and prepared a confidential report. A councilman proclaimed that the document fully exonerated the public officials, but it was never released to the public.

• • •

Exonerated or not, District Attorney William McClusky continued to pay heavily for his actions in the case. When his term of office ended, he accepted an interim appointment as county judge, then ran for a full term and lost. "That plea bargain did it," he explained ruefully. "A city judge ran against me and every one of his ads ended, 'Elect Judge Inglehart and you will sleep better tonight.' It was a subliminal message, very effective. It said I let the community down. But anyone who knew criminal law knew I hadn't."

The McClusky name had been respected in Jefferson County politics, but the public's attitude paralleled Kubinski's—that he'd coddled the child-killer. The former DA kept emphasizing that the plea bargain *preceded* the confessions, that without the plea bargain the state would have had nothing to connect Shawcross with the dead boy and an impossibly weak case in the matter of Karen Hill.

"The people's reaction really shocked me," McClusky said later. "I honestly thought I'd taken advantage of Paul Dierdorf's inexperience by getting him to plead his client to manslaughter. If we'd gone to trial, Shawcross would've been acquitted. Gone right out and killed more kids! The man was a homicidal pedophile and he wasn't gonna change. I thought I did a good job by taking him off the streets for twenty-five years."

But the vagaries and complexities of the case were dimly comprehended by the angry townspeople, and after losing the race for county judge, McClusky quietly returned to private practice.*

* The McClusky family remained star-crossed for years to come. In 1976, McClusky's fourteen-year-old son Leo stabbed, stomped, and shot to death thirty-four-year-old Holly Gilbert, wife of Family Court judge Hugh A. Gilbert, who was Jefferson County Republican chairman and McClusky's former colleague in the DA's office. The boy served eighteen months in a juvenile facility, the maximum allowable, and was released.

12.

Inside Attica, Arthur Shawcross continued his lifelong pattern of confounding the experts. Two psychiatrists, J. O. Carroll and Joseph Loposzko, found nothing more specific than "evidence of personality defect." They described him as being "in good contact, well oriented, no discreet disturbance in thought pattern, pleasant, cooperative, but anxious, apprehensive, mildly depressed. Could appreciate humor but stated had considered taking his life. . . . Delusions specifically denied by inmate."

Typically sociopathic, the killer showed no signs of guilt or remorse. Instead, the psychiatrists reported, he seemed "totally concerned about himself and the penalty which he must endure and is apparently without conscience in the matter." They added, "It is the opinion of these interviewers that need for psychotherapy will be difficult with this inmate because of apparent intellectual deficiency and weakness of superego."

He was placed on ten milligrams of Librium daily.

13. HELENE HILL

A newspaperman phoned me and said, "Helene, I heard that Shawcross was beaten. He's in the prison hospital." He said that convicts hated child-molesters and everybody in Attica wanted to make a name for himself by attacking him.

Toward the end of November, I read that they'd transferred him to Green Haven prison because of information that one of the victims had a relative in Attica and the situation was too explosive. But the Blakes didn't have any relatives in Attica and neither did I. I guess the Department of Corrections wasn't taking any chances. There'd been a big riot at Attica the year before, forty people killed, and they didn't need another troublemaker.

I don't know what got into me, but I decided to stay in Watertown permanently. I wanted to feel closer to Karen, because it was the last place I'd seen her alive. How irrational! If I wanted to be closer to her, I should've stayed in Rochester, where she was buried.

Father Doste located a cheap two-bedroom apartment in Maywood Terrace. I'd saved some money, and my ex-husband was paying support, so we didn't have financial problems. I put the kids in Watertown schools; it was hard on them, but I guess I was so involved with my pain that I couldn't see theirs.

I couldn't stop blaming myself for washing my hair that day. I thought, Was Karen killed because of my vanity? I went through a long list of if-onlys: If only I hadn't kept my head under the faucet so long . . . if only I hadn't spent so much time putting my hair in rollers . . . if only I'd looked out the window more often . . . if only . . .

At night I asked myself questions: Why didn't you bring her in the house while you washed your hair? Why did you drag her to Watertown in the first place? *What kind of mother are you?*

I couldn't sleep. An inch-and-a-half white streak formed in my hair. I was thirty-five and stopped having periods. I went from one-fifteen down to eighty-nine, but I was so bloated I looked pregnant.

One day I read that a few drinks before bedtime helped insomniacs. But drinking never appealed to me because of my alcoholic father. And I couldn't go into a bar alone.

Father Doste dropped by for a visit, and I said on impulse, "Would you take me for a drink? I'm desperate for some sleep and I heard it might help."

He said, "But my pleasure!" in his French accent.

He took me to a bowling hall. I ordered a gin and tonic and he ordered a gin on the rocks and everybody in the place stared at the priest and the redhead. I had one more drink and went home. I slept two hours.

V

HARD LABOR

1.

I was sent to prison for 0–25 years. The first 8 years were hard for me.

—Arthur Shawcross

In the maximum-security Green Haven Correctional Facility at Stormville, forty-five miles north of New York City in a narrow slice of low green hills between the Hudson River and the Connecticut border, Arthur Shawcross was quickly tagged as "mental." Guards passed the word that he could carry on an ordinary conversation, but there was something wrong upstairs.

He seemed uninterested in work, preferring to practice painting on glass. Now and then he slumped to the floor and lost consciousness. "Chest pain," noted a December entry in his file, six weeks after he'd been transferred from Attica for his own safety. "Passed out."

Four days later, another entry said, "Pain right chest—found on Floor B block. ℞ Demerol, Vistaril, Donatol, Dalmane. Diagnosis: myositis muscles rt. side."

Cynical guards suspected fakery. One notation read: "This man appears to have made a miraculous recovery for being brought to the hospital via stretcher and all the commotion he created." Others suspected a childish need for attention.

After more psychiatric interviews, he was diagnosed as a dangerous schizophrenic pedophile, suffering from "intermittent explosive personality." It was also noted that he heard voices when he was depressed, engaged in fantasy "as a source of satisfaction," and had an "oral-erotic fixation with need for maternal protection."

The prisoner seemed bored with the attempts to figure him out and blithely unconcerned about his two young victims. After the Parole Board set his minimum sentence at five years, he continued to show the same coldness that had made earlier diagnosticians write him off as a typically self-involved sociopath. But every now and then he claimed to be upset and even depressed about his crimes. Counselors weren't sure what to believe.

One early examiner noted that the inmate "asks for help in understanding why he did it." The same expert suggested to prison doctors that Shawcross be tested for "possible organic involvement." It was an early hint that his mysterious behavior might have physical causes. A follow-up examination revealed no neurological impairment. Shawcross was described as a "normal psychopathic individual," i.e., sane but suffering from behavioral defects, including a lack of conscience and empathy. The diagnosis fit half the prisoners in Green Haven and some of the guards.

For the first several months, Shawcross was watched closely, both for his own protection and others'. Rapists, informers, and ex-cops were lowest in the pecking order of the 2,050 male inmates, but there was a special netherworld for child-killers. On entering Green Haven, he'd been advised to keep his head down, his mouth shut, and never discuss his crimes. But it wasn't long before word got out. In January 1973, two months after his transfer from Attica, a *Front Page Detective* article circulated inside the prison. It was titled "Karen's Corpse Was the Key to Jackie's Grave" and featured two unmistakable photographs of the killer.

One month later, while the inmate huddled in his cell, an issue of *True Detective* arrived with an article titled "The Kids' 'Friend' Was a Killer." Again Shawcross was pictured, this time with an inflammatory shot of poor Karen Hill, lying facedown in the mud beneath the Pearl Street bridge, her bare buttocks blanked out in an odd touch of consideration for prudish readers.

Word went out that the kiddie-killer would be "piped." Shawcross was warned, and a note in his prison files said, "Upset—starting to cry." By the next day he was still so frightened that he refused to attend a routine meeting with the Parole Board. Ordered from his cell, he bit two guards, cut another with a sharp object, spattered his paints against the wall, and set fire to his bed. Ten officers subdued him and carried him to the infirmary. At first he appeared defeated, but when he burst into action again he was strapped to a gurney and sedated with Thorazine.

Three days later, a guard team approached his cell and Shawcross yelled, "Fuck you! I'll kill you both. Wait till I get out. *I'll kill you both!*" Once again he tore up his belongings and set fires. This time he was sedated with Valium.

Peace returned slowly to the forty-one-man "A-1 Protection Unit," but Shawcross remained a problem. In January 1974 he showed his old aversion to therapy by refusing to attend an interview with a psychiatrist. He complained of frequent headaches and was put on Darvocet, a strong pain-killer.

The animosity against him was slow to abate. He was showered with spit, catcalls, and missiles whenever he ventured from his cell. On September 2, 1974, he was involved in a fight and lost some privileges, and after another battle a week later, an entry was made in his record: "Cut to Adams apple and rt. eye and contusion rt. upper lip and forehead."

But he was a powerful man with a wrestler's physique, and by the time he'd served three years of his sentence, the vendetta had been reduced to name-calling and shoving matches. He remained segregated from the general population. There were nine hundred killers inside the walls, some serving life without possibility of parole, and any one of them could execute a fellow prisoner without serving a single extra day. Shawcross was forced to seek companionship elsewhere.

2. ARTHUR SHAWCROSS

I had sex in prison with a female [staffer]. Had no problem having an orgasm with her. She was heavyset. She was older than I was. It felt great. Maybe because when I was doing it I was just so much in a hurry to get it done and get out of there because I didn't want to get caught. . . . She would tell me about her married life and he's running around and I would just talk to her and I'd pat her on the shoulder and she'd cry. Then she'd hold me and cry. And it just started there.

3. PENNY SHERBINO

I couldn't get to Green Haven—no money, no car. On the phone he said, "Please, Penny, I beg you to believe me. How could anybody think I'd hurt a kid?" Then he cried like a baby. Does that sound like a guy who killed with his bare hands?

I just blocked the idea of his guilt out of my mind. I still had my own two kids to raise. I figured Art would serve his time and get out and we'd take up where we left off. But it was hard on me. I kept laying in bed thinking about him being with the worst kind of scum. You never knew when he'd be killed with a shank.

We wrote back and forth for three or four years. Then his letters stopped. Finally I got a letter that made me want to throw up. He came right out and admitted killing the two kids—in his own handwriting! He didn't even say he was sorry. He told me I was the only person stupid enough to think he was innocent.

I wrote back that he was a rotten stupid son of a bitch and I hoped he died. The nicest thing I wrote was, Fuck you, man. . . .

It messed up my head. I couldn't date because of him. What would the next guy turn out to be? An ax-murderer? I hardly went out of the house.

When he filed for divorce for "cruel and inhuman

treatment"—can you believe the *balls*?—my parents got mad at me for giving in and signing the papers. I said, "So it's a big fat lie. Any way I can get outa this mess, I'm gonna do it."

He said he wanted the divorce because he was writing to a nurse's aide in Delaware County and he was gonna marry her when he got out. I thought, That poor woman, the things I could tell her! But I kept quiet and tried to forget about him. He was just a cloud in my past.

4. MARY BLAKE

They sent Shawcross away but it din't change our life. Big Pete drank more than ever and my kids got into trouble one by one—drinking, dope, disorderly, harassment, you name it. Sometimes they deserved what they got, but mostly they were framed by the piggy-wigs. The caps never forgave us for what we'd said in the papers. They even arrested me for petty larceny at Nichols Department Store on Arsenal Street. I din't take anything, but I wound up paying a seventy-five-dollar fine.

One day Richie, my oldest, got into a fight with some guys outside a neighborhood bar. I heard about it and run down there. A cap was yelling, "C'mon, Richie, where's the knife?"

I run up and I says, "What knife? He don't have no knife." I says, "You caps ya, you coultn't find a cold beer in a phone booth. You're worthless. All you do is try to get in my daughter's pants."

He starts yelling into his police radio.

"Yeah," I says, "you *better* call for backup!"

More caps came and one of 'em musta had a guilty conscience because he says, "Mrs. Blake, I'd like you to know I looked for your son for three days like he was my own kid."

I says, "Who in the hell said you din't?"

He gets hot and he's hallering at me and I took and

grabbed his badge and said, "Tell me, is there really a heart under there?"

He says, "You're pinched, lady. I'm takin' you in."

I says, "You and what airmy?"

He threw me in the back of the police car. At the station, he says, "Can somebody bail you out?"

I says, "What for? You arrested me, din'tcha? Why do you want me out?"

My son Richie got off, but I stayed in jail overnight and paid fifteen dallars for disorderly. Later on they sent him to the penitentiary for burglary. I guess they figured it made us even. After that, I din't grab any more police badges or call 'em "punk" to their face. I figured there's more piggies than there is Blakes.

One afternoon my sister Nancy glanced out our front window and hollered, "Mary, hurry up! It's Jack!"

I ran in from the kitchen, but he was gone. Nancy said he'd been staring up at our house and then stepped behind a tree.

Me and the kids looked all over the neighborhood, in alleys and sheds, even went into some of the caves along the river, tree houses, baxcars. Somebody thought about checking old Agnes Thomas's house, next door to ours. She had a pacemaker and she was one of Jack's best friends —he shoveled her snow and mowed her lawn and liked to drap in and visit. Why, after he turned up missin', Agnes hired some men to hang a bright light on a pole so Jack could find his way back home. She cried about Jack, told me if he was really dead he was the brightest star in the sky and it would never be dark in heaven again.

Anyways, my daughter Robin knocked on Agnes's door and nobody answered. Robin went inside and Agnes was layin' dead on the living room floor.

I believe Agnes saw Jack that day and just died of shack. Yeah, I know the piggies found some bones and a shirt, but stuff like that coulda been faked. I thought about how nobody ever showed me Jack's body. *Never.* Who was in that coffin in the North Watertown Cemetery? There was nothin' in the official reports about no deformed foot. And the sneakers they found, they looked brand-new, but it rained most of May and if those sneakers and clothes was outdoors for four months they woulda been mildewed, weather-worn. The piggy-wiggies planted 'em there to make everybody think it was Jack. Why? Don't ask me, ask them.

After Jack come back that day and Nancy saw him, it made me think about his real father and why he never called anymore. Maybe he took Jack away and arranged for Shawcross to take the blame. He had the power. Mawney talks in Watertown, and Bob had plenty.

One day I seen him driving past. He rolled down his window and said, "How come you din't come up to the hospital and see me?"

I said, "Oh, was you sick?"

He said he'd been *real* sick.

I said, "I'm sorry, Bob. I din't know about that. But I probably woultn't of come to see you anyway."

I wanted to ask him to tell me the truth about our son, but I coultn't say the words. He just drove off and I din't do no more about it. By then I had my hands full with Little Pete.

5. ALLEN "LITTLE PETE" BLAKE

I didn't give a shit about nothin' no more. I thought, They took away my brother, my best friend. I hated the way the caps pushed my mom around and then let Shawcross off easy. I wanted to get even with everybody. It was like the town was telling us, You Blakes are poor, you're crooks, you're dirt. You Blakes are *dogs*.

Some woman made a remark and I chased her down her driveway with rocks. She yelled, "You shoulda been fucked up the ass like what he done to your brother!" One of our neighbors! I couldn't handle it. I was pissed at the world.

I started sneakin' beer outa my father's supply. I stole pills and stuff from my older sisters and my brother Richie. I forgot to take my epilepsy medicine but I never forgot my dope. I was hooked before I was ten.

My mom stared out the front window for hours, waiting for Jack to walk up our driveway. I wanted to say, Hey, Mom, *I'm* alive! Jack's *dead*!

One day I smashed a rock through the window. Mom ducked just in time. Then I busted out some others.

Judge Sanders told me, "I'm sending you to the boys' school for eighteen months. We'll see if that teaches you anything."

I spit at him. It took five probation officers to handcuff me. He was right about the boys' school. I learned plenty.

6.

As the months passed, Mary Blake's survival fantasy hardened into a firm belief. "Jack's *alive*," she would insist as her children arched their eyebrows. "I've seen so many signs from the Lord, but I keep it inside of me because nobody would believe me. Bein' a mother, I'm psychic."

The logic of her fantasy required her to believe that Arthur Shawcross had been railroaded by the same system of justice she'd criticized for years.

"I don't think he killed Jack *or* Karen, either one," she explained. "He was mean, but why call him a murderer? That'd be like saying my son Little Pete was a murderer 'cause when he takes drugs he gets mean. I told him one day, 'If you keep taking those drugs, you could be another Shawcross.' "

Day by day, Mary turned more cynical. Around her house, policemen were no longer referred to as piggy-wigs; the phrase was considered too complimentary. Mary explained, "There's no waste on a pig, ya know? You can eat every part of a pig. I like pigs. I'm against the law all the way."

It wasn't long before larceny became a systematized family activity. "I got stolen coffee from one of my daughters," Mary recalled. "Taster's Choice. Also meat. I coulda had steak every meal if I wanted. My kids shaplifted from the P&C food market, took the stuff out in their pants. Once in a while, they got caught. Little Pete was in jail off and on since he was nine.

"Sometimes my kids shaplifted as a team. One would put the stuff in a cart and wheel it up to the other, and they'd shift the stuff to their clothes while another one blocked the aisle. The Lord watched over 'em, 'cause he knew that if they din't steal, they din't eat. We were living on food stamps at the time. My kids had to steal the clothes they wore. If they din't, they'd get arrested for indecent exposure."

The situation grew worse. One night Little Pete came home drunk. "Here, Mom," he said. "Here's thirty bucks."

"Where'd you get that?" Mary asked. She noticed blood on his sneakers. "Oh, my Gad," she said. "What happened?"

Slurring his words, Little Pete told how he'd stolen an old man's six-pack and wallet after clubbing him to the street with a piece of wood.

Mary's first instinct was to call the police, but then she said to herself, The cops never did nothing for me. They'll hang Pete, and he didn't mean it. Look at him! The poor kid's drunk.

The *Watertown Daily Times* mentioned the assault, and a small reward was posted. "I never told anybody nothin'," Mary confided years later. "I hated the law. Why should I turn my son in? If you tell the truth, it don't work out. If you lie, they believe ya. Anyway, it din't matter. The old man died later of pneumonia."

7. HELENE HILL

My kids and I finally moved back to Rochester for good. I missed my mother and the rest of my family. When we got home, I visited Karen's grave every day. I stared at the angel on the tombstone and talked to her. I never wanted to leave.

One night she came to me, wearing her pink burial dress. Her arms were outstretched and she was going, "Mommy, Mommy, come here!"

I thought, Oh, God, she's home!

I said, "Oh, Karen, Mommy's here." I held out my arms and walked toward her, and she kept backing up. I said, "Karen, stop! Stand still, honey! I can't get to you." Then I woke up.

They say time heals, but I got worse. I couldn't manage my life, couldn't do the simplest things. I'd run out of the market in tears. Every movie made me cry. I wasn't the family comedian anymore, far from it. I couldn't stop crying, couldn't bring myself under control. It wasn't fair to my kids or anybody else.

I decided on suicide but couldn't figure out how. I had enough of my old vanity to say to myself, Don't do anything that'll keep you from looking pretty when you're laid out. Don't disfigure yourself or jump off a bridge.

I collected pills from several doctors. One night I counted 'em up and figured I had enough. I asked my sister and brother-in-law to come over so I could say good-bye. Gary walked in and said, "Helene, you don't look good. You've gotta stop going to the grave every day."

I broke down and forgot all about my plan. "I need help," I said. "You better take me to a hospital."

There were so many disturbed people on the psychiatric ward that I was afraid to leave my room. I had long talks with the therapists about grief, and their treatment saved my life. When I went home after a month, I was sure I could manage.

But I still couldn't see people. Every day after work, I hurried home. I figured if I was inside my apartment and my door was shut, nobody could touch me, nobody could hurt me. I was able to survive, but the pain never went away. People said I should go into counseling, but I didn't want to.

Then the migraines began. My family told me to see a neurologist, but I thought, What's the use? *I should've brought her in the house if I was gonna wash my hair.* I wondered if she'd screamed. *Why didn't I hear her? Was the dryer too loud? . . .*

Friends told me to quit punishing myself. They would call up with the latest information about headaches, the latest treatment, but I wouldn't listen. I didn't take medicine. I figured it was my punishment.

8.

At Green Haven, Arthur Shawcross settled in. He was written up for possession of contraband, stealing food, fighting, running in the corridor, talking out loud at night, but these were minor offenses that occurred over several years and wouldn't be deducted from time off for good behavior. He continued to resist psychotherapy and refused to enroll in the prison's sex offenders program. Some of his counselors believed that he was incapable of understanding his behavior and others concluded that he was too stubborn to try.

"Not much insight concerning maladaptive life dating back to early adolescence," wrote psychologist Michael Boccia at the beginning of the inmate's fourth year of incarceration. "Thrice divorced, aimless existence."

Like most other examiners, Boccia took note of some odd contradictions—"He tells us that he deserves more punishment than he has received for his crimes, which he still minimizes." Despite the killer's long-standing resistance and his "less than complete sincerity in dealing with deep-seated intrapsychic and interpersonal conflicts," Boccia recommended referral to a consulting psychologist or transfer to an institution where intensive therapy was available.

Six months later, on May 27, 1977, a counselor noted in the Shawcross file, "Will not attend group therapy. . . . Has a great deal of shame and remorse about the offense [Karen Hill] and in fact doesn't think he is ready or deserves to be released. Likes institutional life. . . ." He reported that Shawcross suffered depression and nervousness over the killing and saw Karen Ann Hill in his nightmares.

The thirty-two-year-old prisoner told another official that he didn't know why he killed the two children, but "I shouldn't be alive today." The officer listed him as "a grave parole risk" and ordered a psychiatric evaluation. Dr. Y. A. Haveliwala found no evidence of thought disorder and repeated an earlier diagnosis: "anti-social personality disorder [sociopath] and schizoid personality disorder . . . psychosexual conflicts."

After five years in prison, Shawcross seemed adjusted to the role of cellblock loner. "He is prone to be rather simplistic and childlike in his attitudes," a counselor wrote in 1977. "Remains to himself much of the time. Appears unable to establish peer relations, but shows good deal of trust in authority figures."

His attempts to gain parole were routinely denied. Whenever he was scheduled to appear before the Board, the *Watertown Daily Times* alerted Jefferson County residents —*"Shawcross Release Possible"*—and angry letters arrived at Green Haven. David C. Knowlton of Knowlton Specialty Papers wrote to remind the authorities of Shawcross's arsons, including the $280,000 fire at the plant on Factory Street. Various Jefferson County district attorneys, starting with John F. Bastian in 1976, were equally outspoken. Bastian's successor Lee Clary wrote, "If this man is released, no one in this county will have any faith in the criminal justice system."

The New York State Division of Parole agreed. "A release

of this man to the community at this time, given his lack of change in behavior, might result in a murder of several more children," a parole officer wrote in 1977. Four years later, a PO named Thomas Connolly finished what he described as a "pleasant" interview with Shawcross and reported to the Board that "this writer is strongly opposed to parole release at this time. . . . Obviously he is quite dangerous and capable of horrible crimes."

Even after signs that the prisoner had become institutionalized, he remained an outcast. Officials took note that he corresponded with his two sisters, Donna and Jeannie, his mother Betty, and a female pen pal in Delaware County, but there was little or no communication with his younger brother James or his ex-Marine father, Arthur Guy Shawcross.*

About once a month he talked with his mother by collect phone call, describing prison life in terms that sometimes seemed less than appropriate ("the screws caught two guys doin' it last night"). Betty Shawcross was so mortified about her son's crimes that she seldom ventured from Shawcross Corners, and she told relatives that she certainly had no interest in the sex lives of cloistered men.

Now and then the mother mailed off a package, and she faithfully forwarded his monthly disability check from the VA. "He's the same as ever," she confided disappointedly to a friend. "The way he talks, the things he talks about—there's no change at all."

For a while, he told his mother that he was thinking about joining the ministry, but he soon dropped the subject. Then he hinted that he'd married in prison, but a

* Talking about it later, the senior Shawcross almost seemed to take pride in the estrangement. He told a New York State Police investigator that he rarely spoke to his imprisoned son. "My wife used to write to him," Shawcross said, then added emphatically, "but I never did."

relative checked and confirmed that it was just another tall story. Neither of his parents ever paid a visit.

In midsentence, Shawcross began to take advantage of prison opportunities. The ninth-grade drop-out earned a high school equivalency diploma, then scored a B in a horticulture class offered by Pennsylvania State University. He won a certificate in carpentry and worked at various times as a locksmith, earphone repairman, cook, gardener, block porter, clerk, and electrical handyman. Counselors noted that he read an occasional nonfiction book and continued to refine his skill at painting on glass.

For the first time, the unlikely word "industrious" appeared in his prison jacket. Corrections counselor William F. Hutchinson wrote, "He seems to be extending himself more toward other people and has gained the respect of staff members through his pleasant demeanor and conscientious performance of his assignment duties."

A job supervisor named John Beachy reported, "He wasn't the kind of guy to cause disturbances or anything. That type, they usually stay real quiet here."

But exactly what "type" was this man who had killed two children with his bare hands and seemed to have the impulse control of a barracuda? Year after year, behaviorists set about analyzing the killer's personality, with uniformly disappointing results. As in most prisons, psychiatric expertise and therapy were minimal, a circumstance that didn't seem to displease the inmate. In diagnostic interviews, he nodded yes or no, or folded his hands across his belly and remained mute. Sometimes he dozed, or he ignored the examiner as he'd ignored others. In rare bursts of chatter, he played down his killings or hinted that he'd been in the grip of uncontrollable impulses. More often . . . well, he really didn't want to talk about it.

His long and documented history of "passing out" attracted medical attention, but tests showed a normal brain and nervous system. In his first term at Attica, he'd been diagnosed for "syncope" (cessation of respiration and circulation), and frequent notations had appeared in his files: "passed out," "found on floor," "fainting," "dizzy," "fell down stairwell." Counselors had wondered if the incidents were faked.

At Green Haven, the question remained unanswered, like so many others about the killer. He seemed to be aging faster than his fellow prisoners: in his mid-thirties his dark brown hair started turning gray and his waistline expanded. His shoulders sagged sharply, as though his extra avoirdupois were dragging them down. Challengers learned that he was still a powerful man, but some of the snap seemed gone from his muscles. The skin around his green eyes began to crinkle. He complained of abdominal pains, depressions, mood changes, headaches, other ailments. Were they genuine, or was he just seeking attention? No one could tell.

In one interview, he rambled semicoherently about a time when he was seven or eight and "his mother discovered a letter from father's paramour in Australia." A report continued, "From that point on, mother never let his father be a man in the house. The inmate said that for years his mother would swear at father, throw coffee at him, subject him to other forms of abuse. Inmate said his mother ran the house and the father just brought home the money. Says his father did not pay attention to the children."

Later a psychiatrist reported, "He stated he had a very unhappy childhood because his parents were constantly fighting. He was lonely. He felt unloved, unwanted by his parents."

As justifications for murdering two children, the explanations seemed deficient as well as banal. Counselors were accustomed to hearing prisoners blame their parents for their crimes, and few took Shawcross's grumblings seriously.

His recollections of his crimes seemed equally disingenuous, full of strategic omissions. At first he denied all memory of the Karen Ann Hill murder. Later he showed some remorse but said he couldn't recall details of the crime. When his grudging confessions failed to impress authorities, he "admitted that he committed the [Hill] crime and no longer manifested the pretense of blacking out or not remembering the details," according to a report. ". . . The inmate states that he is fully aware and fully conscious of what transpired during the commission of the crime involving Karen Hill."

A psychologist described the expanded new version: "Says he was defecating when she arrived . . . was scared of having his parole compromised by this situation." But he admitted he was under the iron bridge with "sex on his mind." The examiner noted that he "still denies memory of his actions toward the girl after he grabbed her."

The prisoner revealed a little more when questioned directly by members of the Parole Board. He said he was "going to the bathroom" under the bridge when "this girl pops up and I am on parole. I got scared after that, things went haywire. . . . I got scared and I grabbed her and, really, I didn't know what I was doing."

He was instructed to describe exactly how he killed the child. He claimed that he didn't remember. He made no mention of the rabbit that Karen Hill had been carrying, gave no details of how he'd lured her to his side, and insisted that he had no idea how she'd come to be raped and sodomized.

His stories about the Blake killing were more consistent but equally short on detail. He continually repeated the sanitized version that Detective Charles Kubinski and other Watertown insiders knew to be false: "The kid kept following me. I hit him. He hit a tree, fell down. I just kept going." Since the case hadn't been tried in court and no one had testified about the horrifying crime, prison officials were unaware of his earlier attraction for Jack Blake and his attempts to lure the child away from his house. Nor did they know that the boy's clothes had been removed before he was murdered. No embarrassing questions were asked.

In the interrogations, Shawcross spoke about engaging in oral sex with his sister Jean. Sometimes he referred to the incidents as real and sometimes as fantasies. The time frame varied from interview to interview. To counselors, it appeared that he was improvising the story. One noted, "Unclear if sexual intimacy actually took place."

At a 1979 Parole Board hearing, he slyly deflected any blame. "Well," he told the board, "there was an incident, but I told her no." He seemed utterly unconcerned about the reputation of the sister he claimed to love more than any other member of his family.

Once again the Parole Board refused to grant his freedom. Shawcross promptly improved his image by seeking psychiatric help and joining a therapy group, but he sat mute through session after session. As usual, he put the blame for his noninvolvement on others.

9. ARTHUR SHAWCROSS (PSYCHIATRIC INTERVIEW)

Q. . . . You have had a lot of mental treatments at Green Haven?

A. No, I didn't.

Q. But you saw psychiatrists and counselors—

A. I saw a psychiatrist and he fell asleep on me.

Q. Oh, yes.

A. Right. Then he gets fired and then they send me to group therapy. Then I had to cut an inmate in the block, in the yard with a razor blade 'cause he went out in the yard and told people what I did.

Q. Why did you have to cut him?

A. You got thirty guys in a circle . . . group therapy. They told me when I went in there everybody in the room had a similar case as mine. *Nobody* in that room had a similar case as mine but me. When we started discussing things, you know, and the psychologist, he told everybody in the group what my crime was. And

> the guy—this guy couldn't wait to get out in the yard and telling his friends. You know. Then I went in the block and I had just got a couple new razor blades from the officer to go up and shave. So I started up the stairs and he was coming down the stairs, right? And I seen him and I said, "Why did you go around telling . . . ?" and he said, "I'm gonna tell everybody." And that is when I cut him. Right through the paper right in my hand . . . right down the arm.

10.

Unsurprisingly, Shawcross's prison psychiatric records became a hodgepodge of interpretations and educated guesswork, the only consistency being a fear that he would kill again. One early examiner noted wryly that "there are some uninformative psychiatric examinations in the inmate's file." Others simply threw up their hands. Trained to diagnose sociopaths, schizophrenics, manic-depressives, and other specific types, they couldn't seem to sort out the child-killer's chaotic mental processes or classify his behavior. One examiner theorized that he'd been confused and enraged by stunted childhood development combined with addictive abnormal sexual urges, and another cited his "pedophilic fetishes" and mental deficiencies. One pair of experts assayed a more ambitious explanation:

> Inmate grew up in a family situation in which a masculine identity would have been extremely threatening to adopt as a result of his mother's extremely abusive control over inmate's father.
>
> Inmate seems to be the sort of person who easily gets into a downward spiral of poor self image and weak personality structure which exacerbate his sexual hyperstimulation and are in turn further weakened by it.
>
> The inmate then becomes more and more likely to

> vent his emotions in increasingly primal ways such as arson, incest, sexual violence or sex with children.
>
> Because of this inmate's early sexual stimulation and his weak personality structure he is essentially unable to contain his inner drives. For this inmate sexual stimulation is as uncontrollable as heroin addiction might be to others, but because this inmate was brought up essentially by himself, his stimulations are likely to take a ruminative turn toward primal satisfaction and are likely to surface in a manner which will be found socially abhorrent.
>
> . . . The writers do not feel that the inmate had any conscious desire . . . when his blood is cool to be a bad person or to hurt others. [However] the inmate has proved himself to be an extremely unusual person and one whose actual inner workings are probably completely beyond comprehension of any of us. . . .

In 1981, Shawcross's ninth year in Green Haven, he improved his slim chances for parole by agreeing to weekly therapy sessions with a counselor. He also became friendlier with his guards and fellow prisoners, and some were surprised to find that the sullen man who'd killed two children could laugh and smile and exchange an occasional joke, even at his own expense.

Psychiatrists took note of the improvement. A report by Dr. Ismail Ozyaman referred to him as "neat, clean, quiet, cooperative, attentive, pleasant. No bizarre mannerisms. Normal facial appearance and posture. Self-esteem/self-image good. Tolerance for frustration within normal limits. Abstract thinking intact. No hallucinations/delusions. Thought processes logical, rational. . . . Does not manifest any psychotic/neurotic symptoms."

But two years later, his dark side reappeared in another preparole examination. Wrote psychologist Rita Flynn: "Arthur Shawcross initially approached this interview in a very hostile and angered state. Shawcross repeatedly verbalized that he could not participate in this parole meeting as the interview was with a woman. . . . Writer continued with the interviewing process and as time elapsed, Shawcross became less agitated and openly discussed all topics that were questioned."

In recommending against parole, Flynn and colleague Sheldon Sabinsky noted that Shawcross "was interested in downplaying and minimizing his criminal involvements. . . . Focused on what he believes to be the 'unfair practicings of the criminal justice system.' . . . Believes that he is being persecuted by the system as he feels that he has been incarcerated for a lengthy period of time and has 'paid' for his actions. . . ."

They found the child-killer to be "verbal with respect to some crucial incidents as he discussed the facts of his abnormal sexual attraction for younger sister Jeannie. . . . At the time of this interview, Shawcross denied having any sexual type of contact with his younger sibling and indicated that it was purely in the fantasy realm."

For the first time, the inmate claimed a connection between his wartime experiences and his crimes. Sabinsky and Flynn reported that he "appears to have difficulty in discriminating between those activities that he was involved in when deep in combat in Vietnam and the types of activities that are acceptable when living freely among society outside the military. . . . The subject is often prone to compare his past warfare acts with the two killings he committed, as he attempts to minimize his present criminal predicament by informing that he has done much more heinous crimes during his stint in Vietnam."

11. ARTHUR SHAWCROSS (PSYCHIATRIC INTERVIEW)

Vietnam turned country boy into a crazy. . . . I tortured people over there, cut two heads off, took a lot of ears off. The Vietnamese ears, we'd always cut the left ear. We'd string 'em and dry 'em and cut their hair in a mohawk . . . and string bone, teeth, or ear on one of these little amulets. . . .

A lot of guys did that. A lot of guys put a foot on the guy's face, of a dead body, and open up their mouth and get the whole teeth out of there. Knock them out or take them out with bayonets. . . .

One woman I found her hiding a rifle inside of a tree and I shot her. She wasn't dead and I dragged her back to where I was camping and gagged her and tied her to a tree, raped her. Then I take my, I had my machete, took machete out and just sit there sharpening it, looking at her. Then I go over and cut her throat.

12.

The killer joined a posttraumatic stress unit for "help in understanding the motivation of his crime and in effectively dealing with his anger," as his file noted. When it was his turn to share experiences with the other Vietnam veterans, he made vague claims about episodes of "incest" with his sister and an Aunt "Tina." But most of the time he listened quietly to the others. After a while he picked up enough incidental information to file a belated claim for injuries caused by Agent Orange. Although he was a no-show at twenty-one of the seventy-one stress unit sessions, a file entry noted that he "provided role model for patients" and was an asset to the unit.

With his reputation and record slightly upgraded, he returned to the Parole Board to plead again for compassion: "My past I can't dispute. Now I find out [the killings] came out of my past as a child, plus things I did overseas."

In denying the latest application, a Board report noted, "No specific reasons were ever given for both the bizarre acts of burglary and arson or for the atrocities resulting in the deaths of two innocent children. . . . The inmate nevertheless can be classified as a psychosexual maniac based on his behavior alone. . . . Consequently walls could not be erected thick enough to house him. . . . His belligerent reaction represents a foreboding potential for the possible reenactment of his tragic behavior."

After summing up the years of frustration in trying to fathom the inscrutable killer, the report warned: "Though the psychiatric and psychological profession has apparently not as of yet defined a diagnosis for this inmate's aberrant behavior or, even more pertinently, a cure, the society at large deserves protection until such is the case which probably would not be until well past this inmate's conditional release date."

It was still another suggestion, at least the tenth in the Shawcross prison jacket, that the killer was too dangerous to be freed.

Mary Blake's oldest son, Richie, was sentenced to Green Haven for burglary and was assigned the same counselor as Shawcross.

"The shrinks are wasting a lotta time trying to figure Art out," Richie confided to his mother in one of his collect calls. "My counselor says it's simple: the guy's a fuckin' lunatic."

13. MARY BLAKE

Nutty or not, Art Shawcross din't kill my son and I knew it. I still wondered when Jack would come back home for good. I dreamt he was standing by some water with an old man and an old lady, and then they would all come to visit me. Somehow it made me feel better and I finally got some rest.

My husband, he never drew a peaceful breath after Jack come up missing. You never saw a man go downhill like Big Pete—and him not even the boy's real father. He was already an alcoholic, but he turned mad at the world. Woultn't take care of his family or himself. His stomach went bad and he refused to see a doctor. He only ever hit me once, but he constantly abused me with his mouth, called me ugly, stupid, moron. One of his favorites was "pussgut." When I began to think of ways to kill him, I knew it was time to get away.

I told him me and the kids were gonna leave, and he just laughed. He says, "You been singin' that same song for years."

I put my name in at another address, and when he seen I meant business, he let the doctors take out his gall bladder. It saved his life but not our marriage. Me and the kids moved out. I hated to leave Water Street. I lived in that house off and on for thirty-five years. It was my house and my mam's house and all the other Lawtons.

After a while I had to sign Pete into Mental Health for alcoholism. He turned to drugs along with the rest of his cronies and got so sick his liver exploded, blood all over the place.

I went to see him in Mercy Hospital. He was in a coma, roit? I touched his hand and I said, "Pete, do you know who this is?"

He opened his eyes and tried to sit up. Then he went "Ohhhhh" and flopped. I blessed him and told him I loved him and may Gad rest his soul. He never woke up. I always wondered what he would've been like with two good arms.

14.

Separated from Arthur Shawcross by two hundred miles of rolling countryside, Watertown's citizens tried to forget the pedophile and his crimes. Parents released their children's hands. The pool and playground behind the Cloverdale Apartments filled with youngsters, some of them Mary Blake's. Unescorted teenagers walked again at night. With the killer locked away, the citizens had nothing to fear from Arthur Shawcross—or so they thought.

The old town continued in its tired ways. Citizens lined the public square and dabbed at their eyes as bulldozers razed the Woodruff Hotel, where presidents had stayed and high school graduating classes had held their proms for fifty years. Camp Drum expanded to Fort Drum, and infusions of new soldiers brought extra sales to the merchants, but not enough to dispel the familiar economic dreariness. High school graduates returned their rental caps and gowns and left for college or jobs: the town's oldest migratory pattern. Few returned, except to visit.

Those who were left behind tended to discuss well-worn, comfortable subjects: Republican politics, child-raising, hunting, fishing, the game laws, the New York Giants football team.* Yankee baseball broadcasts were played on an old tabletop radio at the bar of the Crystal Restaurant in the public square. Many a lively conversation developed around the latest in snowplows, snow tires, snowblowers, and other devices used to battle the blizzards and freezing rain and "lake-effect snow" that formed over Lake Ontario and blew into town with enough force to knock down signs and trees.

Wherever the people gathered, whether over fifty-cent drinks at the New Parrot or three-dollar dinners at Enrico's and the Crystal or strolling in the public square or shopping for T-shirts at the new Salmon Run mall, one subject came up often:

What changed Arthur John Shawcross from an innocent little boy into a monster? "To those of us who grew up with him," his observant cousin Nancy McBride Baker remarked, "the question was never if he would kill—it was *when*." He remained the North Country's biggest mystery.

* Celebrated in the prizewinning book *A Fan's Notes* by North Country native Frederick Exley, who on most evenings could be found at the bar of the New Parrot Cafe on the Washington Street hill.

VI

KILLER CHILD

Each murder will be solved, but murder itself will never be solved. You cannot solve murder without solving the human heart or the history that has rendered that heart so dark and desolate.

***—Mikal Gilmore [brother of Gary],* Granta**

1.

Historians who examined the Shawcross family tree found a few twisted branches, but nothing to suggest long-running congenital defects or the ultimate appearance of a multiple murderer.

The name was ancient and honorable. According to an uncle who ordered up a coat of arms, "Shawcross" derived from the Old English *crede cruci*, loosely translated as "belief in the cross." Early variations of the spelling were "Shawcruce" and "Shawcrosse." There were about five thousand Shawcrosses in the United States and more in England. Sir Hartley Shawcross, former attorney general of Great Britain and chief British prosecutor at the Nuremberg trials, was a distant cousin.

The child-killer's earliest traceable antecedent was David Shawcross, a footloose preacher who emigrated from England to Canada to Chicago before settling near Watertown, where he married a local woman of German descent, Nettie Busch, and fathered four children, including a son, Fred J. Shawcross, born in 1897. Young Fred quit school in the sixth grade to work in a Black River paper mill, a standard career move in an era when fortunes were built on child labor. Turn-of-the-century women were considered appendages of their men (all the more so in the harsh North Country) and no information survived about Nettie and her own family tree.

At twenty-one, Fred Shawcross brought the first breath of scandal to the family name, a minor indiscretion that would resonate through three generations of Shawcross males. Working as a conductor for the Black River Traction Company in Watertown, he fell in love with Muriel Blake, a comely fifteen-year-old who worked at New York Air Brake. When her parents objected to the friendship, Fred spirited the girl to Oswego, found a job at a shade cloth factory, and rented an apartment in the name of "Fred Shawcross and wife." The parents swore out a warrant charging abduction. Fred explained that it wasn't abduction, it was love. Police threw him in Jefferson County jail.

In stuffy Watertown, the case made juicy reading. A long article on page one of the *Daily Times* of December 21, 1918, was headlined:

POLICE FOIL WEDDING PLAN
Fred Shawcross Is Arrested on Street Car
—Will Probably Marry Girl.

Two days later, on December 23, 1918, the young lovers were married, and charges were dropped. They established residence in Glen Park, just downriver from Watertown. Fred caught on with the Jefferson County highway department, snowplowing, salting, tarring, paving, landscaping, shoveling, and worked his way up to the coveted job of heavy equipment operator, retiring in the mid-1960s. The couple and their four children were law-abiding and tended to keep to themselves, perhaps because of the earlier notoriety. For the rest of his life, Fred seemed preoccupied with the trappings of respectability, and he seldom appeared without tie and jacket. When he died at seventy-three in 1971, three years after the death of his child bride, he was best remembered for his diligent work at the county barns.

Fred and Muriel's younger son, Arthur Roy Shawcross, later to become the father of killer Arthur John Shawcross, was destined for his own premarital difficulties. After dropping out of school in the eighth grade, he took his father's advice and applied for a coveted job at the Jefferson County highway department, becoming its youngest employee. When the Japanese bombed Pearl Harbor, he enlisted in the Marine Corps. He was sent to the South Pacific and landed on Guadalcanal with an artillery regiment of the 1st Marine Division, earning four battle stars. An enemy shell buried him in tons of coral sand and killed a comrade; Shawcross would have suffocated if a buddy hadn't remembered his location. Later his outfit was cut off and forced to live on abandoned Japanese food for months. He told family members, "The rice was full of maggots, and if we picked 'em out there was no rice left." He never ate rice again. Though he saw front-line combat, much of his military career was spent moving heavy equipment with a Caterpillar tractor, a skill he'd learned on the job in Watertown.

Arthur Roy Shawcross was furloughed in July 1944 and immediately became the subject of a *Watertown Daily Times* article that seemed insignificant at the time. The headline read:

MARINE VETERAN
HOME, MARRIED

Four inches deep in the prominently displayed article, readers were treated to a nugget of personal information:

> In February, 1943, after cleaning up on Guadalcanal, [Shawcross] and his buddies were sent to Australia for a rest.
>
> While in Australia, Private Shawcross attended a marine station dance and there he met Miss Thelma June of Yea, Australia.
>
> On June 14, 1943, the couple was married in Melby, Australia. They have one child, three months old, named Harley* Roy Shawcross. Mrs. Shawcross is in Australia residing with her parents. She will remain in Australia until the war is over.

* Perhaps "Hartley," after Sir Hartley Shawcross.

The final paragraph noted that the young husband would report for guard duty at the Naval Hospital in Portsmouth, New Hampshire, when he completed his thirty-day furlough.

The age of twenty-one had been a personal watershed in old Fred Shawcross's life, and the timetable repeated for his Marine son. In his dress blues with the sharpshooting medals and campaign ribbons and battle stars topped by a presidential unit citation, young Arthur Roy was an impressive specimen, soft-spoken and short but well built, wiry, with light brown hair and a strong profile. He'd hardly pulled his first watch at the naval base before he caught the attention of the woman with whom he would spend the rest of his life.

Bessie Yerakes, known as "Betty," eighteen years old, was the daughter of factory workers in Somersworth, New Hampshire, twelve miles north of Portsmouth on the Maine border. She was slight, an inch or two above five feet, with glossy dark brown hair and slightly protruding teeth that gave her an impish look. Her father, James Yerakes, was born in Greece, and her mother, Violet Libby, was variously described as being of Greek, Italian, English and/or French ancestry. Whatever the family's exact ethnic makeup, the children were reared in stern Mediterranean traditions.

Betty quit school in the tenth grade to work in a shoe factory, then took a wartime job as a pipefitter's helper at the Navy Yard in Portsmouth. There she met Arthur Roy Shawcross and married him on November 23, 1944. No announcement appeared in the *Watertown Daily Times,* nor was any public reference made to the earlier article about the Marine's Australian wife and son. It was as though it had never appeared.

2.

Years later, the killer Arthur John Shawcross confided to a jailer that his parents spoiled him as a child. He also claimed that he'd had no problems, mental or otherwise, until the births of two sisters and a brother. But the imprisoned man created so much autobiographical mythology that only his most prejudiced advocates would believe every word. Nor did his parents go out of their way to illuminate the record. As soon as the attention of lawyers, criminologists, social researchers, and journalists focused on the benighted family, the father stopped answering his phone, peeping through drawn blinds and refusing to answer the door for anyone but his closest friends and relatives.

"He's upset, ashamed," explained Betty Shawcross, who also declined to discuss her family in detail. "Can't they understand that?" On the subject of her son's transgressions and any childhood incidents that might have prefigured his future, she retreated into a state of denial so profound that her bathetic recollections made it seem as though little Arthur had lived a North Country version of *The Waltons*.

Those who disputed her motherly memories retained a respect for her veracity. Said one relative, "Betty remembers what she *wished* had happened. She honestly believes what she says. The truth was that Artie was a weird little bastard from the time he learned to walk."

3.

The child was born at 4:14 A.M. on June 6, 1945, five hours after his mother was admitted to the U.S. Naval Hospital in Kittery, Maine, just across the Piscataqua River from Portsmouth. The parents were listed as Bessie Yerakes Shawcross, eighteen, a housewife, and Corporal Arthur Roy Shawcross, twenty-one, both of 38 Chapel Street, Apartment 5, Portsmouth. The length of pregnancy was logged as "8 mo." There was no information about the newborn's size or weight, but Betty Shawcross claimed later that Arthur John arrived two months premature and weighed five pounds, and that she stayed with him in the hospital for twenty days. Under "children born to this mother" on the birth certificate, she answered "1." No such information was required of the father, and little "Harley Roy Shawcross," presumably in his second year of life in "Melby, Australia," remained unmentioned.

A week or two after Betty and the new arrival were discharged from the naval hospital, Corporal Shawcross sent them to Watertown to live with his sister while he finished his tour of duty. No one recalled how the Australian marriage was explained away or if the subject even came up. Years later, certain friends and relatives still believed that the ex-Marine had been married twice. Hadn't the first one been written up in the *Daily Times*? The truth, like so many truths about the Shawcross family, was slow to emerge.

"As an infant, Artie was a doll," a cousin remembered. "He had brown hair and big beautiful dark eyes. His baby pictures didn't look quite normal. Most babies, they're smiling or in tears because they're aware of the photographer, but Artie had a blank look—straight ahead, no expression. Something else odd about him: he almost never cried, but when he did, one eye stayed dry."

Years later, psychologists took note that the adult Arthur Shawcross's facial expressions showed "lack of affect" or "inappropriate affect." It was the same blank look that disturbed Detective Charley Kubinski.

The earliest years of the boy's life seemed to confirm Betty's later contention that her son was a well-loved and happy child. Baby Artie was breast-fed for about two months, spoke his first word at nine months, walked six months later, and was weaned from the bottle at a year and a half. In an early school interview, his mother reported that he caused "no problems as a baby." She observed that he spent most of his time in a crib; the family lived in cramped quarters while the father resumed his prewar work with the highway department and began building a small wood-frame home on an acre of land donated by his father, Fred. When the home was finished, the children squeezed into a cramped little bedroom; Artie and his baby brother Jimmy shared the top bunk of the bed and their two sisters shared the bottom. When another bedroom was added about 1958, the children were separated by sex.

The pastoral acreage, six miles northwest of Watertown on the outskirts of Brownville, became home to four interrelated families and known as "Shawcross Corners." At one time, thirteen of Fred and Muriel Shawcross's grandchildren spilled in and out of each other's homes. They began each day with a seven-mile ride on the school bus, played in fields of daisies, buttercups, thistles, goldenrod, and black-eyed Susans, ice-skated at a local quarry, attended the Methodist church, and summered in the Thousand Islands, just to the north in the St. Lawrence River.

The parents exchanged pies and tools and recipes, bickered over property lines, trudged through snowbanks to share firewood, dug outhouses, arranged games and sports for their children, carried water from the family well in the grandfather's basement, and drove into Watertown to make grocery purchases in bulk. The communal system seemed to work. As adults, members of the clan looked back on childhood with warmth, recalling a gang of rollicking, happy, obedient kids watched and loved by dutiful, contented parents.

Brownville itself seemed lifted from a magazine cover. Founded before the War of 1812, it was the home of twelve hundred lower-middle-class citizens, most of them residing within hailing distance of the roiling Black River. In an era when paper mills were continually shutting down, its two big mills still ran twenty-four-hour shifts, and the townsfolk enjoyed a modest level of prosperity that was denied to most other inhabitants of the area.

Despite bitter cold winters, scorching summers, and temperature spreads of 120 degrees, the families always seemed active. "My son was never left out of nothing," Betty Shawcross recalled years later. "Stock car races, boat races, movies, picking apples, family picnics. Whatever we did, whether we did it as a family or with some of the others, he always went along."

But as far back as most of the relatives could remember, little Artie seemed different from his two sisters and brother and earlier generations of Shawcrosses. "I knew him from kindeegarden on up," said Terry Robbins, who later became a school custodian nearby. "I wasn't close friends with him. Nobody was. He was always . . . odd."

A Shawcross cousin added, "It began to show up when he was five or six. He still talked baby talk—dese, dem, and dose."

Frequent nightmares made the child lose control and wet the bed. Old school files recorded thirty-three days of absence during the kindergarten year. A year later, his attendance record improved, but he began running away from home, not unknown in ten- or twelve-year-olds but rare among clinging younger children.

After one disappearance, posses scoured the woods and fields around Brownville, checking the town's mills, the bar, and the small businesses along the river. Hours later the missing child crawled from under the house, where he'd watched the activity unfold.

"He was always doing things like that," said his cousin Nancy McBride Baker. "He *craved* attention. I don't think he got enough love after the other kids came along. Betty treated her daughters like dolls, and little Jimmy was her baby. It was true that the family took Artie everywhere, but he still seemed left out. Betty's a sweetheart, she always treated the rest of us kids great, we were always welcome in her house, and she'd cry and hug us and tell us to come again. But she wasn't all that loving with Artie."

In later years, repeated tests showed that Shawcross was of subnormal or low-normal intelligence, even "borderline retarded." But despite a teacher's early observation that he had "lazy study habits," he scored A's and B's in the first and second grades.

Then personality problems began to surface. He resented younger children and seemed to enjoy making them cry. Although he claimed that he loved his little sister Jean to the point of imagining sex with her, he was never close to his brother James or his other sister, Donna. A cousin recalled that he hated females.

At seven, he created imaginary friends: a boy his own age and a slightly younger blond-haired girl—" 'cause I wanted someone to play with so bad," as he explained later. They wore silver clothes and spoke in "tinny" voices. He carried on long conversations with his fantasy friends, giving others the impression that he was talking to himself.

Soon called "Oddie" by his classmates, he was made the butt of daily jokes and cruelties. When bigger boys abused him, he screamed and shook his fists, or went home and tormented his sisters, then six and four, and his baby brother. Fellow students remembered him standing at the edge of the playground, looking as though he wanted to join the others but didn't dare try.

He tried to make friends by doing favors or distributing candy purchased with his lunch money or with coins stolen from his mother or a teacher. "If he had a dollar," a male cousin recalled, "he'd split it into equal parts. The kids would take the money and tease him twice as hard. Next thing you knew, he'd be off by himself again. It was hard *not* to tease him. He was so weird, such a perfect target."

The troubled boy often wandered from class and was found daydreaming in empty rooms. School authorities were baffled. The nurse reported:

> Arthur runs away from home, his mother doesn't trust him with the younger children, he brings an iron bar on the school bus and hits at the children. He is a bright boy in school—his grades are in the 90s and he is no serious problem to his teacher . . . because she handles him with a firm hand. . . .
>
> His mother says Arthur was a beautiful baby and she spoiled him. . . . He prefers to be by himself and wanders off whenever he can. Mrs. Shawcross punishes him by spanking him or putting him in his room. She thinks Mr. Shawcross is far too easygoing with him.

The nurse directed her suspicions toward the most obvious target, the mother. The mother-son relationship was clearly complex. The boy showered Betty Shawcross with gifts, never forgetting a birthday or anniversary, but he also showed confusion and resentment. The nurse suspected that the twenty-six-year-old mother might be demanding too much of her firstborn son.

"I encouraged her to tell about the very rigid way she was brought up in her Greek home," the nurse reported. "She said she didn't carry any of her early Greek ideas over [and] wished she knew what made Art act the way he does."

In May of 1953, a month before the boy would complete the second grade and turn eight, the Brownville-Glen Park Central School called for a mental health evaluation. In a comprehensive report, psychologists from the Jefferson County Mental Health Clinic described him as an "attractive, well dressed, neat child":

> School principal states that the . . . problem seems to be unreliability as demonstrated by incidents such as unusual noise and disturbance on school bus [and] the fear his mother has of trusting him because of the fact that he ran away from school last year and runs away from home occasionally. He also spent money which mother had given for lunch. There seems to be a general feeling that one can't tell what he will do.
>
> . . . No problem until he started going to school. Mother says Arthur seems to want to be "first." He may resent attention his grandmother Muriel* gives his cousin. Inclined to be "mean" to younger brother. Reads and likes TV. . . .
>
> Mother says he has no playmates . . . obeys when punished by some means other than a spanking. She says it's hard to always "get the truth" from Arthur because he seems afraid.

* The former fifteen-year-old bride, born Muriel Blake, who continued to live at Shawcross Corners with her husband, Artie's grandfather Fred.

> Betty under doctor's care at present time, nervous, doesn't sleep well. Very thin, pleasant, interested in home and family, anxious to do what is best for Arthur.

After another battery of tests, an examiner described the child as "attractive, well dressed, neat" and noted that he "seemed to be trying very hard to say the right things to avoid getting into trouble." He disliked his school subjects and "is against everything and everyone at home." The boy perceived his father as favoring the other children and his mother as rejecting him. The report continued:

> Still getting high marks, still liked school. Asked which of his brothers and sisters he liked best, he said, "Not any of them," because they wouldn't play with him. Only plays with a cousin who is 10. Harbors a fair amount of hostility especially towards his mother because of fear of punishment and rejection, and seems unable to find many legitimate outlets for it. Defenseless objects (and possibly younger children) seem to take the brunt. He finds it difficult to express it toward either parent but most especially towards the mother. . . .

Still another evaluation noted:

> His conscience does not seem to be strongly developed as yet, but some guilt feelings appear. The mother appears to be rejecting (from Arthur's point of view) and punishing even where it is uncalled for. This has resulted in a great deal of confusion about what he should be like. He feels as if he is a bad boy a lot of the time and is hostile enough in a confused sort of way to want to remain "bad." His confused hostilities make parental identification difficult. He feels he should identify with both father and mother but does not want to identify with either. . . . Is unable to develop moral standards. Instead, he appears to be indulging in a considerable amount of fantasy in which he perceives himself as a new person with respect and dignity. . . . His behavior

> on the school bus seems to be a displacement of hostility aroused by the home.

In the third grade, the boy's interest in school seemed to fall off sharply. His grades slipped, a phenomenon that teachers attributed to attitude rather than lack of intelligence. A confidential report noted:

> He seems to be constantly seeking attention. When the other children are singing he crawls under the radiator. [The nurse] has tried to talk with the parents but they seem indifferent and to feel that it is the school problem and so up to the school to solve. She feels that Mrs. Shawcross is a very immature young mother.

The floundering child was promoted conditionally to the fourth grade, where he remained for two years. He developed a hard blink. When bigger boys bullied him, he made a sound like a lamb's bleat—"wahhh *wahhhhhhh. . . .*" It sounded like an imitation of crying rather than crying itself. And he still lapsed into baby talk, although his normal speech was a blend of his mother's Down East accent and his father's North Country bray.

"He talked baby talk to irritate, get attention," said an aunt. "He knew better." He still had nightmares and wet the bed.

He ran away again, this time after careful preparation. He emptied the box containing his wood-burning set, put in a change of clothes, wrapped the box with a towel, and left a note to his mother saying he was headed south to Syracuse. He was picked up at the Canadian border and returned.

4.

Despite the behavioral difficulties and falling grades, there were no more parent-teacher consultations. The parents, especially the outspoken mother, sheltered behind the belief that little Arthur's problems were the school's fault.*

Family members suspected that there might be another reason for the newly uncooperative attitude of the young mother who'd once been described as "anxious to do what is best for Arthur." Betty Shawcross had learned of her husband's wartime romance and reacted sharply. The killer wrote later:

> Something happend to my mom & dad when I was about 9 years of age. My grandmother, (dads mother) got a letter from some woman in Australia. She claimed that dad was her husband and they have a son. A year older than me. My mother was showed this letter. From that day foreward my life turned upside down. Dad hung his head in shame. He couldn't look you in the eye and say it was not so! Mom took over and she made life hell in that house. Dad can't even watch TV without mom cursing or throwing something at him. Even where he worked he could of done better for himself, but now he started working in a gravel pit. I am ashamed of my father and now I am ashamed of my self. This same woman did it to both of us.

Relatives noticed the downturn in the family spirit. To the close-knit residents of Shawcross Corners, Betty had always come across as a screamer and screecher who dominated her family. If visitors rubbed her the wrong way, she dismissed them in blunt New England fashion—"you get the hell out that doah and don't bothuh comin' back." She spoke her mind and didn't care who liked it, and she cussed in English, Greek, and Italian.

But up to the arrival of the letter from Australia, there'd been no obvious marital trouble in the family, and life in

* Years later, Mrs. Shawcross denied that she'd ever been summoned to conferences or consulted about her son's misbehavior. "The schools didn't even have counselors in those years," she insisted. "There wouldn't have been no reason for me to go to school. My son never misbehaved. He was always a good boy."

the small handmade wooden house had seemed tranquil, perhaps a tribute to the easygoing husband.

"Artie's dad was the happiest-go-lucky guy alive," said a relative. "He had a chuckle, a sense of humor. If you told him a joke, he'd laugh from the bottom of his feet. Lived for his work, never called in sick or vacationed or showed up late. He had zero outside interests—didn't bowl, didn't fish, didn't play bingo or pinochle or chase women. I don't think he was ever inside a bar in his life. He was the kind of guy, he'd drive the snowplow twenty hours straight and then clock in for his next shift. But after Betty found out about the other woman, you never saw him smile or kid around. From then on, he led a dog's life."

Friends noticed that after the revelation from Australia, Betty became subject to jealous rages. "She turned negative, bitter," said a cousin. "If a woman came on TV while Uncle Art was watching, she'd say, 'What the hell *you* looking at?' She'd say, 'You want her, don't you? You two-timin' so-and-so!' He'd have to look away from the screen. You could hear her up and down the road, telling him off. She drove to the gravel pit and picked him up every day, and God help him if he wasn't right there."

To the other members of the Shawcross clan, Betty's favorite pejorative seemed to become "whore," as in "why are you watching that whore?" She started referring to a neighbor as "——— the whore." One night a friend brought a female to the house, and after the visitor left, Betty referred to her as "that whore." A niece thought she understood: "The girlfriend was wearing a miniskirt and Uncle Art said hello. To Betty, that made her a whore."

The husband retreated behind his cigar smoke. He began spending even more time on the job. At home, he busied himself improving the house and making repairs. He'd always been an opinionated man, getting into brisk arguments with his brother Fred Jr. about the merits of Hudson Hornets vs. Fords and whether Art's Marine Corps or Fred's Army Air Corps had won World War II, but now he had less to say.

A cousin explained, "Betty got very short-tempered with

Uncle Art. If he started to say something she didn't like, she'd say *'Arthur?'* and he'd stop. He just shut up and let her take over. The kids were the same way. Young Artie had a different approach. He just stayed t'hell away from home."

5.

It was a recurrent lament in the killer's later life that he loved his mother deeply but couldn't please her no matter how hard he tried. His childhood solution was to spend more time in the corner house of his paternal grandmother Muriel.

"She was always so loving with us kids," a relative recalled. "Artie was one of her favorites. He'd go over there to get her to rub his back. He'd do anything for her. At six o'clock in the morning he'd be mowing her lawn. He mowed lawns perfect and he did it for everybody—that was just his way. But he never worked in his own yard no matter how much his parents yelled at him."

With each passing year, the boy's need for outside affection and approval seemed to increase, along with his quixotic, attention-getting behavior. He stole soft drinks from the walk-in cooler at Brenon's Grocery in Brownville and bragged about his thefts, shoplifted ice cream and shared it with some boys, stole a portable radio from a neighboring house and entertained his cousins with music. There were times when he displayed a droll sense of humor and made people laugh, but sooner or later he alienated every potential friend. When he lost a competition, he wanted to fight.

"He didn't know the meaning of the word 'uncle,' " a cousin remembered. "After he beat you up, he'd keep fighting till somebody pulled him off."

Said another male cousin, "He'd get you down and grind his teeth. He'd hit you and say 'Bang! Zap! Pow!' It was like he didn't know how to express his anger and used words from comic books."

As his anger seemed to intensify, so did his bullying. He

hit a boy in the face with his books, breaking his glasses, and broke his cousin David's nose with a toy rifle. His weaker classmates started fading away when he came into sight.

"We were scared shitless," a fellow student recalled. "He was like a black cloud over the neighborhood. There was talk that he was from Satan, diabolical, evil. Nobody knew how the hell to handle him. He didn't need a reason; he'd just explode. When we turned away from him, he'd only get madder."

After a while, Artie seemed to give up on a social life, slipping instead into the woods around Shawcross Corners, prying out fossils, climbing trees, exploring caves and crevices, always whispering to himself. He insisted that the woods were his private preserve and threatened to shoot trespassers with his .22. If he was an easy child to raise, as his mother insisted later, it might have been because he seldom came home except to eat and sleep.

At nine, he complained that his legs felt stiff. His parents worried about the possibility of polio, a preoccupation in prevaccine days. A year later the Shawcrosses were picnicking at a lake when young Arthur slid from a rock and sank in four feet of water. His father pulled him out. When the boy regained his breath, he claimed that he couldn't walk. He was admitted to the emergency room of Mercy Hospital as "Master Arthur John Shawcross."

Six days of extensive tests, including a spinal tap and an electrocardiograph, provided no clues. Blood, spinal fluid, urine, pulse, respiration, reflexes, cerebral activity—all registered within the normal range. Doctors finally gave up and entered a diagnosis of "encephalomyelitis,* type undetermined," and sent the patient home.

Years later, a few cynical relatives were still insisting that Artie had faked the symptoms in another grab for atten-

* Inflammation of the brain.

tion. According to those who knew him best, he often feigned illness and even unconsciousness.

"I saw him fall six or eight feet down a cliff once," a cousin recalled. "Me and my brother ran over and said, 'Jeez, are you all right?' When he didn't move, we ran three hundred yards home to get help. Artie's sitting on the porch. 'What took ya so long, boys?' he says in his duck voice.

"A while later we were robbing the commercial honeybee hives. Artie's running away from the bees and he goes ass over teakettle in some berry bushes—out cold. My brother says, 'You think he's really hurt?'

"I says, 'I dunno. He wasn't hurt when he fell off the cliff the other day.'

" 'He ain't hurt.'

" 'Let's walk away. If he's hurt, he'll stay here.'

"We start to leave and he jumps up, laughin'."

Back at school after his hospitalization, Artie seemed unable to concentrate. He seldom did homework. When he wasn't daydreaming in class, he was misbehaving. A few teachers suspected that he might be learning-disabled, perhaps even brain-damaged; he showed flashes of intelligence and then forgot the simplest lessons. Less sympathetic teachers wrote him off as lazy, inattentive, and contemptuous. In his latest IQ tests, he scored between 86 and 92, low normal, but gave the impression that he hadn't tried and didn't give a damn. It was his customary attitude.

He flunked the fifth grade and fell two years behind his original class. By now he stood a head taller than the others. He barely made it through the repeat year, then squeaked through the sixth with tutoring from his parents.

Standards were higher and teachers less indulgent at the gleaming new General Brown Junior-Senior High School. In the seventh grade, he scored 51 in English, 44 in citizenship, 53 in arithmetic, 77 in spelling, 67 in science, 80 in reading, 76 in penmanship, and 62 in music, and was promoted conditionally. He failed his first attempt at the eighth grade. Now he was three years older than his classmates and even more of an outcast.

Fellow students remembered him for his moodiness. "He was normal one minute, then hyper the next," said Ronald L. Christie. "He flew off the handle and was punished by school officials for his flightiness."

George J. Haley recalled him as "the one kid who would get in trouble more than anyone else . . . just the typical wise-guy thing."

Both remembered that he had no friends.

6.

By his mid-teens, "Oddie's" patterns seemed fixed. He still had nightmares and wet the bed. A neighbor remembered searching for him with flashlights after he'd run away for the third or fourth time. He sucked in his cheeks and spoke in a squeaky, high-pitched voice. For no apparent reason he would throw his head back and emit a high cackle, trailing off in a low, loonlike warble. No one was ever sure if he was kidding or serious.

"He made weird noises as he walked," his cousin David recalled. "I'd be coming home from Brownville and I'd run into him and he'd be saying 'Die die *dee* die, die die *dee* die. . . .' "

Said another cousin, "It came from his throat, a gurgly sound. We'd wake up at night and hear him walking down the road. At first it sounded like a chant, but later on we realized he was just saying 'die' over and over."

He covered long distances at a fast pace, often making the ten-mile round trip to Watertown after school. He overswung his arms, held his body erect and rigid, and walked in the straightest possible line. Sometimes his reluctance to deviate forced him to slosh through puddles, like an ornery five-year-old. If he came to a mound of earth, he walked straight up and over.

"It was like it didn't occur to him to change direction," a female cousin remembered. "He'd tear his pants on a barbed wire fence rather than use a gate a few feet away.

He'd walk into a swamp and have a hell of a time getting out."

The troubled child called his style "walking cross-lots" and never changed it.*

On some of his travels, he started fires. Fire fighters were called to a brush fire he started near his home. Friends said there were many others. In the outer environs of Brownville, trash collection was undependable and residents used burn barrels. It was the only chore that Artie performed without nagging. "The rest of us would light the stuff and walk away," said a neighbor, "but Artie would feed one sheet of newspaper at a time and then scout around for scrap wood and other stuff. Sometimes he took all day to burn a barrelful."

In school, the boy's behavior edged from odd toward downright violent. "We'd be working on a science project," his fellow student Jim Robbins remembered, "and Art'd throw a book at somebody. I don't think he knew why he did it himself. He hit one kid in the eye with a corner point. He was always doing something like that, then trying to buy us off with money or candy. It got so bad that even the rowdies avoided him."

A few of the older students started calling him "Crazyboy," causing him to sulk and stomp off to the woods. His head was gashed by a deliberately thrown rock. Years later he told a girlfriend that when he was hiding in the woods he heard taunts in his head "and I couldn't get 'em to stop." His cousin Nancy McBride Baker remembered watching him stalk up and down Military Road in a rage, kicking pebbles and swinging a big stick. "When he was like that," she said, "nobody went near."

Nancy wasn't surprised when Artie was arrested years later for murder. Her mother had warned, "Sooner or later he's gonna kill somebody." Nancy recalled:

* He was walking cross-lots when he emerged from the swamplands behind William Murrock's gas station after killing Jack Blake.

"When I was sixteen and Artie was twelve, he was wrestling real rough with my two younger brothers and I said, 'If you kids are gonna act stupid, go outdoors.' That was a mistake. You didn't call Art stupid. First off, he took everything literally. If you told him the cow jumped over the moon, he looked up. Any nasty comment about his intelligence, he'd flip. If you discussed his looks—'Hey, what's that goo in your hair?'—he'd go right off. When he was fifteen he had an old bike with wooden rims and solid tires and no brakes, and if you didn't act like it was a new Schwinn ten-speed he was insulted. He beat my brother Ron on the head with a block of ice because Ron said his fort looked dumb. And he wouldn't stop—we had to pull him off or he would've killed Ron. Then he bit my brother Billy in the testicles. He didn't care *what* he did when he got mad.

"After I told him not to act stupid he must've watched our house through his window till I left to meet my boyfriend a couple hours later. It was dusk, and when I walked past his house he slugged me across the shins with a baseball bat.

"It felt like he'd broken both ankles. He gave that awful laugh—'Heh heh heh'—and then he grabs an ax and says, 'Now I'm gonna chop your head off.' I tried to roll away, but I couldn't get up.

"My boyfriend Jamie ran up and knocked the ax away. There was a big fight and Artie lost. He went home crying, *whahhhh, whahhhhh,* gasping like a two-year-old. As usual his parents took his side and raised hell with my mom and stepdad.

"Word got back that Artie was gonna get even. My mom saw him laying in the ditch watching our house. I never went outdoors by myself after that. He had every intention of killing me, there's no doubt in my mind. Eight or nine years later, when I was living in an apartment in Watertown, he knocked on my door and I wouldn't let him in. I was sure he still had the ax.

"That whole mess turned into a range war, two years of family feud. Artie used to sit up in a tree with his .22 aimed at us. One day he told my brother, 'Your stepdad was riding the lawn mower and I had the .22 on him the whole time. It woulda been like shooting ducks.'

"Finally it came to a fistfight between the fathers. My stepdad was six-four, 225 pounds, and Artie's dad, my uncle Art, was short and lean, maybe 140, 150, but he was all muscle. They fought in the ditch and Uncle Art got my stepdad down good. The feud blew over after that, but we never shook our fear of Artie."

When the angry boy wasn't menacing neighbors and relatives, he was tormenting animals. His cousin Linda Cobb told reporters how he skinned fish and toyed with their bodies: "He liked to watch them suffer. He'd like to see how long it took them to die."

In one of Betty Shawcross's rose-colored reconstructions of early family life, she told investigators that her son enjoyed many pets, including a dog, a hamster, chickens, rabbits, and a succession of abandoned kittens that he found in nearby woods. Friends confirmed a preoccupation with animals, both wild and domestic. He snared rabbits and snapped their necks. He caught bats and put them inside parked cars, then watched as the drivers panicked. He tied cats together, pounded squirrels and chipmunks flat, shot darts at frogs nailed to his dart board, scraped the feathers from baby birds.

One day he carried a burlap sack to the lake. "Who says cats can't swim?" he told a friend as he tossed a kitten into the water. When the cat swam to shore, he heaved it farther. After three or four throws, the other boy turned away and left—"I knew what was gonna happen."

On a Sunday morning when the problem child was about sixteen, a relative looked out the window and yelped, "Jesus Christ, look at this!"

Cousin Artie was marching down the road with a stick held against his shoulder. "He looked like a one-man drum and bugle corps," the woman recalled, "and he had a big-ass snapping turtle run through from one end to the other.

His pants were stuck in his socks, the way he always dressed. He stopped in front of our house and you could hear his mother holler at him all the way to the four corners. 'You stupid son of a bitch! What the fuck's the matter with ya? Don't you know how stupid you look?'

"Uncle Art must've said something to her, 'cause we heard her yell, 'I don't give a fuck *who's* listening!' "

Members of the extended family claimed that Betty Shawcross had no match for profanity, especially when dealing with her oldest child. "She didn't mean anything by it," said one. "She was a good woman and a good mother. It's just the way she talked."

Some considered the salty language an understandable response to an impossible situation. "It would've taken a saint not to cuss Artie out," said a close relative. "I can just imagine what his mother and father went through at home. I remember when they were putting an addition on their house and Artie stole the lumber and shingles to build a fort. He lined the walls with crushed velour that his mother'd brought back from a visit to New Hampshire. He didn't understand why they were upset. He said, 'I was just trying to build a fort!' There were lots of incidents like that. Artie just didn't *get* it."

No amount of discipline smoothed out his behavior. "Art would get on Artie verbally, ride him a little, make fun of him," a relative remembered. "He'd tell Artie to stop acting like a big baby, things like that. He even called him crazy sometimes. When it got down to the tough disciplining, Betty ran the show."

In later years some of the townspeople speculated that the hot-tempered mother might have crossed the line into child abuse and thereby helped to create a murderer. Everyone agreed that her cheerleader daughters Donna and Jean and her youngest child Jimmy had been treated reasonably, but they weren't so sure about her handling of Artie. Years later, an anguished Betty Shawcross told an investigator: "I spanked Art only a few times, always with my open hand on his bottom. I never spanked or hit Art with a paddle, switch, belt, broom, or any other article." There was no evidence to the contrary.

7.

By the time Artie Shawcross reenrolled in the eighth grade, after being left back for the third time in his school career, he had turned sixteen. Surprisingly, he continued the sterling attendance record that he'd maintained since the first grade, and he was never tardy. His mother took pride in dressing her children neatly and getting them off to school on time.

In most other ways Artie remained different from his classmates. Although his voice had deepened, he still lapsed into his duck squawk. He was the tallest member of his class and the first to shave. His upper body filled out, and his powerful shoulders took an odd downward slope that gave him a slightly simian look.

For a time it appeared that he might regain his lost social status by excelling in sports. He was fast and well coordinated. His teammate Jim Robbins, brother of Terry, recalled wrestling with him in the 145- to 154-pound class: "He had a lot of natural talent and he was as hard as an anvil, but he couldn't concentrate. He was always too mad. You don't wrestle from anger. He'd forget his holds and use sheer strength. Or he'd try the TV crap—body slams, airplane spins, flying mares. If he lost, he went nuts. I saw him throw a chair at a guy that pinned him. If he won, he'd keep beating on the guy till we pulled him off. He slammed one opponent across his knee and threw another one into the seats. Coach'd yell, 'No, Shawcross. *No!*' Sometimes he was disqualified. He'd throw punches till his face was red and his veins stuck out."

After failing as a wrestler, the boy moved on to baseball, football, lacrosse, and track. It upset him that no one from his family watched him compete. "You go to football games and you see the kids' fathers there or something," he complained later in a typical denunciation of his family. "You'd never see my family there."

He suffered from occasional blackouts, once after hitting his head on the crossbar while pole-vaulting. The coach broke smelling salts under his nose and his green eyes fluttered open. Teammates were baffled. It was the first time anyone had seen a vaulter knock himself out on the thin bamboo rod.

He showed early promise as a runner, but tried to turn track into a contact sport. He hit a teammate in the chest with a twelve-pound shot and was on the verge of being thrown off the team when he was skulled by a discus thrown from fifteen feet away. He spent four days in the House of the Good Samaritan Hospital in Watertown with a hairline fracture, one of a long string of insults to his brain. Within a few years, he would be rendered unconscious by a shorted electrical switch, knocked out for a half hour by a sledgehammer, hospitalized overnight after falling on his head from the top of a forty-foot ladder, and hospitalized again when he was hit by a truck.

In the classroom, the lean, wiry boy remained a pariah. The few friendships of earlier years had long since dissolved, and he showed no interest in establishing new ones.

"It wasn't that he was shy," said his former classmate Terry Robbins. "He'd talk and laugh as much as the next guy. Fact is, he could be funny as hell. But he was just too damn much trouble."

In the crowded halls, he gained attention by jabbing boys with his pen, "goosing" girls, snapping bras and sliding away with a smirk. In class, he slouched behind a closed book with his eyes closed. Later he explained, "I didn't go to school to learn. I went to school to either sleep or look out the window."

Most of the time he seemed to block out the classroom. Classmates laughed as frustrated teachers called out, "Art? *Arthur?* Is anybody home?" On the rare occasions when he bothered to respond, it was usually to squawk "What?" or

"Huh?" in his duck voice. Sometimes he said, "I didn't hear ya." His hearing was tested and found to be normal.

Toward the end of his second year of eighth grade, his misbehavior escalated. His mother remembered that he broke a girl's glasses (quickly adding, in her revisionary style, "but he didn't mean it"). He sifted gunpowder onto his desk and ignited it with sunlight focused through a magnifying glass, creating a hissing sound and an acrid smell. He boasted that he could throw his farts like a ventriloquist. He trained his pet hamster to nibble ankles and jump back into his pocket at a signal. He sprinkled Ex-Lax on fudge that had been prepared for a bake sale and pulled less imaginative stunts like yanking seats from under classmates and littering chairs with thumbtacks.

After a mistreated girl took a roundhouse swing at him and missed, the teacher ordered him to the principal's office. As he left, Artie shouted, "Shove this fucking room up your ass!"

A few days later, he made the mistake of challenging a popular teacher to a fight. The burly instructor slammed him against a wall and the boy slithered to the floor like the flattened cat in a movie cartoon.

Other teachers opted to work around the problem, seldom calling on Artie or bothering to offer remedial assistance. His parents doggedly tried to help with his homework, but they were reaching the end of their own educational resources. The bottom dropped out of his report card: 25 in citizenship education, 48 in English, 20 in math. He was promoted on sufferance, but after scoring a few more subterranean grades as a freshman, he followed the example of his parents and grandparents and dropped out. He was seventeen.

8.

With time on his hands, young Shawcross turned to thievery. He'd been light-fingered for as long as anyone could remember. As a boy, he'd stolen apples and potatoes from farmers. He routinely stole from his cousins and neighbors and pilfered the collection plate at church. Now he burglarized neighborhood houses, took a rifle and a rowboat, looted summer cottages, lifted money from the till of the gas station where he worked briefly, broke into a store called Jean's Beans and took food and cash, and shoplifted on a regular basis.

As a schoolboy he'd developed a system for explaining contraband. He would stash his loot and pretend to stumble on it later. A cousin recalled how the system worked:

"Artie says, 'Let's go to the dump to look for bike parts' —that's how we made our own bikes. He was leading the way across a field and takes a header. He picks up this rusty old paint can and he says, 'Look what I tripped on. Hey, look, there's sumpin' inside!' There was money, stamps, paper clips, stuff like that. The school called that night. He'd taken the stuff from a teacher's desk.

"Another time Artie threw a ball over my head and into a ditch. He beelines past me and says, 'Jeez, look what I found!' It was three fishing poles and some lures. A coupla days later, I'm up at Pete Murdock's house and he says, 'Somebody stole my dad's fishing poles.' "

Footloose from seventeen on, Shawcross bumped about from job to job, baling, milking, roofing, working as a stock clerk. To the few Brownville boys who made contact with him, his main interests seemed to be thievery, fire, and sex. He'd always shown an unusual interest in females, dating to the imaginary fair-haired friend of his earliest childhood and the fantasy affair with his sister Jean. At night he peeped into neighborhood windows and spied on his sisters and parents. He told neighbor children, "Dad got Mom last night," then took them inside his house and showed the peepholes he'd drilled in the wall.

"He was always bragging about the women he 'got,' " cousin Nancy Baker reported, "but all the boys talked like that. When he was five, a doctor told Betty that he was built like a sixteen-year-old. My brothers joked that he needed two women: one to get it up and one to hold it up. I think most of that talk was hot air, like so many other things about him. Artie's first wife gave him his first sex, I don't care what he claimed later."

A male cousin confirmed that Artie had problems with females. "He started late," he said, "because every girl in town hated his ass. He did *everything* wrong. One day me and him went up to a girl's house. After we made out on her bed, I come out and watched TV, and Artie goes into the bedroom. After a few minutes, she jumps up and says, 'You guys gotta leave. My parents are comin' home.'

"Artie turns red and goes into a crazy little dance. He says, 'Well, if I gotta go,' and grabs her crotch. He squeezed so hard she cried. We had to get the hell outa there. That was his idea of romance."

Years later, at a time when Shawcross was acting insane to avoid being returned to prison, he described other sexual activities in his imaginative, semiliterate style:

> After I was first introduced to sex by my Aunt Tina, my mothers sister I became obsessed with sex. I was very upset when my aunt went back home. I was about 9 then. After that I would play with my self, either in bed at night or in the bathroom, or outside in the woods near home. One time I was just walking around near home and fell in the swamp. I was up to my neck in muck and was screaming my head off for help. A little while went by when all I could do was cry, a boy my age showed up and helped pull me out of that hole. Went to the creek and soak off the muck and then walked around to dry off. We stopped in some pasture near some woods and I took off my clothes and hung them in a bush to dry more. . . .
>
> Then I went to a stream near there and cleaned my self off more. Mike took his clothes off and jumped in also. After awhile when we were sunning our selves off I started to jack off. No reason, just did it, Mike did too. Then we would touch each other then we did oral sex. That was my first experience at that. Mike and I got to be good friends. Only once in awhile we would have our touching sessions.
>
> Then I started to have oral sex with my sister Jeannie.

. . . One time at a farm near by, about $1^1/_2$ miles away Mike and I started playing with sheep. We didn't know that sheeps had organs like a woman. It felt good at the time.

When I was 14, one night I stayed after school for wrestling practice then I got off the school bus in Brownville, N.Y. and walked home. It is only two miles. I was within a mile from home when a man in a red car, convertable stopped to give me a lift. I didn't think about, just got in. Then he grabbed me by the throat and told me to take my pants down! Then he held on to my balls and sucked me off. I was scared and crying. Then the guy got mad because I couldn't cum. He raped me. I was let off near home. I couldn't tell anyone what happened either.

After that when I masterbated I could not cum until I inserted a finger in my ass. Why I don't know.

One day I did it too a chicken, it died. Then a cow, dog and a horse. I didn't know where this was leading up too.

9.

By his eighteenth birthday in 1963, Shawcross had turned into a slender six-footer with sharply accented dark sideburns, pronounced cheekbones, and dark green eyes that sloped downward from the bridge of his slightly curved nose. Early pictures showed a resemblance to the comedian John Belushi. Although he claimed later that he was dubious about his parentage, no one in his extended family entertained any doubts. "He looked a little like his mom and strongly favored his dad," said an aunt. "The resemblance was unmistakable."

On the edge of manhood and emancipation, Shawcross replaced his homemade bicycle with a '54 Hudson Hornet that his grandfather Fred Shawcross sold him for a dollar, but he continued to wear his socks tucked into his pants, biker-style. He wrecked the Hornet and returned to a bike because, as he told his cousins, "driving makes me nervous." Then he put the bike aside and bought a souped-up 1958 Pontiac that once had belonged to the sheriff's department.

As his circles widened, he met more people but still failed to make friends. His behavior continued to defy explanation. Strolling along Military Road toward Brownville, he would break into a sprint, then resume a natural pace after twenty or thirty yards, then make a mad dash as though chased by demons. He continued his habit of hiking from point to point in exaggeratedly straight lines. When he got out of a chair, he grabbed his buttocks and pretended to lift himself upward, a technique he employed long after he'd been advised that it wasn't funny. At dances, he whirled and spun and made outlandish moves.

"Years before spazziness was in style, Artie danced spazzy," an acquaintance recalled. "He was ahead of his time."

Predictably, it was burglary that caused his first serious trouble with the law. At eleven-forty on a frigid Sunday night in December 1963, Watertown police responded to a silent alarm at the downtown Sears, Roebuck store on Arsenal Street and found a front window smashed. Eighteen-year-old Arthur Shawcross was dragged off a shelf in the basement and locked up in Jefferson County jail. After he explained to the judge that he was overwhelmed by the Christmas spirit and needed money to buy presents for his beloved family, he was sentenced to eighteen months' probation as a youthful offender.

Relatives hoped that a steady new girlfriend named Sarah Louise Chatterton might settle him down. The teenagers met in the stock room of the Family Bargain Center in Watertown, where both held menial jobs. From time to time Artie amused himself by making droll comments to customers. He was fired after he told a woman who asked for a 44-D bra, "Hey, lady, you got to go to Syracuse. We don't have nothin' that big here."

Sarah quit in protest over the firing. She lived in Mannsville, twenty miles south of Watertown, came from a respected family, and enjoyed a good reputation. She was tall and slender and had green eyes the same shade as her boyfriend's. She'd graduated from Sandy Creek Central School and he told her he'd finished high school, too.

On a hot September day in 1964, the unlikely marriage took place in the nearby Sandy Creek Baptist Church while both sets of parents and Art's beloved grandmother Muriel watched and fanned themselves. The Chattertons hosted a reception, the newlyweds departed for a honeymoon in Canada, and the *Watertown Daily Times* memoralized the event in a polite article headlined: MANNSVILLE GIRL IS BRIDE OF ARTHUR J. SHAWCROSS.

The couple moved into a trailer on land owned by Sarah's parents, and the nineteen-year-old groom found a job in construction. From the beginning, there were puzzling aspects to the marriage. Artie seemed oddly uninterested in his twenty-year-old wife. Relatives didn't know whether he was shy, bored, or preoccupied with other interests. After laying down his tools at the end of each shift, he would walk to a nearby diner on Route 11, order a cheeseburger, play the pinball machine, and flirt incompetently with the waitresses.

A few weeks after the wedding, a cousin reported to other relatives that Artie's marriage hadn't been consummated—"I asked him how it was going, and he said, 'I ain't got her yet.' I thought maybe he couldn't get it up. He'd hinted about that problem before."

Although the young husband followed his father's example and put in a good day's work, he still jumped from job to job, sometimes walking off and sometimes being cashiered for misbehavior. He worked in a Watertown bowling alley, dug graves at Elmwood Cemetery for twenty dollars a hole, performed unskilled labor in a paper mill. To the dismay of the highly moral Sarah, he refused to attend church, lied about his past, and engaged in various dishonesties and infidelities. He learned about sick leave and workmen's compensation, then faked injuries to collect.

One job held his interest longer than others: apprentice butcher at a meat market in the nearby town of Adams. His salary was eighty-five dollars a week plus whatever meat was left in Cooler No. 1 on Friday nights. Fellow workers noticed his deep involvement in splitting and boning steers and lambs. He told a cousin, "Boy, at the end of the day that crick runs *red*!" He sickened his wife with drawn-out tales about the killing.

After he was fired, he caught on at a dairy, bagging powdered milk. He smuggled out fifty-pound blocks of butter, far too big for Sarah's refrigerator, and sliced off chunks for girlfriends and acquaintances. He liked to fill a gallon jar with ice cream mix, insert a broom handle, freeze the whole mess, then drive home in Sarah's '56 Buick, licking the monster Creamsicle. He drew a lot of stares.

10.

The young husband's parole for the Sears break-in ended in the same week as his twentieth birthday on June 6, 1965. A son, Michael, was born that fall. A few weeks later Shawcross faced another criminal charge.

"I went to visit him and Sarah in their trailer," a cousin recalled. "It was cold as hell, ice and snow everywhere. When I walked in, Artie says, 'I just got her. She's in the back resting. Go in and get her if you want.'

"When I said no, he kept on—'She's still back there. Go on. Go *get* her!' I said no thanks.

"After a while we leave in his hot Pontiac and a kid hits the car with a snowball. Artie slammed on the brakes. He always run funny, bent over frontwards, but he could cover ground. When the kid went into his house, Artie busted through the storm door and slapped the kid around. On the way out he got caught in the broken door. A girl started yelling inside. Artie pretended his shoulder was broken and cried like a baby: *whahhh, whahhhhhh.*

"The two kids ran to a neighbor's house and Artie got loose. He says to me, 'You're gonna have to drive. You don't mind, do ya?'

"All the way to Watertown he kept moaning. He'd pass out and wake up and moan again. But then he'd say things like 'How's it drive?' and 'Lotta power, right?' Son of a bitch was faking, as usual. I knew his act."

Mrs. Kathleen Cascinette brought a complaint on behalf of her thirteen-year-old son, and Shawcross was arrested on a technical charge of second degree burglary. After three days behind bars, he pleaded guilty to unlawful entry and was sentenced to six additional months of probation. The judge took note of the offender's behavior and ordered a psychiatric workup. A mental health clinic found him to be an "emotionally unstable personality [who reacted] with excitability and ineffectiveness when confronted by minor stress."

After the latest incident, Sarah Shawcross decided on a divorce. It wasn't that Art beat her or treated her badly, she explained, but he "always seemed to be getting hurt at work and getting laid off," and she was tired of having to pick up and move. She didn't mention his numerous acts of adultery or his crazy ideas, such as his plan to impregnate a neighbor whose husband was sterile "as a favor."

His own explanation for the impending breakup was Sarah's refusal to engage in oral sex. It was his favorite technique. Later he observed in a typically discursive memo:

> When I was 17 I had sex with a girl that lived near us, only oral sex. She wouldn't do the other. Then I went and did the same thing with another girl near by who lived on a farm. I got to like going down on girls. When I was 18 I had sex with a girl of 27 where I worked at the Watertown bowling alley. She was a waitress there at the bar. I learned everything that night. . . . I met my first wife. We got married in 1964. Had a baby boy on October 2, 1965. Everything was okay for a while then I started doing strange things again. I'de pick up girls near where we lived near Sandy Creek, N.Y. We had sex. Sometimes with others as well. I couldn't stop myself. . . .

11.

A bachelor again, Shawcross rambled from Watertown to Adams to Pulaski to Sandy Creek, still unable to hold a steady job, maintain friendships, or behave normally. There were few social activities available to a young North Country male who lacked religious or school ties. After the final separation from Sarah in August 1966, he wrecked his souped-up Pontiac and stuck her with the final payments. He sought female companionship in fast-food joints and dance halls but seldom showed up in bars; like both his parents, he had an aversion to alcohol.* He seldom saw old acquaintances or relatives.

A measure of enforced stability came into his life when he was drafted on April 7, 1967. By then he was dating Linda Ruth Neary and didn't object when Sarah served divorce papers at Fort Lee, Virginia.

The rookie soldier's first encounter with military justice occurred when a sergeant criticized him for "goofing off." Official Army records showed that Pvt. Arthur John Shawcross, 52967041, responded, "What do you think I'm doing, pulling my pud?" He was fined twenty-seven dollars.

He completed basic training at Fort Benning, Georgia, and was designated a supply and parts specialist. When he failed to show up for a work detail, he was fined eleven dollars and restricted to the post for fourteen days. After that, he appeared to accept Army discipline, and his records showed no subsequent charges.

On various intelligence tests, he scored from subnormal to slightly above. His efficiency ratings ranged through "fair" and "good" but were mostly "excellent." It was an early example of his improved behavior in structured settings.

After coming home on leave to marry his second wife, Linda, he was ordered to Vietnam with the 4th Supply and Transport Company of the 4th Infantry Division. Later he recalled a scene with the father whom he'd claimed to have

* And later to cigarettes.

been "ashamed of" since age nine: "When I got on the plane to go to Vietnam in Syracuse, he grabbed me and hugged me and said, 'Don't bring a goddamned Purple Heart back.' "

He said it was the only time he ever saw his father cry.

12. ARTHUR SHAWCROSS (HANDWRITTEN ACCOUNT)

About the middle of October 67 I went by transport c-130 prop-planes to Pleiku, Vietnam. 20,000 men went there to replace the same amount already there. I was sent to S&T unit, transportation. I drove 2½ ton trucks full of ammo or men. Sometime I would carry two or three kinds of ammo on my truck. Against the rules but it was needed up north. I took chances. In December 67 I went to the first of the 14th, 1-35th, 2-35th infrentry as a armor, weapons spec., spec-4 in rank. I had a tent quite large to hold 16 conex metal boxes. These were big enough to hold 600 guns, food, sundry packs and equipment. I even slept in one. The tent was heavily sandbaged all around. In these boxes I had 45's, M-1's, M14, carbines, M60,s M50s, M15 & 16's, BARS, flares etc.

. . . In February of 68 one of my men got hit in the face. Something happened to me then. I started to smoke, even drink rice wine, or smoke pot. Then in May I was given R&R to Haiwii. I met my wife Linda there. We had a good week together, but I couldn't wait to get back to Nam! When I got back there I would go off by my self and look for the enemy by my self. Some days I'de be out 2 or 3 days at a time. No one asked me where I was for I would always show up at a firebase on foot. I'de go to the C.P. and let them know what I seen, then they would send off a petrol. I killed the enemy as I found them. All had weapons! Most of them didn't hear the shot that got them. I was a ghoast in the jungle.

. . . I shot one woman who was hiding some ammo in a tree. She didn't die right off. I tied her up, gaged her, then search the area. Found the hut with another girl inside of the age about 16. Knocked her out with the butt of the gun and carried her to where the other girl was. There was alot of rice, ammo and other stuff in the hut. I tied the young girl to a tree, still gaged, tied her legs too. They didn't say anything to me at all. I had a machete that was very sharp. I cut that first girl's throat. Then took off her head and placed it on a pole in front of that *hut*. . . .

That girl at the tree peed then fainted. I stripped her then. . . . First I gave her oral sex. She couldn't understand what I was doing but her body did! I untied her, then retied her to two other small trees. . . . She fainted several times. I cut her slightly from neck to crotch. She screamed and shit herself. I took my M16, pulled on a nipple then put the gun to her forehead and pulled the triger. Cut off her head and placed it on a pole where they got water. . . .

This was war! I didn't kill any one that had nothing to do with the conflect. Another time I went on a petrol and shot a kid chained up into a tree. He killed one GI, with an M1 our own weapon too. That made three. Again on a petrol I killed two women in a river, after they had killed two GI's. They had a map of base camp, plus AK47 rifles and ammo, food and $2800.00 in money belts. I split the money with some guys. Smashed the AK's and ammo, took everything else back to camp. We let the bodies drift in the current down stream.

. . . Didn't need food. Those days I ate wild bananas and monkey. I carried C-4 plastic explosive. Use a little ball of it and you can cook with it, but to put it out you've got to be careful. Take loose sand or dirt and cover, leave it.

. . . All and all I know for a fact, I killed 39 people in *Viet Nam*. Scared alot and wounded more!

When I left Viet Nam, I wasn't ready for the states. I was to keyed up too hyper! I should have stayed another 6 months!

I left Viet Nam and flew to Japan . . . Alaska . . . Washington State . . . Chicago . . . Detroit . . . Syracuse. Stayed overnight. The next morning people started calling me names, babykiller *etc*. If I had a gun!

. . . I was home three days before I was asked if I was going to see Linda. I said Linda who, I had forgotten that I was married.

13.

Still on reassignment furlough from Vietnam, Shawcross ran into Jim Robbins. "Hadn't changed a bit," his old high school teammate recalled later. "Same weird look, weird voice. Talked a lot about the war, body bags, killing. He wore a bunch of ribbons and a stripe.

"I took him for a drive and he had to stop to take a leak in an orchard. He says, 'Jeez, them apples look good.'

"I said, 'Art, you better ask the farmer.'

"He just shook 'em out of the tree. A deputy runs us down and wants to know which one shook the tree.

"I says, 'That guy right there, and I warned him not to.' Art paid the farmer fifty bucks. I thought, Gee, when's the guy gonna grow up? Twenty-three years old, a combat veteran, still stealin' apples."

Other acquaintances noticed how the returning soldier babbled about the war. He told how a baby crawled into Pleiku and blew up a crowd of people with a grenade wired to her body, and how a Vietcong whore's cleverly implanted razor blade split a sergeant major's penis "like a banana." He spoke of American soldiers "skinned from their neck to their ankles," eyelids and lips sliced off, tongues cut out. He told how he'd acquired jewelry—"you'd take the body, put your foot on his mouth and you smash the teeth out with the butt of the weapon, and you collect his gold teeth and you'd string those."

He described his overseas sex life as "one gook kid after another" and told of teenage whores who charged two dollars a night. He seemed to regard his penis as a weapon and told how he and his fellow troopers raped enemy females to "teach them a lesson."

Said a male cousin, "He told me he was bangin' a Vietnamese girl and blew her brains out just when they came.

What bothered me was the way he said it—jackin' around, giggling, using his duck voice. Goofy! If you were telling a story like that, wouldn't you be serious? But it was all fun to him. 'Boy, did she quiver when I shot her!' A few days later him and his new wife, Linda, took off for Fort Sill. I didn't know what to think."

In Oklahoma, Specialist Fourth Class Arthur Shawcross repaired weapons for four months, made reluctant visits to the camp psychiatrist, and was honorably discharged in the spring of 1969. With his second wife, he settled in Clayton on the St. Lawrence River. He promptly put in a disability claim for war injuries. A Veterans Administration examiner reported, "Vet alleges shrapnel wound left arm and cut left thumb May '68," but noted that there was no substantiation in the service record and no field recommendation for the Purple Heart, routinely awarded to war casualties. Shawcross insisted that his wounds had been treated at the 4th Medical Battalion at Pleiku. After a futile investigation, he was awarded a $23-monthly disability pension (later automatically increased to $73).

With the local boy back in the North Country, it wasn't long before articles about his misdeeds began appearing in the *Watertown Daily Times*. Insiders clucked and said "I told you so" as they read about the burglary of the gas station, the three arsons, other offenses.

Seven months after his discharge from the Army, Arthur Shawcross was divorced again and back in a structured setting, serving five years in Attica. During an intake examination, he reported that he had "a weak back due to polio" and suffered from occasional blackouts. Twelve days later, he buttressed his claim by fainting dead away and was revived in the prison hospital.

Two and a half weeks later he was found unconscious again, this time after being shoved by a convict and hitting his head against a door latch. He wrote his own version of the incident years later: "Got raped in Attica prison by 3 black guys. I was lost, threatened and in pain. I got all three my way, their way!! I hurt them like they did me, but I used a sock with soap as a *black jack.* Knocked them out and screwed them and then smashed them once in the nuts. I was never bothered after that!"

He explained to counselors that sexual incompatibility was responsible for his divorces from Sarah and Linda and that he'd loved both women. After a brief flurry of adjustment glitches, he seemed to come to grips with his losses and accept the prison routine. He was transferred to Auburn Correctional Facility and suffered one more blackout, on September 22, 1971, after trying to do too many push-ups after lunch.

As his first parole hearing approached, he was examined by the prison's supervising psychiatrist. In a prescient report that was quoted and requoted years later, Dr. William A. Tucker wrote:

> Inmate is an immature adolescent with schizoid personality who decompensated [disintegrated or broke down] in ego functioning under the influence of unemployment stress, employment stress, rejection by wife. The [gas station] burglary is minor compared to his three arsons.
>
> He should be viewed as a schizoid arsonist who requires supervision, emotional support and immediate referral to a mental health clinic upon parole.
>
> *Latent projected homicidal intent* of at least two of his arsons should not be underestimated.
>
> He is a fair parole risk . . . will require psychiatric treatment plus close supervision.

A parole officer observed that the inmate's parents were "anxious to help him in whatever way possible" and were willing to accept him into their "well-furnished, tastefully decorated home." On October 18, 1971, after serving twenty-two months, he was paroled to Shawcross Corners. He was immediately hired by Frink Sno-Plows in Clayton but laid off after four days when it was learned that he was an ex-con. He collected public assistance and his Army pension while he sought another job. Just after Christmas, he was hired by the Watertown Public Works Department under the Federal Emergency Employment Program. A supervisor assigned him to a far corner of the sixty-acre landfill at the end of Water Street. Mary Blake and her brood lived a mile away.

Parole officials insisted that Shawcross undergo outpatient psychotherapy at a VA hospital. In a repetition of earlier behavior, he failed to keep his appointments. No action was taken by overworked parole officers. The psychiatrist's recent warning that he "will require psychiatric treatment plus close supervision" seemed forgotten.

Never gregarious, the ex-convict became even more of an odd man out. A steady job and a third marriage, this time to Penny Sherbino, didn't keep him from continuing a lifelong pattern of abusing others, including children. Early in 1972, he attacked a sixteen-year-old girl in an underground room of Watertown's old railroad station. "I seen her again in front of her appartment building a few days later," he wrote later. "She asked for $10.00, I gave it to her. She could have called the police that I raped her, but she didn't."

A few months later, he was arrested for the killing of Karen Ann Hill and implicated in the death of Jack O. Blake. No one who knew his background was surprised.

VII

ODYSSEY

The Saddet day of my life was when my sister Cheri diod. Shc got murdered. . . . My dad and mom started to cry when the cops came back about 4 hours after. I didnt know what was going on.

My Mom an Dad told me about two mounth that Cheri was dead and then I started to cry and then I stoped when my dad took me to K mart to buy a toy or two.

I went to the furnel home to watch her get beared. I was talking to her because I thought she was still alive. But she wasn't and my dad told me she was not alive.

Ever since it was okay

—David Lindsay, Jr., eleven years old

1.

It was March of 1984, and as far as anyone in the North Country knew, Arthur Shawcross was serving the twelfth year of his sentence for the killing of Karen Ann Hill.

In Binghamton, a sunny, sparkling city set in rolling hills and watered by the Chenango and Susquehanna rivers, the citizens were unaware of the child-killer's existence. Watertown was 130 miles to the north, the Pennsylvania coal fields just across the border to the south, and the Catskill Mountains a short drive eastward.

Unlike Watertown, Binghamton was a prosperous place with community spirit and steady jobs. Its sixty thousand inhabitants rode the city's six free carousels and ate a traditional local specialty called "spiedies," chunks of marinated pork charbroiled on a skewer and eaten with Italian bread. The city's Roman flavor dated to the first wave of immigrants who arrived around 1900 to roll cigars; they stayed on to make Endicott Johnson shoes and work for Thomas Watson's IBM and hi-tech light industries such as Link flight simulators. Rod Serling of *Twilight Zone* once lived in Binghamton, and baseball's pugnacious Billy Martin had a house a few miles up the road.

The peace was kept by 140 members of the Binghamton Police Bureau, whose biggest problem was spillover dope peddlers from New York City, three hours distant by freeway. In the peculiar dynamics of the drug trade, pushers sometimes found it expedient to abandon the Big Apple and set up shop in Broome County and other less populated points north and west. Prostitutes rode a similar circuit—Rochester, Binghamton, Scranton, Utica—and on any night fifteen or twenty women walked Binghamton's side streets and alleys, earning twenty or thirty dollars a trick and moving on when public pressure forced a police crackdown.

Crime rates were low in the riverside city. Murder was almost unknown until sporadic drug skirmishes broke out in the '80s, but even in its bloodiest year the police bureau counted only six homicides. The city was small enough so that sex criminals could be monitored. Parks and playgrounds were reckoned safe for children of any age.

2.

Everyone on Mulberry Street was fond of Detective David Lindsay's twelve-year-old daughter Cheri, a peanut-sized seventh-grader with blue eyes and brown hair and a .300 batting average in softball. Cheri played clarinet in her school band, marched in parades with the American Legion auxiliary, and roughhoused with her miniature collie Muffin. She was proud that her forty-two-year-old father was a vice squad cop. "My dad—man, he's tough!" she told a teacher. But she admired her father's patience and gentleness, too. As a Little League coach, he'd helped to smooth out her swing.

Cheri delivered the *Binghamton Evening Press* to thirty-five customers and was usually back at her house on the North Side by 5:00 P.M.; her parents forbade her to work the route after dark. She would check in with her sixth-grade boyfriend by phone, and thirty minutes later he would return the call: their own adolescent ritual.

On Monday afternoon, March 26, 1984, Cheri presented her homeroom teacher, Cynthia Antos, with an unusual problem of discipline. The child had been named "student of the month," and her picture beamed at the class from atop a tulip pot. That day she'd helped to correct papers, and she'd been so upbeat and joyful that Mrs. Antos considered telling her to cool it. What the heck, the teacher admonished herself. She's happy about something and she's a good kid. Let her alone.

The problem was that the class owed Mrs. Antos nine minutes of penal servitude. But Cheri's ebullience made the teacher issue a blanket pardon. The smiling child rushed off at the last bell.

She didn't reach home on time, nor did she keep her evening telephone date. Her boyfriend told the upset parents not to worry; Cheri had planned to shop for a secret shower for her pregnant teacher before serving her route.

When she wasn't home by seven, the mother and father began knocking on doors in the working-class neighborhood. A neighbor reported seeing her at Chenango and Bevier around 5:00 P.M., and someone else said he'd spotted her on nearby Deforest Street a few minutes later. It looked as though she'd been going door to door, making collections.

By 9:00 P.M., the Binghamton Police Bureau was on the lookout for Dave and Jeannie Lindsay's child. Fifty state troopers sped toward town to assist, and volunteers swarmed the headquarters of the Broome County sheriff. Firemen searched the brush on the wooded hillsides east and west of the Chenango River; two helicopters flew grid searches; tracking dogs nosed for a scent on Deforest Street. Roadblocks were manned by off-duty cops and civilians.

Friends on the Lindsays' block left their unpretentious two-story wooden houses to sit up with the parents and discuss every possibility—except kidnap and murder, which were carefully avoided. Someone advanced the theory that the irrepressible child was making a point by running away.

Impossible, David and Jeannie insisted. The family ran on love. Cheri had shown flashes of adolescent rebelliousness but never bore a grudge. The hardest nose in the family belonged to her policeman father, and Cheri worshiped his shadow.

"If she walked through that door right now," her mother said over coffee at 3:00 A.M., "I'd just run up to her and grab her in my arms and kiss her." She tried not to cry. "I sure wouldn't holler at her."

In his firm soft voice, David Lindsay added, "But we'd take care of it later."

"No we wouldn't."

"Yes we would."

"Well, maybe a *week* later," Jeannie conceded. She dabbed at her eyes and said, "Cheri can't even go to bed at night, no matter how mad she is, without giving both of us a kiss. Oh, she'll still go to bed mad, but she has to give us that kiss."

His wife's words reminded Sergeant Lindsay of the day his daughter had been hit in the eye while trying out for Little League catcher. No one had seen her cry.

He stepped into a bedroom to be alone.

3.

By morning, ten thousand flyers were being printed, citing a three-thousand-dollar reward. An all-points bulletin instructed police to look for a handsome gray-haired man who'd been seen sitting in a light blue car at Chenango and Cary late Monday afternoon. Search teams canvassed the homes on the child's collection route. Any kidnaping was a serious matter, but the kidnaping of a policeman's child was considered an affront to everyone on the force.

At 3:00 P.M. detectives arrived at the home of James B. Wales, a thirty-five-year-old laborer who'd owned the neighborhood paper route before Cheri. He was a short, stocky man with thickly textured red hair and mustache, a blocky face, an Elvis pompadour and odd, staring eyes. He usually dressed like a dandy—hats and jackets and florid ties—but today he was in a blue T-shirt and sweat pants.

Police had been informed that Cheri Lindsay was terrified of her predecessor. A month earlier, she'd told a friend, "The route is fine, but the person who is showing me the route is weird and gives me the creeps." Whenever

Cheri went to the Wales home to collect, her mother rode shotgun—until this Monday.

"If anything happened to Cheri," Jeannie Lindsay had advised the searchers, "take my word—it's Wales."

To detectives, the prime suspect seemed open, honest and concerned. He described Cheri as "kind of a quiet girl and real pleasant . . . a real nice girl." He had a solid alibi: his wife had been out, and he'd spent the afternoon at home with his eleven-year-old stepson. Neither had seen the missing child.

Wales nodded agreement when his wife added, "I've always preached to my son not to go with strangers. You can't trust anybody today."

During the interview, the two Wales toddlers played on the floor, and when the two-year-old handed up a toy, Jim Wales smiled and said, "That's good, honey." He impressed the detectives as a loving husband and father.

Influenced by Jeannie Lindsay's continuing suspicions, headquarters detectives ran "James B. Wales" through a computer and came up with a half-dozen hits. Neighbors and relatives filled in the rest of his background. In school, he'd been a troublemaking truant and certified brawler before his permanent expulsion at fifteen. Two marriages ended in divorce after his wives charged that he beat them. He was a drinker and doper and suffered blackout spells; he couldn't hold a steady job, and he supplemented his income with burglaries. At twenty-six, he'd barricaded himself in his house and fought an imaginary war until he was carried off and hospitalized. He regaled psychiatrists with tales of his exploits as an army squad leader in Vietnam and cited his grief over a buddy who "took a bullet meant for me." Military records showed that he'd been dishonorably discharged from the Navy for homosexuality and had never been overseas. He was diagnosed schizophrenic, treated, and released. At thirty he was arrested for committing oral sodomy on one child while forcing another to watch; the case was dropped for lack of evidence.

At nine o'clock on Tuesday night, twenty-eight hours after Cheri Lindsay failed to come home for dinner, police returned to the Wales home on Sturgis Street and asked Wales to accompany them downtown. En route, he referred to the child in the past tense and offered his expert opinion that she'd been murdered. He seemed nervous.

With the suspect removed from the premises, officers questioned the eleven-year-old stepson. The boy said that Cheri had knocked on the front door at around 5:00 P.M. to collect for the *Evening Press*. He said he summoned his stepfather, then went back upstairs to watch TV. A little later he heard screams from the cellar. He'd taken a few steps down the basement steps when he saw the girl's feet dangling in midair. As he retreated, he heard a child's voice say, "My head hurts."

The boy said he stayed in his room out of fright. Wales advised him to forget what he'd seen.

Detectives confronted Sue Ellen Wales with her young son's story. "I had a feeling something was wrong," the wife admitted. With a trembling hand, she signed a "consent to search" form.

Cheri Lindsay's body was found in a basement fruit cellar under several pieces of paneling, an old suitcase, a blue blanket, and a pair of children's jeans. Her shirt had been torn down the front and flipped up to cover her face. The body lay atop a pair of sneakers and an *Evening Press* bag.

Wales told police that he'd been preparing pork chops for his stepson and two toddlers when Cheri showed up at the door. In a five-minute frenzy, he dragged her into the basement, clubbed her with a table leg, choked and raped and hanged her from an overhead pipe. He said he hid the child's coins and her broken glasses in a dresser drawer, stuffed her folding money under his mattress, and went back to the kitchen to finish preparing supper.

At the funeral, snow sifted onto the epaulettes of fifty uniformed officers standing at attention. Jeannie Lindsay leaned heavily on her husband. Friends said that the sergeant's face showed more anger than grief. A newspaper editorial spoke for the citizens: "We are drained of color.

The city is bleak and foreboding. In the coffee shop, the faces seem tense, drawn in gray. The radio plays a sweet melody and it reeks of dissonance. . . . The melancholy is etched on everything."

4.

James Wales entered a plea of insanity and enlisted the aid of a local psychiatrist. The trial was a minute-by-minute ordeal for the Lindsays, especially when some of the jurors seemed moved by the details of the killer's pathetic life. It turned out that Wales had an IQ of 84. He'd been put out for adoption at five and was obsessed by a need for revenge. He claimed that when Cheri Lindsay appeared at the door, he was deep into a fantasy, and the child "suddenly took on the appearance of my mother."

Dr. R. David Kissinger, director of the Counseling Center at the State University of New York at Binghamton, testified that Wales had lost control of himself during an episode of "intermittent explosive disorder" and was under the impression that he was killing his mother. The psychiatrist averred that Wales's fatal misapprehension might or might not have had something to do with the pork chops he'd been cooking, but "once it happened he just plugged into the fantasy and there was no getting out."

While the Lindsays fidgeted on the hard wooden seats, state witnesses set about refuting the defense scenario. Forensic psychiatrist Mokarran Jafri testified that Wales had told him a similar story and turned red-faced as he acted out the killing, but "in my opinion it was just dramatics."

Dr. Syed Farooq, a psychiatrist from Buffalo, testified, "If he sees himself as standing before his mother, he would behave as a five-year-old, not as James Wales as he appears today. A little child does not have the force or control over the mother that was shown in this killing." Wales was described as an antisocial personality whose relations with his wife had soured and who killed Cheri Lindsay in a rage after the child spurned his advances.

The jury returned a verdict of guilty and the judge handed down a sentence of 33⅓ years to life, with no chance of parole. David Lindsay grumbled that he would have preferred a sentence of "slow death." After the killer was sent to Green Haven, the grieving sergeant told a reporter, "They oughta cut the bastard up and throw him down the sewers."

5.

Underneath his professionally tough exterior, David Lindsay was a mild man—his wife had never seen him lose his temper—and he tried to channel his sorrow and rage into constructive tributes to Cheri's memory. Not far from the family home, a landfill above the Chenango River had served North Side children as a community park; Lindsay had played baseball on it as a child and so had his daughter. He convinced the city fathers to rehabilitate the area and rename it the "Cheri A. Lindsay Memorial Park." David and Jean helped a North Side boosters club raise thirty-five thousand dollars, and soon children were swimming and playing tennis and bicycling and playing ball in a playground named for their daughter. The parents framed a copy of the proclamation creating the park and displayed it in their small living room.

Lindsay requested a return to uniform and became a patrol sergeant. The park was on his beat, and he made sure that his officers kept it safe. At least twice a day he cruised the place himself. A father couldn't be too sure, and neither could a sergeant.

As the years passed, a measure of his rage dissipated, although he still couldn't discuss his daughter's killer in a calm voice. Jeannie gave him good advice. Instead of remembering how Cheri died, she suggested, they should remember the joy she'd brought, the memories. Everyone on their block recalled the tomboy fondly. A teacher wrote, "In all the years I've dealt with children, no one has ever touched my life like Cheri did. I loved your daughter as if she were my own child."

Life returned to normal on Mulberry Street, and Lindsay began to think about stretching the family budget with an inexpensive swimming pool in their small backyard. A few blocks away, the Cheri A. Lindsay Memorial Park resounded with the cries of children romping in the shadow of a handpainted mural featuring the unmistakable profile of Cheri's dog Muffin. The North Side relaxed. So did David Lindsay. No one knew who was coming to town.

6.

By February of 1987, almost three years after the Cheri Lindsay atrocity, Arthur John Shawcross was forty-one years old and looked much older. He'd served fourteen years of his sentence, and if he stayed out of trouble inside Green Haven, his conditional release would be mandated by state law in two years. But he wanted his freedom earlier and continued to improve his jailhouse image—"walking the walk and talking the talk."

In preparation for his latest appearance before the Parole Board, he submitted to another exhaustive evaluation. An anonymous psychiatrist described the strangler as "neat, clean, quiet, cooperative, alert" with "positive attitude," "no evidence of any perceptual disorder," "no delusions, no morbid preoccupations, memory intact," "intelligence good, good reality contact, denies suicidal or homicidal ideation," "not depressed, not elated, mood neutral, affect appropriate, motor activity normal, no bizarre gestures or mannerisms," "emotionally stable" and "not mentally ill at present." The only dark brushstroke in the picture was a suggestion that the inmate "utilize psychotherapy to maintain his ability to control his emotional conflicts once he is placed on parole."

Years later, Shawcross admitted that his biggest fear as he prepped for this latest Parole Board appearance was that he would get out and kill another child. It was a fear that he carefully concealed.

7. MINUTES OF PAROLE BOARD HEARING, MARCH 24, 1987

Q. Good afternoon.

A. Good afternoon.

Q. You are Mr. Shawcross? Arthur Shawcross?

A. Yes.

Q. And you are reappearing for parole consideration today?

A. Yes.

Q. Now, when you were last seen, it was September of eighty-five . . . ?

A. Yes, sir.

Q. And you were instructed to involve yourself in some form of counseling?

A. Yes.

Q. I understand you see the psychologist every Wednesday?

A. Yes, sir.

Q. How is that going?

A. Good.

Q. Been helpful to you?

A. Yes, sir.

Q. Now what are your plans for the future?

A. I sent job applications out. I have got two nice letters back from Delaware County, Delhi, New York, and I have got three areas for housing. . . .

Q. Okay. I noticed a letter from you indicating that a

friend of yours who had been contacted was called out of town.

A. Yes. She had to go to Florida because her mother was sick.

Q. And she was going to assist you with housing?

A. Yes. One was a hotel. One was a private place in Delhi which has apartments and rooms, and another one was like a co-op place. You know, a terrace house.

Q. Okay. Now how would you get to the Binghamton office, where parole—

A. That's about twenty-six miles from Delhi, I believe.

Q. How would you get there?

A. Cab, or have somebody drive me there.

Q. You have never lived in that area before?

A. No, sir, I haven't.

Q. And the only person you know there is your friend?

A. No. I have Reverend Duthie, who takes care of my bank account for me.

Q. Where is he located?

A. He's in Twenty-one Second Street, Delhi, New York. He's the Baptist minister.

Q. Hmmm. There is some concern about, you know, your going to a new area. I think it has been discussed with you. And people, you know, recognize your desire to go to a new area. I just want to see what kind of ties you have, what kind of support system you have, because Delhi is a pretty remote area.

A. Well, I like country life. City life, I don't care for it. It's too crowded, and I figure like—[my] family tells me to go to an area I have never been, start a new life.

Q. Your family still lives in the Watertown area?

A. Yes, sir.

Q. Have you ever been to Delaware County? I guess Binghamton is the major city?

A. I have been to Binghamton years ago, just passing through.

Q. Binghamton is about the same size as Watertown?

A. I don't know. It's a pretty big-sized town.

Q. Now, it appears that you have, you know, followed through on the directives of the previous panel in terms of getting involved in counseling.

A. Yes, sir.

Q. You recognize the seriousness of the criminal activity that you were involved in?

A. Yes. The psychiatrist advised me to seek counseling on the outside, and I agree.

Q. Hmmm. Well, what we need, though, is an approved residential program for you, which we don't have at this time.

A. Yes. I'm still waiting word from the parole officer.

Q. Anything else you'd like to say to us today?

A. I think we pretty well covered everything.

Q. Okay. We will have to discuss the matter further to make a determination on the appropriateness of your parole plan, you know. You served a lengthy sentence, but you were involved in the most heinous of crimes.

A. Yes, sir.

Q. So we want to make sure that you receive the supervision that is necessary to protect society.

A. Yes.

Q. I know this happened a long time ago, but there is an eight-year-old girl who is dead now and will remain dead. So we want to make sure that there is no repetition of any criminal activity. You were on parole supervision when this crime was committed?

A. I was.

Q. So we will look into it and you will be notified of our decision shortly. Thank you very much, Mr. Shawcross.

A. Thank you.

8.

On April 28, 1987, fourteen years and six months after he was sentenced to an indeterminate term of up to twenty-five years, Arthur Shawcross became one of the approximately eighteen thousand convicts released each year from New York's overcrowded penitentiaries. His face lined and soft, his body bloated from starchy food, he expected to be met at the prison gates by Rose Marie Walley, his mail-order fiancée, but she couldn't get away from her job as a nurse's aide. The couple intended to live in the sylvan village of Delhi while she divorced her elderly husband and Art readjusted to the outside world, but local parole officers put a crimp in the plan by ordering him to move into the Volunteers of America shelter in Binghamton. The Parole Board had insisted on tight supervision, and Delhi was too far out of town for the overburdened PO's.

There was apprehension about the decision to free the child-killer two years earlier than required by law. A report by a parole officer named Gerald Szachara attempted to synopsize the psychiatric bouillabaise in the Shawcross file: "An evaluation of August 1985 done by a Dr. Charles Chung described a lack of any emotional disturbance. . . . An evaluation of August 1983 conducted by Dr. Ismael Ozyaman referred to Shawcross as being in good contact with reality and in good control of his mental facilities. . . . An evaluation of June 1977 conducted by Dr. Haveliawala referred to Shawcross as showing evidence of schizoid personality feature as reflecting low self-esteem and in all probability being a personality disorder, antisocial as well as schizoid type. . . . An evaluation of September 1979 conducted by Dr. Boyar referred to Shawcross as being of abnormal character with psychosexual difficulties."

Szachara's subtext seemed clear enough: no one knew what was wrong with the man.

Robert T. Kent, senior parole officer in the Binghamton area, read the report and warned his superiors in Elmira: "At the risk of being dramatic, the writer considers this man to be possibly the most dangerous individual to have been released to this community in many years."

Kent and his colleagues set up a strict routine for the pedophilic killer: weekly visits to a parole officer, abstinence from drugs and alcohol, 11:00 P.M. curfew, restriction to Broome County [Binghamton], regular attendance at a mental health clinic, and avoidance of playgrounds and other areas where children congregated.

But caseloads were bursting, and only so much attention could be paid to one parolee, no matter how threatening he might be to the community. When the tether loosened, Shawcross slid into his old ways. He resisted psychotherapy, sitting glum and uncooperative. A psychiatrist concluded that he had "orgasmic and ejaculatory problems," "no unusual sexual fantasies," no insights into the child-killings beyond "having problems with anger and experiences in Vietnam," and "no mental disorder requiring any specific counseling or treatment at this time."

Shawcross cited the ambiguous report as proof that he was healed and stopped attending his therapy sessions. He seemed to crave action. He rendezvoused with his pen pal, Rose Marie Walley, and achieved a rare orgasm during a romantic weekend in the Best Western Motel in Johnson City, a few miles from Binghamton.

After Rose returned to Delhi to care for her ill mother, Shawcross began hanging around parks and playgrounds and routinely ignoring his 11:00 P.M. curfew. He did some cooking at the shelter but avoided steady work. Sometimes he was seen lying on his bunk, apparently lost in thought.

After five weeks of freedom, he slipped up behind a female acquaintance as she worked on some drapes, grabbed her by the crotch, and body-slammed her to the bed. A curiously incomplete parole report noted that he backed off when "she told him to let her alone, that she was not that type of woman," but he stole "several hundred dollars' worth of property from her residence." No action was taken.

The long arm of the Green Haven Correctional Facility reached out on a less momentous matter. The parolee had walked away from a $48 commissary bill and was threatened with arrest for petty larceny, a violation that could have ended his freedom. In desperation, he phoned his mother.

"He said he wanted some small amount of money," Betty Shawcross recalled later. Neither she nor her husband had visited their firstborn son during his years in Green Haven, but mother and son had stayed in touch by mail and phone. "He said they overpaid him when he was released," Mrs. Shawcross continued, "and he spent the money. He said, 'If you don't send me any money I'm gonna have to go back.'

"I thought, It's only money, and I sent it." Her tone turned self-derisive. "Oh, sure I did! I knew it sounded like a cock-and-bull story, but I thought, Well, heck, I don't want him to get in Dutch."

Out of trouble for the moment, the parolee purchased fishing tackle and trudged down the grassy riverbank toward the Chenango. It had been a long time since he'd killed a fish.

9. SERGEANT DAVID LINDSAY

I was working days as a street supervisor, six-thirty to two-thirty, when somebody read a delayed flyer from the Division of Parole at roll call. A child-killer had been paroled to the Volunteers of America. It made my hair stand up because that was only a few blocks from the Cheri A. Lindsay Memorial Park. I thought, Hey, this is a first. We've had a lot of bad apples paroled to Binghamton, but never a child-killer. I gotta check this out fast.

I memorized the mug shot and drove to the parole office for more information. The secretary told me the guy murdered a little boy and raped and strangled a little girl in 1972. That came a little too close to Cheri's case to suit me. I said, "How come he's out so soon?" and she explained that he should've been sentenced to consecutive twenty-five-year sentences, but there was a plea bargain.

I said, "Did the murders happen at the same time?" and she said, "No. It was two separate murders."

I'm thinking, It's 1987 now. This son of a bitch murdered two kids and he didn't even serve fifteen years?

I said, "Why'd the Parole Board send him to Binghamton?"

She said they didn't want to send him home to Watertown because they were afraid he'd be killed. I'm thinking, So they dumped him in *my* neighborhood?

I saw red. Every PO in town knew about my daughter—my God, it was only three years. I didn't think it showed a hell of a lot of sensitivity, putting a guy like that in my backyard.

I drove over to the Volunteers. It was an old brick church that was converted into a shelter for the homeless: ex-cons, dopers, winos, New York City rejects. The street behind it was kind of a run-down area where a lot of kids played, mostly unsupervised. I thought, Some bureaucrat's flipped his gears.

This Shawcross guy wasn't home. They told me he was either in the park or fishing in the river for carp and walleyes. I drove to the park and no adults were around. A couple kids said a guy with a pot belly invited them to go fishing, but they were streetwise and backed off. I didn't learn till later that he usually took his victims fishing before he strangled them. My God, he was still using the same MO!

I drove the patrol car to the river just below the park and spotted a guy standing on the bank. He had one pole in the water and he was rigging another. The flyer said Shawcross was forty-one, but this bum looked fifty. I pulled right up on the grass and opened my window. My face was about three feet from his. I recognized him from the flyer, so I didn't ask for ID.

I wouldn't want to repeat the language I used, but it went back to my Navy days when you weren't a man unless you cussed and got tattooed. I told the guy I knew who he was, what he was, what he did, and what I thought of guys like him. I pointed up the bank and said, "That's the Cheri A. Lindsay Memorial Park. Ya know who Cheri A. Lindsay was? She was my daughter." I told him she was killed by a rotten pervert like him and I didn't want him anywheres near her park.

He looked at my uniform. "Yes, sir," he said, nice and quiet and respectful. "Yes, sir, I understand, sir."

"Stay the hell outa my park," I said. "If I ever see your blankety-blank ass up there," et cetera, et cetera.

He said, "Yes, sir. I won't go in there. No, sir."

I wanted him to get outa line so I could deck him, but he never raised his voice. The whole thing lasted two or three minutes, but I hung around for a long time, observing from the bank up above. When I left he was fishing.

I don't know who I was maddest at, the parole office or Shawcross. I told my wife Jeannie all about him and she was as upset as me. We agreed, This guy has killed twice; what's to keep him from repeating? You can't put a convicted child-killer in a neighborhood full of kids. How could the parents ever relax? I mean, your kid's an hour late from school and you're convinced he's dead, right? How could anybody live like that?

After dinner I took a spin around the Cheri A. Lindsay Memorial Park, but he wasn't there. I went back a couple more times before I went to bed.

Neither one of us could sleep. Jeannie kept trying to figure out how it happened and I kept explaining that it was simple: the Parole Board lost their mind. It was like a slap in the face, an insult to my daughter's memory. I sat up all night and finally went for a walk.

In the morning I talked to a few neighbors. They were as shocked as me and Jeannie. The original Parole Division flyer about Shawcross was marked "for police use only," but I decided to spread it around. If I got fired, I got fired.

I steamed all day at work and finally figured out how to run the guy outa town.

10.

WBNG-TV newsman Paul Daffinee paid close attention. As a police beat reporter he'd covered Cheri Lindsay's murder and often dealt with her father. Now the soft-spoken detective sergeant was on the phone telling him in a tense voice that another child-killer was loose in the community, but "you can never say where you heard about him or I'll get fired."

By the time Lindsay finished reciting the details, Daffinee was as outraged as the cop. "The guy killed two kids?" he said. "And they dumped him in *your* neighborhood?"

"Yep. The son of a bitch has been fishing down by Cheri's park."

The newsman said, "Leave it to me, Dave."

Daffinee was the father of two small boys, and his instincts as a parent told him that the child-killer had to be driven out of town even if it took a scare story. But his instincts as a TV journalist made him reluctant to use his power for personal reasons.

His colleagues in the Channel 12 newsroom were split. Several wanted to flash the killer's picture on the next edition of *Action News*. But another reporter asked, "Doesn't this guy have a right to privacy? Doesn't he deserve a fresh start?"

Daffinee told Lindsay that it might take a few days to sort out the ethical questions. Lindsay replied that his neighbors had collected fifty signatures on a petition to be sent to the Parole Board, but they weren't sure it would bring results. Couldn't the TV people move a little faster? The reporter asked for patience.

• • •

At thirty-five, Paul Daffinee had won awards for investigative reporting. He was a short, lean man with a sharp up-pitch delivery and a reputation for beating the opposition. He also tried to observe an old journalistic dictum: get it first, but first get it right.

To get this latest story right, he checked into Shawcross's background, then described the situation to three local psychologists and asked each, "Is this man likely to kill again?"

All agreed: Arthur Shawcross appeared to be an antisocial personality, a psychopath, and such types seldom learned from their experiences or altered their behavior. The man might not kill again, but at forty-one years of age he would almost certainly continue to molest children. His years in prison would have changed nothing; indeed, they'd probably twisted him more.

Daffinee worked out a compromise with his boss and his colleagues. The Shawcross story would be reported as part of a comprehensive three-part series on problems confronting the New York Division of Parole.

"That's the only way we can justify it," Daffinee explained to David Lindsay. "Otherwise it looks like a hatchet job."

Daffinee scheduled a taped interview with local parole officials, and while waiting outside the office with his crew he noticed a heavyset man in a soiled white T-shirt sitting on the other side of the room. The man clicked a knife open and shut, and avoided eye contact.

The POs refused to identify the man, nor would they acknowledge the existence of anyone named Shawcross. Daffinee knew a conspiracy of silence when he saw one. He decided on his next step: a trip to Watertown.

11.

Alerted that the killer's cover was about to be blown, parole officials tried to decide what to do. No one wanted to repeat the nightmare scenario of the California rapist who cut off his young victim's hands, was released on parole after a long imprisonment, and then was hounded from town to town until he had to be shipped out of state under deep cover.

The option of returning Shawcross to Watertown was revived and quickly dismissed. The parolee didn't like the idea, and neither did the North Country. The *Watertown Daily Times* had already carried a critical article headlined "KILLER OF 2 CHILDREN WINS EARLY PAROLE."

But Binghamton authorities also knew that the killer would be in grave danger after Channel 12 aired its story. Local citizens had vivid memories of the Cheri Lindsay case. How would they protect another pedophilic killer?

12.

Paul Daffinee and his crew drove the clunky WBNG-TV van two hundred miles north and confirmed from old photos in the *Watertown Daily Times* that the potbellied man in the T-shirt had been Arthur John Shawcross. Neglecting to shoot the killer's picture was a missed opportunity, and Daffinee planned to correct it as soon as he returned home.

Police files on the case, many of them unpublicized, made the father of two boys shudder. "When I found out what the guy'd done in Watertown," he told a friend, "it eliminated any doubt about whether we were doing the right thing. There were cinders embedded in Jack Blake's feet. He must've broken loose from Shawcross and run to the railroad tracks, and Shawcross caught him and dragged him back in the swamp. I thought, What if my son was stripped and hunted down like that?"

The TV piece opened with Daffinee standing on the Pearl Street bridge narrating the story of the killer's crimes. A local police official appeared and said, "It would be better if he didn't come back to Watertown probably for his well-being and for the community's peace of mind."

Then Daffinee dropped his bomb: "Shawcross did not return to Watertown. Instead he came here to Binghamton. He was paroled on April 30, and has been living at the Volunteers of America facility at 320 Chenango Street. Sources say Shawcross eventually plans to move to Delaware County."

Within a few minutes of the broadcast, the Channel 12 newsroom heard from its first outraged caller. "I live around the corner from the Volunteers," said a male voice, "I'm goin' over to take care of that bastard right now." Similar messages poured in.

"Christ, Paul," a staffer yelped, "I told you this was a mistake."

Daffinee alerted the Volunteers of America by phone. A night clerk told him not to worry. Shawcross was gone.

13.

The stranger hadn't been in the Catskills foothills for more than a few hours before he was noticed.

"This is the kinda place where strangers stand out," Police Chief Frank Harmer explained in his Humphrey Bogart voice.

Delhi, the seat of Delaware County (population, forty-eight thousand), was a one-stoplight village thirty miles south of baseball's Hall of Fame in Cooperstown. It was a fifty-mile drive from Binghamton, the last fifteen miles on a twisting two-lane blacktop that wound past willow and dogwood trees, clapboard houses with canted walls, crumbling rock fences, and meadows mantled in wild narcissus, buttercups, and dandelion.

In summer, the village's thirty-two hundred residents were joined by hundreds of outdoorsmen, and in the remaining months the permanent population was swelled by twenty-three hundred undergraduates at the two-year State University of New York at Delhi ("SUNY Delhi"), a cow college that included plumbing, nursing, carpentry, and hotel management in its curricula. The townies wore cammies, drove pickups, owned hounds, and supplemented their food rations with venison; Delaware County had the most deer kills in New York State, some of them legal.

"But we're not a woodchuck redneck community," the prideful Chief Harmer hastened to point out. "There's plenty of upscale people here."

Convivial chatter and Genesee beer were available at the village's only bar, and mixed drinks were served at the American Legion. Two or three nights a week the chief found himself sitting at "the Legion" and reciting the details of his most interesting cases in his gravelly voice. He was a short, affable Air Force veteran who boosted his height with thick-soled high-top "cop shoes." He was barely fifty, with thick glasses, clear blue eyes, a suntanned face and a genial manner. His speech included locutions that he'd learned as a child in the Fishtown neighborhood of Philadelphia: "alls I know," "beauteeful," "wooder" for water, "liggle" for "legal," and a colorful twisting of his vowels not unlike Mary Blake's.

14. CHIEF FRANK HARMER

You can see why the guy wanted to come here, besides the fact that his girlfriend Rose Marie Walley had worked here for years. He didn't have a car but he could walk a half block from downtown and fish by Twin Bridges. And there's brookies in Elk Creek and Falls Mills Creek where you enter town. The east and west branches of the Delaware River rise in our county. We're famous for our trout wooders; the guy coulda fished till he dropped and never worked the same hole twice.

The day before him and Rose arrived, I got a call from a State Police detective out of Margaretville, says, "Frank, I thought I better tell ya. You got a bad dude comin'." He gimme a little background.

Next day, the Division of Parole informed me that the

guy was on his way. They told me what he did, how long in prison, et cetera. They forgot to mention there'd been a problem in Binghamton. I thought he was coming straight from Green Haven.

One way or the other, I didn't like it. I said, "I really think this is the worst place you can put a guy like that. This is a very quiet community except for some noisy college kids. Down the line there's gonna be problems."

The parole guy interrupts me: "Frank, there won't be any problems if you don't tell anybody."

"Hey," I says, "what kind of an atteetude is that? Delhi pays my salary—not the state of New York, not the Parole Board. I eat with these people and socialize with these people, and if I didn't say something—"

He says, "We'd prefer you kept this as quiet as possible."

The first day Shawcross was here I saw a dumpy-looking guy come out of 84 Main Street by himself. It was an old frame building over Oliver's Five-and-Dime, across the street from the Mobil station and the Dairy Delight. Without Rose being with him, I wasn't sure who he was. He kinda stood on the corner for a while, then ducked back inside. Later I saw him and Rose taking a walk, so I knew it was him.

That night several of the boys at the Legion asked me who's the new guy. I said, "Alls I know is he's on parole and he's gonna be living here."

They says, "On parole for *what*?"

"Murder," I says. They buzzed about that all night.

The next day I went to 84 Main and the landlady told me that Rose Marie Walley had rented a third-floor rear apartment in her own name. I knocked on the door and the guy come out. I says, "I'm not happy with you being here, 'cause ya know it's gonna create problems for me and the community *and* you."

He just stood there, didn't talk much, didn't look ya in the eye. Finally he says, "Well, I got my rights, too."

I says, "I'm just telling ya, you're here and I got no choice in the matter. But myself, my department, the sheriff's department, and the State Police are gonna be watchin'. You're gonna have family you never knew you had. I'm not threatening, I'm just tellin' ya."

He said, "Uh, yeah, um-hmmm," looking at the ground and everywhere except at me.

The next few days, I watched him like an iggle. He got an odd job with an outside painting contractor, cleaning up, doing a little brushwork. Every morning he'd have coffee in the Delhi Diner across the street from the apartment. He sat in the back by himself, never talked. It was unusual, 'cause the diner is the hubbub of gossip in our village and everybody's friendly.

Technically I was supposed to keep it under my hat about the parolee, but I told friends, a couple of teachers, law enforcement. God forbid if this guy hurt some kid and I'd kept it quiet that he was living here. They'd've hung me and throw my body to the crows.

People began calling and asking if it was safe to let their kids come downtown—imagine, in a place where my biggest problem use to be overtime parking! There was a run on pistol permits by folks that never owned a gun; they'd ask me, "Should I buy a six-shooter or what?" A couple of families moved out of 84 Main. There was a nice older couple that lived right across the hall for twenty-eight years, and they were afraid to let their grandchild visit. Another couple took their four-year-old boy and their baby girl and moved to his mom's. People that'd never locked their doors bought padlocks. Kids up to fifteen or sixteen went straight home from school and stayed inside.

The guy would stroll along Main Street and everybody would cross. Waitresses refused to serve him *or* Rose. A petition started, and people called Senator Moynihan's office in Washington and threatened to sue the Parole Board.

When folks called the police station, I said, "Don't worry. I know who he is. I'm watching." They told me that's not good enough. What about three o'clock in the morning when I'm asleep? Couldn't he strangle some little girl then? Molest some boy?

One night I got a call on my car radio from the sheriff's department, said go to 84 Main, third-floor apartment.

They didn't use his name but I knew who they meant. I thought, Maybe somebody's gone up there and solved my problem.

Turned out it was Shawcross that called. He said he was getting phone threats, but he wouldn't go into details—"They just told me I better get outa town."

I said, "Well, the only thing we can do is get the phone company to put on a tracer for seven bucks a month."

He says, "I just wanted to let ya know. I want it on record."

"You don't want to pursue it?"

"No."

I said, "Listen, Shawcross, don't you think you'd feel better somewhere else?"

He says, "You cops are all the same. You all try to run me outa town."

I said, "Take it whatever way you wanna look at it. People don't want you here. Eventually one of these mountain men is gonna coldcock ya, if nothin' worse."

He says, "I'm paying three hundred a month for this apartment. I got as much rights as anybody else."

I'm thinking, No you don't, you son of a bitch. You're a convicted child-killer, you're on parole, you lost your civil rights, can't vote, can't even carry a BB gun. They'll restore your full rights the day those two kids come back to life.

But I didn't argue with him. I just left.

The Walley family weren't too happy that Rose was shacked up with an ex-con, and after three or four days I heard that her daughter-in-law Nancy tipped the press. Nancy was quoted later: "I don't care. I figure I saved somebody's life."

All this time the newspaper and TV reporters had been looking for him, but Parole wouldn't give up his address. When it finally got out, reporters rushed here—TV, radio, newspaper, weeklies, the *Oneonta Daily Star* and the *Walton Reporter* and the *Delaware County Times*, the Binghamton papers, Schenectady, Albany, Syracuse. Throw in a few clowns and an elephant, it woulda been the circus. They not only reported that the child-killer was in Delhi, but they ran pictures of the building and even gave his apartment number.

The landlady was a village trustee, and she didn't like the situation any better than me. Her tenants were making a fuss and she had her own grandchildren to worry about. She calls her lawyer and says she wants the guy out. He asks her who did she rent the place to.

She says Rose Marie Walley.

He says, Well, then, she's violating their lease. If the guy won't leave, that's grounds for eviction.

The landlady warned Rose, and her and Shawcross began to pack that evening. Next thing I knew, they'd left by the back alley and went around the corner to the Day Care in the basement of the Baptist Church, a block off Main.

I got a call from Reverend Lawrence Duthie. A nice guy, I knew him well. He says, "Chief, the press is harassing Art and Rose and they got no call to."

I go to the church and there's Shawcross, all red-faced and stammering. He says, "The press keeps trying to get statements from me. I don't want my picture taken and I don't wanna be bothered. I have a right to my privacy."

"Well, look," I says, "don't go outside then. If the reverend tells 'em they can't come into the church, they can't. If he calls me and makes a complaint, I'll make 'em leave." I'm thinking, Yeah, but it might take me a day or two to get here.

He says, "When I go outside, reporters harass me. I can't even leave this basement!"

"Look, mister, I told you a few days ago you're gonna cause problems. Now you see what I meant. And this is only the beginning. Everybody in town knows who you are and where you live."

He kept saying, "I got my rights!"

I said, "We're not talking liggle rights, we're talking reality. The reporters are just doing their job. That's freedom of the press. You're news." I'm thinking to myself, Yeah, *bad* news.

He says, "Well, I'm gettin' the hell outa this town anyway.

They kicked me outa Binghamton. Now they're kickin' me outa here."

That was the first I knew there'd been trouble in Binghamton. It woulda been nice if Parole had mentioned it.

He says, "You can't expect me to stay in this basement all the time."

"Well," I says, "fame brings people. You can't blame 'em. They wanna see the celebrity."

15.

Rose Marie Walley was confused and hurt. A stout, motherly woman with massive breasts, short brownish hair, and a voice that rarely rose above a mumble, she'd expected to begin a quiet domestic life with her ex-convict. Their correspondence had started a dozen years earlier after one of her daughters paid a visit to Green Haven Correctional Facility and returned with the name of a potential pen pal. Rose claimed later that the letters from Art were the warmest contacts of her life. Her first marriage seemed to have left her with bad memories. Her husband was twenty-seven years older and they'd lived apart for years. She attended a Mormon church but didn't believe in plural marriage. Art wrote her that there were ten and a half women for every man on earth and he intended to get his share before he died. When she asked what he would do about the half, he wrote back, "I'll get a midget."

Rose's children were grown; she was slightly hard of hearing, her teeth didn't fit, and it had been years since she enjoyed a social life. In his photos, Art looked like a handsome man, but she'd been too shy to visit him in the penitentiary or even talk to him on the phone, and they hadn't laid eyes on each other until a few weeks earlier when she'd gone to Binghamton for a romantic weekend in a motel.

16. ROSE MARIE WALLEY

I never thought Art would be run outa Binghamton and I never thought we'd be run outa Delhi less'n two weeks after we got there. I'd worked in Delhi for years! And I didn't think my family would turn on us, either.

I knew we were in for it when a couple of drunks tried to kick our door down. Then I came back from doing laundry and the woman who owned the building called me over and says, "Rose, the State Police just took your friend away for a talk."

"What?"

"Two state troopers. You didn't tell me he'd been in prison."

Well, I never thought I had to.

That night Art got a phone call from his mother. After he hung up, he went into the bedroom and cried. Later I found out he always reacted that way to his mother.

When I realized he was being pushed out of Delhi for good, I walked into the nursing home where I worked and told 'em, "I'm quittin'. I'm goin' with Art."

They says, "You may be sorry for this."

I told 'em it was just something I just had to do.

17.

The beleaguered couple tried to find a place that was near enough for Rose to stay in contact with her friends and relatives. On the steps of the Reverend Duthie's church, Shawcross stalled for time by holding a short press conference. He said he'd been rehabilitated in prison and needed only a final psychiatric interview in Binghamton to receive a clean bill of health.

"I'm fine," he told a reporter from the *Oneonta Daily Star,* "if people would just leave me alone."

But his publicity campaign was too short and too late. Duthie found the couple new quarters and helped them pack. On Sunday he admonished his parishioners in a sermon, "We are called to love one another and to forgive. I thought we could have done that a little better."

In the predawn hours of Monday, June 22, the travelers and their earthly goods left town in a loaner van provided by the Division of Parole. Twenty-one miles southeast of Delhi on State Route 28, they pulled up in front of an apartment building on the outskirts of the Catskills village of Fleischmanns. Shawcross could hardly wait to unpack so he could drop a worm in a stream that he'd spotted en route.

It took reporters a week to hunt them down and publicize the new address. The ensuing scenes were reminiscent of the mob scenes in *The Bride of Frankenstein.*

18. ARTHUR SHAWCROSS (HANDWRITTEN ACCOUNT)

It was a nice cozy building, two stories high with two appartments and 11 bed rooms. We had the whole thing for $300.00 a month plus utilities and phone. We spent a week there and then I went to the postoffice to register for mail. The woman at the window told me that I will not be getting my mail from there! Two days later a deputy sheriff stopped by and told Rose and I that there was a linch mob comming to kick me out of town. The mayor was leading them.

I refused to move. We were scared sure. When the people got out front with flash lights and tourches, they started screaming my name to come outside. I had all the lights out. I opened that front door and one guy started talking, making threats. I made one statement. Who ever made one step into the yard was a dead man. Who ever, man, woman or child. That stopped them for awhile.

19.

The couple's sojourn among the four hundred residents of Fleischmanns lasted until the first newspaper article hit town. Mayor Edward Roberts Sr. proudly took credit for leading the eviction party. "I had him out of town before dark," he boasted to the *Oneonta Daily Star.* "I called his parole officer in Binghamton, but I can't repeat what I told him."

The mayor insisted that he'd had no choice; the reaction of his constituents had been "like wildfire. Get him out of here!" Later His Honor told a reporter, "It was my responsibility. I didn't really care what the town thought, especially the assholes who complained about his civil rights."

20.

Shawcross and his girlfriend packed hurriedly, stashing their few sticks of furniture in Delhi with the kindly Reverend Duthie. The Division of Parole hid the exiles in a motel in the town of Vestal, three miles west of Binghamton on busy Route 17, while higher-ups tried to decide where to send them next. On the first night in Vestal, Rose was afraid that vigilantes would kick in the motel door. Shawcross stood watch at a window shade. Neither slept.

They had asked to be taken to Utica, conveniently located midway between Watertown and Delhi near the geographical center of the state. They were sitting outside the motel atop their three battered suitcases when a Parole vehicle pulled up and a PO announced that they were leaving for Rochester, 100 miles northwest on Lake Ontario.

"Rochester?" Shawcross asked. "Why Rochester?" As a young truck driver, he'd made a delivery in the old industrial city and come away unimpressed. He complained that he wouldn't feel safe in the same community as Karen Ann Hill's parents; they'd been out for blood from the beginning. And Rochester was too far from Rose's people in Delaware County and his own family up in Brownville. And . . . where would he fish? Everyone knew that Lake Ontario was a dead sea.

The parole officer explained that there'd already been three highly publicized failures and the story was ballooning out of proportion. One more failure and they'd have to move him to another state. Rochester was big enough (population, 250,000) and an excellent place to live, known to its boosters as "The Number One City in the U.S.A. for Quality of Life." Also, it was far enough from Binghamton so that the killer could be smuggled into town without attracting attention. This time the Division of Parole wouldn't inform local police. There would be no Sergeant Lindsay or Chief Harmer or Mayor Roberts to stir things up.

When Shawcross continued to protest, he was reminded that he was on parole.

The couple arrived in New York's third-largest city at 4:30 P.M. on Monday, June 29, and were booked into room 314 of the Cadillac, an unstylish hotel on a seedy block in the center of town. They had two suitcases and twenty-nine dollars. The parole officer advanced Shawcross fifty dollars and told him to stay out of sight "till we see what happens."

When the PO returned to check at 8:00 P.M., the couple had just returned from dinner at a fast-food restaurant in the Midtown Mall, just about the least private place in Rochester. He ordered them to remain in their room for the rest of the night and prepare to leave on short notice.

The next morning they were quietly moved to the top floor of the Hudson Avenue Group Home, a halfway house on a threadbare street near the Amtrak station. The place was home to a collection of mental patients, most of them poor and black. The newcomers were assigned a bare room with no stove or refrigerator, no electricity, and only a few pieces of furniture. The daily report to the chief parole officer in Rochester noted, "Subject was pounded* out of Delhi NY by media, i.e. press and TV. Area Supervisor Murray to withhold information of subject in community from police until initial adjustment is made."

For a week the lovers camped indoors and dined out, quickly going broke. A stove was provided, but there was no gas line to the bare room. Shawcross seethed at the situation. He snaked a wire under the door so they could cook on a borrowed hot plate. The harsh living conditions caused Rose to miss her period, and for two weeks they sweated out a pregnancy scare.

Shawcross found temporary laboring jobs through an employment agency, earning minimum wage as a general laborer, box loader, and warehouse worker. He also registered at the New York State Employment Service for itinerant farm work at $25 or $30 a day. At the end of each shift, he was required to check in with his parole officer.

Rose landed a job as a "health home care assistant," earning $4.35 an hour assisting the infirm and elderly in their homes. The couple began to talk about an apartment of their own.

When no embarrassing articles appeared in the local press, it looked as though the transplant had taken. After two weeks, higher-ups ordered parole officers to inform the Rochester police department about the parolee's presence, "but not regarding his criminal background."

The situation remained touchy. Rochester Police Chief Gordon Urlacher had once blown the whistle on a parole plan to import a criminal who was described as a person with "great potential for extreme violence. . . . Any contact with the individual by law enforcement should be made with extreme caution." The angry Urlacher had trumpeted the information at a press conference, and the felon was shipped elsewhere.

Against this sensitive background, local POs had to consider the uproar that would ensue if Shawcross caused trouble, especially if he approached children, and they kept a

* Probably "hounded" was intended.

priority watch on him despite caseloads that included thirteen hundred parolees in their area, eighty of them killers. The pedophile and his paramour were the subjects of frequent unannounced visits and terse reports: "RMW [Rose Marie Walley] says not feeling well . . . $20 emergency funds provided. . . . S & RMW interviewed. . . . Said had quiet weekend, did some exploring in Rochester and went up to Charlotte Beach. . . . $10 emergency money provided. . . ."

Shawcross dyed his hair black and planned to change his name to "Ara Yerakes," after a maternal relative. He gorged on fast food and put on twenty-five pounds, mostly around the middle. He explained to Rose that the increased girth would make it harder for reporters to recognize him.

When his parole officer reminded him that he was disregarding a strict requirement to undergo therapy, he grudgingly visited the Genesee Mental Health Center and was found to be suffering from a grab bag of behavioral problems, including inhibited sexual excitement, inhibited orgasm, adult antisocial behavior, mixed personality disorder, secondary impotence, sexual sadism, and a prostate ailment. His assets were listed as "physical health, intelligence, social skills, psychological mindedness, successful use of treatment in prison."

Psychologist Gary Mount took note of Shawcross's resistance to treatment but observed that the reason might be financial. "As you know," he reported to the Division of Parole, "he has a very limited income and the cost at this time, although on a sliding scale, still is quite difficult for him. When he does obtain fulltime work and possibly some health insurance, this may no longer present a difficulty for him."

The therapist recommended a treatment goal of "increased performance" and advised the client to read a book called *What You Still Don't Know About Male Sexuality.*

Despite the somber tone of Mount's report, he sounded a hopeful note: "Shawcross reports extensive and what sounds like rather thorough counseling, both for his posttraumatic stress disorder while in Viet Nam, as well as his sexual difficulties which led to his imprisonment. He does report extensive self-awareness and what sounds like very appropriate use of psychiatric and psychological resources while at Green Haven. . . ."

Hardly a word was true, but the killer had cleared another hurdle.

VIII

MURDER IN ROCHESTER

I had a problem. A problem that I couldn't keep an erection. Couldn't have an orgasm. My wife knew about it. I went out with a lot of women in that area over the last few years. . . . I went out with at least 85 to 100 or more women. . . . I was trying to find out why I was impotent, something like that.

—Arthur Shawcross

1.

Life improved for the exiles. In mid-October, three and a half months after their surreptitious entry into Rochester, they received permission from a parole officer to move into a brownstone and brick apartment house at 241 Alexander, two short blocks from one of the city's busiest thoroughfares, Monroe Avenue. Reverend Duthie drove up from Delhi with Rose's furniture and helped install the couple in 107 B, a first-floor studio with a kitchenette, bathroom, and bedroom-living room. A bubble-front window provided a view of the Genesee Hospital across the street. The blocky apartment house was plain but functional, with fifty-two comfortable units. Fire escapes hung like crab claws from the sides of the three-story building. The manager kept potted plants at the top of the stone staircase leading to the big front door, and several turrets and a set of groomed hedges completed a vague Tudor effect. A small sign warned, "No Soliciting."

Rose described those first few months as "a happy time" and life with Art as "marvelous." She enjoyed her daytime job fluffing up pillows and emptying bedpans for the aged and infirm. A van from the Visiting Nurse Service picked her up just after dawn and returned her at the end of the day. The neighborhood was a little run-down and shopworn, but less demoralizing than the one they'd left behind. As in even the grubbiest parts of Rochester, there were canopies of trees, splashes of flowers, manicured hedges, green lawns clipped like the flanks of prize poodles. Some of the older homes had been razed to create parking lots, and others had been turned into medical offices or small shops. Ambulance sirens whined around the clock and a steady stream of cars pulled into the parking area for "Prank's," a disco and nightclub next door.

Shawcross didn't seem to notice the din; he seldom slept more than three or four hours even on quiet nights. But he was jumpy about unexpected loud noises; he explained to Rose that it was a holdover from Vietnam. One day a truck backfired as they strolled past the school at Monroe and Alexander and he slumped to the sidewalk.

"I'm shot!" he gasped. He turned pale and seemed to stop breathing. Rose revived him and helped him up. After a minute or two he continued walking. Rose said she was more frightened than he was.

2.

Overworked parole officers pronounced themselves pleased with Shawcross's adjustment and made plans to cut back their unannounced visits. A report noted, "His relationship with [Rose] appears to be a strong one and both appear to support each other. Once [her] divorce is finalized, they indicate they will be married and both hope to remain in the Rochester community where they can assume a quiet life."

Privately, the POs gave Rose the credit. She'd learned early to bend to his will, to run on his schedule and according to his needs. When she forgot her obligations to the master of the house, she was quickly reminded.

Shawcross had been a nonsmoker since 1977, his fifth year in Green Haven, and one day she carelessly opened a pack of cigarettes in front of him. "Did I get it!" she told a friend later. "I thought I was gonna get licked! He yelled, 'What're you doing with these things?' I got rid of those cigs in a hurry."

Rose had lived a lonely life and enjoyed her role as a strong man's mate, subservient or otherwise. She only wished they talked more, shared their daily experiences, but Art didn't seem interested.

"Rose," he warned her when she started to tell him about a balky old woman, "I don't want to hear no more bullshit about your goddamn patients. When you come home, your job stops when you walk in the door."

Rose never complained, nor did she think she was getting a bad deal. It wasn't as though Art demanded obedience and gave nothing in return. She suffered from recurrent headaches, and he was a sympathetic helpmate, drawing the curtains and shooing others away in his deep, masculine voice. He enjoyed music, especially Hawaiian guitar, but he didn't object when she tuned to her favorite country and western station. He liked to cook and proudly prepared gourmet meals ("he cooked salmon *hundreds* of different ways," she said). He did more than his share of the housecleaning, hung up his clothes, washed dishes and scoured pots. He had a strong aversion to clutter. When he came home from work, he seemed agitated until he'd put things back where they belonged. He read paperback books on Vietnam, plus *Reader's Digest, Yankee, World Earth News, Cable TV News,* and tabloids like *The National Enquirer* and *Star.* He attacked crosswords and other puzzles, seldom worked them out but never quit trying.

His biggest interest was TV, and sometimes he would shut Rose out as he stared at the screen, his lips moving silently. He told her that his mother hadn't allowed him or his father to watch shows featuring good-looking or half-dressed females, that Betty had described them as whores.

"Look at that bitch!" Art would say excitedly. "Did you ever see tits like that?" It was as though he were talking to a man. He didn't seem to realize that his overweight girlfriend felt uncomfortable about his comments.

Rose tried to be understanding. She knew he had sexual hang-ups, and who didn't? In a rare confidential moment, he claimed that his aunt had paraded in front of him in bra and underpants when he was nine, then fondled him and taught him oral sex. It helped Rose to understand his tastes in bed. He'd seemed sexually excited ever since they reached Rochester, but he complained that he couldn't reach a climax. He'd had one orgasm since they'd been together, on that first weekend together in the motel near Binghamton.

Rose felt he was more than worth the trouble. They'd had difficult lives, gambled on each other sight unseen, and now were making their relationship work. They would show the doubters! She loved him and told him so twenty or thirty times a day. Sometimes he would turn away and tell her to shut up—"It makes me nervous when you talk like that"—but she didn't intend to stop.

3.

Neighbors couldn't decide what to make of the moody newcomer. Sometimes he was pleasant and helpful; sometimes he scowled and ignored their greetings or friendly remarks. He would carry on an interesting conversation and then blurt out something that made no sense, something totally disconnected, or answer questions that hadn't been asked.

He paid his $255 monthly rent on time and went out of his way to please the middle-aged manager, Yvonne LaMere, even offering to baby-sit for her grandchildren and inviting her to go fishing with him. He tended the small front lawn without being asked, and when the snows began in November he was the first to grab a shovel. It was true that he didn't radiate warmth or human kindness, but he seemed to want to be appreciated, even by people he hardly knew. He was a skilled handyman and acted pleased to be asked to fix an appliance or solve a plumbing problem. He distributed candy and coins to children of tenants and gave matchbooks, old magazines, newspapers, and other oddments to the adults. He seemed bent on giving away all his possessions. He even gave handouts to the teller at his bank.

"If people needed something," Rose said later, "Art would get it for them. If they were hungry, he gave 'em our food or went out and bought more. He took bags of clothes to the neighbors because they didn't have nothing. He brought people in off the street and cooked them a meal."

"Yes, he'd give you the shirt off his back," said neighbor Susan Ristagno. But along with a few other residents of the brownstone, she was disturbed by his cold stare and his offbeat reactions. "There was a dark side to him," she said. "Sometimes he scared me."

For months, apartment manager LaMere accorded him the triple status of volunteer handyman, personal friend, and favored tenant, but in the end she decided to back away. She'd judged him to be a simple, sad, lonely man who was drawn to the warmth of other families, but after she invited him to join the LaMere clan on a few of their outings, he seemed to misunderstand her friendliness.

"He was becoming fast friends with my entire family," her husband James reported to authorities later, ". . . starting to become involved in many of our family activities. It was bad, almost as if he was taking my place. At one time he even took my grandchildren out trick-or-treating on Hallowe'en. On one or two of our family outings Art even made a pass at my wife. I remember at a pig roast we had, Art grabbed my wife's breast. . . . My wife was very upset that Art did this and told him so. She even told him that if he ever did anything like that again she would kill him. Art told her that she better watch out what she says to him or she would suffer the consequences."

The social problem didn't end until the LaMeres moved from the brownstone and broke off contact.

4.

From the beginning, the parolee seemed drawn to the hot lights of the intersection at Monroe Avenue, a two-minute walk to the west. On the corner stood a fire station, the Raj Mahal restaurant ("Authentic Indian Cuisine"), the New Delhi Deli, and a Dunkin' Donuts set at an angle so that it faced both Alexander and Monroe. A few blocks in either direction were pornie magazine and video stores, thrift shops, coin-op Laundromats, a 7-Eleven, Enright's Thirst Parlor and Liquor Store, the Monroe Theater ("adult movies"), and a gallery of fast-food restaurants including McDonald's and Arby's. And there was the Monroe Middle School, a dusty old edifice backed by a big grassy athletic field and a disused quarter-mile running track. Children were always around.

In between his part-time jobs, Shawcross took to hanging out at the Dunkin' Donuts, idling over coffee while he perused *USA Today* and the *Rochester Times-Union.* Habitués found him approachable and easygoing, though he said little of substance. Given a choice, he seemed to prefer the company of women. He was no strain on the restaurant's small parking lot; he traveled on foot or on a ladies'-style blue Schwinn bicycle with a shallow basket and an American flag on the front and two deep baskets on the back. He explained to an acquaintance that he'd bought the bike for Rose, but she couldn't learn to ride.

He bounced from one temporary unskilled job to another—laborer, loader, warehouseman, farmhand—and in August he caught on at Fred Brognia Produce, a wholesale fruit and vegetable business in the public market south of town. Brognia and his brother Tony started new employees at minimum wage but provided side benefits including free food and pleasant working conditions. Their big airy market smelled like a roadside vegetable stand. The brothers sold only the freshest produce and went out of their way to fill specialty orders—prickly pears for Sicilian-American clients, pomegranates for Greeks, chile peppers for Hispanics, bok choy and matsutake mushrooms for Orientals, persimmons, acorn squash, chayote, morels, chanterelles. If an item was "touched," it was thrown into a separate bin for employees and the homeless.

The owners noticed that the new man was filling the baskets of his five-speed bike every night and coming to work the next morning a little thicker around the middle. But he worked hard, and they figured they were still ahead of the game.

5. FRED BROGNIA

Shawcross fooled us, all right. He was a strong-looking guy, paunchy, sloping shoulders, big hands, black on black hair. He was a hardworking son of a bitch. One day I said, "Hey, you look like you're on the ball. How come you're working on a minimum-wage job? You got a drinking or a drug problem?"

He says, "Naw, I'm an ex-convict. It's a little hard to find a job."

We put him in the prep room where we prepare items for hotels and restaurants. He peeled onions, cored and shredded cabbage for cole slaw, sliced up peppers and removed the seeds, made carrot and celery sticks, broccoli and cauliflower florets, stuff like that. Never complained, kept to himself.

We carried him as a temporary at first, but after a while he went to my brother Tony and said, "You see the good work I do? Why don't you put me on full time?"

We talked. Tony said, "Ya know, Fred, the guy's right." It was an easy decision for us. So we never took an implication on the man. We figured he was clean—flaky but clean.

He rode his bike to work right up till winter, must've taken him an hour each way, six, eight miles from his apartment on Alexander. He was either on time or early. He worked 7:00 A.M. to three or three-thirty. He shut his mouth and did his job, so when he wanted a key to come in extra early, we gave it to him.

After a while he started having a few problems with his temper. He grabbed a part-time kid by the neck and ran him into the wall. He told weird stories about being a soldier, how one woman wouldn't admit she was a Vietcong so they tied her legs to a couple of saplings, slashed her down the crotch and let the trees rip her apart. He smiled when he told that one.

I found out he was bothering Loretta Neal, a kid from West Virginia. She was twenty-three, twenty-four, chubby, one of our best workers. At one time or another, almost the whole Neal family worked here—Roscoe, Rex Allen, Don

William, Robert, James Eddie, Loretta—all good workers. The mom, Clara, she wanted a job, too, said she'd been a cook and knew how to handle food. She told Tony, "I'll show my kids how to do things and they'll do a better job for ya."

Tony thought about it and said, "Yeah, we'll hire them, but you stay home, Mom." God bless my brother, he had a feeling.

Loretta came in the office one day and said, "Shawcross won't leave me alone. I don't trust him."

So I took the guy aside. "Art," I said, "what you do outside is none of my business, but when you're in here, leave the women alone. Especially Loretta."

He got a little hot. "Everybody else in this joint's fuckin' her," he said. "I don't know why I can't."

"Wait a minute!" I said. "Slow down right there." I happened to know it wasn't true and I didn't know where he got the idea except that Loretta kidded around a lot and in his simple mind he probably got the wrong idea. So I said, "I don't know of anybody else is fucking her here."

He still wanted to argue. I finally said, "Keep your fucking hands off her! If I find out, you'll be thrown out on your fucking ass. *Nobody*'s fucking her. That kind of talk's no good for business."

He backed off, said, "I didn't mean anything."

Loretta did tease him sometimes—I heard her myself. She told him, "I'd be the best piece of ass you ever got."

I said, "See, Loretta? It's your own fault he bothers you. You're teasing him."

But he stopped bothering her. By then he'd met her mother.

6.

Clara Neal lived a mile north of downtown Rochester with as many of her ten grown children as elected to shelter under her wing at any given moment. Some stayed a while, some just hung out, and some were as permanent as

"Bones," born Robert, her youngest at twenty-three, a night-shift metalworker, and her oldest son, Roscoe, thirty-nine, who'd worked at Brognia Produce since 1980 and could barely read or write but according to his boss knew "a hell of a lot more than he let on."

The Neals' sagging one-story house looked as though it had been shipped intact from Tobacco Road. It was in the shadow of the Hickey-Freeman plant in a neighborhood so tough that pizza parlors refused to deliver. The matriarch didn't serve much fast food anyway. Her formal education ended in the fifth grade, but Clara was a virtuoso cook with specialties like golden-fried chicken dripping with butter and fluffy mashed potatoes with West Virginia mountain gravy and soup recipes that had been in her family for generations and featured subtle touches of salt pork and bacon.

Cooking for her offspring took time and care, but it was one more way to show the love that had held the Neals together. Everyone saw Clara as the strength of her family, a survivor. She was usually to be found on her hands and knees, cleaning house and demolishing cockroaches.

"We spent a hundred and fifty dollars to get rid of 'em but the war goes on," she said, throwing her head back in a raucous laugh that set her latest stray dog to keening under the back porch. Some of her children credited their mother's high spirits with seeing them through the bad times, choosing not to mention that the bad times continued.

Clara had a blocky face, wide-set blue eyes, high cheekbones, and a robust head of dark blond curls that seemed to require the constant attention of her pudgy fingers. She worked so often and so persistently on her hair that sometimes it looked like a wig. A furrow ran from each side of her nose to just outside the corners of her lips. When she talked about her big love affair in her coquettish voice, she rolled her eyes upward till only the whites showed, creating a resemblance to Orphan Annie.

"Art Sharcross," as she called him in her Appalachian twang, could be discussed only in reverential terms. Even after fifteen years in the Rochester area, Clara retained her childhood drawl. She was an animated, expressive talker, and sometimes she employed a few slightly altered clichés with a sly smile, as though she'd just thought them up: "sharp as a tick," "four sheets to the wind," "thick as fleas on a coon. . . ." She pronounced "TV" southern-style: TEE-vee. For emphasis, she used a few trademark phrases: "Now I'm gonna be plain about it," "I'm gonna say it," "I'm gonna come right out and tell ya," and the ubiquitous southernism, "Tell you what," pronounced "Tell ya hwut."

The arthritis in her back had been worsened by years of standing over cooktops and counters; sometimes she blinked with pain and turned away. She drank an occasional seven-and-seven or a bourbon and ginger ale, dieted unsuccessfully but often, and had a sparse social life. She avoided most residents of her neighborhood; not that she was antiblack, but the young males made her feel squirmy.

"They bounce around in their sweatpants up there on Clinton," she explained, "and it looks to me like they don't wear nothin' underneath. They just look nekked. I'd ruther they wore a old pair of pants with patches in 'em than run around like 'at."

Every day she fed squirrels and birds. A twenty-four-inch TEE-vee flickered in her small front room while C&W music played constantly on a radio: the Ronnies and Randys and Hanks, Dolly Parton, the Judds.

"I admire Loretta Lynn above all," Clara explained. "Named one daughter after her. I like music I can understand."

She read supermarket tabloids and shared the stories with her children. "Listen at this," she told daughter Linda over the phone, her eyes rolled up in wonder. "There's a story today about a two-headed baby. . . . Why, shor that's why I bought it! I saw a two-headed baby at a fair when I was a small girl. In a big jar of formaldehyde. Sometimes I think about it at night."

But mostly she pondered her great love.

7. CLARA NEAL

I'm mountain-born and -bred. Wished I never left, 'cept I never would've met Art. I was born Clearidee Drennan in a little mining and timber town in Clay County, West Virginia. It's God's green place on earth, but there's never been no work there since the mines give out. We lived in the holler of Sycamore Creek, mountains reaching up on both sides of us and the growing season short. I'll be plain about it—I was born in nineteen and thirty-one, so I got a few years on me. I went barefoot till I was eighteen. My father and stepfather worked in little old scab mines, no union, took 'em forty-five minutes to get down to the coal face. There was plenty of accidents. We doctored our men ourself.

Never knew anything but work, that's why you won't hear me complaining. Sometimes all we had to eat was good old beans or a pan of baked bread. We raised what we ate: chickens, pigs, a cow for milk and butter, corn, tomatoes, cabbage, string beans. I cooked my first meal for the whole family when I was seven. Mommy was outside weeding.

Some folks, they say I made a pet out of a killer. Well, I always had pets, I'll admit it. When I was a little girl I had a hen that was named "Toppy" 'cause she had a big toppyknot on her head. She was coal-black, but when the sun would shine on her, her feathers turned blue and green and different colors—oh, God, she was pretty! Followed me around like a puppy dog, got up on my bed, and laid her egg. I had a little mountain mare, mix breed, name of "Pearl," rode her bareback all over the mountain. Always had pets. If Art Sharcross was my pet, he was a long way from bein' my first.

When I was little, my uncle asked me what're you gonna do when you grow up, Clearidee? I said, "I'm gonna get married and have a dozen kids." Well, add 'em up. I have eight boys and two girls living, miscarried two more. We're a tight family. One of my son's serving a short sentence out in Albion. He used to be in a maxim-security prison. Phones me whenever he can. All my kids do.

I was married when I was almost eighteen. There was no work in the mountains so me and my husband, we started doin' like a lot of folks from Clay County: comin' up here to Rochester. Kodak, Hickey-Freeman, Bausch & Lomb, places like that didn't want us because we were unskilled labor, so we hired out on small farms. We'd work hard, but then we'd pack up and go back 'cause we missed West Virginia so much; anybody would've. It was a hard life, back and forth, and my husband didn't make it any easier. I'm gonna just come right out and say it: I lived with that man from nineteen and forty-nine till seventy-four and all he ever give me was sex. I never had love, never had compassion. He slapped my face one time, made me feel so bad I drank a bottle of turpentine, but it only made me sick.

He accused me of larkin' around with another man, this and that, made me out to be lower than a snake's belly. I told him if I gotta bear the name, I'm gonna play the game, and I went out and had a child by another man. When my husband found out that our new baby son wasn't his, we got divorced.

I come back up here to Rochester to support my kids. Sometimes we went hungry, but I refused to go on welfare. I was housekeeper at Brockport State College, worked at Burger King across from the produce market, worked at nursing homes as cook and assistant cook. Tried to hire on at Brognia produce, but they had enough Neals on the payroll. I took odd jobs cleaning offices. Tell ya hwut, hard work don't bother me. All my life I been pickin' up after others.

It was like a 'lectronic shock the first time I seen Art. It was just after Christmas 1987, and I drove over to pick up my daughter Loretta at Brognia's. He was cutting carrots and cabbage and stuff. I took one look and the hair went up on my neck. He didn't look like anybody I'd ever known. He had the blackest black hair and I thought he was an Italian. I wouldn't call him handsome, but there was something about him.

He was running a slicing machine with razor-blade knives, and one of the guys started acting playful. Art told him, "Hey, listen to me! This is no time to act the fool! I could lose a hand in this thing."

Women like men that speak up, men that's *men.* I thought to myself, Some way I'm a-gonna meet that guy. So I talked to Loretta, and she invited him to our house. Why? *Because I asked her to!*

A few nights later he shows up and we're setting in my living room, him and my kids and me, and he looks at me, and I look at him. . . .

I'm sorry. I can't talk about him without getting all teary. . . .

We look at each other and just stare. He's got a way that he don't wink with one eye, he winks with both of 'em, and he did that, and it was just like a 'lectric shock. So I started pickin' at him, just touchin' and pokin' at him 'cause I couldn't help myself. After a while we went into the kitchen and I kissed him. But that was all.

The next day I seen him at Brognia's again and I drove him to his place on Alexander Street. Before I dropped him off, we made a date for a couple nights later. We went out to my daughter Linda's on the ridge in Brockport, then to my son Rex's place to watch the rasslin' on TV. We came home around midnight and I kissed him again, but nothing more.

He had a way of making you feel tenderhearted toward him. I didn't know the details about his prison troubles, but I just felt that when the time come, his arms would be something comfortable. And he carried hisself so nice and clean.

8.

Shawcross's consort, Rose Marie Walley, was already dealing with another woman in his life. Art hadn't seen his mother in seventeen years, but as far as Rose was concerned, she might as well be living in their front room. He loved his mom and always told her so on the phone, but he claimed that he never could please her. He went out of his way to take offense at anything she said. He admitted that he was still hurt and angry about her failure to visit him in prison. He kept coming back to that insult like someone worrying a hangnail.

He didn't say much about his father, but Rose could see how much he yearned for his mom. Somehow the visiting arrangements never worked out. After a long, imploring phone conversation one night, he slammed down the phone and began sputtering: "Mom was, she says, 'Well, they, uh—you should have died. You never should have come out.' "

He went into the bathroom and slammed the door. "Art," Rose called, "what can I do for you?"

He said, "Just go out. Leave me alone." She could hear the sobbing.

After a while he explained that his mother had blown up at him when he said that he intended to visit Shawcross Corners by bus. His mother had told him to stay the hell away; he wasn't wanted in the North Country.

The couple discussed the situation and decided to invite the parents to Rochester, a four-hour drive by freeway. But once again Art was rebuffed. This time he slammed down the phone and stalked out the front door. Rose checked and saw that his bike was gone. He stayed away for hours, and she didn't dare ask where he'd been.

His black moods deepened with every call to Watertown. Rose wondered how long he could contain so much annoyance and rage. He would phone his mother, ramble on about his job preparing salads, and his friends at the Dunkin' Donuts, all the facets of his new life, and after the conversations he would snap at Rose about the least little thing, or drop into his chair and stare blankly at the walls.

These days he was spending most of his free time in front of the TV. She found the shows uninteresting. He usually made a comment or two during newscasts, but whenever the subject of murder came up, he went silent. He seemed to prefer the jiggle-and-leg shows on cable. She didn't complain, as long as it kept him around the house. If she interrupted his concentration, he would throw instant temper tantrums that ended as fast as they started. He slammed a potted plant on the floor, then calmly swept up the pieces. He heaved a frying pan against the kitchen wall, then finished cooking dinner. He broke dishes, a lamp, a few appliances. When Rose asked why, he said, "Rose, do you want me to break up *you*, or do you want me to break up the appliances?"

Once he raged about having three flat tires in a day. "You poor thing," Rose said. "What'd you do?"

"Threw the goddamn bike in the river," he answered.

"How'd you get home?"

"Went up the road and caught a cab." Later he replaced the dunked bike at a garage sale.

He came home one night and found that she'd broken a promise to him by drinking some wine. As he put it later, he "smacked her a few times."

Sometimes he seemed in a daze, drifting in his own space. He awoke from nightmares about Vietnam, once becoming so upset that he vomited in bed. He would jump into his clothes and tell her he was going out for a while, or she would wake up and find him gone. Where was he going at three in the morning? She didn't dare ask.

9. ARTHUR SHAWCROSS (HANDWRITTEN ACCOUNT)

There is something in Viet Nam that is still bothering me. Its got to be bad because as yet I am unable to bring it out.

I was with some guys who took a whore and put a firehose inside her and turned the water on. She died almost instantly. Her neck jump about a foot from her body.

Another time we took another prositute and tied her to two small tree's, legs to the trees, bent down. She had a razor blade inside her vagana. She was cut from her anus to her chin. Then the trees were leg go. She split in half. Left her there hanging between the trees. . . .

Viet Nam was a haunting experience in my life! Girls over there were whores from the age of 9 to 15. After that I don't know! The girl I had in Pleikue was 13 (Kie), Kontum 24 (Lyn), Daktoa 11, her name was Froggy. Clean girls. But the others were something else altogether. . . .

I remember one time in Pleikue a small little girl about 6 walked into a bunch of GI's and exploded. Another time there was a fat little girl sitting on a pile of dirt and was not moving, crying, yes; but not moving. We did not get to close but walked around her. Good thing too, she had a wire around her waist going down the crack of her ass into the ground. We had a jeep with we put a loop under her arms and a good hundred feet of rope between her and the jeep. That jeep took off and that girl came off that pile two ways, pulled and pushed. She left a 30 foot crater, lost one foot also.

There was a lot of stuff going on over there that no one reported. I bet if people were to talk to some of the people who came back, then they might begin to understand more. There is so much I can't shake. I lay here, don't sleep when sleep does come I dream. It hurts!

. . . Maybe what bugs me is those two women and this I butchered or helped with. I lay here and wake up crying. Why? All these years I've tried to forget and now it haunts me. I break out with sores from my nervousness. I did hit [illegible] in the forehead. Didn't knock him out but he did bleed pretty good. He had a toy of some kind. I thought different. . . .

That other girl in the jungle that I killed where I had taken off her head and placed it on a pole by a creek. I took her and butchered her like a steer, neck down. I had use the machetti a cut her or the body down the middle. Then cleaved the back bone and wash the blood out. Why? I wish I knew for sure! The same way you cut a deer I did to the body. Back in 1965 I had a job at the Adams Meat Market. At Adams, N.Y. just south of Watertown. N.Y. This is where I learned to butcher, 19 cows and bulls a day. . . .

I guess the only thing really that hurt was my mind, my thinking . . . I think the word is *aberration*.

10.

As Art's nightmares intensified, the couple began to bicker over sex. Rose could never be sure he would stay in bed. She had to go to work at dawn and couldn't always wait for him to return after an eruption. His phone squabbles with his mother continued. He would stomp around the apartment and punch the walls and wind up drinking coffee at the Dunkin' Donuts. When he came home, all hyped up, she would be asleep. When she awoke in the morning, he would be flopping into bed.

His sexual problems grew worse. Rose had always been patient about his difficulties and tried to help. He seemed to find it easier to blame his problems on her, complaining that she hurt him when she rolled on top. She went on a crash diet, but it didn't stop the complaints. Soon he was winning their arguments by force.

Her headaches intensified and her upper body was bruised from his blows. One night Betty Shawcross phoned while Art was out, and in desperation Rose complained that he'd slapped her face and grabbed her leg so hard that he left marks.

"Well, tell his parole officer," Betty snapped.

Rose couldn't take the risk of losing him. Instead she told the interviewing PO that they were closer than ever. She wished she knew how to improve matters, but nothing suited him lately—the apartment wasn't neat enough, the toothpaste tube wasn't rolled up, the dishes didn't shine, the furniture was off line. She could only conclude that he had some unknown personal reason for being annoyed with her. She could hardly stand the thought of losing him. So much of him was lovable and kind. Everyone in the apartment building admired him; children knocked at the door and asked if he could play; he'd made friends at the Dunkin' Donuts, including the Pakistani manager. She hoped Art wasn't bored with her; some men needed constant change, and life at 241 Alexander wasn't all that inspiring.

She wished her divorce papers would come through; maybe he would treat her better if she was Mrs. Arthur John Shawcross. Whatever was in store, she had no intention of leaving. She'd given up her job in Delhi and alienated half the members of her own family to be with a man who'd killed two children. If she'd made a mistake, she wasn't going to admit it now, even to herself. She was Art's woman for life.

11. CLARA NEAL

One rainy midnight early in '88, my phone rang and it was Art. We still weren't courtin' heavy. I went out with him a couple times after our New Year's Eve date, but it wasn't a big romance. He says, "Come and get me."

My heart just fluttered. I says, "Where you at?"

He says he's at a phone booth down on Main. It sounded like he was upset. I told my kids I'll be back in a few minutes and I drove down there and found him slumped over the guardrail by the river. His face was wet from the rain, but I could see he was crying.

I said, "Honey, what's the matter?"

He says, "Rose pulled a butcher knife on me. Said she'd cut my nuts off."*

He stayed all night, cried hisself to sleep in my arms.

After that, he'd ride over on his bike and peck at my front bedroom window to get in. He always did the shave-and-a-haircut knock. At first I think he appraised me more like a mother type than a lover or girlfriend. Even at forty-two, that's what he needed most. He'd scoot down the end of my couch, lay his head on my lap and go to sleep, me holding him jes' like you would a baby. He'd pull his shirt

* A charge that Rose vigorously denied and for which there was no substantiation.

off and I'd take a hairbrush and rub his back gently. What a boy would want from Mama!

We went to bed together, but that wasn't the main thing on his mind, or mine neither. He made sure I was happy in the sexual way, and I did him. I'll come right out and say it —he told me more than once how good I was. He said, "I've been down the road quite a while, I've been everywhere, and you're the best."

He couldn't get enough hugging, tickling, touching. One night he came here and asked me to do his back the way his grandma used to do when he was a kid. I was sitting on the couch and kicked my shoes off and he laid his head on my lap and went to sleep. Laid that way for an hour, and I scratched his back with a comb and didn't dare move. Oh, gosh, I had to go to the bathroom *so* bad. Finally I said, "Honey, you got to move. I'm *paralyzed*!"

I guess I only knowed the good side of Art. I'm gonna be plain about it—I told him, "I don't want you for just sex." I wanted something out of Art I never had: love, compassion, kindness. I got it and I give some back, too.

At first he wouldn't talk about his personal life. I would say, "Baby, why don't you talk about your family? I've told you all of my life's history."

He said, "I don't know any life's history."

When he finally did say a few things, I give him my full attention. We were out driving in my little blue Dodge Omni when he told me about hearing voices when he was a kid. He'd be off in the woods by himself, 'cause the others wouldn't play with him, and he could hear kids talking to him, and he'd look around and he was alone. He'd put his head on my shoulder and cry. He said he never understood himself and he only wished he did. Said he did some terrible things in his life. He had a son that was knocked off his trike and killed by a car when he was three—poor little fella. And Art was always a offcast when he was growing up. He said his two sisters and his brother always come first.

He told me, "Mom was pregnant when her and Dad got married." Jes' saying that made him get mad, looked like a rooster with his feathers ruffled. When he calmed down he said his mother was forced to get married and she always took it out on him. He said his father paid no attention to him and his mama was mean and locked him in a closet all day. He showed me a knot on the back of his head where she hit him. He wouldn't allow me to rub him back there 'cause it still hurt.

Tell ya hwut, he *always* seemed upset about his parents. Told me they'd think nothin' of drivin' clear to Virginia to visit his sister Donna, but they couldn't be bothered to drive to Rochester to see their firstborn. He'd say, "My mom won't come and see me, and every time I send her a gift she says it's junk. How would you feel if that was your mother?"

He said that every time he called home, his mom would get to talkin' hateful. He'd slam the fone down and beat the walls till he near broke his hands. A coupla times I saw the blood. He'd bandage his hands and ride his bike down here or call me to pick him up in my car 'cause he'd be shakin' and sobbin' so bad. Many's the night I cried right along with him.

He said, "Know why your children are so good to ya? Because they know where you are and they know they can see ya whenever they want." He said his mom didn't ever want to see him again and neither did his dad. He'd just set there talkin' and talkin' about it, shakin' his head, till I tried to change the subject. No matter what we were doing, his mom was always on his mind. And when it wasn't his mom, it was the things he saw in Vietnam.

12. ARTHUR SHAWCROSS (PSYCHIATRIC INTERVIEW)

We were on a patrol and came out of the jungle area onto a riverbank and I was walking like left point and right point. I was left point. And I still had a machine gun and one of the other point men, he only had a M-16 and walked out into the river and there were two girls in the water and from the waist up they were nude. And they must have taken a bath or what. And this guy, he walked out into the water and started talking to them and one girl reaches under the water and pulled out a long knife that had a wiggle blade and sticks him in the groin and rips him and then I just let go. I hit one girl across the thighs and one girl across here.

Q. Did they go down immediately?

A. Right.

Q. Did they jerk?

A. Oh, yeah.

Q. Convulse?

A. Yes. The first one died, the second one didn't.

Q. What happened to her? Did she fall in the water?

A. Right. And we walked out there, grabbed her and pulled her back up on the beach and the lieutenant comes out and he had an interpreter try to talk to her and she wouldn't say nothing, kept spitting at everybody. Finally the lieutenant put a forty-five to her head and shot her. . . .

Q. And what did you do with the bodies or did you just chuck them in the river?

A. Chucked them in the river. . . . They'd float downstream.

Q. And rot?

A. Most likely.

13.

Dorothy "Dotsie" Blackburn, prostitute, cocaine addict, and mother of a six-month-old boy and two older children, lunched with her sister at Roncone's Grill on Lyell Avenue, then deposited her baby with a friend and hit the streets with her black pimp and live-in boyfriend, the baby's father. It was late on the afternoon of March 15, 1988, and their welfare checks wouldn't arrive for a few days. They bought three six-packs of beer on credit and scored twenty dollars' worth of crack on Dotsie's promise to pay after turning a few tricks. Soon they were high, and Dotsie lost some of her characteristic nervous jitters. As the boyfriend recalled later, "Everything was great." Things were always great when they were high. It was their main goal in life.

Dotsie was a small-boned woman of twenty-seven, with a slender figure, brown eyes, and long brown hair. She looked petite and dainty, but she'd dealt with all kinds of men and fought her way out of bad situations. She was careful and streetwise, even when she was high. Like most Rochester prostitutes, she worked the riverside area around Lake and Lyell, a section of town marked by eyesore shops, bars, small business establishments, adult bookstores, and other evidences of urban blight.

Dotsie preferred oral sex in the belief that it would protect her from AIDS. For the same reason, she refused to date strangers, Latinos, or blacks, and she tried to maintain a clientele of "regulars." She usually performed her services in her customers' cars or in a favorite motel off Interstate 490, where she was known and protected.

At 5:15 P.M. on the blustery March day, she left her pimp and went to work on Saratoga Street around the corner from Lyell, an area where hookers and johns converged at all hours. Rochester was a city of "clean" well-paying industries like Kodak, Xerox, and Delco, and there was money to be made both on and off the street. Her boyfriend wasn't concerned when she walked off; it was business.

By 2:00 A.M., Dotsie hadn't returned to their apartment, but her thirty-eight-year-old paramour remained unperturbed. She'd been gone overnight before; sometimes one date led to another and sometimes she would get too geeked on crack and forget her address and sometimes she would totter in at dawn with money or dope hidden in her clothes or her body. On such occasions he would confiscate her holdings, often leading to fights and temporary breakups. Once he'd broken her nose and she'd walked out, but as usual the pimp and the prostitute were reunited by their community of interests—crack, beer, and their son.

When the boyfriend awoke the next afternoon and realized that Dotsie still wasn't home, he checked out the street, but none of the regulars had seen his woman since the previous night, when she'd disappeared in a late-model gray van or a brown Bronco or a compact light blue vehicle; in daylight, the street people's memories tended to be hazy. He realized that she could have tricked in all three vehicles and others. No one kept watch or score, and an enterprising prostitute might serve fifteen or twenty johns a night. And Dotsie was not only enterprising but had pressing financial needs. She owed one of her customers four hundred dollars and had been trying to avoid him and some of her other creditors.

Early in the afternoon the boyfriend took his little namesake to his sister's for safekeeping. It was unusual for Dotsie to leave her baby for such a long time, and for the first time, the father began to worry.

When three more days had passed, he conferred with Dotsie's sister Kathleen, who knew that something was seriously wrong because she was holding Dotsie's uncashed welfare check. The sister filed Missing Persons Report #91980 with the Rochester PD.

The downtown cops were acquainted with Dorothy Blackburn—she and the boyfriend had minor police records—and some of them bore a grudging admiration for her gritty professionalism. Her description was read and reread at roll calls—white female, twenty-seven, five feet, ninety-five pounds, brown hair, brown eyes, very fair, no marks or tattoos, wearing white sneakers, white socks, brown-white rabbit jacket, faded jeans, and a black sweatshirt with a hood. Her apartment on Lyell Avenue and popular hangouts like Mark's Texas Red Hots restaurant were checked. A clerk at her regular motel on I-490 said that she hadn't been around for at least a week and it was unlike her to stay away for so long.

The cops suspected foul play.

14.

A week after Dorothy Blackburn dropped from sight, parole officer Leonard DeFazio made an entry in the file of Arthur Shawcross: "Everything the same. RMW has her divorce and $100/mo. settlement. Health counseling of S noted. S states that he does not feel he needs it. However, due to the sensitivity of the case, parolee has been advised to re-contact the counselor, Gary Mount, at Genesee M.H. Center. Parolee also advises that he is going to secure driver's license."

15.

Two days later, on the morning of March 24, a crew of laborers peered into Salmon Creek in a remote part of Northampton Park, a public play area a few miles northwest of Rochester. Dorothy Blackburn had been missing for nine days and friends were convinced she was dead—"Nobody could hold Dotsie this long," one of them explained.

The work crew was checking for debris or garbage that might have clogged a culvert, but instead one of the men pointed out a mannequin covered with a layer of silt. It was fetched up against an oddly shaped chunk of concrete that appeared to be the missing home plate from the park's baseball field. The men were convinced they were looking at the latest prank by bored teenagers.

In the forty-degree weather, a light rain turned a mantling of snow to slush as the crew tried to figure out how to remove the object from the middle of the creek. The mannequin was dressed in jeans and sweatshirt, legs and feet barely submerged in the shallow winter runoff, head half concealed beneath an icy garland of weeds and brush.

One of the men produced a steel rake, caught a belt loop on the jeans, and tugged the object toward the bank. The face came into view and the workers realized they were looking at a frozen body. The woman had heavy eyebrows, full lips, dark curly hair, and slightly irregular teeth. Her left eye was shut. She wore jeans, a hooded sweatshirt, a white "Soda Pops" brand sneaker. Her navy blue top was pulled up from the beltline, giving a bare midriff effect. Except for the closed eye, there were no signs of struggle.

At the morgue, Kathy Lafleche identified the body as her sister Dorothy Blackburn, and police bore down on Dorothy's lover, partly because he was the last person to admit seeing her alive, and partly because he'd been known to beat her. When his alibis held up, they interviewed some of Dotsie's regulars: Don, a businessman whom she paged in his black pickup truck; Steve, a white male in his mid-thirties who drove a Cadillac; a nameless Canadian who wore a baseball hat, dressed like a farmer, and paid her a hundred dollars an hour to lie alongside him and play dead; Roger, who lived with his mother in a Rochester suburb; Dave, who had a big house and plenty of money and liked to get high with her and her boyfriend before she "did" him; Jim, a fifty-year-old Kodak shiftworker who allowed the pimp to drive his car while Dotsie served his needs in the backseat; and another Kodak worker who sometimes lent her money. All were cleared.

After some difficulty, the medical examiner's office determined that the tiny woman had been bitten ("multiple lacerations vaginal area, right labia minora has 3 cm vertical and 1.5 cm horizontal laceration from clitoral area. Lateral to this, laceration labia majora left of clitoris"), and probably strangled ("contusions to right supraclavicular area and hemorrhage into right neck strap muscles, consistent with manual strangulation").

Detectives reexamined the deaths of two other prostitutes, one found dead of a gunshot wound behind the Dirty & Co. bar on Lake Avenue and the other a stabbing victim, but found no apparent connection. The investigators were accustomed to dealing with men who derived sexual pleasure from punishing women; there were sadists in high and low places, and when they weren't killing or abusing females, they resembled normal adults. Prostitutes were their targets of choice. Every year a few of the three dozen women who rode the mattress circuit from Rochester to Scranton and back were badly beaten or killed. It had always been a high-risk occupation.

In years past, pimps ran the streets, but dope peddlers had taken over. Experienced cops were hard-pressed to name a single Rochester prostitute who wasn't an addict. The peddlers were a special problem because of their power; they were quicker to take offense and exact revenge, and if they didn't have a personal taste for murder, they could afford hit men. Police had a good idea what had happened to Dotsie.

16. ARTHUR SHAWCROSS (HANDWRITTEN ACCOUNT)

In December of 1987 we ask my mom and dad to come for a visit. Never came! In January we asked again. Still no one showed up. In February 1988 one Friday night I had Clara Neals car, a 1987 Dodge Omni, light blue. I was feeling OK but there was something in me that was wierd. I started to sweat. Why it was chilly outside with snow on the ground.

I drove up Lyle Ave. toward RT 31. Got as far as tent city and a girl stepped into the street in front of me. I stopped, she got in and asked me if I wanted a date. I said OK then asked where do we go. She guided me to an area behind a warehouse. I was a dummie. Going out I thought ment to a resturant or something. She laughed at that. Then she asked if I wanted to fuck! Point blank.

I was surprised for I've never done it this way. I asked how much, she said $20 for blow job and $30 for half & half. Half blow job, half screw. gave her the $30 and told her I would like to give her oral sex while she did me. She agreed.

I had my zipper down and my penis out, she took off her pants and underware, shoes and socks. Why all that I don't know. The car was real warm though. I had my penis in her mouth and I on her. It was OK for about 3 minutes then she bit me. I screamed and pulled back. There was blood all over. I was scared I thought I was going to die, I really did I grabbed my penis and screamed why did she bite me.

She said not one word but had a smile on her bloody face. So I reached over and bit into her vagina. Something tore loose. I didn't care. So now she was bleeding also. But I could not stop the pain. I grabbed her by the throat with one hand, my right and squeezed until she passed out.

I got out of the car and got some handi wipes and wrapped my self up, then zipped up. I got back in and turned her around so she was sitting up. She was breathing OK. I took her pants and tied her arms behind her. She came too and ask me what I was going to do. Mean while we were outside the city. I told her to shut up. Then she stated I was not the same person she got into the car with.

I pulled over and stopped. Grabbed her by the hair and asked her why she bit me. Because she felt like it! I got her shirt and tied her feet together. Then drove out to North Hamton Park. Pulled in by a small bridge. Turned off the engine, and sat there. This time I smacked her in the face and asked again.

I took the flash light and inspected myself. What a Bloody mess! All Miss Blackburn said was; she felt like it! I told her I won't be able to love a woman again!! Then she started calling queer, faggot and cursing me. I took off my pants and got out of the car and put snow on my penis. That cold stopped the bleeding. I put a rubber on as slowly as I could and got back in.

Now I told her she is going to be raped. All she did was laugh. Then I got mad and started to sweat real bad. Pulled her close to me and fondled her. Then whispered in her ear she was going to die, and what did she say now!

She must have been on drugs. Just smiled at me. I took her shirt off her feet and her pants off her arms then told her to get dressed. She did, then called me *little man.* I choaked her for a good ten minutes, or near as I thought. She went limp.

I sat there half the night with her. Took her out of the car and dropped her into the creek. She was face down. Watched for about a half hour, then drove away. Came back to the city and stopped at Marks on Lake Ave. Had coffee, calmed down then went back to the car.

Then I drove to a parking lot to clean up the car. Her shoes, socks, and coat were still in there. Dumped them in a trash can, minus any ID. Then went home. At daylight I cleaned the car as best I could, but still the blood was in the seat.

I was in a daze for over a week. Even Rose and Clara ask me what was wrong with me. I didn't say much to anyone. I felt I wasn't me, not the same me.

17. CLARA NEAL

I didn't know what come over him, just that he was quieter than ever and drawed into himself. Maybe if I'd known about his record, I'd suspected something, but he held that back. All I knew was he was on parole. He said he was in jail on some li'l old misdemeanor thing. I didn't know about Green Haven, didn't know he was from Watertown, didn't know about his family.

My daughter Linda told me she heard a rumor that Art killed the man that murdered his son or run over his son, one, but then lots of stories came back from Brognia Produce. I didn't know and didn't care. I loved him. I didn't know that he killed two kids and it was gonna break us up. I'd already laid myself liable by lending him my car, 'cause he still didn't have his learner's permit.

On March 25, I drove to Brognia's to pick up him and my daughter Loretta, and Art asked, Could I drive us back in town? So we drove off. Loretta and two of my little grandkids were in the back and I was sitting in the front next to Art when a cop come up behind us and flipped on the lights.

Art said, "Holy fuck, I'm fucked now." Of course I didn't know that some woman was missing or that Art ever picked up whores when he borrowed my car. He seemed too neat and clean for that. He didn't slow down right away, so I said, "Pull it over, honey. We don't want no big deal. He can't do more'n give you a ticket."

The cop wrote him up for driving without a license and improper child restraints, and I had to take over the driving.

I dropped Art off, expectin' to see him later, but that night he didn't ride over on his bike and peck on my bedroom window as usual. He dumped me. It was a long time before I found out why. That eighty-five-dollar traffic ticket got him in trouble with his parole officer for cheating on his wife and violating his parole by being with little kids. Rose raised hell, too.

So I lost Art. I cried many a night wondering what happened, but it wasn't his way to explain.

18.

By April 11, 1988, twenty-seven days after he'd killed Dotsie Blackburn, the strangler was "out of my slump," as he wrote later, and putting on another bravura performance for Gary Mount, M.S.W., the social worker who'd examined him at the Genesee Mental Health Clinic nearly nine months earlier and recommended that he read a pop study of male sexuality.

In this second evaluation, Mount seemed impressed with Shawcross's steady progress: "For one thing he is engaged to be married to his fiancée and consort and he reports that their sexual relationship is greatly improved. She has lost a great deal of weight through dieting and feels more competent so they are no longer experiencing sexual difficulty. . . . Social adjustment shows great improvement. . . . He has reestablished contact with his parents after eighteen years, has a pleasant apartment with his girlfriend and seems to have made friends. He has managed to conceal his prison past so that he is not dogged by journalists or others and is not an object of ridicule. He reports that he is doing well at his employment, is now working full time. . . . And he will soon get a raise. In brief, he has no real complaint and his coming is only in response to request of his PO."

For the benefit of the Division of Parole, the psychotherapist pointed out that "there has been no recurrence according to his report of any impulses or inclination toward the sort of behavior which landed him in prison for a number of years." This time Mount shortened his diagnosis to sexual sadism, adult antisocial behavior, and mixed personality disorder, taking the parolee's word that he no longer suffered from inhibited sexual excitement, inhibited orgasm, and secondary impotence.

Mount also mentioned the strangler's tendency to ignore certain subjects, his reluctance to answer direct questions, and the difficulty of pinning him down. It appeared that Shawcross was still "unwilling and unable to be involved in treatment at this time." But the resistance didn't keep the strangler from impressing the social worker as "genial," "convivial," "quite warm," showing "fair to good" judgment, "good" insight, and "average" intelligence.

The report concluded, "I have left it with him that he can contact me on his own initiative should he feel the need for ongoing help with any personal problems. At this time I've scheduled no further visits and do not feel he should be compelled to come."

One month later, Shawcross left his front-room apartment and walked across Alexander Street to the same Genesee Hospital to complain about the sexual difficulties that he'd concealed from Mount. The patient's main problem, according to a pair of diagnosticians, was "sexual dysfunction," as manifested by "retrograde ejaculation." The physicians recommended an aspirin a day.

When the medication failed to improve his worsening

sex life, Shawcross turned to Urology Associates of Rochester.

"He feels he does not ejaculate," said a report, which also noted "occasional dizzy spells" and low blood pressure. A staff physician reported that the patient "has strong erection and good sensation of orgasm," "scattered white cells," and "mild prostatitis."

The powerful antibiotic tetracycline was prescribed. Once again, as Shawcross reported later, nothing changed in his bedroom. He told Rose that he thought his problem might be that he was ejaculating inward, and he seemed more tense than ever.

19. FRED BROGNIA

All through that spring of '88, the guy did whatever we asked him. But he seemed to get weirder and weirder, not that I paid a hell of a lot of attention. The other workers were breaking his balls about Clara Neal, so my brother Tony went and asked him, "Art, did you fuck that old woman?"

He said, "Yep. She's as tight as a banjo string."

Tony said, "You're sick, pal." Shawcross just laughed.

Me and Tony, we'd made a lotta cop friends through the years, and whenever one showed up, Art would go way in the back, outta sight. Tony noticed it after Loretta Neal told him, "Don't you realize every time your police buddies come here, Art ain't around?"

A few days later, Loretta says, "Did you know Art was in prison?"

Tony says, "Yeah." Art told us when he first started here, but he didn't tell us what he was in for, and we didn't ask, 'cause in this line of work, when you got a good worker, mum's the fucking word.

So Loretta says, "Do ya know what he was in for?"

Tony says, "Musta been robbery or somethin'."

Loretta says, "I think he's a convicted murderer."

That about floored Tony, so he goes and confronts the guy: "What were you in prison for, Art?"

He says, "While I was in Vietnam, a drunk driver killed my wife and son, and the guy got off with only six months. I killed him and burnt down his house."

Tony was too busy to mention this to me, and a week later I just happened to ask, "Say, Art, what were you in prison for?"

"In New York City," he says, "I was working for the Mafia." I guess he thought that would impress a guy with an Italian name.

I says, "What?"

"Yeah. I killed somebody for five hundred bucks."

I says, "You must've been pretty stupid to do something like that and get caught."

He didn't say anything, so I dropped it. What the hell, he was a good worker.

Then we began to notice that a guy came in to talk to him every coupla weeks. Turned out he was the parole officer, but I could never catch the two of 'em together. It got my curiosity up, so I called a friend of mine, Charlie Militello, an investigator for the State Police. Charlie's a tough guy, a great cop—he was one of the first troopers inside Attica when they broke up the riot.

I asked Charlie, "What rights do I have to find out something about a guy working for me?"

Charlie says, "Every right in the world, Fred."

I gave him the name of Arthur John Shawcross and forgot about it. Two weeks later, in walks Charlie and another guy. I thought they were just dropping by on their lunch break to talk about hockey. We go inside my office with my brother, and Charlie asks us, "Did Art tell you what he did?"

Tony says, "He told me he killed a guy that killed his wife and son."

I go, *"What?* He told me he was a hit man in New York."

So then we knew he was lying. The investigator with Charlie says, "Do you wanna know what he *really* did?" and he spread a copy of Art's rap sheet on the desk. Oh, my God, it was a half a mile long.

I says, "Oh, shit!" I'm really pissed about this whole thing. A murderer working for Brognia Produce? I says to Charlie, "You gotta lotta fuckin' balls letting a child-killer out."

Charlie says, "Wait a minute, Fred. We didn't let nobody out. We didn't even know he was in town. The Parole Board kept it quiet."

The other cop says, "Never mind all that bullshit. What're we gonna do about this guy?"

I says, "I'm not looking for no trouble with the Civil Liberties Union or none of that bullshit, but he'll be outa here in three weeks."

April comes, the weather's breaking, and Darien Lake Theme Park's about to open, one of our biggest clients. So me and Tony, we call Shawcross in and tell him Darien Lake made a big order. We need him to peel and slice five hundred pounds of onions.

I expected him to say, "No problem" like always. But that processing room's enclosed like a vault, and he didn't like the idea of being sealed in with all those onions, so he starts to bitch.

Tony says, "Hey, pal, you don't wanna do the job, you can leave."

Art goes to work. We usually keep a big fan in the processing room, but we'd taken it out—told him it wasn't summertime yet and we never used the fan till it got hot. We shut the door and he began to feed onions through the power slicer. He'd almost finished the whole five hundred pounds when somebody come yelling to the office: "Art's leaning against the counter moaning. He's having a heart attack from the onion gas."

We called 911, put him in a chair, made him comfortable. The sheriff put oxygen in his nose and took him away.

Two weeks later he calls in and says, "The doctor says I can't work for you no more."

I tell Charlie Militello the news and he says, "We gotta keep an eye on this asshole. He's already killed two kids."

Then one of our workers sees Shawcross on Main Street, selling hot dogs from a cart, so I called Charlie back and told him. He says, "Well, he's the Rochester PD's problem now." Little did we know.

20.

Alert parole officers took note of the temporary downturn in the Shawcross family fortunes and were relieved when he quit his street job and went to work for G&G Food Service on East Main, a few blocks from his apartment on Alexander Street. He earned $6.25 an hour and his schedule was conveniently flexible; he arrived around eight or nine at night and stayed till he filled his assigned orders: making macaroni and olive and pasta salads, peeling vegetables, slicing roast beef, turkey, salami, and pepperoni, preparing bulk foods for morning delivery to stores and restaurants. Around 3:00 A.M. he biked to the Dunkin' Donuts for a snack, then went home.

By now he'd resided quietly in Rochester for eleven months, and Charles Militello and a few state troopers weren't the only lawmen who knew that a child-killer walked in their midst. Some were no more pleased than Binghamton Sergeant David Lindsay had been a year earlier.

21. SERGEANT DANIEL WOODS

Parole finally sent a flyer to the Rochester Police Department and we all saw it. I kept it in sight and made a copy. I told the younger officers, "See this picture? This guy murdered two little kids. He's out here riding his bike around, enjoying his coffee at three o'clock in the freakin' morning, and those kids are gone forever."

I told the guys to keep an eye out for him. My daughter

was eight at the time, same age as that little Karen Ann Hill. It infuriated me that he was loose. Guys like that don't change—every cop knows. They may lie dormant for a year or two, but a pedophile's a pedophile forever, and they're as common as flies.

When I worked nights I would see Shawcross at Dunkin' Donuts. He liked to talk to policemen, but I wouldn't have anything to do with him. One night he edged over toward me, and I held up my hand and said, "Don't say a word! Don't say *nothin'* to me." He just turned away, no reaction. He knew that I knew.

He talked to the regulars, mostly about fishing. He was helpful to people, anything to get on their good side. If you told him you had to wash your car, he'd be out there helpin' ya.

One night I saw him parking his bike with the fishing tackle strapped in the back. It pissed me off that this guy could be out having a good time, while the kids he murdered, they're dead and gone forever. I thought, One of these days he's gonna ride his bicycle out in front of me, and . . .

I'm not a killer, but I could see it in my mind, see him hitting the front of my van, flying up in the air. I wondered what I'd do if I ever got my chance.

22. FRED BROGNIA

Me and my brother Tony find out that Shawcross is working at G&G Food Service, up on Main. We both called, told 'em this guy's a child-killer, he don't even belong in this town. We told 'em, That guy belongs strung up by his fucking big toes.

They said he's a hell of a worker.

23.

On the next-to-last day of June 1988, Arthur Shawcross and Rose Marie Walley marked the first anniversary of their backdoor life in Rochester. They hadn't wanted to come to the Lilac City but seemed to be making the best of it, despite sexual difficulties that were clouding their relationship.

Parole officers took note of the killer's progress in another encouraging report: "Shawcross's adjustment to parole supervision to date has been most satisfactory. He has been responsive to supervision requests of the parole officer. He reports regularly and notifies the PO of any changes immediately. He works regularly . . . plans marriage within next two months."

Under "noteworthy information," the report warned: "This case is very media sensitive. A review of case folder points out the problems of adjustment in the community caused by press involvement. RPD [Rochester Police Department] is currently aware of parolee's place in the community. No repercussions have resulted to date. Nature of the crime obviously warrants special attention and supervision."

As a part of the "special attention," another psychological opinion was requested by wary parole officers, and once again the killer found himself looking at funny pictures, recounting his adventures in Vietnam, and claiming that his mother "abused" him and his aunt "fondled" him, this time to Carl Christensen, a clinical social worker and psychotherapist at Family Service of Rochester, Inc.

After two lengthy sessions, Christensen diagnosed post-traumatic stress disorder and severe adjustment problems in dealing with women, stemming at least in part from "childhood incest and sexual abuse." Like other clinicians before him, he saw no danger signs or pressing problems, "no particular symptoms, discomforts or behavioral difficulties which would benefit from mental health treatment."

Christensen reported to the Division of Parole, "I find

that Art is a well controlled and fairly stable individual. Although he continues to exhibit some discomfort or flashes related to anger, he is able to manage these episodes extremely well.

"The one feature which continues to be present in his current functioning which was probably predominant in his past is his general inclination or personality style of dealing with guilt or bad feelings by becoming angry rather than becoming or experiencing serious discomfort, depression or low self-esteem.

"Given his history of childhood and early adult difficulties, traumas and anti-social behavior, it is logical that Art has developed elaborate and somewhat dysfunctional defenses in managing his feelings. However, this functioning style does not appear to present any current emotional or behavioral difficulties and Art does not have any particular motivation to pursue treatment at this time. Consequently I see no need for pursuing counseling with Art at this time."

The date was June 29, 1988. Psychotherapy wouldn't be discussed again until much too late.

IX

BODY COUNT

A. . . . Certain women ticked me off.

Q. And that is when you gave them the death sentence?

A. If you want to call it that.

—Arthur Shawcross

1.

On July 8, 1989, Anna Marie Daly Steffen, an emaciated twenty-seven-year-old cocaine addict, was arrested by Rochester police for prostitution. The ninety-five-pound woman was pregnant and wore a bright maternity dress. In a hospital emergency room, she was found to be dilated and in poor general health. At her insistence, doctors released her and warned that she could go into labor at any time. An attendant noted that she left with "some guy."

Anna Marie, known as "Ann," had a cameo face and the typical history of a drug-drunken prostitute. She'd spent most of her childhood caring for a paraplegic half sister, Tina Louise, born with spina bifida. Relatives recalled how the teenaged Ann had bathed and dressed the stricken child, played with her, pushed her to school in a wheelchair. After the sister died of gangrene in 1980, Ann seemed to lose direction. She could never discuss the death. A quiet woman, she married and bore two children but became estranged from her husband and family after she was "overwhelmed by drugs," as another sister put it. From then on, her life was a succession of beatings by pimps, risky encounters, suicide threats, comas, bad trips, nightmares.

When Ann became pregnant for the last time, she hired a voodoo woman to chant over her abdomen, then announced to friends that she intended to sell the child for five thousand dollars to pay her debts. With some degree of accuracy, she raved, "Everyone's against me." She was last seen soliciting customers in the prostitution corridor.

At first, no one was concerned when she failed to return

to the small apartment on Gladys Street that she sometimes shared with a pimp or a boyfriend or fellow prostitutes. A long time back she'd lost contact with her relatives and ex-husband, and her street friends figured that she'd gone away to have her baby in peace. She might even have returned to the circuit—Binghamton, Scranton, Syracuse, and back to Rochester—to earn some quick money to pay off her pusher, a routine procedure.

After several weeks, a rumor circulated that she'd died in jail of AIDS. Someone said that she'd finally carried out one of her frequent threats to kill herself with a heroin hot shot. In the drug-hazed street world, no one was even sure when she'd disappeared. A friend reported seeing her scurrying across the Driving Park Bridge over the Genesee River, but he couldn't pinpoint the exact date. Her face was red and she was crying; she yelled that someone was after her. No one bothered to check the story or report her disappearance. Prostitutes were frequently roughed up. They changed addresses. Sometimes they disappeared. It was part of the job description.

Two months passed. Around 6:00 P.M. on September 9, Hector Maldonado, a short, swarthy man with luxuriant black wavy hair, climbed down the steep slope of the Genesee River Gorge to search for deposit bottles so he could buy cigarettes. In an hour he found eight bottles, good for forty cents at the nearby Topps Supermarket.

On his way back up the embankment, Maldonado spotted something on a narrow ledge below the rim of the gorge, under a canopy of maple trees, weeds and ferns. He worked his way over to check out a dark green plastic garbage bag that was covered with sticks and chunks of black asphalt. A leg bone protruded. He thought it was the remains of a deer until he noticed the clothing.

The body was so decomposed that technicians couldn't detect the cause of death. A rock about fifteen inches in diameter covered a hank of medium-length brown hair that appeared to have been ripped from the skull. The eyes were gone from their sockets and most of the skin had rotted away in the summer heat. A few gnarled brown ribs lay in disarray. A white tank top with red shoulder straps was bunched around the left wrist bone and a pair of Calvin Klein jeans had been pulled down to the right ankle and turned inside out. An unbuckled brown belt was looped through the jeans. Fifteen feet from the body, police found a pair of blue flip-flop sandals.

The body was left on the steep ledge overnight and the crime scene was reworked the next morning by crime lab technicians, detectives, and top brass. In Rochester, eight or ten missing women usually appeared on police blotters at any given time, but this summer the number stood at eleven, almost all of them prostitutes, and four others had died of violence. Police began the tedious job of eliminating suspects.

2. ARTHUR SHAWCROSS (PSYCHIATRIC INTERVIEW)

I walked up Lake Avenue toward—back toward the city, and I get up there by the Princess Restaurant and, ya know, a girl seen me. She recognized me before. I seen her before, and she says, "You want a date?" and I says, "All I got is twenty dollars." She says, "Well, I'm not doing nothing for the rest of the day." I said, "All right."

She said—we went across behind the YMCA over there and went back down to the Driving Park Bridge and, ya know, she says, "Go down this way," and there was an area where there was some construction. A field was all mowed, right? There was an area with tall grass, ya know, maybe four, five feet high, ya know, overlooking the river itself. . . .

She start doing oral sex, ya know, and I got an erection, right, ya know? Then we started having sex itself, intercourse, right? And, ya know, some kids showed up, ya know. There was four, five kids coming down the trail that we came down, and they were going down to the riverbank itself, and she says, "What's all that noise?"

I says, "Don't move," right? "There's kids maybe twenty

feet from us. Don't say nothing,'' ya know? And she gets up on her knees, right? And she sees the kids and she says—ya know, she was going to—she wanted to get up, get her clothes on, get out of there, and I says—I had to pull her back down, says, ''Just keep quiet,'' ya know? Because I was panicking when—the parole officers, they want me—I ain't got no clothes on, kids around. Ya know? That's the only thing I thought of, and the more she, ya know, made—ya know, struggle around, the more I panicked, ya know? And I told her, I says, ''Keep quiet,'' ya know? And she says—just kept telling me, ''Let me up,'' right, and I just laid across her.

I says—ya know, I says, I can't explain it, I says, ''We just can't have these kids see what we're doing,'' ya know? And she says, ''You don't let me up, I'm going to scream,'' ya know? And at that moment the same thing happened to me happened with the first one: I started sweating, ya know? Water just rolling right out of me, and I panicked, and I just grabbed her by the throat, ya know? Just held and squeezed her until she quit.

Then I took and I rolled her off—we were about maybe four foot from the edge of the cliff, and I rolled her over there behind a bush. . . .

Q. And did you say that you were concerned that if you were found naked around kids, your parole would be violated for exposing yourself?

A. Yeah. That's—yeah, that was the only thing on my mind.

3.

At the approach of their second Christmas in Rochester, Arthur Shawcross and his roommate decided to send his mother a nice gift. After a year and a half of freedom, he still hadn't given up on the idea of a reunion, either in Watertown or Rochester, and he hoped that an offering might improve his chances. For her part, Rose thought a gift would help to mellow the stormy mother-son relationship. She was tired of seeing Art cry after talking on the phone.

To Art, nothing in the Salvation Army secondhand shop seemed good enough. "This?" he said as he discarded a saltshaker and pepper mill. "For *my* mom?" He didn't approve of a single item in their price range.

They finally settled on a silver dish that they couldn't afford. At home, Art polished it to a high gloss and sent it off to Watertown between sheets of soft white tissue.

A few nights later he put down the phone and dug his knuckles into his eye sockets. "What's the matter?" Rose asked. "Didn't she get the dish?"

Art nodded.

"What'd she say?"

"She said, 'If you're gonna buy something, buy something new.' " Then he stomped out of the apartment.

4.

The Monroe County medical examiner spent two months studying the skimpy remains found in the Genesee Gorge and decided that the cause of death was "probably asphyxia." He couldn't be positive because the neck tissue had rotted away.

Detectives proceeded on the theory that the victim was another prostitute, but they couldn't match the body with anyone on their lists of missing persons. They checked dental records and physical descriptions till they'd run out of possible local victims. A statewide canvass produced 138 possible matchups; 112 were eliminated by using a narrower age range; of the remaining 26, 22 were eliminated after police obtained more information. That left 4, and dental records ruled them out one by one.

Frustrated officials hired a forensic anthropologist, William C. Rodriguez III, to mold a clay face around the carefully preserved skull found in the gorge. A wig and plastic eyes were added, and photographs of the likeness were sent to the media.

After a picture of the reconstruction appeared in the flagship newspapers of the Gannett chain, the *Rochester Times-Union* and the *Democrat and Chronicle,* a fifty-year-old man called from his home in the nearby town of Albion to tell police that the head might be his daughter's. Dental records confirmed that the victim was Anna Steffen. The father told police that he hadn't seen her since Christmas 1988, thirteen months earlier, and hadn't reported her missing because she moved often and he didn't have her latest address. He said that Anna had been involved in drug dealings and probably had been killed by a dealer or a pimp.

The woman's powdery bones and a lock of her brown hair were buried in the family plot near Naples, New York, alongside the coffin of the paraplegic sister, Tina Louise, whom Anna Steffen had nursed and loved till death.

5. ARTHUR SHAWCROSS (PSYCHIATRIC INTERVIEW)

I got involved with a woman who, ya know, lives on Clinton Street, ya know, and she pressured me, ya know? She wants me to live over there. I said, "No, I'm living with Rose," ya know, and I told her, "I'm on parole," ya know, and I says, "I got to do what my parole officers—they told me I got to live here. This is where I'm going to stay," ya know? A couple times I was riding home from work, and she forced me off the road with the car coming down that hill by Mount Hope by the cemetery, ya know? She forced me off the road, and I went right over a hedge, ya know, messed up the bike. . . .

Q. Why was she doing this to you?

A. She wanted me. . . . And I broke it off finally, about six–eight months, ya know? Then she started coming around again, ya know, and I don't know, I tried to, tried to tell Rose I want to be a Mormon. She says, "They don't do that no more." Sure they do!

Q. Now who's the woman that you're describing?

A. Clara Neal.

6. CLARA NEAL

All through that winter, '88 and '89, I was just sick from missin' Art. Every now'n again, he'd phone and ask how I was doing, but he never came around. Then he called one night in late spring. The snow and ice was still on the ground. He asked how I was getting on and I just taken the bull by the tail and I says, "When am I gonna get to see ya?"

Every time I said something like that he'd fob me off, but this time he says, "Well, I'm goin' fishin' in the morning."

"Yeah?" I says. "Where at?"

He told me he'd be at the outflow at Charlotte, near where the Genesee River run into Lake Ontario a few miles north of town. So when I got off work I drove down there in my little Dodge Omni. It was bitter cold; they was ice all around but the outflow was warm and the perch swam up there from the lake. I rode by twice and didn't recognize Art from the way he was dressed: a big old coverall, waders, a heavy coat. He recognized my car and walked up toward the road.

I got out and I said, "Why don't you hide yourself a little more?"

He says, "Well, it's cold. You got the car warm?"

"Yep."

"I'd like to get in there and get warm."

"You know where it's at."

He put his fishing gear away and we both got in. We set there and talked and talked and *talked.* So it started all over again.

After that day, we saw each other four, five times a week.

Went out to dinner at the Ponderosa on Ridge Road at least once a week. I was always so excited I couldn't eat. He said, "God, I take you out to a good dinner and you eat like a mouse."

I told him how much it hurt to go all those months without seeing him, and he said, "Don't let me hear not one word more. That was yesterday and this is today."

He told me he didn't want to make love to Rose now that he had me. We'd drive past a pretty girl and he'd say he had all he needed sittin' right next to him in the car. He was in love with me, not Rose, and love goes deep. She used to tell him she loved him and he said he couldn't handle all that pressure. He'd just holler, "Quit saying that!" A real man don't like gush.

He worked nights and Rose worked days, so they had a hard time getting their bedroom life worked out. She liked to get on top of him—"ride the pony." If he got home early from work and tried to sleep, she'd flop on him and just maul maul *maul*. And he hated to be wakened. He'd tell her, "Lemme sleep till I wake up. Then we can do it." But she never wanted to wait that long. He'd get so mad at her he'd come over to my house and I'd have to gentle him down.

Art always drove my little Omni. When I was low on money, he'd take it to the Thrifty station and fill it up. He called it *our* car. I had the radio set on 92 FM, country and western, but he preferred soft dinner music—he called it "orchestra music"—so I told him, "Any time you're driving my car, if you want to change the damn thing, change it." But instead of changing it, he was glad to listen to my station. He was always talking about getting aholt of some money, winning the lottery, this raffle or that raffle, and 92 FM had a deal where they call off serial numbers on dollar bills and you win five thousand dollars. So Art took to carrying a wad of dollar bills around in his wallet and whenever they'd call off a winning number, he'd stop and check. Sometimes I helped him. I figured, What the heck, five thousand bucks might take us to West Virginia for good.

He'd come over to my house early every morning, drive

me to work, then borrow the Omni for errands and fishin' and stuff all day. Friday he was off; he'd make an excuse to Rose and come pick me up. One time me and my daughter Loretta had taken him home from work and he invited us right inside his apartment and there was Rose, big as life, didn't suspect a thing. Then he give a party and me and Loretta were invited.

After he kept showing up at his apartment house with my car, Rose began to wonder. He told her we were just good friends, so to throw her off we started takin' her along with us once in a while.

I guess she was willing to accept just about anything by then, 'cause he was turning hard against her. The things he said! She had a tendency to mumble, not open her mouth wide enough when she talked, and he'd say, "Rose, speak up so I can hear ya." Then he'd say, "Get the mush out or don't talk at all."

A couple of times he went too far. He told her, "Rose, me and my friend Clara are going out and you cain't go."

I said, "No, no, I ain't gonna have it that way, Art. We're friends, me and Rose."

I took her aside and said, "Tell ya hwut, Rose. When I come over to pick him up, you have your coat on, 'cause you're comin' along!"

Sometimes we taken Rose fishin'. We'd go down in that Genesee Gorge, pretty a place as any you'd see in Clay County, and right in the middle of a big city. Rose didn't say much, just slumped down in the seat so far that you couldn't hardly see her. She was always freezing to death. Wouldn't talk or nothin', acted annoyed. But she never made no accusations about me and Art, 'cause if she ever climbed my frame, I'd of climbed right back, and the toughest damned dog'll come out on top. I'll say it plain: whichever bitch whips the other one, that's the one that gets the man. Lucky for her, it never come to that.

Art wanted to dump her, but he couldn't because he was paroled in her custody. That's what he told me, anyway. He said she was just somebody to write to in prison, but now she was tying him down. Sometimes she wouldn't even talk to him and it upset him and he'd come over to my place. He hated to be alone. A man likes attention. He'd be here an hour or two and he'd jump up from my sofa and he'd say, "Oh, my God, she's gonna be home before I have supper ready."

I said, "Let *her* cook."

He'd already be out the door. He was afraid of her in a way. He always said he was just holding out till April 1990 when his parole was over and him and me were gonna head south for good. Where? Unbeknownst. Wherever the wheels stopped. Maybe that would be Clay County, maybe someplace else I'm not sayin'.

By this time I had an idea what he did in Watertown way back when. The workers at Brognia had started the rumor of it, and one of my sons came home and said, "Mom, Art was in prison for murdering a little girl."

I told him to shut up, I didn't want to know. I loved Art Sharcross at first sight, so I never brought it up. Neither did he. It was the past. He served his time. Why cain't they let the man live in peace?

Me and Art, we went to yard sales that summer of '89. He loved old things, said they reminded him of his time in Sharcross Corners. He loved antiques and old cars. He was an outdoors type of person, and we were always hunting or fishing or going on cookouts. Didn't go to movies or concerts. Sometimes he'd just set around my house and read, or I'd scratch his back till he fell asleep. We had sex maybe once a week, but no kinky stuff. He asked me a couple times to lick him, but I said no, not as long as you're living with Rose. We did it the usual way and we satisfied each other every time. *Every time!*

June six was his forty-fourth birthday. Rose was working, so I threw him a little party at my house. I bought him cake and ice cream and we drink a bottle of Niagara wine cooler. I saved the bottle and I'll have it forever. He loved his birthday card. Little 'membrances like that meant a lot to him, especially since his mom told him to stay away from Watertown.

I began to notice he never showed up on Wednesdays, and I asked how come. He told me that was Irene's day. I thought, Who the hell's Irene? Turned out she was an old lady, ninety-two, lived in a high-rise apartment downtown.

"Clara," he says to me, "Grandma Irene is like a mother to me." Said he met her through the visiting home nursing deal when Rose went there to clean. Every Wednesday Art would go up to Irene's apartment on the twentieth floor. She'd stretch him out on the couch, put his head in her lap, and set there and comb his hair till he fell asleep. He told me if he didn't show up, she'd call and ask where he was. And if he was feeling down in the dumps, she'd cheer him up.

Most people get a little antsy around old folks, but Art, he liked 'em. He even give Irene a couple of rings he bought off a guy at North Clinton and Main. Rose said he was always doing favors at the old folks' home, give 'em anything they wanted. He brought a bag lady home one time, fed her, put her up right in his own apartment! That's the one that they never found her head.

7. ARTHUR SHAWCROSS (PSYCHIATRIC INTERVIEW)

One of the women that lives on the street, Dorothy, she came—she would come clean our apartment, ya know? I give her three, four dollars an hour, ya know, just clean the apartment. I'd go to work, Rose go to work, she'd stay there, clean the apartment, ya know? Everything's all right for a while, ya know? Then she start stealing the laundry money: quarters. We had a washing machine downstairs, we'd wash clothes and dry them down there.

One day she came in, she's all dirty, and she says, ya know, she was sleeping over here by the river under the trestle, the loop, and she's all dirty, and she says, "Can I take a bath?" And I said, "All right, go take a bath."

And she wanted to know if I'd take her clothes downstairs and wash them. So when I came back upstairs, right? she's sitting in the living room, no clothes on, no—not even a towel, just sitting there smoking a cigarette, no concern at all, ya know? So I went and got a blanket. I said, "Here. Put this around you."

She said, "What are you, nervous?"

I said, "I ain't nervous."

I took just the blanket, threw it back in the closet, ya know? I was sitting there talking to her, ya know? Then we just started a little affair there. It went on for about maybe two months. And one day I was down, I went down usually when the fish start biting in the river. I was down there every day, and I was catching bass and different things, and I went down there one morning and Dorothy's down there, ya know?

She says, "Where're you going?"

I says, "Well, I'm going across this little creek here," part —an offshoot of the river and onto an island. I went over there, and I take the bicycle I had and I chain it to a tree, and somebody had a little small camp set up there, and somebody went in there with a chain saw and cut up one of the logs.

And we're sitting on the ground, talking, and I told her, I says, "You got to quit stealing money out of the house." I says, "When you clean the house, I give you four dollars an hour, right?" Ya know?

I says, "That ain't enough, if you want more." I says, "I'll go get somebody else," ya know? Then she knew, says to me that she's going to tell Rose that we got an affair, right? And I just got peed off, ya know? I just picked up a—one of the pieces of cut lumber, a log. I just swung on her, ya know? And she dropped. And that's—I started sweating again, ya know? Same thing: the brightness, the—the no sound, closeness, and that's—ya know, I just picked her up, carried her over behind one tree that was rotted out, and just laid her down in the high grass off the trail. And I took her clothes and shoes and stuff, put them—laid them over there beside her and stayed a while down there because I didn't believe what happened.

And that same day, not even five, ten minutes after I put her over there, somebody else was on the island, and we—I didn't know it, ya know? He come right up the trail ten feet from me, didn't even see me, just kept right along.

Q. How were you feeling then?

A. I was—bad panic, ya know? Crying. And I stayed down there most of the day.

Q. With her?

A. Yeah. And I went home, and I just pushed it away like it didn't happen. And another time—another—maybe a couple weeks later—I say it was over a month later, went down—and I been down there every day in another area—but went down there, and you could smell it from the island, right? Ya know? Because you get a lot of dead salmon and fish around there, something else, and I just seen like a skeleton there, and the skull was all cracked in, and I just took a stick and picked up the skull and threw it in the river and then just left out of there.

Q. . . . Did you have to weight it down or did it sink?

A. No. It was—the water was pretty fast. It must have went probably thirty feet, and it float, and just went under.

Q. Now you mention that you had taken her clothes off—over and put them by her?

A. Yeah.

Q. What—you didn't mention that her clothes were off.

A. We were fooling around before that.

Q. You were having sex with her . . .

A. Yeah.

Q. . . . Before you got into the discussion about the money?

A. Yeah.

Q. Had you both been naked at that point?

A. Yeah.

Q. So when you hit her, you were stark naked?

A. Uh-huh.

Q. And as soon as she was down and you saw that she was . . .

A. Blood coming out of her ear—out of the ear and the corner of one eye.

Q. That's when you started to sweat all over and everything changed? Was Rose home when you returned from that?

A. No. . . .

As in the case of Anna Marie Steffen, no one reported the homeless woman missing.

8. LINDA NEAL

When my mom talked about Art, she left out a few things. Some she ditn't know; some she knew and pretended she ditn't. She had such a good West Virginia heart, and she loved Art so much it made her blind. But me—I seen him plain, and it was scary.

I noticed that he took an interest in little boys, bought 'em presents, tried to take 'em places. He offered to take one of my nephews sledding, and he was always interested in my little sons—he'd watch cartoons and play with them for hours. Liked to wrassle with them, but he always got too rough. I'll say it right out: he bit my fourteen-year-old son on the nipple on my mother's kitchen floor, and he sat on my oldest son till the boy coultn't hardly get his breath. I told my mom to make him stop, 'cause I was scared to tell him direct. I ditn't like him or trust him.

He was always after my sister Loretta's three-year-old son, Roy, told Loretta he wanted to have a relationship with her and take care of Roy, but she woultn't have nothing to do with Art 'cause he put her in mind of our dad with his big stomach and all. That was before Art started seeing our mother; Mom thought him and Loretta were just friends. But even after Mom and Art started going out, he'd sneak over to Loretta's house and try to do sick things with her, try to push his weight on her just like he did with me.

The first time he hit on me was in the summer of '88. He'd started killing, only we didn't know it. I picked up an abandoned box spring and mattress from in front of a furniture store and called Mom to help me get it into the house. She showed up with Art, and when we got the stuff upstairs he threw me on the bed and jumped on top. I fought, I turned my head away, kicked at him, but he was strong. I don't know why my mom and my sister-in-law stayed downstairs; they must've heard all the racket.

When I finally broke free and ran downstairs, they were laughing. I said, "It's not fuckin' funny."

Art says, "Let's go back upstairs and try that bed out."

"No way," I says. "I'm not going near you till you leave."

That seemed to turn him on, and from then on he went after me every chance he got. We'd be riding in my mom's car and he'd try to grab me by the crotch. With my mom sitting next to him! He'd grab my butt or my breasts and squeeze so hard it hurt. It ditn't matter who was around—my mom, my kids. He pinched my nipple at my mom's house and I got mad and I said, "Don't ever fuckin' do that again." He gave me a dirty look, but after that he stopped bothering me. After that he just said a lot of gross shit to me: "You're Kentucky Fried Chicken, finger-lickin' good. . . ."

My mom thought he was kidding around, but I knew better. There was something wrong with that man, something I ditn't understand and my mom ditn't *want* to understand. It wasn't just that he was a badass, because he could be nice, too. He could do something *so* nice, and then while you're thanking him he'll stick his hand up your dress. It was like he coultn't stop himself.

That man never acted right. He had a violent streak a mile wide, and he hated women. He told my son Stephen that he killed a Vietnamese lady and cut her from neck to crotch. Stupid thing to be telling a kid, Stephen being emotionally disturbed and all. My son kept that story to himself for months; he coultn't bring himself to repeat it 'cause it scared him so bad.

Art ditn't know that we'd heard about his crimes from the grapevine at Brognia's, so he never stopped bullshitting us about how he had to kill the guy that killed his son. My mom ditn't want to hear any different. She was one of Art's worst victims, only she'd never admit it. I never seen him hug her or kiss her or nothing like that. She talked about their big love, the big romance, but he ditn't show one sign of affection or warmth. She was lonely when he come along, that's all. Mostly he just sat around her house and watched the kids out of them mean green eyes. Like he was looking to pounce.

After a while I found out what was going on in my mom's car and bedroom. He bit my mother. Not love bites—*hard*! I saw the marks on her breasts and upper arms and inner thighs. I saw him pinch her so hard she almost cried, and I saw him bite, too. From the first times she ever went out with him, she carried black-and-blue marks, bite marks, pinch marks.

Whenever I said anything, my mom swore he never laid a finger on her. She said he was just horsing around and ditn't mean nothing.

I got so upset, I told her to fuckin' forget about him. She giggled and said, "Cain't do that!" Then she kinda grinned and said, "I know what's in store and you don't," like the two of 'em had a secret. He kept telling us how much he hated his wife Rose, but I notice he didn't get no divorce.

To be plain about it, all that son of a bitch ever did was use and abuse my mom. What he wanted was somebody to pinch and bite and beat on and give him free use of a car. I guess it was getting too hard to find women on a bike.

9.

Arthur Shawcross marked the second anniversary of his arrival in Rochester by visiting his ninety-two-year-old friend Irene Kane on St. Paul Street and falling asleep during a back rub. Refreshed by his nap, he cooked dinner for his partner Rose at their studio apartment, then treated Clara Neal to an hour of sex in the backseat of her Dodge Omni, parked near a favorite fishing hole in the Genesee Gorge. As usual, he couldn't reach a climax.

Toward midnight, he took Clara home and then drove her car to the Lake-Lyle area. This time he found a cliché prostitute with a heart of gold; when she failed to satisfy him, she waived her fee. He calmed himself over coffee at the Dunkin' Donuts, chatting with a few of the regulars. As he explained later, it was just another typical evening in the summer of 1989.

To his neighbors, Shawcross was beginning to come across as an oddball with an unusual interest in women. He stared at females and seemed obsessed with breasts. The apartment house manager, Yvonne LaMere, hadn't spoken to him since the day he'd mistaken her friendship for a sexual invitation. Friends like Silla Rossler and Susan Ristagno were giving him shorter shrift. He'd made advances to Susan and once tried to nuzzle her lap with his face. He griped about his home life, complained that his "old lady" didn't turn him on and he hadn't enjoyed sex in months.

Theresa Lamanna, a friend of a friend, visited the brownstone apartment building and while walking home in the evening discovered that she was being followed by a man on a bike. She was relieved to see that it was good old Art. He invited her to go fishing with him, then asked if she knew that pinching female breasts could cause cancer. He wondered if he might check hers on the spot. She declined and hurried away.

He even made some prostitutes nervous. There was murder in the air, and a working girl couldn't be too careful. He usually called himself "Mitch" or "Joe" and employed a blunt approach. Most johns and streetwalkers spoke in euphemisms—"dates," "tricks," "going out"—but Shawcross would say, "Hey, you wanna go to the river and fuck?" He didn't seem to understand that a minimum of politesse was expected, even on the street.

One woman, mindful of the fact that the pregnant body of Anna Steffen had recently turned up in the gorge, told him that she didn't conduct business near the river.

"Joe" asked, "Well, how about the used-car lot across the street?"

The woman told him that a backseat adventure would cost fifty dollars. "Joe" replied that the price was too high and pedaled away on a bike with a fishing rod protruding from a rear basket.

Another prostitute treated him in a friendly manner and found him to be a reasonable client. Later she described their first date in a police statement: "I was working Jones Park, right on the corner of Jones Avenue and North Plymouth. I was approached by a light metallic blue compact vehicle with bucket seats. The driver was a male white, with blue to green eyes. I asked him if he was a cop, of course. He told that he wasn't a cop. He asked me if I was a cop, and I said no. And I asked him if he wanted to date and he said yes.

"I got in the car and we settled on the price, which was fifty dollars, which was for a blow job. That was all he was going to get for that price. We went behind the Mapledale Party House. He paid me up front, it was COD. I started to get busy and things were going pretty slow. That is when he told me that he sometimes had a problem getting it up. Those were his words.

"I said, 'That's all right, baby, because I won't have no problem getting it up'.

"Then it went, and we went. And we left.

"While I was with him, he stated to me that his name was Joe and I asked him what he did for a living and he told that he worked at G&G Food Service."

The prostitute dated the man four or five times and said she never felt threatened; he was just another john named Joe.

10. ROSE MARIE WALLEY

Art and I finally decided to get married. He invited his mother to our wedding, and they talked back and forth on the phone. She told me we shouldn't be in such a hurry. I thought, A *hurry*? It was August '89 and we'd been together for two years and wrote letters for years before that. She said, "Why don't you wait till he's off probation?"

Art took the phone and I heard him tell her that he loved her. When he put down the phone he was near crying. I got it out of him that she told him to wait till him and I could "start over." Well, wasn't that what we were doing?

He said she told him, "You'll have a second chance. You can go anywhere and start a new life." She also reminded him to never come back to Watertown.

He was so upset, he said, "Well, if she's gonna be that way I'm not gonna bother mailing her no invitation."

Then she turns around later and says, "I don't have to get you guys a wedding present 'cause you didn't invite us to the wedding." That was her excuse for not sending nothing.

Art had our place decorated two weeks before the wedding. The lady upstairs' daughter made us a nice layer cake, two tiers.

We were married outdoors in front of the courthouse and Art took some nice pictures. He wore a nice white shirt and I wore my best dress and we each had a nice ring. We'd sent out a lot of invitations, but nobody showed up except my daughter's boyfriend and his mom. Art made a big spread, done most of the cooking himself. Ended up, he give it all away.

11.

Before she traded her health for cocaine, Patricia Ives bore a slight resemblance to the actress Julia Roberts in *Pretty Woman*, the story of a sanitized Hollywood whore who romanced and won her wealthy suitor in a world devoid of herpes, AIDS, syphilis, gonorrhea, vicious pimps, and killer drugs. In high school, Patty had been a slender five-two, weighed 110 pounds, with dark eyes and blond hair. She read poetry and talked about becoming a writer. Friends described her as "gentle, kind, loving," if a little oversexed. She was also naive. "Like the streets could swallow her up," said another Rochester prostitute, "and they did."

Patty discovered drugs at sixteen and dropped out of school. From then until her death, she was preoccupied with getting high. Married briefly, she worked as an "exotic dancer," appearing nude and inserting foreign objects into her vagina to titillate the audience into throwing money. Between numbers, she performed oral sex through holes in the wall of her dressing room. When she was too debilitated to work, her pimp, "Ratface Billy," a burglar by trade, shot her up and shoved her into the street. She gave birth to a cocaine-addicted son who was placed in the care of county authorities. Every few months she was jailed for prostitution or dope.

She made frequent attempts to clean up, joined AA, went through drug rehabilitation three times, but always returned to the life. Said her mother, "They wave bye-bye at the door of the rehab center and don't do any follow-up. She goes right back to where she came from, and when everybody around her is using, it's hard to resist the temptation."

At twenty-five, Patty Ives was a walking skeleton, ragged and unkempt, with long, dirty hair, a sliced-bread complexion, and ragged needle tracks from her elbows to the backs of her fingers. She'd become known as "Crazy Patty" because she couldn't seem to shut up. She was believed to have AIDS and perhaps herpes. A front tooth was missing and another was rotten. Once regarded as bright, she was now described by a friend as dull, stupid—"her brain's burnt out."

Crazy Patty disappeared on Friday, September 29, two months to the day after the homeless Dorothy Keeler had vanished from the neighborhood of the Shawcross apartment on busy Alexander Street. Ives had been missing for two weeks before Ratface Billy reported her absence. Liz Gibson, one of the street's most outspoken prostitutes, theorized that the pimp had overdosed her and dumped the body. Several times he'd injected Patty with heavy hits of cocaine, trying to make her work around the clock. Police agreed with Gibson's theory and scheduled an interrogation with the man whose street name referred both to his feral countenance and his willingness to "snitch off" his friends.

Ratface Billy told a detective that his woman had gone out to do drugs in an apartment at the old Jewish home off Hunting Park, then left for work. He hadn't seen her since. She sometimes disappeared for two or three days, but always checked in so he wouldn't worry. But this time he hadn't heard a word.

Later it developed that a passerby had been the last to see the missing woman, but the witness didn't know the significance of his sighting and made no report. The man told police that he'd been driving past the corner of Lake and Driving Park at about 7:30 P.M. on Friday, September 29, when he noticed a prostitute of his acquaintance walking alongside a white male who was riding a bike with balloon tires. Fishing rods protruded from baskets in the rear. The cyclist parked his bike behind the YMCA and followed the woman through a hole in the fence behind the tennis court. The onlooker presumed they were going into the bushes for a quick "date" and drove on by.

12. ARTHUR SHAWCROSS (PSYCHIATRIC INTERVIEW)

I was down fishing and came up toward Lake Avenue from Driving Park, and on the corner . . . there was a girl there, and, ya know? She says, ya know, she seen me before, says, "Let's go over there in the bushes," ya know? I didn't have two dollars in my pocket, and I says, "Maybe the weekend . . ."

So Friday morning after I got paid, about eight o'clock in the morning, right? I went home, changed clothes, had shorts on. I went down to the river about nine in the morning . . . puttered around a while, then came up about ten, ten-thirty, and the girl was up on the bridge, and she says, "Well, you ready to go up in the bushes?"

I said, "All right," ya know? She wanted thirty and all I had was twenty-five. And we're up there behind the Y, and, ya know, we're making out, having intercourse, and a bunch of kids are behind the swimming pool area over there running around in the grass, and she said, "What's all the noise out there?" You couldn't see, ya know? The tree came down within a foot of the ground, ya know? All leaves on it, and I told her, I says, "Well, I got to get dressed." I said, "We got to leave out of here," right? And, ya know, she grabbed ahold of me, says, "Not yet," ya know?

So we continued doing what we was doing. Then, about four, five kids chasing a volleyball or something over there got near the tree, ya know, and I tried to hide her with myself up against the fence as much as possible, ya know? And something happened. At that moment I'm paying attention to the kids, right? And she's going through my wallet, right? Ya know? And I just got paid. She's got everything in her hands, ya know?

So I grabbed it. I said, "What're you doing?" Ya know? And I figured she's on drugs or something, and I just panicked. She didn't scream, didn't holler, didn't struggle, didn't fight.

13.

Saturday, October 21, came up rainy, cloudy, slightly windy, the temperature in the low forties. Three men from Pennsylvania trudged down the steep sides of the Genesee Gorge to fish for spawner salmon. The trio splashed through shallow water and across a string of rocks to the brushy, five-acre Seth Green Island, and set about gathering firewood against the chill.

Just off the well-worn trail, they found what a policeman described later as "a buncha bones in clothes." The bones lay in the fetal position, knees bent, and were nearly hidden by a canopy of weeds and small maple branches just off a narrow trail. They appeared to be the remains of a woman. Her jeans were unzipped and pulled down to her thighs. Three pullovers encased an assortment of upper-body bones, including a fractured rib. An untied pair of reddish-brown low-heel shoes lay under weeds a few feet to one side. There was no ID and no head.

The skeleton was taken to the medical examiner's office, and police enlisted the aid of twenty-five Explorer Scouts and five dogs to search the small island. The ME reported that the woman had been thirty-seven to forty-five, her rib injury was old, two of her front teeth were missing, she'd had a hysterectomy, and both of her heels had bone spurs "common in prostitutes." He made an educated guess that she might have been killed by "blunt impacts to the body."

An employee of the Monroe County jail read an account in the *Times-Union* and informed her superiors that one of the jail's regular clients, Dorothy Keeler, a petite bag woman who lived on welfare and refundable bottles, hadn't been seen lately. Inquiries on the street confirmed that she'd dropped from sight around the end of July. Acquaintances from the Blessed Sacrament Church homeless shelter said they weren't worried; Dorothy was an unlikely murder victim—suspicious, distrusting of strangers, wary of men. An alcoholic, she frequently dried out at Genesee Hospital on Alexander Street.

The Keeler woman hadn't been reported missing, and there was no way to match the remains to a name. The puzzle was handed over to a forensic anthropologist, along with a plastic bag containing bones, clothes, a few strands of hair, dirt samples, and two jars of maggots and insects.

• • •

Six days after the latest find, a boy wriggled through a hole in the fence behind the old brown-brick Maplewood YMCA building to retrieve a baseball. The neighborhood was mixed commercial and residential, on the fringe of the prostitution area that paralleled the Genesee Gorge. The boy wasn't surprised to find junk and garbage along the weedy border of the fence, but he was shocked to see a human foot protruding from under a flattened piece of cardboard. He ran for police.

Patty Ives lay face up in black pants and a heavy black-striped sweater. She wore no underwear or socks and had been dead for weeks. The gold wedding ring that she'd steadfastly refused to sell was missing. The leathery skin on her thin face had turned mahogany brown, obliterating the final faint resemblance to the heroine of *Pretty Woman.* Maggots had eaten most of her flesh.

The medical examiner attributed death to "probable acute asphyxia," but admitted it was a guess. Ratface Billy, the pimp who'd battered and narcotized "Crazy Patty" for years, sobbed as police questioned him. Now he would have to return to burglary. Pimping was easier.

14. CLARA NEAL

The last few months I was with Art Shawcross was the happiest I ever was. There was just something about it that words cannot tell. He seemed happy with me, too. He was a country boy at heart, always talking about the woods and the rivers up in the North Country. Myself, I talked about Clay County, West Virginia.

Me and Art did country things together—hunting, fishing, picking apples, picnicking, just driving around in my little Omni and smelling the fresh air. Sometimes we'd get lost at night, way out of town, and we'd follow the glow back to Rochester.

That man was crazy about fishing. Well, he didn't have no growing-up life, did he? Ya know how it is with little fellers eleven, twelve, thirteen? How they like goin' fishin'?

That's him: fishin', fishin', fishin'. Now do you get the point? That's all that was wrong with him. *He never grew up.*

He took me and my kids and grandkids all over Monroe County fishing. Tell ya hwut, he was the best fisherman they ever was. We'd go down to the sewer outfall and the backwater and in less'n fifteen minutes he'd have a dozen brown trout. Just waded into the shallow water and scooped 'em up. You're only allowed three fish a day, but after you cut 'em up the warden can't tell.

Art caught so many salmon in the Genesee River he overflowed my freezer and fed everybody back at his apartment house and his friends at the Dunkin' Donuts, including a couple cops. What he did was, he snagged spawners. They'd come up from Lake Ontario and have to stop at the old Rochester Gas and Electric power plant by this big waterfall. You had to have a permit from the RG&E to drive in there. There was maples, oaks, birch, some ash trees, all growing in that steep canyon, and rust-colored cliffs, and when the sun came out, half a rainbow would hang in the spray from the falls. You'd think you was out West somewhere till you looked up and saw the Kodak Tower to the west.

Fishermen lined up shoulder to shoulder on a gravel bar at the bottom of the waterfall, and they'd be dozens of big Chinook salmon whirliggin' around, and Art would jerk that treble hook into their backs and drag 'em up the bank a-wigglin' and floppin'. He'd smash their heads till they were dead—thirty-pounders, forty-pounders, some full of eggs. Most of the fishermen sold the eggs to a guy who bought 'em on the spot for thirty bucks a pound and then discarded the carcasses. But the ones that Art caught, he always taken 'em home, and sometimes he went to the discard box and grabbed more. He gave everybody fresh salmon. That's just the kind of heart he had.

We used to take a four-pack of wine coolers down there and Art would drink one and get to acting playful. He was always so sly with words and comments. He slipped and fell between the rocks one day and just laid there like he was dead. My son Don got scared. He leaned over the body and said, "Art! Art! You all right?"

Art jumped in his face and said, "No, I'm not all right!" And he waved his left arm and said, "I'm half *left*!"

Another time, he hurt his ankle in the gorge and two guys in a pickup truck taken him home. He wanted to know if I'd loan him an old pair of crutches I had around the house.

I drove them over to the apartment and he was laying there in pain. Rose was out and I couldn't get his shoe over the swelling. He screamed while I put a pair of socks on the one foot and walked him across Alexander Street to the Genesee Hospital on one leg and the crutches, put him in a wheelchair and taken him to the doctor's office. Turned out he'd been walking around with a hairline broken ankle and four torn ligaments! They gave him a walking cast. I wondered, You poor guy, what do you do when I'm not around?

Rose still went out with us once in a while, but you could see they weren't getting along. I'll say it plain: she was quiet, sullen. I s'pected she knew about our secret love affair but didn't dare make anything out of it.

When the hunting season began, Art bought me a new scope for me and my sons' twenty-two rifle, and we went to Orleans County to spotlight deer. It was a seventeen-shot automatic—dit dit dit *dit*! Art was crazy about that gun. One night the moon was shining bright and there stood two deer, right in the road, and Art cut loose and got 'em both. He laughed and said, "Them poor son of a bitches! They just stepped right into my line of f'ar!"

We slung 'em into the back of the Omni. Art was driving and he asked Rose to reach over and steer while he rolled down his window to look for another deer. She near put the car in a ditch and he started cussin'.

"Well," she says, "ya *know* I don't know how to do this."

He says, "No, you don't, you goddamn fuckin' cunt." He was *mad*! "You don't know how to go to the bathroom. Now either straighten your act up or I'll put you out and you can walk your ass home."

I jumped in and I said, "No, you won't do no such thing, Art!" I knew just how far to push him and when to stop. I told him, "You shut your mouth, Arthur Sharcross, or I'll bop you right upside the head."

He says, "You're gonna hit *me*?"

"Yes I will!"

Well, that set him to laughing. My son Don dressed out the deer. It was near Holley, where my daughter Linda lives. Art said, "I want the pussy off'n this deer." He was gonna give it to my youngest son Robert, nickname "Bones"—it was kind of a long-run joke between the two of 'em. Art felt around the carcass and he says, "Bonesie's shit outa luck. It's a boy." He cut off the penis and said he was gonna taken it home. We never laughed so loud in our life. Even Rose laughed a little.

Come time for my daughter Loretta to have a C-section back in Clay County, and I told Art I had to be with her. He says, "You're driving all that distance?" It was five hundred miles, a eight-hour drive. I would pick up the New York Thruway just south of Rochester and run ninety miles an hour to Erie, P.A., and take Interstate 79 straight on down to Clay County. My little Dodge Omni done it so many times it could steer by itself.

I says, "Yes, I gotta be there. Loretta's my baby."

He says, "You're coming back, aren't you?" Sounded so mournful and all.

"Yes," I says. "I'll be back."

I was supposed to stay two weeks but I come back in one week 'cause I missed him. I called and he said, "You're back already? When'd you get home?" He said, "Oh, my God, you made my night! I feel better already." He was *so* excited.

He came right over to borrow my car and we exchanged love vows. He give me a wedding ring from one of his ex-wives, size 7, ten-karat gold fill. Said he'd carried it in his wallet for years. That ring was so nice, it made me cry. I hated when they took it away from me later. They can tell me a thousand times, but I'll never believe it belonged to no dead whore.

15.

Rochester police wondered if they had a genuine serial murderer on their hands. Even after the finding of Patty Ives, some remained doubtful. The only solid link among the killings was that most of the victims were prostitutes or street people. To many of the top cops and detectives, the cases seemed to add up to nothing more than an unusual string of isolated homicides:

Linda Lee Hymes, killed by a car under suspicious circumstances.

Patty Ives, probably strangled.

Nicola Gursky, shot on Lake Avenue.

Jacqueline Dicker, strangled and dumped on a highway entrance ramp.

Sharon Eady, knifed.

Dorothy Blackburn, probably strangled, thrown in a creek.

Rosalie Oppel, strangled on a railroad embankment behind the Kodak parking lot.

And two undiagnosed deaths: Anna Steffen, found dead in Genesee Gorge, and a headless woman, still unidentified, found on Seth Green Island.

Privately, police strategists suspected the existence of three or four killers. Bodies had turned up in downtown Rochester, some farther out, and at least one, Dorothy Blackburn, in an area under the jurisdiction of the Monroe County sheriff. From the beginning, hard evidence was in short supply.

"You can't get prints off maggots or old dead bodies," an evidence technician complained. "You can't establish identification without a head. On TV they get prints off running water, off a cinder block. But this is the real world."

Investigators theorized that the murderers might be using ether, chloroform, drug overdoses, an overcharged stun gun, or some other offbeat form of killing that left neither clues nor residue. Technicians were puzzled because they found no fingernail scrapings and no semen. Plainly, the murderer was killing quickly and easily. But how? And why were hard-bitten streetwalkers giving up their lives without a fight?

It was difficult to reconstruct the final hours of the victims, especially those in advanced states of decomposition. Although prostitutes were at the highest risk of any other social group, they distrusted police and lied about their activities. Laying false trails and covering up for friends came as naturally as cheating one another in dope deals. The street people filed missing persons reports only as a last resort, and all too often detectives would expend major effort only to learn that a missing woman was tricking in Scranton or Binghamton or New York City, or she'd dropped out of sight to evade her family or her pimp, or she was drying out in an alcohol program or kicking drugs in a rehab center.

"We were upset as hell about the killings," said Deputy Police Chief Terrence Rickard, a master tactician who ran the department while Chief Gordon Urlacher specialized in shaking hands and public appearances. "We were scratching our heads figuring what was going on."

After the Ives murder, a veteran homicide detective named Billy Barnes took note that the bodies of three of the victims—Ives, Steffen, and the unidentified woman on Seth Green Island—had been carefully covered, as though the perpetrator was concerned about aerial reconnaissance. It suggested the possibility that his homicidal career might have begun in Vietnam. Barnes was convinced that the serial killings would continue and might even accelerate.

"Nobody listened to Billy," said his longtime partner, RPD investigator Lenny Borriello. "Nobody wanted to admit we had a problem. All police departments hate to admit they got a serial killer, because the media starts right in. 'When are you gonna catch the guy?' 'Serial killer strikes again,' that kinda crap. Makes us look like assholes."

An elite Tactical Squad supplemented the work of detectives from the Physical Crimes Unit and the outlying precincts. Thirty-two strong, its permanent assignment from Chief Urlacher was to "go where the crime's happening and kick hell out of it." At the moment, the squad was committed to Operation Clean, wresting ruined neighborhoods from drug dealers. In an election year in a highly political town, it was a good way to please the mayor.

The squad was directed by Lieutenant James Bonnell, an athletic ex-Marine sergeant who ran a hands-on operation. The former star quarterback for the U.S.M.C. "Warhawks" was known as a hard-hitting cop who issued orders in simple English and commanded admiration and respect. The eight-hour day was almost unknown in the Tac Squad and soon would lengthen.

Bonnell had been on the squad for twenty-two years, his first and only assignment as a cop. At forty-six, he ran on adrenaline, coffee, and a hatred of criminals.

"Imagine an old fart like me," he said, his thin blue eyes narrowing, "getting paid for a job like this. We catch a good armed robber, we take down a good mugger or a child molester—that's why I'm here. I just wanna look him right in the eye, feel his breath."

He worked the streets hard. "You got to," he explained. "You got to make your men realize you're just like them, and you got to make the bad guys think you're behind every tree." He despised press conferences. "Tell ya the truth," he went on, "I gotta be ordered to be at them fuckin' things."

After a meeting with the top brass, the old quarterback assigned a sergeant and six men to the prostitute murders.

16. LIEUTENANT JAMES BONNELL

We knew most of the dead girls, so we took the killings personally. The street makes prostitutes seem hard, without fear, but we see them as human beings. They're vulnerable as hell, and they're no harder than an emergency room nurse. They fascinate me; they're a unique form of life. I've arrested grandmas whose grandchildren are now on the street. Three generations of hookers! Act the same, look the same.

I guess you could say we had a tolerance policy in Rochester, but we never thought of it that way. For any cop, the bottom line on prostitution is you can't stop it but you gotta keep it under control. Sweeps were an education process for everybody. When we arrested young johns, we always took 'em aside like we would our own son. "What the hell's the matter with you? Don't you understand AIDS?"

And they say, "Well, we're just getting a head job."

"Don't you *read*? Don't ya know you can get AIDS from body fluids?"

When our prostitutes go to jail, something like 25 percent test positive for the HIV virus, and the others have everything from jock itch to herpes. They're not a glamorous group, tell ya that—underweight, bad skin, bodies wrecked from drugs and alcohol. At twenty they look thirty. At thirty they look fifty. At forty they're dead.

There were maybe a hundred that rode the circuit in and out of Rochester, but only about thirty-five were here at any one time. They worked an area of fast-food restaurants, run-down homes and apartments, rinky-dink redneck bars, and legitimate businesses that shut down at night. A lot of 'em carried a knife or a razor for protection—they'd use it, too. Ninety-nine percent were addicts, which meant they'd lie, cheat, steal, whatever it took to feed their habit.

They came in all shapes and sizes, wore jeans, flannel

shirts, sneakers, heavy jackets 'cause it got so cold. They were basically unkempt and unfriendly, except to johns. Only two or three of them could even be called attractive. The highest-paid whore on the street was a man, a transvestite. When he got his drag together he was the most beautiful thing out there and had the most customers. When the girls saw him coming, they moved to another corner. There were three or four other men working, but they were dogs compared to him.

When these killings started, we figured we're gonna need the cooperation of every prostitute. We had to observe the guy picking up a hooker or killing one or driving around with a dead body. So we made a friendly arrangement with the women: do your business as usual and we'll cover your ass. We had to keep it quiet that we were working with prostitutes, but we couldn't let this guy kill more women. It was strictly a survival deal between the Tac Squad and the hookers.

Every night from 7:00 P.M. till 6:00 A.M. we tried to watch the girls' action. They felt safe 'cause we were there; they knew our unmarked cars. There'd be a girl on every corner and we're a half block away with binoculars, radios, the whole nine yards. Every john that hit on her or drove her off, we'd tail 'em, get a full description of him and his vehicle. Then we'd back off and turn everything over to the detectives from Physical Crimes. So if the hooker turned up missing or didn't come back to her corner in a half hour or so, we put out a pickup on the car. Of course, she might be dead by that time, but that was the chance they had to take. They accepted that risk the day they went into the business.

To help out a little, I started watching Liz Gibson's operation. She was a typical whore, in a car, out of a car, in a car, out of a car, quick blow jobs all night long. I'd been hearing that the prostitutes were being real careful these days. Bullshit! Liz wasn't careful at all. It showed me what we were up against. Most of these woman were addicts, and they weren't gonna change their ways. They couldn't break out a whole new style and still make five hundred a day to maintain.

One night Liz pops into a van, two guys in it. Then they take off. I figure, this is how the son of a bitch is getting away with murder. It's *two* guys!

They drive down a dark street and park. I beep my horn at Liz and show my badge. Turns out the driver is her husband and she's turning a trick in the back of the van. He can't let her out of his sight 'cause she earns their coke money. Coke is king, right? It runs the lives on this street.

In the beginning, we thought we had a pretty good rapport with the girls, but we couldn't let ourselves forget that these weren't the Junior League. We told 'em in front: don't jack us around. Don't try to scram or hide on us or take on private tricks that we don't know about. 'Cause your private trick could be the killer! We told 'em, If you hold out on us, you're going to jail.

A few couldn't resist. They were used to a small amount of indulgence from the police department, but nothing like this, and they couldn't handle the freedom. One of the older girls would turn a trick, then jump out of the car and look for another john without returning to her original corner, like we'd arranged. Scared us into thinking something had happened. We told her to cut it out but she wouldn't.

So we separated a plainclothes team and one of 'em hit on her, got a proposition. When we arrested her, she got all upset, then calmed down and started to laugh. We asked what the hell was so funny.

She'd just put a roast in the oven for dinner, figured she'd grab a coupla quick tricks while it was cooking. She wondered if we'd take her by her apartment so she could put the roast back in the freezer, 'cause she knew she was going to jail. We did her that little favor and thirty days later she thawed out her roast.

After a while some of the girls started turning nasty about the surveillance. Their johns would complain and the girls felt uncomfortable doing blow jobs while an undercover van watched. All we were doing was trying to keep them from being strangled to death and maybe beheaded, but what dope fiend could ever be accused of logical thought?

Once in a while we had to make an arrest to keep the pack in line. We'd say, "You're no longer working with us. Now you're gonna work *for* us. We'll go to bat for ya, talk to the judge, but you're gonna have to work off the favor with a little cooperation." That was how we reestablished our contracts with girls who forgot how to be friendly and nice, because otherwise they'd get thirty to ninety days, and their habits wouldn't allow them to be off the street that long.

Some of the girls, if they didn't want to be with a certain john, they'd point us out and say, "Don't mess with me. Those cops are watching me." A few times a john would come over and challenge us. We made 'em believers quick.

One guy kept popping up in our surveillances, and we began to wonder if he was the killer. We stopped his car and he turned out to be a harmless mental. He was gonna solve the case—a junior G-man, right in the middle of our detail. Just for a joke, one of our teams deputized him. "Raise your left hand and swear to this tree here that you'll be a good cop."

The joke backfired. He became a bigger pest than ever. The prostitute would drive off with a john, the Tac Squad would follow in our van, Physical Crimes would follow the Tac Squad, and the mental case would bring up the rear. The prostitutes and the johns were pissed off. All they wanted was a twenty-dollar blow job and go home. They didn't want a Rose Bowl parade.

So I had one of our investigators pick up this guy and tell him, Hey, enough is enough. Stay the hell outa this area, you're causing problems. It took some conversation, but he caught on.

17.

After a few weeks without progress, police officials became jumpy. In normal times, a report of a missing prostitute would generate yawns, but reporter Corey Williams of the *Rochester Times-Union* had been asking probing questions about missing women, and a big story was expected to hit any day. So when Maria Welch didn't come home to her sixty-six-year-old boyfriend and her five-month-old son, police took the disappearance seriously.

Friends and colleagues reported that the twenty-two-year-old woman had been having problems. She'd been bothered by a man who posed as "Officer Finn" and demanded free service. She'd received calls from men who asked, "How many dicks did you suck today?" and promised to kill her on sight. Two weeks before her disappearance she'd been forced to perform oral sex on a stocky man in a blue two-door Impala; he'd threatened to kill her with a screwdriver, and when she jumped from the car and fled down Daus Alley, he tried to run her down. Barely recovered from the experience, she learned that a favorite trick named "Ed" had also dated the murdered Dorothy Blackburn and Patty Ives—"Whoever he dates turns up dead," one of the street women reminded her.

Just before midnight on November 5, 1989, Maria left her baby son Brad in the care of her elderly boyfriend and said, "I'm scared to death to go out."

Like the other working girls, Maria had been limiting her clientele and tightening her safety practices, but the frantic need for dope created occasional sloppiness. After the normally reliable woman had been out of touch for eighteen hours and her baby was caterwauling for attention, police and prostitutes presumed the worst.

At roll calls Welch was described as five-two, about a hundred pounds, light complexion, brown eyes and brown hair, wearing low white sneakers, a thigh-length blue jacket, jeans, a purple T-shirt, and a gold chain around her neck. Her body was dappled with tattoos: a unicorn on her forearm, a marijuana leaf and a rose on her left arm to cover up the name "Leo," another leaf on her leg near the ankle, and "L-O-V-E" on the knuckles of her left hand. She was described as a lesbian who tricked only to support a big habit. She was known as a good mother to Brad and a soft touch to anyone with a story.

Maria's roommate apparently had made the final sighting of the missing woman. Just after midnight, the two women had been working the intersection of Lyell and Saratoga. Maria drove off in a maroon car but returned quickly. "Fuck that asshole," she told her friend. "He didn't want to go to the apartment."

A small blue hatchback cruised past, slowed, then went on. The driver, a male who appeared to be in his late forties, circled the block and looked them over three or four more times before the roommate hooked up with another customer and drove off for a tryst of her own.

When she returned to the street corner, her colleague Maria was gone. She wasn't worried; she figured Maria was on the job and would check in soon, following their new security procedure. She slept by the phone all night, but it was silent.

18. ARTHUR SHAWCROSS (HANDWRITTEN ACCOUNT)

On November the 9th or there about I picked up Maria Walsh at Marks [restaurant] on Lake Ave. No. 7. We went down behind that area and parked. We sat and talked for she was cold. Had the heater on high, gave her $30. She took off her shoes, socks and genes. Then took off the rest of her clothes. I only unzipped. I ask her if she was on the rag and she said no. But when I put my hand in her I felt a Tampax and blood. I've never done it that way!

I ask for my money back she told me to go fuck my self. I choked her until she past out. Had some rope in the car and tied her hands behind her, plus her feet to her hands. I had take out that Tampax and pushed in a bar-towel. She came too and ask me what I did to her. Then she wanted me to untie her. I was sweating like crazy. Kept wiping my head and face off. I pulled out that bar-towel and it was almost clean. Then I mounted her. My sweat dripping into her face. That was when she said I love you. I kissed her then and killed her.

19.

The day after Maria Welch disappeared, her roommate spotted the maroon vehicle she'd seen the night before and jotted down the license number. Police interrogated a mild-mannered Kodak engineer who admitted that he patronized the Lake-Lyell area every two weeks. He confirmed that he'd picked up a hooker named Maria but said he broke off negotiations after she insisted they trick at her apartment and cussed him out. He passed a polygraph examination and was released.

Detectives asked neighborhood pimps and prostitutes for suggestions on where to look for the Welch body. Her roommate and fellow prostitute reported that Maria preferred to steer her customers to the cubbyhole apartment they shared at 90 Saratoga, where sadistic johns might be less likely to hurt her, but she also performed her services on both sides of Diamond Trucking off Emerson, in the brushy areas behind two houses on Jay Street, on Boswell behind the Mapledale Party House, in weeds behind Wendy's on Lake, and in an abandoned building on Lyell. The haunts were carefully checked by police cadaver dogs, but there was no trace of human flesh among the trash and whiskey bottles and used needles. Nor was any useful information elicited at a free-basing house run for prostitutes by Jamaicans.

Mindful that several bodies had turned up in the Genesee Gorge, detectives called in a State Police helicopter to search the river from the upper falls to where it emptied into Lake Ontario. There was brief excitement when the pilot spotted a patch of blue on Seth Green Island, where the headless body of an unidentified woman had turned up three weeks before, but a ground party determined that it was a plastic tarp, rolled and tied with rope. Tests were negative for blood or prints.

20.

Maria Welch had been missing for five days and nights when a fisherman trudged down Seth Green Drive past the "Public Access Prohibited" sign and another advisory warning fishermen not to "discard any fish carcass or parts thereof into the waters of this state or upon any public lands contiguous to and within 100 feet of such waters." It was 3:00 A.M. and no one was around. An eye-watering smell of decay floated up from two big rusty cans marked "Only deposit fish remains here."

The fisherman walked past another sign that said "Watch for Fallen Rock" and started to urinate over the steep bank. Dawn was still hours away, but there was enough light to reveal something that looked like a discarded mannequin about forty feet down the slope. Still only mildly curious, the fisherman worked his way to a narrow shale ledge and found the body of a young woman in a pile of old grass clippings, bushes, and twigs. In the dim light, he saw that she was naked except for white go-go boots. Shoulder-length blond hair framed an attractive face. She was in a slightly off-center kneeling position, facedown, and appeared to be clutching a cement block. It looked as though she'd been pitched from the top and came to rest against a small tree on the ledge.

Police noted a homemade tattoo, "KISS OFF," on the bare buttocks, a tattooed cross on the right ankle, a wing on the left shoulder, and a butterfly around one wrist. Word went out that the search for Maria Welch was over. Deputy Chief Terrence Rickard was awakened at home and asked if the family should be advised. "Not yet," he said. "Let's make sure."

The medical examiner, dealing with a fully preserved body for a change, noted the pinpoint hemorrhages behind the victim's eyes and observed that the woman had been asphyxiated, exact method unknown. Abrasions and bruises showed that she'd also been beaten. As in earlier cases, there was no semen in the body cavities. Whatever sexual satisfaction the serial killer was seeking, he wasn't reaching a climax, a possible explanation for the increasing frequency and severity of his attacks. Further examination revealed another significant fact: the dead woman wasn't the missing Maria Welch. This victim was petite, like Welch and the other victims, but the tattoos didn't match.

By noon, detectives from Physical Crimes and plainclothesmen from the Tac Squad were collaring pimps and prostitutes and knocking on doors, trying to determine who had a "Kiss Off" tattoo. On Lyell Avenue, investigators Billy Barnes and Lenny Borriello ran into sixty-four-year-old Clem Brown and, on a hunch, showed him a mug shot of the corpse. Brown said the woman looked like his granddaughter, then confirmed the identification at the morgue. Frances Brown was a twenty-two-year-old wanderer who'd been seen alive just the day before. She was described as a nice blond kid, a high school dropout who wore glasses and liked music, poetry, and heroin. The story on the street was that Cuban drug dealers had kidnaped her the previous summer and forced her into prostitution in New York City. In August, she'd called her grandmother from a bus station in Massachusetts and said she was returning. Asked how she was doing, she'd answered, "You don't want to know."

On her return, her family had seen little of Franny. Her last known date was over the previous weekend with a man named Mike, who drove a two-door Monte Carlo. Family members said they didn't plan to tell the woman's little daughter about the murder. "She doesn't know what is going on," said the grandmother, Viola Brown. "She doesn't know what 'dead' is yet."

21. ARTHUR SHAWCROSS (HANDWRITTEN ACCOUNT)

Frances Brown I found walking on Lyle Ave. She took me to Seth Green Drive to a parking lot where a lot of people go fishing; including me. She was wild and somewhat crazy, didn't act right. I gave her $30 and she took off all her clothes and got in the back of the car. The Dodge. I let down the back seat, then we had sex-69-oral. She ask me to deep throat her so I did but got carried away. I didn't pull out so she could breath. She peed into my mouth and I kept pushing. Uncontrol reaction to doing it that way. She suffacated. I used her then also while still warm. Even to kissing her and sucking her tongue and breast. Didn't have an orgasium. This was October 89. I put on my clothes and got out. Opened her door and rolled her over the cliff.

22. SERGEANT JOHN EYGABROAT

About the time Franny Brown was found, I was on night patrol, and I usually stopped for coffee at the Dunkin' Donuts on Monroe Avenue. I kept running into this gray-haired guy who talked about the prostitute killings. I kept my distance. You don't encourage talking to the general public on breaks. A lot of nuts come out of the woodwork. You run into some guy that got a ticket thirty-four years ago and it's "Hey, Sarge, it wasn't right. It wasn't fair!"

This guy, they called him "the fisherman." He'd ride up on his bike at three in the morning, a coupla poles tied in the back and a salmon or two in the basket. Said he caught 'em in the Genesee Gorge. I don't know who the hell would eat those fish—they were half dead by the time they reached the falls and the river was polluted anyway, but once in a while somebody would accept a gift salmon and make him happy. He'd look pleased and say, "Hey, come in tomorrow night. I'll have another one for ya."

I tried to just say hi to the guy, nothing more. He'd talk to some of the uniformed men and he'd always bring up the killings. "I hope you get that guy," he'd say. "What a shame."

One night he comes right up in my face and says, "Hey, Sergeant, you got any leads on them murders?"

I just said, "Well, on Patrol we're really not that close to the investigation."

I didn't get his name.

X

MANHUNT

We do not even know if when animals tear each other to pieces they do not experience a certain sensual pleasure, so that when the wolf strangles the lamb, one can say equally well "He loves lambs" as that "He hates lambs."

—*Theodor Lessing*

1.

When Joseph Tibbetts read about Frances Brown's murder, he felt a jolt of fear and decided it was time to report that his girlfriend had been missing from his bed and board for eighteen days. Tibbetts was a retired Monroe County Parks employee, a wizened little man with stark black eyebrows, protruding ears, and pomaded hair that looked a little like combed tar. He wore army shoes and a dark brown cap, usually carried a shiny plastic pack, and spent much of his time walking around the center of town and placing bets.

Three years earlier, he'd met June Stott, known as "J," sitting on a bench inside the Midtown Plaza. "J" didn't seem to have a home and had difficulty answering his questions. He bought her coffee and learned that she was neither an addict nor a prostitute, but only a shy, homeless woman who sometimes heard voices. Since the death of her mother two years earlier, she'd taken to sleeping in parks and doorways on Lyell Avenue. In winter, she sought out heating grids. She believed that spirits were after her and had a deep fear of being assaulted. She lifted weights and carried a pocketknife against attackers. She was twenty-six, wore thick glasses with conspicuous rims, had a plain roundish face and a full figure.

Soon Tibbetts and "J" were sharing his one-room walk-up on the fifth floor of a rooming house on Chestnut Street. "I took her in," the retiree explained later. "I was afraid if she was on her own something would happen to her. She was like a daughter to me." After moving in with

Tibbetts, "J" continued her meanderings, but every afternoon at four she joined him at the Midtown Mall.

On Monday, October 23, he'd left her at 9:00 A.M. to go to an off-track betting parlor. Later in the day a friend saw her drinking a beer at the nearby Hotel Cadillac, a treat she allowed herself about once a year. She was seated at a table alone. She didn't keep her usual 4:00 P.M. rendezvous with Tibbetts and failed to come home that night.

The dapper little man decided that she'd found someone new. Now and then he'd seen "J" talking to males, and three or four times he'd noticed her drinking coffee with a potbellied man of about fifty in the food gallery of the Midtown Mall. Tibbetts didn't want to know who the man was and didn't ask, but one day he'd followed him and seen him unlock a bike with several fishing rods sticking up from the back. A few nights later "J" had shown up with a salmon steak wrapped in newspaper. Tibbetts didn't ask her to explain.

In reporting his friend missing almost three weeks after she disappeared, Tibbetts told police that he doubted that she met foul play because he'd schooled her carefully to avoid people she didn't know and to stay out of cars. He admitted that she was a little slow, but she was too fearful to have fallen for a stranger's con, no matter how slick. He said she'd been wearing a red-and-white jacket, a blue over red skirt, plastic black sunglasses, brown loafers, and jeans. He said he hoped police would find her and return her to his apartment so he could stop chain-smoking and crying.

2.

Rochester PD Major Lynde Johnston parked his car on Seth Green Drive and walked to the edge of the slope to look down. It was a Sunday, normally his day off, but June Stott had just been reported missing and Maria Welch still hadn't turned up and he was wondering if other victims were hidden in this same Genesee Gorge. A thoughtful man whose piercing blue-gray eyes, sandy hair, and bushy blond eyebrows gave him a slightly Nordic look, Johnston commanded the Criminal Investigation Division and was directly responsible for finding the killer.

From his vantage point near the barrels of discarded fish, he could see past the ledge where Frances Brown had been found in her go-go boots, then across the island where the headless skeleton had rotted in the sun, and up the far slope to the site of Anna Steffen's bones. Not far beyond, the body of Patty Ives had been hidden under a big piece of cardboard near the Mapledale Y.

My God, Johnston said to himself, the son of a bitch thinks he's dumping garbage. It was past time to engage in airy theories. No matter how many maniacs might be out there killing prostitutes—and Johnston and his colleagues still suspected there were several—a single murderer was clearly responsible for these four deaths and probably others. How many more would be killed before he was caught?

Lately the CID boss had been reading up on serial criminals, and he knew that they seldom moderated their activities. It was much more likely that their tastes would broaden and their crimes turn more savage and frequent—"the crescendo effect." Not far from the most recent killings, hundreds of girls attended Nazareth Academy, a Catholic high school. If case-hardened prostitutes weren't safe, neither were the students or any other woman in Rochester.

Johnston had already established a "war room" adjoining his office, with blown-up pictures of victims and vital information about their cases plastered on the walls—a gallery of the missing and the dead. Every morning when he arrived at work, the worn sallow faces, most of them blowups of police mug shots, seemed to berate him for not doing his job. After two dozen years as a cop, Johnston still firmly believed that no matter what rights the street women might have forfeited for money and dope, including the right to live healthy and happy lives, they deserved to be protected by society and not wind up with maggots in their eyesockets and bare backsides exposed to strangers.

He picked his way to the ledge that had held Franny

Brown. Normally the evidence technicians were thorough, but it never hurt to double-check. Johnston noticed that the ledge, Seth Green Island below, and the two murder sites up the far side of the gorge lay in a straight line. He wondered if the positioning was an accident or if it said something about the killer. He also wondered if other bodies might lie in this same trajectory. He went back to his office and arranged for more reconnaissance of the Genesee Gorge.

Coast Guard helicopters swooped over the river from the lower falls upstream to the Main Street bridge. A patrol boat searched from the Veterans Memorial Bridge north to where the river flowed into Lake Ontario. Police climbers belayed one another on ropes and rappeled down the sides of the steeper slopes.

Another body lay in the weedy shoreline, but it was overlooked.

3.

To the discomfort of police officials, the prostitute killings went public in a front-page article by Corey Williams in the November 14 edition of the *Rochester Times-Union.* A big headline read, "POLICE LOOK FOR LINKS IN DEATHS OF EIGHT WOMEN." The phrase "serial murderer" didn't appear, but a box titled "THE DEAD WOMEN" made the point. For the first time since the bodies had begun to turn up, the citizens of Rochester were in on the RPD's dirty little secret.

Deputy Chief Terrence Rickard was quoted in a damage-control mode:

> An argument can be made either way as to whether the deaths are linked, Rickard said. "You have common trends," he said. "Some of the women were prostitutes. All have drug habits and several were found in the river gorge area. Some of these things are not unique or uncommon. I do not believe that every prostitute's death

> in the city or county in the last two years is related. There may be four or five perpetrators to these acts."

Privately, the DC and his fellow officials were less sure of themselves. There were definite links in the murders of Blackburn, Steffen, Ives, Brown, and the unidentified body on Seth Green Island. And two other women, Maria Welch and June Stott, were missing under similar circumstances. But the RPD had a built-in distrust of the media and little inclination to pool information, even with other police departments.

The hard-driving Rickard issued a confidential intradepartmental warning. Beware of nosy reporters looking for awards, he advised. He also warned that November was the time of "the infamous Nielsen ratings" and the electronic media would be "vehement" about the killings.

George Ehle, a hard boiled veteran serving out his years as the RPD's crime analyst, put the situation more baldly: "I told everybody from Chief Urlacher on down, 'Get away from the papers. They're treacherous. They'll try to pull us down.' "

4. CLARA NEAL

Art rode his bike to my house and asked did I see the newspaper. I said no and he read me some old article about missing women. He seemed upset and said, "When is this gonna stop?" He told me to make sure I kept my doors locked. Then he borrowed my car. He said he felt like going out to Northampton Park and shooting a deer.

5.

The day after the *Times-Union* ran its first article about the killings, it was obliged to run another:

WOMAN'S BODY FOUND
Fourth discovered
in past three weeks

A man named Jimmie Thomas had checked out his trailer behind a house on Meigs Street and stepped on something hard. He scraped away a covering of leaves and found the body of Kimberley Logan, a thirty-year-old black prostitute who frequented the neighborhood. Her face was battered and she'd been hit in the abdomen. She was naked; leaves had been stuffed deep into her throat; her blood-stained bra lay on the frozen ground near her foot, and her bloody purple sweater was tucked under a fence. Police learned that she'd been drunk the night before and was seen with a hustler named Ronald who shook down prostitutes for money. The case seemed unrelated to the bodies found in the gorge, but the top brass took no chances and added it to the investigators' caseloads.

In his office at 4:00 A.M., Major Lynde Johnston poured another cup of black coffee and tried to make sense of the latest find. He wondered if the new killing was a "Catch me if you can" move, a middle finger for the PD. Certain criminals operated that way.

The CID commander had been to the Logan crime scene and marveled at the efficiency of his evidence technicians. But once again there'd been next to nothing to find. Had the police driven the killer from the gorge? Would he start dumping bodies all over town? Every answer led to more questions.

By afternoon, Corey Williams's latest article was being passed around in Mark's Texas Hots No. 2 restaurant and other establishments along the Lake Avenue prostitution corridor. In alleyways, abandoned houses, and cheap apartment rooms, tears flowed along with alcohol and cocaine. At nightfall, the working women had to decide what to do.

Six or eight returned to business, leading one of the more prudent to exclaim, "They're out doing the same thing!"

Others, like the roommate of the missing Maria Welch, decided on a policy change. "I'm making sure I'm not on the street," the prostitute said. "I'm not stupid enough to do that. There is no way nobody can get me out there." Henceforth, she said, she would trick in her apartment.

A woman known as "Barb" said she wished she could afford such a luxury. She was interviewed by Williams as she walked against a cold wind on Spencer Street near North Plymouth Avenue. "I just want one twenty-dollar date and then I'm going home," she told the busy reporter. "I have to feed my kids. I'm a widow and get Social Security—only $368 a month. I only come out once or twice a month." She said that for the first time in her career she was armed.

6.

She worked under the name "Barbara Gammicchich" (a cousin's married name), but when the sun came up she reverted to "Jo Ann Van Nostrand," taxpayer and public-spirited citizen. By either name she was in a state of annoyance at just about everyone in the Rochester demimonde: overbearing pimps, rip-off pushers, mouthy cops, ex-boyfriends and husbands who failed her in one way or another. But mostly she was disappointed in her fellow prostitutes. In her waning years as a wage earner, Jo Ann viewed them as a bumbling bunch of amateurs.

If she spoke bluntly about certain sexual activities and/or body parts, she wasn't being deliberately dirty or vulgar; she was just another craftsman discussing her trade, as a machinist discussed his lathe, a logger his chain saw. Jo Ann Van Nostrand had passed through stages of shame and humiliation to a degree of professional pride. At forty, she was a grandmother and looked it, underneath the tintings and paint. Her manner was mildly flirty and coquettish, and she seemed unexpectedly vulnerable for a woman who earned her living on her back or her knees. She had big round brown eyes, coffee-colored hair with red highlights, penciled eyebrows, and a figure so voluptuous that it still caused traffic problems.

"Course I'm a little overweight now," she said demurely. "I'm a forty double-D bust and a thirty waist. You shoulda seen me when I was a twenty-two waist and double-C cup. I'm walking down the street in go-go boots, hot pants and a halter, and a driver runs into a fire hydrant. The cops gave me a ticket for impeding traffic. God gave me these tits, and I've always had good legs 'cause I swim and I dance."

Although she was a white woman of Cuban, Indian, English, and French ancestry, she preferred the company of blacks and usually spoke rapid-fire black talk: "Ya hear what I'm sayin'?" "Ya follow my meanin'?" "In yo' eye," "the brothuhs," "suckah," "the man" for "police," "ho" for "whore," "bitch" for "woman" (and sometimes, oddly, for "man"). She called blacks who earned her disfavor "niggers" but bristled when others used the epithet. Her girlfriends, most of her neighbors, and all of her beaux were black. White men had never interested her romantically.

Van Nostrand (the name came from a three-week marriage in her teens) was proud of her erudition—"I graduated from the eighth grade but I been reading ever since."

She lamented the ignorance and lack of sophistication of her colleagues. "Those other ho's don't even read," she complained. "It was weeks before they knew there was a killer around. I heard about him when Frances Brown died. I'm an avid newspaper reader and news watcher, learned it from a madam when I was sixteen. She said, 'If you can speak on any topic, you'll get a higher type of clientele.' All us ho's followed the newspapers so we could talk about current events. We didn't just fuck."

She was raised in a poverty section of Detroit by a deaf-mute couple and was fluent in sign language. She had all the problems of childhood poverty plus a few of her own.

"I grew these curves early, and the men in my family couldn't keep their hands off me. When I was five my father began, and after that it never stopped. It made me nervous, gave me fainting spells, but when I told my mother what was happening, she said it was my imagination. Later my father said that I enticed him by running around naked. Maybe I did. What the fuck did I know? I was just a kid. He said he'd kill me if I talked about it."

She started running away at five and was in and out of juvenile facilities. At eleven she was sent to a Catholic school for wayward girls. "I was there fifteen months and I got on the honor rolls. When they ordered me back to my parents they had to peel me off the nun, Mother Helen, a Good Shepherd. I still love her, think about her every day. She explained that they couldn't keep me 'cause I wasn't wayward anymore."

Six months later, after she'd turned thirteen, she found herself fending off her father again. "That bitch tried to get me to suck him and jacked off in my face. That was the farthest he'd ever gone. He said, 'You're big enough to have sex.' But I wasn't. I was a tomboy. Sex bored me. I thought it was repulsive."

She fled again and wound up in a reformatory in Adrian, Michigan, twenty-three miles northwest of Toledo. "I was always getting thrown in the hole, a cement room smaller than the smallest jail cell. Steel bars, rats, lousy food. The PA system shook your brainpan; I swear they used it for torture. You wore gunnysack dresses. I escaped many times. Once me and another girl took a guy hostage."

At fourteen she was back in Detroit and working "bellboy to bellboy," tricking with traveling salesmen and pedophiles. At fifteen she fell into the hands of a married pimp. "It was the standard story," she said ruefully. "That brother had too much *savez quoi* for me to resist. I left when the beatings got bad."

A black singer offered to take her to New York. "I thought, Oh, boy, New York City. I didn't know he meant Rochester."

The singer found her a job at a go-go joint called The

Pussycat on the wrong part of Main Street. She became a skilled dancer and hit the road. From 1967 to 1972 she appeared in various cities as "Paddy LaMonte, the powder-puff girl," dancing naked behind a three-foot-wide powder puff and staying high on drugs. "Coke and heroin hung in the dressing rooms like dust. I became a full-time ho to afford my habit. In New York I got busted by the pussy posse a thousand times. I worked hotels for Xaviera Hollander and Dirty Rose's house uptown, off Eighth Avenue. Rose did the biggest ten-dollar business in the East. For twelve hours you'd turn ten-dollar tricks, then give her half. Flatbacking! After the first two days I couldn't walk! I went to Rockin' Chair Helen's on East Grand Boulevard in Detroit and then to a black madam on Cherry Street in Buffalo and then I worked for a ho agent that would book you into houses all over the South, from Peachtree Street to Bourbon Street and points west. I worked on call for another madam, went out to the big hotels, dated David Janssen and some other actors, a couple of senators, judges, I don't know how many cops, police chiefs, mayors. My body drove 'em nuts, and my personality commanded good money. I took my time, talked to guys, made 'em feel comfortable. Ya know what I'm saying?"

She shook her head and frowned. "Almost every girl I knew from the sixties and seventies is dead now."

At eighteen, bothered by asthma, she completed a course as a toupee and wig specialist, but by then she was so addicted to heroin and cocaine that she couldn't hold a straight job. "I ran [injected] that shit till I was twenty-six," she recalled. "Been off heroin ever since. I use coke, but it's not a regular thing like it is with these sluts in Rochester. I may binge for days. It's like a little vacation from the street, ya hear what I'm saying? Then I'll be clean for five, six months. I don't act any different when I'm high. I'm not erratic. I might talk a little more, but I'm not frantic like most geekers. It mellows me out."

Looking back, she figured she'd had one solid opportunity to turn her life around. "I went into this boutique in Rochester to steal something so I could eat, and I fainted from hunger. The owner was a forty-two-year-old musician. Instead of prosecuting me, we fell in love and started living together. Oh, God, a fine, lovely, decent man. He taught me that black men don't have to be pimps or geekers or kick your ass. He taught me to respect myself. We got married on a Monday in 1975 and on the following Sunday we went swimming at a motel and he sank to the bottom, dead. Heart attack.

"I ran home to Detroit and laid down in a snowbank. I prayed, 'God, I want to die.' I went crazy on drugs and hit the streets again. My father started in on me, but I wasn't a kid anymore and I whipped out a knife and told him I'd cut off his dick. Later he was dying in a hospice in Detroit and he had the balls to ask me to forgive him. I told him to look elsewhere for absolution. He had tumors inside his body; he was suffering real good. He got his just deserts. Then I went back to the streets in Rochester."

At the time of the serial killings, one of her sons was doing penitentiary time for assault and grand larceny, and the other lived with relatives in Detroit and attended high school.

"My big boy has a baby of his own," she said with pride. "I'm a grandma." She lived in a small apartment in the blackest part of town, paying the rent and supporting her habit with occasional dates, a small stipend from an old man who ejaculated when she bathed him like a baby, and a monthly disability payment for her asthma and epilepsy and the rheumatoid arthritis that had twisted her left hand into a claw.

7. JO ANN VAN NOSTRAND

The cops made a mistake by shadowing us. It forced the girls with habits to sneak around, trick on side streets, dark alleys, where the Tac Unit couldn't watch. They promised not to arrest us, but how could we be sure? Some of the cops were total motherfuckers. "Hey, bitch, get off the street." "Hey, pig, get your fat ass over here." They'd stop me on Lyell and say, "Listen, cunt, I better not see you coming back this way. Get the fuck over to Lake." Then a cop on Lake would order me back to Lyell. Musical whores!

They spread us so thin to where we couldn't watch over one another and the strangler could pick us off. We like scattered, you follow my meaning? After a while most of the girls just quit. Some figured it was a good time to go into a drug program or rob cars. Some hitched to Scranton, Binghamton. When Maria Welch disappeared, one girl got so scared she left her baby with a black guy and disappeared—never seen again.

Pretty soon there were only three or four hos out at a time, along with the faggot Lucian. He was *always* working. A thin, light-skinned brother, a dancer's build, wore a white miniskirt with a fringe jacket, an auburn wig that picked up glints from the neon. I thought he was female till he showed me his brass knucks, told me if he ran into the strangler he'd smash his fuckin' face. He knocked one trick right out of the cab of his semi.

Lucian worked without a pimp, like me. Rochester pimps were so country, ya know? No class, no finesse. There was one who had about five girls, an ugly guy, looked like an Alabama sharecropper. He beat on this girl and I tried to help her and he started to jump on me. I told him, "Look, I'm not the coward she is. You fuck with me you got problems." That same nigger showed up drunk and asked where was my pimp. He told me, "You can't work down here unless you got one."

I said, "Well, kiss my ass. I work anywhere I want. I don't need no one to stick his nose up my ass. I was workin' when you was wearing diapers, boy."

He gave me a lot of problems and I had to stay away from Lake and Lyell for a while. I didn't give a shit. I never had much to do with those hos anyway. They were even stupider than the pimps, and the coke made 'em twice as stupid. Farm girls, most of 'em. All night long they did industrial-strength blow jobs, because the tricks thought that made 'em safe from AIDS. My ass! It's like girls saying "I can't never catch clap because I suck." These locals, they didn't even know how to check a guy for diseases, how to milk a guy down, check for crabs, *nothin'*! It don't take but two seconds.

Everything these stupid cokeheads did, it made things easier for the strangler. They were so reckless, untrustworthy, couldn't think past the next fix, wouldn't work together. In New York City there were twenty hos on each block, but you didn't stab each other in the back. Hanging together kept the bad motherfuckers from bothering you. When I worked Boston, this guy was hurting my neck on a street corner, and as soon as the shit jumped off, the other girls whaled on that bitch good. "Hey, we don't allow that kinda shit on our corner. Get the fuck outa here!" And they didn't even know me! They had pride of profession, pride of craft. In Detroit, broads would steal from the poor boxes in church, but they'd starve to death before they'd rob each other. I used to say, "I don't steal from old folks, babies, or God." But these Rochester hos, they'd steal from God or anybody else.

It wasn't long before the strangler emptied the streets. There was more johns than hos—and that meant big bucks. Let's see, who was left? Me, Darlene Trippi, June Cicero, Lucian, a couple girls I didn't know their names, and a paranoid bitch named Madeleine that thought every trick was the killer.

Being thirty-eight, I had seniority, but I preferred to keep to myself. Cicero considered herself the queen bitch. She came from Brooklyn, had a funny accent like Joan Rivers. She was thirty-four, a plain face but a great shape. She'd pour that muscular ass into a tight pair of Levi's and make a grand a night. She was what the cops called a 24-7, meaning she tricked twenty-four hours a day seven days a week. She'd work even when she was high. She ran in front of cars on Lake and nearly got hit. Her problem was she was always in love with two or three guys at a time and supporting their habits. She was fifteen years on the street—suspicious, mean, hard. The word at Mark's Texas Hots was that if the strangler hit on her, he was dead meat. Any time a john tried to drive her away from her comfort zone around Lake and Lyell, she'd give him an elbow and dive out the door.

If you ever tried to warn her about a bad john, she was like, "Fuck you, bitch! You're just trying to take away my trick." Feared nobody, trusted nobody, always geeked. If you went near one of her dates, she'd be, "That's my regular! *That's my regular!*"

One night I told her to back off a guy in a gray van because he'd been acting squirrelly and two police units were watching him. She says, "Fuck you! You date your tricks and I'll date mine. Get the fuck outa here." Her typical charm-school rap.

I says, "Look, you stupid broad, you guys may be used to stabbing each other in the back, but where I come from we help each other. You get more sticking together than you do fighting."

While I'm at it, I says, "Why don't you quit running out to cars all that time? Where's your fucking pride? All that crowding around, running in the street, pushing yourself on the johns like pat rats. There's more than enough guys to go around." I says, "You're stupid, June. If you wanna trick with guys that'll kill ya, go ahead. Date whoever you want. But I'm warnin' ya. If I want your trick, I'll take him. Don't nobody own no tricks out here."

After they started finding bodies in the Genesee Gorge, some of the girls paired off to keep an eye on each other, which I didn't want to do because I'm a lone operator. Madeleine, a fat kid with a big butt, a baby face, and short brown hair, she approached me and said, "Hey, you heard about the strangler?" She says, "Look, I don't see you on the street that much, but since we're out here tonight, how about you check the license plates of my cars and I'll do the same for you?"

I made the mistake of agreeing. I'd get in a car and tell the guy, "That's my girlfriend Madeleine back there and she's got your license number and if I ain't back in twenty minutes she's gonna flag the cops. If you wanna buy extra time, tell me before we get started."

A lot of guys would get scared and tell us to get outa the car, but most of 'em took it okay. This Madeleine, she turned out to be flighty. She'd disappear, or she'd leave the street to get high somewhere, and I wouldn't know whether to report her missing or what. So I went back to being a single. What the hell, I been doing this for twenty years. Who'd bother an old ho like me?

8.

Disquieting articles were beginning to appear almost daily in the *Times-Union* and were echoed by stories in its sister newspaper, the more conservative *Democrat and Chronicle* (known to its detractors as the Demagogue and Comical or, simply, the Dumbocrat). Radio and TV picked up the tempo with live interviews from the area of Lake and Lyell. Shoplifting and petty theft increased as frightened prostitutes sought new ways to support their habits.

Sande Sommers, spokeswoman of the National Organization for Women, issued a public apology to the victims: "We did not know you, but we mourn the loss of each of you. We recognize the violence you received as violence against all women. Your deaths could be ours."

The United Church Ministry started a reward fund with five hundred dollars. The Reverend Raymond Graves appealed to the murderer: "We beg you to stop killing the women and come and talk to us."

Police officials thanked Graves and the ministry publicly, but in their nightly drinking sessions at an oasis called Shields, just across the freeway from the drab gray Public Safety Building, they complained that do-gooders were making their job more difficult.

"We're already overwhelmed," said a frustrated sergeant. "We don't need more public cooperation. Lead packages are piling up in Crime Analysis because there's only six investigators in Physical Crimes and they haven't got time to check 'em out." Besides, he added, no one in the department could remember a single murder case that had been solved by a reward.

9. INVESTIGATOR LEONARD BORRIELLO

We got a million false leads from hookers alone. They turned in their own pimps, other pimps, people they owed, people who owed them, johns they didn't like, johns that looked at 'em cross-eyed. Hookers live in an unreal world; they con, they exaggerate, lie. So they always hyped up their information, made it sound better than it was, which drove us nuts. We kept hearing about a gray van. We must've worked a thousand man-hours trying to find it. The girls said the driver acted suspicious, he had rough hands, a southern accent, mid-forties, a torn sheet on the front seat. We stopped one gray van and the guy turned out to be an ordinary john, scared shitless that his wife would find out he used whores. He had solid alibis for every killing. As soon as we dropped him as a suspect, we got three more reports of a suspicious man in a gray van. It wouldn't stop. That fucking gray van!

Pretty soon we had four thousand license numbers to check out. Sixteen hours a day my partner Billy Barnes and I were interviewing boyfriends, ex-boyfriends, pimps, jail inmates looking for a deal, hotel clerks, transvestites, addicts, chasing every lead, the good ones and the stupid ones. Every violent john had to be checked out, and for a while it seemed like they were *all* violent. We'd been conducting prostitution sweeps all summer, issuing tickets, and we had a thousand johns to check out.

I saw a guy back a woman against a car door in an alley. He's got a screwdriver in his hand, trying to steal some sex. I grabbed him and figured I had our man. He turned out to be clean.

After a while we noticed that one guy's name kept surfacing. Night after night the girls saw him sneaking around, peeping, hiding in doorways. And he kept asking questions about the police, what were we doing, did we have a suspect, stuff like that. Serial killers like to keep up with the action.

I stopped the guy and it turned out he was in love with one of the whores. It happens to a certain type of mentality. They pay thirty dollars for a blow job and then convince themselves she did it for love. This hooker was living in a van with her pimp and this john was dying of jealousy. I checked him out and he was clean—obsessed, stupid, but clean. Like a hundred other guys we checked.

10. JO ANN VAN NOSTRAND

The night before Thanksgiving I picked up a trick on the Bausch Street Bridge near the Upper Falls. It was a spooky place—empty factories with busted-out windows facing the river and a big brick smokestack and an abandoned glass plant. I hadn't gone out for a while 'cause I was bingeing on coke at my boyfriend's house on Clinton. I liked to get high for twenty-four hours and then sleep for two or three days. This night I wasn't high, but I was thinking about it. But first I needed money.

Three or 4:00 A.M. was scabville in my business. In Rochester the best traffic was like early evening, when the shift workers got off, and like 5:00 to 7:00 A.M., when there were no cops and the johns were on their way to work. Kodak workers, Bausch & Lomb, bankers, et cetera. It's one quick trick after another, twenty to fifty bucks a pop. In an hour I'd have two hundred, three hundred bucks. Then I could dissolve a little coke in hot water and run it in my arm and sleep for two or three days.

I'm walking west over the bridge and this little silver-blue car's coming at me and I waved. I never ran out and flagged cars—a lady lets the man come to her—but I don't mind doing a little soliciting. There was no traffic. The guy stops in the middle of the bridge, calls out, "You dating?"

I says, "Yeah. You goin' out?"

"Yeah."

"You the heat?"

"No."

"Prove it."

He says, "Hey, lady, *you* prove it!"

Every city had its own system, but in Rochester the way you proved you weren't a cop was you showed bare tit and the john showed dick. Supposedly that was one thing that cops won't do—only they *will*! That was how I got busted my only time in Rochester. I was so pissed! When we got to the police station I said, "I wanna see the sergeant, 'cause this pig showed his dick!" The next morning they told me to plead no contest and in six months they'd expunge the record, which they did.

So this john on the bridge pulled it out and I lifted my shirt. Before I got into the car, I took a good look at him: Fifty, fifty-five, stocky built, dark eyes, thinning gray hair. He was wearing a dark baseball cap, a quilt jacket, a V-neck pullover, white T-shirt, bluish poplin work pants, white socks.

I said, "My name's Barbara. What's yours?"

"Mitch," he said. "You got some time? I don't like nothing fast. You gimme some extra time, I'll take care of ya good."

I says, "You gotta pay me first."

"That's no problem," he said. "When we get there I'll give you the money."

I said, "You gotta give me my money now. Whattaya you wanna do?"

"I want a straight fuck."

That was unusual these days, so I said, "Straight fuck? I don't like to fuck. Don't you want a half and half?"

"Yeah, maybe."

"What're you spending?"

"I can give you forty bucks."

I was gonna push for more, but I figured I'd wait a while. I used to charge fifty dollars just to take my pants off. But at 4:00 A.M. forty bucks is okay, ya hear what I'm saying?

He drove north on St. Paul. He said, "You don't mind if

we go out a ways? I don't like to do it down here. With that strangler around, the cops are kinda bad."

Three minutes into the ride I caught the bad vibes. This guy was a nonstop talker. When he slowed at Seth Green Drive, I said, "You're not headin' down there, are ya, honey?"

He said, "Oh, no. I was just lookin'. I wasn't gonna park there."

"Well, you better not."

"Yeah, I don't blame ya. I heard about that dead girl down there."

I said, "You ain't going near Driving Park Bridge, are ya? There was another dead girl over there."

"No," he says. "That's where I broke my ankle."

We headed north, toward Lake Ontario. That didn't bother me, some guys like to take you way out. I had one guy took me to a trailer park in the next county. I had a pig farmer that took me twenty miles and always brought me back. Pros don't mind a little travel time.

En route he's telling me how he married an older bitch, she wasn't worth shit in bed, he kept a girlfriend, he worked late at night making salads, et cetera. As we're getting near the suburb of Irondequoit his voice turns growly and he starts telling me about hos that ripped him off—one grabbed his wallet while she was blowing him, one tried to steal his wedding ring, et cetera. One girl brought him into this apartment and went out the back door with his money, so he stole some of her stuff. He said he told her later, "Go ahead and laugh at me, bitch. I got your VCR and TV." And she said, "So what? It wasn't my apartment."

I'm thinking, Something isn't right about this guy. Something doesn't hang together. I spoke right up: "Hey, look, I'm not young, and I'm not into ripping people off. I'll try to make you happy. If you got a problem or you been drinking too much, I'll take my time, and if you ain't—after a certain length of time, then it's *your* problem, ya hear what I'm saying?"

He says, "Yeah. Okay," in this tight, tense voice, and

then he tells me how a black ho jumped in his car down on Hudson, which is a bad area, and she pulled a knife on him and went for his wallet.

He said he told her the car had an automatic lock and she couldn't get out. She believed him and panicked, and he kept on with his story, only I'm not listening because I'm checking the door. It didn't look like it had an electrical lock. What a relief! I figured if he keeps up this rap I'm gonna do the old June Cicero—give him a chop in the ribs and jump out.

He started talking about his wife again, said they had six kids. Said he'd worked in a boys' school as a cook.

I said, "Where ya workin' now, Mitch?"

He said, "At this grocery place, G&G Cheese. And before that I worked in a nursing home."

He asked me about my kids, and when I put him off, he asked again, in a nicer voice. Well, I never tell tricks the truth about my sons. Ya hear what I'm saying? I told him I got three kids, eight, eleven, and twelve, 'cause I don't want him to know my age. People on the street think I'm in my late twenties.

He said he could take my sons fishing. I says, "No, thanks. I don't play that. I don't involve my kids with nobody."

He says, "You don't seem like the kind of girl to be hooking."

I said, "Well, I gotta feed my kids. I don't get enough money from Social Security."

He said, "I got some potatoes and apples that I found in the country. Farm forage." He laughed. "I do most of my harvesting when I get off work at three in the morning."

By this time we're way out Lake Avenue, and I'm beginning to wheeze from my asthma and my arthritis is kicking up and I'm wondering where the fuck we're headed. He says, "You seem like a nice girl. Maybe I could bring some food by your house. Maybe I could come by and take you out. I kinda like you." He said he didn't get to go out all the time because he didn't always have access to the car—"My kids use it all the time."

He said, "I like to hunt deer." He showed me a rifle scope on the floor by the hand brake. He said he'd dropped his gun and it broke off. I'm thinking, This motherfucker's getting weirder and weirder. My brain clicked. *This son of a bitch has got a gun in this car. . . .*

I'd been carrying a knife because of the killings. I opened it nice and slow and held the blade flat against my thigh. It was a hunting knife with a brown wood handle, razor sharp. When you pressed a button on the side, the blade folded out and locked so it wouldn't collapse if you hit somebody. I cut my finger two or three times with that knife when I reached into my pocket to open it up on dates.

Pretty soon we turned down a dark street. I said, "Where we going?"

He says, "To the park."

I spotted this sign: "Durand Eastman Park Golf Course." He pulled off the road and backed up to a tree. I knew the lake was somewhere near, but I couldn't see a thing. I'm thinking, I'm keeping this knife open till I see what shakes out. I held it in my right hand. I was scared shitless. I mean, it was *dark*!

He counted out the forty bucks. Then he says, "There ain't nobody out here. Take your clothes off."

I'm like, "*Unh*-uh." 'Cause I don't get naked unless I'm in a hotel room or my house. In a car, I'll do a ho's strip, which is you take your pant legs down and ball 'em up around your ankles nice and tight, so you can pull 'em back up and haul ass. Then I take my blouse and whip it up, 'cause they all wanna see big tits, right? Part of the price of admission. So that makes me bare from the neck to ankle. What more can a john ask?

I said, "Hey, man, we're in a park. The rangers could come." I did my little ho's roll and got out and shuffled around to the backseat. The car was a four-door hatchback with bucket seats, blue or blue-gray. It looked like a Chevette.

He joined me in the back. I asked him to use a rubber, but he didn't want to hear about it. He pulls down the front seatback to flatten out a place. Then he spread a quilt under us and motioned me to lay with my head toward the dashboard.

I did an acrobat spread, feet against the back window, head propped on the passenger bucket seat. Then I went into a Georgia Buck, which is you push your chin tight against your chestbone so the john can't get at your neck—hard on the breathing but it may save your life.

He says, "Wouldn't you be more comfortable with your head in between the seats?" Something told me, No, no, you gotta keep this suckah in sight. If I put my head between the seats, I wouldn't be able to see him and my neck would be in a blind-side position. I've been raped and I don't let nobody get me in a vulnerable position. Also, I saw clear plastic bags in the car and I thought, Maybe this guy's not strangling women, he's *suffocating* 'em. It would've been a cinch with my head between the seats.

So I says, "No! I'm fine just like I am."

He wasn't hard and he couldn't get it in, but he seemed cool enough. He talked all the time he was trying to fuck. His three favorite subjects were his wife is a bitch, hunting and fishing in the country, and all the shitty things the other hos did to him. I was being careful. I'm thinking, Could this goofy guy be the strangler? Ya know what I'm saying? Was this weirdo smart enough to be killing girls right under the cops' noses?

He finally gets it up, but only semi—you follow my meaning? Like when you're on diabetes or blood pressure medication, it takes a long time to come. Mitch was big: big and soft.

I said, "Hey, hon, you got diabetes or something?"

He said, "No, but it takes me a while." Then I hear his teeth grinding together and he's saying, *"I asked ya did ya have time?"*

"It's okay, hon," I said, real gentle. I took a good grip on my knife. That blade felt nice and warm.

After a while, I peek at my watch. He's been pumping away for forty minutes. His hands keep fluttering toward my neck, and I'm telling him, "Don't *do* that! I have asthma." If I was closer to the city I would've walked home.

The seat hurt the small of my back. My arthritis was flaring and I was having trouble catching my breath. I was crying inside, but I couldn't let him know that. Some guys, it turns 'em on and they can be dangerous. Don't get me wrong, I can fight good. A guy in Rochester bit my tit and I whaled on him with a cast iron skillet till I thought he was dead. When I was seventeen in the Plaza Hotel in New York a guy on amyl nitrate went berserko and I coldcocked him with a lamp. I stuck a Niagara Falls guy in the leg to get out of his car.

So when it came to violence, Mitch wasn't getting cherry. But I couldn't get a handle on him. He acted scary *weird,* scary *goofy.* One minute he's gonna give me apples and potatoes and the next he's flaring up.

After a while the back pain got unbearable. I started to say, "Look, hon . . ."

He stops pushing and says, "What the fuck are you?" He looks me dead in the face and his voice turns mean: *"What the fuck are you, one of those bip bam thank you ma'am bitches?"*

He shoved at my chest. I went to myself, Fuck, this is the strangler and you're next! You better start playing this motherfucker right and let him know you can handle him.

I says, "No, honey. I *told* ya, I'm not used to fucking this long. Calm down! I'm so out of practice. I haven't fucked in a long time, ya know what I'm saying?"

He chilled out. In this soft, gentle voice, he says, "It's because of my wife. She don't ever wanna fuck. I work hard, I got all these kids, and I can't go out that often."

I'm feeling a little weak, but I kept on playing him. His eyes kinda relaxed and he did a nervous giggle. Then my hand brushed against his leg and I felt something plastic. I thought maybe it was a gun.

I said, *"What's that?"*

He raised up his leg and showed me. "I got a brace. I told you about hurting myself at Driving Park Bridge."

All this time, I was still on my back in my acrobat spread

and my Georgia Buck. Feet on the rear window, head on the front seat, him on top. I was *tense.*

He says, "Hug me, hug me."

I reached up with my right arm, the one without the knife.

He says, "Use *both* your arms."

"No, I—I—I can't."

He groped down my arm and says, "What's *that*?"

I said, "I got a knife. Hear what I'm sayin'? It's sharp and it's open. You bother me, I'll fuck you up. There's a killer around. I'm prepared to meet my maker and take that motherfucker with me."

It's a Mexican standoff. He knows if he makes one move on me, I'm gonna stick him.

He laughed. He said, "Well, I don't blame ya."

I stayed on guard. Something still ain't right. Then he tries to get me to lay my head between the seats again. I kept telling him I had to be able to see everything.

A headlight flashed and he pushed me down and said, real vicious, "Shut up!"

I pushed him off. That suckah weighed two hundred pounds. I said, "Get off. I can't breathe. I got asthma."

He said, "Wait a minute. Wait a minute!"

I pushed him hard and yelled, *"Get off!"*

He bumped his head on the ceiling and I thought the shit was gonna jump off right then, but he said, "Okay, okay, okay. . . ."

His hand went back up above my tits. I said, "Hey, I told ya. *Don't* do that. I'm too ticklish." That was about the fifth time I had to tell him. I'm thinking, It's normal for a trick to reach up and grab my tits, but this guy was interested in my *neck.* See, my tits are so big they're over to the side. I don't wear a bra or underwear when I'm working. So his hands got no business up around my neck when my tits are over to the side, see what I'm saying?

He pumped for another five or ten minutes. The sweat was pouring off. I'm hurting all over, I can't breathe, I can't take any more, so I said, "Look, we been out here for a long time and this seat is killing me."

He told me, "Just play dead for a few minutes, okay? Close your eyes."

I kept my eyes open a slit so I could see what he was doing. The crazy son of a bitch was still talk, talk, talk. Then he says, "C'mon now. If you'll just play like you're a dead body, we'll have this over with."

So I says "Okay" and let out all my breath and sank down like I'd been dead a month.

He was still talking when he came. Just like that.

Then he lets out a deep breath and says, "You know what *that* was, don'tcha, baby?"

I played stupid. I said, "No," in a tiny voice. I knew it was all over for me. He got what he wanted, now he's gonna make his move. I shifted my knife till it was almost touching his side. I'm saying to myself, This motherfucker's the definite *killer.*

He says, "Well, goddamn, I'm finished." Like he's proud of himself!

I figure I'll jolly him along so he won't kill me, so I said, "Oh, wow, man, that was the best fuck I ever had."

He said, "I haven't fucked like that in twenty years."

He just laid there on top of me till I had to say, "Honey, I can't breathe." I pushed him again. The windows were fogged. He was making me claustrophobic. "I gotta breathe, baby. I got asthma."

When he didn't move, I opened the door and wiggled out from under. The change fell out of my pants. He raised up and said, "Wait a minute. We'll look for it together."

I was so happy to be alive, I said, "Leave it for the sweeper." I pulled my pants up and my shirt down. He gets out the other side of the car, raises the seatback, picks up three white plastic grocery bags of potatoes and apples, and hands 'em to me. Thin-skinned potatoes, the kind I like.

I got in the front seat and sat with my back to the door so I could face him. I figured I was probably safe at this point.

On the way back to town, he says, "Can I call ya?"

I said, "I don't have a phone, Mitch. But you're gonna drop me off where I live, so you'll know where I'm at."

"I don't always drive. I ride a bike. When I get the car, I'll come getcha. We'll take a ride in the country."

All the way home he's doing the motormouth again. When I didn't respond, he said, "Why're you so quiet? Are you shy?" Sounded kinda annoyed, like it was a social error if you didn't comment on every word. You see that in johns.

I had him drop me off, and when I went inside, I told my boyfriend, "I coulda swore I was out with the fucking strangler tonight."

He laughed. My man's a very *cool* guy. He said, "How could that be? You're still alive."

I laughed, too. I went out and got high with my earnings —four dime bags, good for about five hours. I was so ragged out I didn't get the full effect.

11.

Just before noon on the next day, Thanksgiving, November 23, 1989, Mark Stetzel was walking his dog in the northern Rochester suburb of Charlotte, just upriver from the place where the polluted Genesee River stained Lake Ontario a murky brown. It was a damp, cold day, a hint of snow in the air. High-tension wires stretched to the cement plant up on the bluff. The swampy area had the pervasive smell of canal water. It had been named "Turning Point Park" for the widening in the channel where small ships and motorized barges put about before returning to Lake Ontario. It was an isolated spot, reachable only by cutback road off Boxart Street, and it was usually empty of life except for an occasional deer, raccoon, or muskrat.

Stetzel followed a narrow cinder road alongside a rusty old barge that seemed to be settling into the muddy water inch by inch. His dog ran down a game trail that led to a stand of reeds and cattails five or six feet high. The man followed his pet to a flattened area where deer bedded down for the night. He came to a swatch of ice-encrusted carpeting, burlap side up, its color almost matching the vegetation. A bare foot protruded from a corner. Stetzel left to find a phone.

The discovery interrupted Thanksgiving dinners. Among the first to arrive at the desolate spot were Deputy Police Commissioner Terrence Rickard, CID major Lynde Johnston, Physical Crimes commander lieutenant Tom Jones, and First Assistant District Attorney Charles Siragusa. Despite their rank and power, they were forbidden entry to the deer trail by a tightly disciplined team of evidence techs and other investigators.

The first word was that this find was different from the others. The female body lay facedown, but a large area of lividity showed that it had been face up long enough for the blood to settle along the backbone, which meant that the corpse had been moved after death. The right leg was bent backward at the knee, elevating the buttocks and suggesting the possibility of anal intercourse, probably postmortem. The decomposing skin was covered with a milky-white gelatinous coating, mottled with varying shades of brown and dark red. The body looked as though it had been under the rug for three or four weeks. There were no tattoos; thus the victim couldn't be the missing Maria Welch.

The medical examiner commented that the woman probably had died of asphyxia, but the neck area was too decomposed for a positive diagnosis. The body was slashed from breastbone to crotch—"a deer hunter's cut," as a cop observed. The privates were clotted with blood, and the genital lips appeared to be missing.

After the body was removed, evidence techs came across a pocketknife among the reeds, along with a bloody towelette. Apparently the killer had cleaned his hands before walking back up the access road to the busy streets above. But what else had he done to the corpse? An act of necrophilia? Masturbation? Once again there was no trace of semen.

"Now he's switched the ball game on us," Lynde Johnston complained when the officials returned to headquarters. "He's changed his dump site to seven miles downriver. And he's into mutilation." It was the escalation that everyone had feared.

Atop page one, the *Democrat and Chronicle* trumpeted, "GORGE YIELDS BODY OF ANOTHER WOMAN. It's area's 11th mystery death."

A photo showed prosecutor Siragusa, Johnston, and two others trudging, heads down, along the path where Mark Stetzel had walked his dog. The photo was taken from the rear, and there was an air of frustration and desolation about it.

"I don't remember the caption," Johnston said later, "but we all felt it should've read 'In the shit.' The Rochester PD had a great rating. In an average year we'd handle thirty to forty murders and clear 90 percent, against a national average of 62 percent. But in the last half of '89, our murder rate nearly doubled and hardly any of them were being cleared. This guy killed nine or ten women and we didn't even know how he was doing it, let alone his name. He was making us look like Laurel and Hardy."

It didn't take long to establish that the dead woman was June Stott, missing for a month. Her murder reduced speculation that the bodies found in the gorge were victims of a vengeful drug dealer administering "hot shots." Stott had never been known to touch drugs and was terrified of addicts.

Johnston added the "slightly slow" woman's photograph and vital statistics to the gallery of victims in his war room, using up the last inch of space on his wall.

12. ARTHUR SHAWCROSS (PSYCHIATRIC INTERVIEW)

Q. What was next?

A. I think it was a girl named June Stotts who I knew as "J," and I—she's been at the house before, had supper, dinner with us. She lived on the street. When I first met her, she was skinny, and I told her, I says, "Any time you want something to eat, you just stop over, ya know? Or if you're cold, ya know, somebody's home, you get warm." Most of the time I see her down at Midtown [Mall] where they have all the little tables and stuff, and she'd be hanging around down there at breakfast, lunch, and suppertime. Somebody would buy her something to eat. Never knew where she lived. . . .

I had a car—the car, a Dodge Omni. I came up on Dewey Avenue and came across up near some park area behind—between Dewey and Sarasota, over in that direction—North Plymouth—and J was sitting on a park bench over there right on the curb, and she seen me, waved her hand. I stopped the car and pulled up to the curb, and she says, "What are you doing?"

I says, "Just driving around." I told her I was out fishing, and she says, "Want to go for a drive?" and I said, "All right." At that moment there was a cop coming up the street, right? And I just went across past the cop, went over to Lake Avenue, and left.

She says, "You know you went up a one-way street."

I says, "I'm only going one way." It was weird. Cop just looked at me. Turned around in the car and just looked at me, ya know? At that moment, ya know, it was weird.

And we went down to Charlotte, went into a gas station, a store, diner thing in the village of Charlotte, bought a couple loaves of bread and some potato chips, soda, and stuff, and we went down and parked at the beach parking lot, the big parking lot by the Genesee River, right up by the Genesee, where the warehouses are. And we locked the car, walked out on the pier at the beach, and we started feeding the ducks and the sea gulls the bread. We walked out the end of the Charlotte Pier, hanging out there, watching the boats coming in and stuff. There about a couple hours, came back, and we stopped where they put the boats in the waters—a lot of ducks there—walked back to the car, went up and back to the same store, got some more bread and stuff and drove up to Turning Point Park.

We walked down the—that way, down the big steep hillside, and there's a bunch of concrete docks there with a small railing, goes way out where the ship turns around, the dredger. Down there feeding all the sea gulls and a few ducks, a muskrat running around there. . . .

We walked back from there, and we just followed the river toward where the barges were tied up, get down the end of that little cinder road . . . and there's a concrete block sitting there with a ring on it like where you'd tie something up to, and on the right-hand side there's an area that was all short grass, and somebody had an old rug laying there, a gray rug, two pieces of it, so instead of sitting on the ground, took the rug. We're sitting on the rug.

And we were just laying back, talking, ya know? And I don't know what we said, but after a while she, ya know, asked me, she—"Can you teach me how to make love?" And I said, "How old are you?" And she said, "Thirty." And I says, "You never been with a man?"

She said, "No," ya know, so she took her coat off. I took my shirt off. I took everything off but my shorts, and she got everything off but her panties and bra, and I'm laying beside her. I start kissing her, and I look back at her, says, "You can't tell me you never been— Where'd you learn how to kiss like that?"

She said, "TV."

"Yeah, sure."

So I'm fondling her, and I just lift up the bra—no reaction, nothing. And I massage her vagina—no reaction. And I told her, I said what I was going to do, and she said, "All right."

It wouldn't—I couldn't get it in, right? She wasn't a virgin, but I couldn't get it in, and at that moment, ya know, she gets up on her hands, back. She says, "Oh, my God," right? Ya know, she says, "I'm going to tell the police," ya know? I panicked, ya know? I pushed her back down on the ground.

I says, "You're the one asked me to do this for you." I said, "Now you want to, ya know, spoil it and go—say you tell the cops?" Said, "Well, I made a mistake," and that's when I started to sweat again, and the brightness, the quietness, ya know? You usually hear a lot of sea gulls, and the boats are going up and down the river, guys that are going up toward Driving Park, catching salmon up there. And I panicked. I strangled her. She didn't fight, nothing.

And I took her clothes off that were—that she had, took her bra and panties and rest of her clothes, and I just, dazed, walked over to the river about maybe thirty feet away and dropped her clothes in the water. And there was a big metal barge there, and the force of water pulled everything underneath. And I went back, ya know? And I felt bad, and I'm talking to her, ya know? Why, ya know? I said, "It didn't have to be this way."

I stayed there about maybe two, three hours late in the afternoon, and I walked back—back up the top of the hill to the car, and I sit in the car for about an hour, ya know, trying to, ya know, think things out, and I drove back to the city. I went over to Clara's, wherever, I can't figure. She was working somewhere, I don't remember. Took the car back to her—her place and got—got the bicycle, rode the bike back to the house.

And about two days later I took a bus down to that area. . . . I walked back down there just to see if it was true, ya know? I was thinking, ya know, see if it was something really happened. And she was still there, and she was—the body was stiff, rigor mortis, whatever, and it started getting warm out, and I'm sitting there beside her, talking to—just talking to the—the body, and I start looking around, see if anything dropped on the ground from the previous time, and I find some change, a set of keys, and I found a little ID thing, and that's when I knew what her name was and where she lived.

And she had the jackknife laying there, and I just picked her up under the elbows, the armpits, and dragged her off in the swamp area where the cattails are, probably about sixty feet, took the rug back there and, I don't know, I just took that knife and I cut her from her neck down to her anus. But I didn't cut the stomach wall. I just opened up the fat tissue, and I cut out the vagina and ate it. Why, I don't know. I just ate it, and I took, went back. I covered her up with the rug. First I rolled her over on her stomach, covered her up with the rug, went back, picked up all the excess stuff that was there, threw it in the river, and left.

Q. . . . And you have no idea why you cut her?

A. No.

Q. Can you imagine any reason you might have done that?

A. No.

Q. How did you remove the vagina?

A. I cut it, around it.

Q. Then did you cook that flesh?

A. Why should I cook it? I said I ate it.

Q. I was asking you if you cooked it before you ate it.

A. No.

Q. What did you do while you ate it?

A. That's a stupid question. I'm just sitting there in a daze.

Q. You were sitting there next to the body?

A. I was eating—I just ate it, looking at nothing, ya know?

I don't know what I was thinking about. I was just there.

Q. Sitting . . .

A. Yeah.

Q. . . . Down by the water with her?

A. You're stupid. . . .

13.

After the Stott body was found, Deputy Chief Terrence Rickard asked crime profilers for assistance. State Police Lieutenant Ed Grant and Special Agent Greg McCrary of the FBI's Behavioral Sciences Unit studied police files and concluded that one man was responsible for the deaths of Dorothy Blackburn, Anna Steffen, Patty Ives, Frances Brown, June Stott, the headless woman on Seth Green Island, and perhaps one or two of the others.

They reported that the murderer was most likely a white in his mid-thirties, a bullying and difficult husband, a stickler for neatness. He probably had a troubled relationship with his mother and a criminal record. He lived or worked in or near the Lake and Lyell prostitution area, felt inadequate with females, had minimal social relations, and didn't stand out in crowds or groups. He might be a security guard or a police buff, perhaps even a policeman "dropping tin" (showing his badge) or using a gun to force his victims into his car. Despite his antisocial tendencies, he was capable of faking conviviality and friendliness. If questioned by police, he might babble on about how he hoped the killer would be caught before he caused more heartache, point out that he was familiar with the neighborhood and ask if he could assist in the manhunt. In general he would play the role of a cooperative citizen. He was, of course, a sociopath, or as the plainspoken Terry Rickard put it after reading the report, "A guy with a line of bullshit."

Neither the profilers nor the police brass knew exactly

what to make of the killer's tendency to conceal his victims under coverings like cardboard and asphalt tiles, but they agreed that the clumsy method was more efficacious than they'd first believed. Stott's body might not have been found if it hadn't been for Mark Stetzel's dog. Police helicopters had flown over the murder scene and Coast Guard vessels had searched the banks of the river while the corpse lay under a rug. The killer's peculiar MO had to be considered one more stroke of offbeat cunning.

The profile was kept in Rickard's office and reserved for a few top strategists. The deputy chief didn't want the information to influence the thinking of beat cops and detectives who were supposed to keep their minds open and check out all suspicious persons, not just those who matched their own preconceptions or a profile.

A hit soon unreeled from a police computer. The suspect was a white male sociopath, thirty-eight, who'd once served a sentence for rape. He enjoyed kinky sex and had tied one of his victims to a tree in Durand-Eastman Park. He was often seen around Lake and Lyell and had numerous hangups about women, especially prostitutes.

A lieutenant dropped the printout on Rickard's desk and chortled, "Here's your killer, boss. It'll be over by Christmas."

A stakeout team watched the suspect pull out of his suburban garage in a gray van. "A gray van!" Rickard recalled later. "Exactly what we'd been looking for. We were about to pop the corks."

But a check with the suspect's employer disclosed that the time lines were off. The man had been out of town on three or four of the killing dates. He was kept under observation.

In the middle of an early-morning snowfall, a prostitute ran up to a police car and reported that she'd just been approached by a werewolf in a light-colored van. The creature was wearing a mask and a hat.

At a traffic light, detectives stopped a white GMC van and

questioned a forty-one-year-old carpenter wearing a ladies' straw hat, blond wig, three-quarter-length imitation leather coat with fur collar, blue and red skirt, and black pumps. His full beard was concealed under a lumpy mask of brown gauze and adhesive tape.

He explained that he was looking for a prostitute to rip off, his favorite method of sexual release. He slumped down and moaned, "I don't want to live anymore." Then he popped up and said, "I don't know, I just lost it for a minute. I'm okay now."

He admitted that he'd been arrested for cross-dressing and for lying on the floors of public bathrooms to watch women. One of the detectives cracked, "Is that how the limbo was born?" A lie detector test confirmed the bizarre story, and the trembling "werewolf" was released.

Then a factory worker was overheard at a drinking fountain threatening to "off another one this weekend." He was thirty-five, had a record, hated his mother, and had sexual problems with his wife. A company security guard searched the man's car and found pornie videos and a snuff film. The man lived above a carpet store and sometimes borrowed a gray van from a relative.

Once again surveillances were set up and deep background checks begun. "We didn't stop working our other leads," Rickard emphasized. "Everybody was on the case: Chief Urlacher, clerks, meter maids, elevator operators, *everybody*. I had to order some of the guys home before they collapsed. Then this factory worker came along, and it was bells and whistles again. Except that once again it was the wrong man."

The frustrated Rickard doubled the personnel of the Physical Crimes unit and ordered all thirty-two members of the Tactical Squad to break off "Operation Clean," their campaign against neighborhood drug dealers, and concentrate on the murders. Something had to be done. The media were circling.

14. JO ANN VAN NOSTRAND

A few days after my date with that weird motherfucker, I slept late behind an antidepressant and didn't go out till two in the morning. I was walking across the Bausch Street bridge toward Lake and Lyell and here comes the same asshole driving the same little silver-blue car.

I said to myself, Oh, shit, I'm not going out with this guy again. But I waved, 'cause I pride myself on being a friendly ho.

He turned and there's a girl in the car. I thought to myself, Better her than me! I'd seen her around, but I didn't know her name. She was twenty-nine or thirty, Italian extraction, short, maybe five foot, with teased-up dark hair. She always stood under that sign in front of the hangout—"Texas Red Hots, Mark's No. 2, Open 24 Hours." No matter how cold it was, she wore the same pink jacket. Most of those girls, they sold their good clothes for their habits. That's why they wore cheap high-top sneakers in three foot of snow.

This ho, she was trying to pass AIDS to every john in town. Her and her husband were heavy users. He took her to drop-off spots and she worked till they scored coke money. Used to be respectable people, lived in the suburbs, two nice kids, nice house, the American dream. They went to a party one night and somebody laid out a line of coke. After that, they weren't suburbanites anymore.

Now here she was, disappearing up St. Paul Street with that crazy son of a bitch that couldn't get his rocks off unless you played dead.

I turned a few tricks, got high, went to bed, and I woke up late in the afternoon at my boyfriend's house up on Clinton. Pretty soon I heard the TV news come on. I'm in the bathroom and he calls out, "Oh, shit, they found another girl. Facedown in a crick in Wayne County." That's next to Rochester.

I rushed in as they were flashing the face on the TV. I looked at the pitcher and I said, "That looks like the girl that was in a car I saw last night."

I said I was gonna go out and do a little investigating, and my friend says, "What're you, *crazy*? This guy just killed another girl."

I said, "I gotta go."

I found fat Madeleine on Lyell and I said, "That dead girl, is it the one that's always in front of the restaurant? Short black hair? Pink jacket?"

"Yeah," she said. "Liz. Hangs with her husband."

I said, "Oh, shit. I know something I got no business knowing. I—I . . . I know who the strangler is."

Madeleine's eyes got big and she slapped her mouth with her hand. "Hey, girl," she says, "you gotta flag a cop."

There was a warrant out for me for a hair-pulling fight with a bitch roommate. I'm wanted for harassment. So I'm like, "Oh, no, Madeleine, I can't."

She said, "Girl, if you know somethin', you gotta tell 'em. What're ya gonna do, wait till he kills us all?"

So I'm thinking, Well, the worst I can get on the warrant is thirty to ninety days. Maybe it's worth it if this is the guy. Maybe the judge'll gimme a break.

I waved down a uniform in a car. I looked at his name tag and said, "Listen, Walker, I got something to tell ya. It's about the killer. But hey, listen, I got a warrant out on me."

He said, "If you know something about these killings, just tell me. We don't care about chippy warrants."

So I told him how the guy took me out to a park and his hands kept going up to my neck and I had to pull my knife.

Walker called his sergeant and a squad car took me to the Physical Crimes office for an interview. They told me the dead ho's name was Elizabeth Gibson. A hunter found her in a swamp, just before noon. Shit, I saw her ten, eleven hours before! They said it looked like strangulation. She died on the same day she was supposed to check into the hospital for an abortion.

My memory was fucked by all the coke I was runnin', and I couldn't remember where Mitch said he worked or the exact time we tricked or even where he took me. The cops said thank you very much and drove me home.

A couple nights later this little red car passes me several

times and one of the sisters is driving. I don't turn black tricks, 'cause there's a certain element of nigger that's a pain in the ass, period. They rip you off and they're too tough. And anyway, I never been into females.

She rolls down her window. I says, "No, baby, I don't play that shit."

She flashes a badge and says, "Are you Barbara?" Turns out she's a cop from the Tac Squad, and my presence is desired at headquarters.

So that's how I met this cute investigator, Lenny Borriello. He had eyes like slits, gave him an Oriental look, said he was Ukrainian on his mother's side and his father was a well-known boxer in New York City. Lenny's hair was in spikes, like a half-grown crew cut, and he had this big grin. After I got to know him, I realized that all he did was grin and work. Most of the cops took part-time jobs, but not Lenny. He spent *all* his time on police cases. He blew a marriage 'cause he was never home. That's why they gave him the prostitute murders.

He took me to one side and said he'd read the reports and he was convinced "Mitch" was the strangler and he'd intended to kill me. The other detectives, including Lenny's partner Billy Barnes, took a different view of me. They said he was crazy to believe a ho that ran coke.

I didn't know what the hell to think. Lenny looked wobbly—it was his night off and he said he'd had a few pops over at Shields. I thought, Yeah, man, a few *dozen.*

He interviewed me for an hour, kept checking back and forth with my first statement to Physical Crimes. Took nothin' for granted, ya get my meaning? He kept asking, "Are you sure? *Are you sure?*"

Well, no, I wasn't. Sometimes I'd wake up after runnin' coke and not know how long I slept—two days, three days? I told Lenny I remembered talking to a Puerto Rican guy on the night I saw Mitch with Liz Gibson and maybe the spic could help straighten out the dates. His name was Junior and he hung out at Mark's.

So we get in Lenny's car and he drove like a maniac. I thought it was because of the drinking but I found out later it was his natural driving. I said, "Sir! Investigator Borriello! You're drunk," and he said, "I can drive, I can drive. Call me Lenny."

I spot Junior's car on Lake. He was shaky when he got out—"What I did? What I *did*?"—but he gave us some good help on the dates. 'Cause he kinda kept track of me, gave me rides home. The dates were important to Lenny 'cause he had to connect 'em with the night Liz Gibson disappeared. Whattaya know? They matched.

Then Lenny followed my directions to the spot where I tricked with Mitch in Durand-Eastman Park. After we got out of his car to look around, Lenny said, "Look where he was gonna throw your body." There was a sharp drop-off.

He kept on me to remember where Mitch worked. The part of my brain that remembers conversations was wrecked. I did a little better on the car. I told him it was a blue hatchback, probably a Chevette. It was definitely a four-door. And it had bucket seats and a rifle scope on the front floor and white plastic bags in the back.

Lenny told me he was gonna use my car information to crack the case. He put the description on the radio and it was read at all the roll calls. The deputy chief made a video that went to every station in town and ordered 'em to be on the lookout, and pretty soon the cops around Lake and Lyell were checking out blue compacts and especially Chevettes. The girls on the street were briefed to yell for the Tac Unit if the car came in sight.

Lenny promised it wouldn't be long before I'd be picking Mitch out of a lineup. I'm thinking, I hope so. The guy's gotta know he's gonna be caught and he's gotta know I saw him with Gibson—shit, why did I wave? And he's gotta know I talked to the cops. He must be asking himself, Why'd I let that bitch live? First chance he gets, I'm history. Ya know what I'm saying?

15. ARTHUR SHAWCROSS (PSYCHIATRIC INTERVIEW)

I stopped at Mark's on Lake Avenue, pulled into the parking lot right by the restaurant. I was in there having a —I think it was a steak dinner I ordered, or a chicken dinner. And it was cold outside, and I came out into the parking lot and . . . there was a girl, this Elizabeth Gibson, was sitting in my—the car I had. . . .

I said, "What are you doing in the car?" She says, "Cold outside." And so I got in, started the car up, and the heater's on. I just flipped the heater on full blast. I sit there about twenty minutes talking to her, and I says, "Well, you warm enough now?" Ya know, because I wanted to go home.

And she says, "You wanna go out?" and I told her, "All I got is ten dollars because I just spent the rest of it in the restaurant," and she says, "All right."

So . . . we started making out and, I don't know, she panicked. She grabbed me by the face, ya know, with her fingernails right into my eyes, and her left foot broke the gearshift . . . the housing, the plastic, ya know. And I'm pushing—trying to push her back away from me. I says, "What's the matter with you?" Ya know, I'm pushing with my arm. Her head's down over the edge of the seat, and I just panicked again. . . .

When she quit struggling, ya know, I got back into my seat of the bucket seat of the car, and I'm sitting there, ya know, and I look at the floor, and I see the gearshift, and I try to figure—I couldn't even put the car in reverse, ya know? Didn't know what to do. . . .

There was some rags in the car, and I just wiped the windshield and the rear window down and got back in the car. I didn't have my clothes off, just my zipper was down, and put her back down on the seat, fold the seat back up into the normal position, and she just laying against the door, so I got my door open and I just took the gearshift and just bent it manually, ya know, by physical force pretty much up to where it was before, but the housing itself, I couldn't. . . .

I just took the plastic out, only way to get the car into reverse, backed out and drove down in St. Paul past the zoo area, and I got lost somewhere out St. Paul somewhere and ended up going toward Wayne County. . . .

And there's a little path goes off into the field somewhere there, and I pulled into there, or backed in . . . about fifty, sixty feet, got out, and I was just standing there beside the car for a while, ya know?

There was snow on the ground and cold out. I didn't feel it. Went around to her side. While she's in the car I stripped her down, took all her clothes off her, and picked her up, carried her back probably a few hundred feet, and laid her down. . . .

Q. Had you strangled [Gibson] with both hands?

A. No. I didn't strangle her. When I went in, pushing against—I'm laying on her . . .

Q. I see.

A. . . . Right, but she's dug into my face, and I'm panicked, and I just—pushing her away up under the neck.

Q. Until she stopped scratching?

A. Yeah. . . . Then I tried to give her mouth-to-mouth, ya know, and the air would go in and come back out—nothing.

Q. Was that the only time you did that?

A. Yeah.

Q. Who noticed the scratches?

A. When I got to Dunkin' Donuts, everybody that was working that night noticed the gouge marks on my face. One girl, ya know, the girl I knew, she says, "What did you do, get in a fight with a girl?" I said, "No, I was out chasing a deer. . . ."

16.

Three days after the Gibson killing, Clara Neal was driving home from her cooking job in Spencerport and thinking about Art. Lately he'd been tapping on her bedroom window with satisfying regularity. He usually packaged his last salad at two or three in the morning and bicycled straight to her house. Ice and snow and zero temperatures didn't slow him down; he told her that Rochester seemed balmy after growing up in the North Country. He took shortcuts through parks and alleyways and empty parking lots—"riding cross-lots," as he described it to Clara. She'd never heard the expression before.

The lovers would enjoy each other's company for a while and then he would borrow her Omni for all-night hunting, fishing, foraging in farmers' fields, or running errands. He was a good provider; he kept gas in her tank and brought food that helped sustain her sons Robert and Roscoe and the rest of her brood. Sometimes he drove out to the countryside and prospected for new trysting spots. A few nights ago he'd found a lovers' lane so close to the lake you could hear the waves. He said it was called Durand-Eastman Park and promised to take her there for a little outdoor recreation. She knew what that meant. It wasn't easy to enjoy each other at home, with her children watching TV outside her bedroom door.

Lately the lovers had been fine-tuning their plan to set up housekeeping in West Virginia as soon as his parole ended. He told her he would be liberated in March, just four months away.* Clara was counting the days. For her, their flight would combine two dreams: a new life with Art and a return to her childhood home. Over and over she told herself, I'll be Mrs. Art Shawcross of Clay County!

Musing about the future as she drove toward town, she slowed for a stoplight on the Spencerport–Brockport Road. The paving was damp, but the hatchback had good brakes,

* In fact, parole supervision was scheduled to continue until September 2, 1997.

and Art had promised to repair the broken shift-housing. She felt a jolt and her body jerked against the seatback. She'd been rear-ended by a pickup. She wasn't hurt, but the Omni's rear end was smashed.

A tow truck hauled the little blue-gray car away and she took a bus to a downscale rental agency. She selected a gray four-door Chevrolet Celebrity, bigger and faster than the hatchback. The rental manager told her it had been used by the police Tactical Unit, and showed her the electric windows and the RPD number on the dash. She figured Art would get a laugh about that.

XI

CLOSING IN

. . . Because in my household I had been made to feel like shit, so no matter how handsome I might have seemed, I looked in the mirror with disappointment. It was only because of the way some women looked at me that I knew I was worth something more, but if you left it up to me, I would have spent my life hiding like a monster.

—*Oscar Hijuelos,* The Mambo Kings Play Songs of Love

1.

On November 29, 1989, two days after the body of Elizabeth Gibson was found in Wayne County, the personable police chief Gordon Urlacher made his first public admission that a serial killer was at work. The *Democrat and Chronicle* broke the story the next day under a page one headline:

COPS: KILLINGS "SERIAL"
13 Women Dead;
12 May Be Linked

The *Times-Union* opened its coverage with pictures of eleven dead women just below the masthead on page one. Headlines proclaimed:

VICTIMS LONELY, VULNERABLE
Rochester's Serial
Killer Preying On
Troubled Women

A twelfth panel was filled with a question mark and captioned, "Unidentified skeleton found Oct. 21, 1989." Almost every inch of the front page was devoted to the case, and two full pages inside detailed the life and death stories of the victims. Completing the saturation coverage, a lengthy "PORTRAIT OF A SERIAL KILLER" appeared on the first page of the second section.

The *Democrat and Chronicle* followed up on its original newsbeat with a picture gallery and a thoughtful story titled

"MARGINAL LIFESTYLES MADE WOMEN EASY PREY." It opened:

> She was a troubled woman.
>
> Drugs or mental illness or just terrible judgment made her take risks most women wouldn't.
>
> She spent a lot of time on the street, searching for drugs, searching for customers or searching for her sanity.
>
> She had been in trouble with the law. She came from a family of broken relationships, or started the pattern herself. She moved a lot and lived in a rough neighborhood. She had very little to her name, except maybe a child or two—or even six.
>
> Her name was Niki, or Dotsie, or Anna, or Rosalie, or Jackie, or Linda, or Patty, or Kimberley, or Frances, or June or Liz. She had another name, too, but we may never know it because she was just a headless skeleton when she was found. . . .

In their article, *D and C* reporters Diana Tomb and Leslie Sopko quoted crime writer Ann Rule: "They're all somebody's little girl. They don't deserve this."

The next day, the competitive *Times-Union*'s team of Corey Williams and David Barstow turned up the heat. Under a black-bordered logo, "Rochester's Unsolved Murders," the headlines read:

PROSTITUTES ANGRY, ARMED
"I feel like I'm on a mission" to find killer

Chief Urlacher was quoted as saying that he wasn't surprised about the prostitutes' new attitude. An angry and pseudonymous "Stacey" said, "I'm carrying a switchblade now." Another woman offered the opinion that the killer was "a man that a girl robbed or gave AIDS to. I think he is trying to get revenge." Still another added that her pistol-packing boyfriend would be following her every night until the killer was caught.

2. LIEUTENANT JAMES BONNELL

That December, Lake and Lyell was like a Chinese fire drill, even at three in the morning. The hookers would tell their johns, "Don't fuck with me. That cop behind us is my pimp." Every whore had a purse stuffed with police business cards. Pimps followed their women, amateur detectives followed johns, *johns* followed johns. Neighborhood people took license numbers. And right in the middle, my guys are out there trying to be inconspicuous. We were surveilling hookers, and guys from Physical Crimes were surveilling *us*. That burnt the shit outa me. Here's my people following a suspicious-looking john that just picked up a hooker, and Physical Crimes pulls us over with flashing red lights and then says, "Oh, you're the Tac Unit? Well, excuuuuuse us."

I went into one of our crime coordinator's meetings on a Thursday and said, "This is bullshit. Physical Crimes people don't belong on surveillance. You guys gotta be pursuing leads. You got no business sitting out there on some whore. That's *my* job."

The Tac Unit and Physical Crimes, they're both the cream of the crop, so it was prima donnas against prima donnas. It was hard for us to turn over our leads to them, and it was hard for them to work our leads. I'd give 'em a suspect and they'd say, "Aw, shit, Jim, no way he's the guy," and I'd say, "Okay, you go out and spend fifteen hours *proving* he's not the guy. Don't just sit there telling me no way!" So there was plenty of friction.

My kids took every new killing as an insult—"This guy's out there laughin' at us. He's *flaunting* it!" At first I had six men on the case, then the whole unit, thirty-two people in two-man teams, and then the pressure got so big we had to split our teams, use rental cars and vans, our personal cars, the neighbor's cars, vans, pickups, everything except the Good Humor truck.

It was a cold winter, and I knew what my people were going through. At roll call, I'd tell 'em, "Listen, I got you on a ten-hour shift tonight. I'm sorry, but that's the way it's gotta be. I can only make you as comfortable as possible. Grab your early cuppa coffee, get your thermos filled, do whatever it takes, but when you're on that surveillance you gotta give it your undivided attention. When you got that hooker in front of you, when you're looking at that piece of bait, you can't afford to miss anything. The one time you miss a car or a john, that could be the guy. Just think how you'd feel if you're on a woman and she gets killed. Think about living with that."

We spent hundreds of hours working the case and the guy never changed his basic MO and yet we weren't catching him. We knew he had to come to Lake and Lyell to pick up his targets. We'd probably stopped his car more than once. We knew a little bit about him from the profiles and what little evidence we had, like there was an indication in the Liz Gibson case that he was into anal but wasn't ejaculating, so we know we're not only looking for a killer, we're looking for a creep, a sodomist, a—whattaya call 'em?—a pederast. And we're being dragged up to the sixth floor for these depressing gatherings, and the chiefs are saying, With all the study and work and critique you're doing, *why aren't you catching this son of a bitch*?

Well, things got too complicated, that was one reason. Chief Urlacher contacted the serial killing experts in Seattle and they advised him to dig in for a long siege. That was probably good advice, from their point of view, but not necessarily from ours. For eight or ten years they'd been looking for a guy that killed fifty prostitutes: the Green River killer. Fifty unsolved murders! Seattle wasn't alone. Thirty-one hookers were killed in Miami since '86 and sixty in Kansas City since '72. San Diego had forty-two in four years, New Bedford, Mass., had nine. John Douglas, the head of the FBI's Behavioral Science Unit, told some reporter, "They're just all over the place."

So our deputy chief, Terrence Rickard, planned for the long haul. He got hold of a thirteen-thousand-dollar phosphorescing beam called Luma-lite, very useful at crime scenes, and a terrific new Kodak technology called Edicon, a computerized video mug book that helped us keep tabs on street people and criminals and others. He started doing videotaped briefings to background the whole department. He recalled men on disability leave to help with paperwork. One guy put off surgery to come in and help. We set up a computer system to check car licenses, fishing licenses, hunting licenses. The only trouble was, nobody knew how to run the fucking computers. So we had to go through a schooling process. It became so complex—computers, paperwork, stacks of leads, a superhuman job.

After a while I began to notice a morale problem, especially among the hardest-working detectives, guys like Tommy Jones, the Physical Crimes boss. It was an attitude that no amount of paperwork's gonna solve this, it's gonna take street work and a stroke of luck, some young bluecoat'll drive around a corner at four o'clock in the morning and stumble on this guy killing somebody. That's how serial murderers are caught. It wasn't very inspiring.

3. LIEUTENANT THOMAS JONES

My attitude was, People got killed all the time, and our job at Physical Crimes was to find the killer. That's what we *did,* and we did it all year 'round, twenty-four hours a day, and we racked up a fantastic record. The only difference between the prostitute murders and other murders was the number of bodies. My instincts were to hit the streets and hustle, assign a couple of hot teams, give 'em their head and let 'em go.

But after the chief went public that we had a serial killer, we went into an unaccustomed mode. Too damn many hands were involved. From Frannie Brown on, the direction of the investigation was controlled by the sixth floor, by administrators, not by working detectives. All we heard was, "*This* has gotta be done." "*That* has gotta be done." When we should've been on the street using our imagination, acting like professional homicide investigators, improvising, going with the flow, following our instincts and our noses, we were too busy taking orders.

The sixth floor did all kinds of crazy things. Changed our schedules, broke up our teams, revised our methods, then revised 'em again. It was distracting. There was too much paperwork, and every time we looked up, the DC wanted more. On one of his video briefings, he mentioned his ancient hero, a detective nicknamed "Trapper," and he mentioned that Trapper's strength was attention to detail. He said that Trapper used to tell patrol cops, "If you bring me the bear, I'll make bear soup." He said, "That's what we need today. The bear is *information*."

So every beat cop and traffic cop and desk cop in town was bringing him the bear—stopping cars, interviewing guys whose socks didn't match, passing on every two-bit lead they could find, burying us in information that nobody had time to process. I heard they had the same problem in other places with serial killers.

One day I look up and there's a utility cart coming down the hall with two more computers on it. I thought, What the hell's next?

4. LIEUTENANT JAMES BONNELL

A naked body washed up at Sodus Point, over in the next county. Turned out she was a suicide, jumped off a bridge and floated a hundred miles in Lake Ontario. But at first everybody thought she was Maria Welch. That kept us jumping for a while.

Then one of our teams spotted a john picking up a girl in front of us. An ex-con, long police record. I'd arrested him myself, years ago. His MO was to sodomize his victims, then leave them tied to a tree. Sometimes he posed as an undercover cop. He was six-two, muscular, had the right build and background. Chill the champagne again!

We talked to the hooker and she said the guy hadn't done anything unusual during the trick. We didn't believe her. A lot of the women were lying to us, protecting their johns. So we started a deep surveillance on the asshole. You can't imagine the excitement. We watched his house, his car, followed him to and from work. He was clean.

A few days later I walked in on a meeting between Lynde Johnston, head of CID, and Deputy Chief Rickard. I said, "All this detail work is bullshit. It isn't working. Let's try something else." It wasn't anything I hadn't said a dozen times before.

Rickard looks at me and says, "Well, why don't you get a suit outa mothballs, 'cause you're gonna be wearing two hats for the next three or four weeks." Turned out Tommy Jones had to go to Florida on family business, and I was taking over Physical Crimes.

I was really rocked. I had no aspirations that way and I hadn't seen it coming. And it didn't seem logical. On the other hand, what *was* logical that December?

After I thought about it a while, a charge went through me. I'm thinking, Now I can make some changes. But I had to do it without stepping on toes.

The morning Tommy left, I grabbed the lead packages that had piled up in Crime Analysis and assigned them to Physical Crimes investigators. I called a staff meeting and said, "Nobody in Physical Crimes will do any surveillance at any time. That's Tactical's job. Your job is pursuing these lead packages. I want a daily report on my desk on each lead." I figured that would keep 'em too busy to interfere with surveillances.

It didn't take long for one of the detectives to come in and complain, "This lead shit isn't gonna give us our killer."

I said, "Unless you got a better idea, get busy."

The DC approved all my changes. He was confident we were gonna nail the killer. Chief Urlacher challenged the asshole in the paper: "We're gonna getcha!" We all felt that way. It would happen any day—or night. The murdering son of a bitch had to drive his gray van or his blue Chevette back to the street to do his thing, and we were waiting.

Of course, it would've helped if we knew he was driving my old unmarked car.

5. ARTHUR SHAWCROSS (PSYCHIATRIC INTERVIEW)

Q. Had there been any unusual things that have excited you sexually?

A. Unusual things?

Q. Umm-hmm.

A. Not that I know of.

Q. What about corpses?

A. That doesn't bother me.

Q. Does it excite you?

A. No.

Q. The thoughts of sexual activity with the dead have not excited you?

A. No.

Q. Did you find it exciting to have the women tied to the trees [in Vietnam]?

A. Well, what was I supposed to do? Let them walk around? They got enemy weapons, they know the area.

Q. I'm not criticizing you for it.

A. All right.

Q. I'm asking if you found it sexually exciting.

A. No. But you want me to say yes.

Q. I want you to tell me the truth.

A. I'm telling you no.

Q. There's some questions you don't like. Have you noticed that?

6.

As Christmas approached, the people around Art Shawcross noticed an improvement in his disposition, especially toward his wife Rose. He'd always been a generous man, pressing gifts on strangers, but now he seemed bent on becoming Alexander Street's designated Santa. He gave a drawerful of his clothes to a family that had lost everything in a fire. He delivered bags of groceries to a destitute female friend. He handed out newspapers, magazines, half-empty packs of cigarettes, lighters, other items that he claimed he'd found in places like the Midtown Mall. His neighbor Silla Rossler wondered where he got a woman's cigarette case containing a soggy pack of Winstons.

Working alone on his overnight job at G&G Food Service, he prepared extra helpings of olive salad, macaroni salad, and sliced vegetables, wrapped them in clear plastic, and bicycled them around town to his friends, including ninety-two-year-old Irene Kane in her high-rise condo on St. Paul Street. He appropriated soup spoons, butter knives, teaspoons, napkins, dishes, dinner sets, giving away his plunder with a smile and a Robin Hood flourish. He continued to liberate potatoes from farmers' fields and extract gifts from Salvation Army donation boxes. He jacklighted deer and snagged brown trout and traded the meat to hookers for friendship or services.

After two years, he still seemed to covet Clara Neal's daughter Linda and Linda's four sons, and he lavished gifts on all of them, including cash for the boys and silverware for Linda. Several weeks before Christmas, he pulled up at her ramshackle house in exurban Holley with an evergreen bush tied to the roof of Clara's rented Chevy Celebrity.

"Here's your Christmas tree!" he exclaimed as he barged through the front door without knocking, his usual style. Linda was annoyed. Her boyfriend had already promised her a real Christmas tree, not some fat round bush that looked dragged through a swamp.

"Where'd you get *that*?" she asked.

"From a lady's yard," he said. He sounded proud of himself. "I cut it last night."

Linda knew what "last night" meant: sometime between 3:00 A.M., when he finished at G&G, and 6:00 A.M., when he returned her mother's car so she could drive to her job at the old people's home in Spencerport, where Linda also worked as an aide.

Art reached into his pocket and pulled out a Timex watch with a round face and a black band. "This is for you, baby," he said.

Linda was wary. All too often, his handouts were followed by a sudden grope or a wisecrack about "Finger-lickin' good." You never knew what mood he'd be in or when he'd get that weird gleam in his green eyes and make his move. To Linda, there was something satanic about him. She'd done a little shoplifting herself and hadn't refused the towelettes and napkins he'd brought earlier, but that gift had been followed by a dozen silver teaspoons, a dozen soup spoons and thirty butter knives, all of unexplained origin. And now he was upping the ante. She wondered, What does the crazy bastard expect in return for a watch?

"Where'd you get this?" she asked.

"Don't fuckin' worry about where I got it," he said. She was relieved when he drove away in her mother's gray car.

7.

In the neat little studio apartment on Alexander Street, Rose listened nervously as Art explained that this Christmas they were going to give his mother a present that would *really* get her attention. He reminded Rose that he hadn't seen his mom in seventeen years and wanted to show how much he missed her. Betty Shawcross had refused to come to their wedding and was still urging Art to stay away from Watertown, but they talked once in a while on the phone and he seemed more relaxed about the relationship.

At the downtown department store, Rose watched as he

pored over costume jewelry, lamps, hats, kitchen appliances, radios. Finally he selected a clock—"but not just a clock," as she explained later. "It was a set, nine pieces carved in wood, including two candle holders. The clock had an inlaid Christ on the Cross under a clear glaze. We made a down payment. The total was sixty dollars."

Three weeks before Christmas, the gift was sent to Watertown, marked "Do not open till Xmas," and within a few days Art's sister Donna phoned to report that their mother had described the set as "trash," a "waste of money," and said that her son "got taken."

Rose wished she knew how to comfort him. He punched the wall, then left the apartment. As she prepared for bed, she told herself, I hate to see him leave, but I wouldn't want to deal with him tonight.

8. JO ANN VAN NOSTRAND

I was back on the street picking up a little change and also to see if I could spot the guy in the blue-gray Chevette. Some nights I cruised with Lenny in his undercover car, but we kept tripping over the Tac Squad. They were too obvious. I mean, who wouldn't notice big, handsome guys following *men*?

A trick was taking me home and they followed us to my apartment, made the guy so nervous he drove the wrong way down a one-way street. This Tac cop flashed a big spotlight and started asking questions. I said, "Hey, man, he's just giving me a ride home."

After a whole bunch of questions, I jumped in. "Hey, man, he's not the strangler. I would know. I *dated* the fucking strangler."

The cop jumped back. "Oh," he says, "are you Barbara?"

"Yeah."

"Oh, I'm sorry."

Well, they were cops and that's the only way they knew to protect us. Things were *bad*. You picked up a newspaper or turned on the TV, you heard about another missing girl. Everybody was teaming up, so I doubled with Darlene Trippi. She was less flighty than the other hos, and much nicer. She'd say, "Look, I'm taking off to get high and I'll be back at such and such a time," and you could depend on it.

Darlene wasn't real open, a little hard to know, but if she liked ya she liked ya, know what I mean? Not bad-looking, kinda short with curly hair. She started tricking after her baby died of crib death and she discovered coke. Her apartment was near the street corner where I worked, and on cold nights she'd let me come in to warm up. She liked to work Jones and Emerson, which is a dark corner off the park, across from the church. You can't see a john's face there and it's a dangerous place, but she wouldn't go nowhere else. I told her, "Dar, the strangler's around. The cops figure he's somebody we know. How're you gonna save yourself if he grabs you?"

I told her about Mitch—the car, the leg brace, the potatoes, his style of fucking, everything. All the girls knew about the blue-gray car. Dar told me she was sticking with her regulars. Told me she'd been tricking with a guy that brought her deer meat. I didn't pay much attention. She didn't say his name.

When I didn't see her for a while, I asked one of her faggot pals where Dar was keeping herself. Bitch said he didn't know. Dar's roomie told me that the last anybody'd seen her, she was on her way over to Lyell. She'd been looking kinda depressed 'cause her boyfriend dumped her for putting his money up her nose. The roommate had already filed a missing persons report.

I thought, Dar's *missing*? My fucking hair stood up. I was half geeked when I got ahold of Lenny Borriello and I was talking so fast he had to slow me down. I said, "You don't think the strangler's got Darlene, do ya? She wouldn't be stupid enough to get in his car. She knew as much about him as I did."

Lenny went, "Nah. Don't worry about it." But he didn't sound like he meant it, ya know what I'm sayin'?

I figured if the strangler snatched Dar, he'd snatch me, too. I went to a church and asked 'em to help me get off the street. What a bum trip, Sister Benjamin's halfway house for hos. I stayed there a couple days, then split for a shelter. I called Saint Lenny Borriello to help me out—he was always good for a few bucks—but the motherfuckers at Physical Crimes wouldn't pass him my message.

I kicked cold turkey and little by little my memory came back. It was like a movie in my head. Every day I remembered something else about Mitch. I hadn't been able to tell the cops where he worked, but now I remembered he made salads at a restaurant and the name of the place began with C or maybe B. It definitely rhymed with B. I spent hours trying to get the letters straight. My mind was still fucked. Lenny gave me ten bucks for some healthy food and told me to keep thinking.

9. ARTHUR SHAWCROSS (HANDWRITTEN ACCOUNT)

No. 8 was Trippi. Picked her up on Dewey Ave. went behind a warehouse somewhere. I couldn't get it up and she cursed me, I told her to shut up. She called me a little boy then baby talked at me. I choked her.

10. LIEUTENANT JAMES BONNELL

Just after midnight I'm with Tim Hickey, one of our best sergeants. It's a week before Christmas and we'd been on this operation for over a month and hookers were still being killed. Tim and I're driving along Lyell in an unmarked car and up ahead we see the toughest hooker in town sloggin' through the ice and snow. It's windy out, miserable, but nothing's gonna stop Cicero. She's got a big habit. She was a short woman, well built, maybe five-two, had on white boots and a white jacket with a fur hood.

We stopped and she leaned in the window and said,

"How the fuck are ya?" Her ladylike greeting. She was high, per usual.

"June," I said, "what're you doing out? This is ridiculous. It's nine degrees."

She says, "I don't give a shit about the cold. I'm a working girl."

Her face is about a foot from me. I said, "There can't be much business tonight."

She says, "I got some steadies that'll be driving by, but you gotta do me a favor first."

I says, "What?"

"You gotta get ridda them assholes over there." I looked and saw a car from Physical Crimes; they must've been surveilling me and Tim in our red Toyota Camry. She says, "Business wouldn't be so bad if it wasn't for them. They're ruinin' my whole fuckin' night."

As we're talking, a Puerto Rican couple walked by on the sidewalk and the guy said something about June's ass and she turns to bitch 'em out. "You filthy motherfuckers," et cetera, and they're exchanging a few words while we watch.

Tim whispers to me, "This has gotta be the nastiest bitch on the street. Listen to her! She's just filthy."

I said, "Yeah, she's the queen, the toughest, the oldest, the meanest."

Cicero sticks her head back in the window and I said, "Listen, June, not for nothin', but aren't you worried about being out here? This guy's killed a lot of people. We'd hate to see anything happen to you."

She said, "Fuck him! He's great for the economy."

"Whattaya mean?"

"There's only six or eight of us working steady because all them other bitches are afraid. I'm gettin' forty bucks for a two-minute head job. Supply and demand, Lieutenant. The johns're still there, but there ain't no broads."

I says, "What're you gonna do the rest of the night?" It's 1:00 A.M. and the street's dead.

She says, "Aw, it's getting late. I'm getting tired. Maybe I'll go home."

"Where ya living now?"

"Over on Plymouth. About two blocks."
"You want a ride?"
"Naw. Maybe I'll grab one more trick on the way home."
"Watch out for the killer, June."
"Fuck him!" she says. "Let him watch out for me."
Three blocks away we notice the Physical Crimes unit is on our ass. We slowed down so they could see who we were. They waved and pulled away.

Next morning we get a call. Cicero didn't come home. We checked Mark's Red Hots and a few other places. No one had seen her since she talked to us on the street. I tried to remember what she said—something about waiting for her steadies? Her roommates said she wouldn't even approach a car unless she knew the guy. So if she was dead, she was killed by a regular, somebody everybody knew.

I called Major Johnston and the DC and told them we were in a ton of shit.

11. ARTHUR SHAWCROSS (PSYCHIATRIC INTERVIEW)

The next one was June Cicero . . . She flagged me down. And she was pretty high-strung, and she got in the car, and we were driving out 31 somewhere, and—right at the moment I can't think, I can't remember, ya know? I just remember where I put her, and it was snowing, and snowplows were on the road, and I pulled up by this place, this culvert area, just pushed her out of the car, and she went over the guardrail. And what clothes that were still in the car, I put at a Salvation Army box on Manitou and 104.

And I think about two, three days went by. I went back, and I had—I cut her, cut the vagina right out of her, bone and—bone and all. And I was driving around with that somewhere out there, and I ate that, too.

Q. While you were driving?

A. Yeah.

Q. And that was when you went back several days later?

A. It was frozen.

Q. Did you cut her anyplace else?

A. No.

Q. And what did you use to cut her?

A. I had a saw.

Q. What kind?

A. A hacksaw. . . .

Q. You had the hacksaw along that day for some reason?

A. I bought one just that morning. It wasn't a hacksaw. It was like a—you know, a little—like a regular one-bladed thing.

Q. What had you bought it for?

A. Probably for that purpose. I don't know.

Q. Had you used a saw on any of the others?

A. You fail to realize what I said earlier? I said I used a jackknife on the one . . .

Q. Yeah, I remember that.

A. . . . And the saw on the other. And there's only two of them.

Q. There wasn't any other time when you used a hacksaw?

A. Why you trying to get me mad?

Q. Just asking you questions.

A. But you know already.

Q. Well, I know some, some things.

A. You know everything about everything and some things I don't know, but you're trying to antagonize me! I only cut one person with a—with a saw, one with a knife after they were dead two or three days. *Nobody else!*

Q. You don't like it if I challenge you, do you?

A. No. But you know the facts already, but you just antagonize.

Q. You think the things I've done so far are antagonistic?

A. At the moment.

Q. Just a couple of those questions?

A. Nobody else was cut up and nobody else was sawed up. Now if they found somebody out there that was cut up or something, I don't know nothing about it.

Q. I'm going to ask you about a hacksaw that was found at the apartment.

A. Yeah, I had one.

Q. Had you cut any meat with that?

A. Yes. Deer meat.

Q. Deer?

A. Yeah.

Q. But never any victims?

A. You're—you're—I'm gonna walk out of this room! I already told you, I cut Cicero with a . . .

Q. Uh-huh.

A. . . . like a saber saw and Juno Stott with a jackknife, her own jackknife. Nobody else got cut anywhere, right?

Q. Well, *is* that right?

A. Yeah.

Q. And you say there are parts you don't remember and that you haven't seen the reports?

A. I didn't use the hacksaw at my house to cut no body, just deer meat that I had from a half of a deer, and Clara and her family got the other half of the deer. They got their own knives, they got their own saws, and . . . I had my own knife right over the sink in the kitchen, and the hacksaw was sitting on top of the refrigerator.

Q. Okay. So it's the, the murder of June Cicero you don't remember, and—

A. See, you're trying to trick me for some reason! I don't remember Trippi. I only know where I found her, and I can't remember too much about Cicero, just where I put her a few days later.

Q. Am I wrong? You do remember the murder of June Cicero?

A. No.

Q. So you don't?

A. Just where—dumping her a few days later.

Q. And is that all now?

A. All of what?

Q. That's all of them?

A. No, there's one more. . . .

12. JO ANN VAN NOSTRAND

It came back to me in the middle of the night: Mitch worked at a place that began with "G." I couldn't wait to call Lenny Borriello. He asked if I was certain and I said yeah and if you guys'll just show a little patience I'll come up with the whole name. Then Lenny told me Cicero was gone.

I said, "*Shit!* He got June? I'm taking the bus to Detroit!" Lenny told me to stay put, he needed my help.

After I got it together a little bit, I tried to come up with a list of possibles from the yellow pages. There was a meat place out in Irondequoit that began with "G," a couple of restaurants, two or three other joints in the suburbs. I remembered that Mitch said he rode his bike to work, so it didn't seem likely the place would be out of town. I called

Lenny back and told him the name was "G *and*" something, but I couldn't remember the rest.

The next morning he wakes me up at the shelter and says his girlfriend took a Rochester phone book and figured it out. The place has to be G&G Food Service on East Main, near Goodman. As soon as he said G&G, it came back to me. He said they made salads and stuff for restaurants.

He told me to meet him at Physical Crimes in the Public Safety Building as fast as I could get there. I took a cab and Lenny was busy and I had to wait a while. Those detectives schooled around me like a bunch of fucking hyenas. "You're fulla shit, Barbara. Why're you runnin' this scam on Lenny? You're just looking for dope money."

I said, "Dope money? You stupid fuckers, I can make more on the street in ten minutes than I can make hanging around this dump all week." I said, "Lenny gives me five or ten bucks for food or cigarettes. How much dope do you think I can buy with chump change?"

Another plainclothes guy sticks a picture of a body under my nose. I didn't recognize the girl; she was covered with spots and cut up the middle. He says, "See this? This is June Stott. She ain't even a whore. This is serious shit, bitch. You're in here jerking us around when we could be out working." He says, "Lenny's the only one that believes you, anyway."

Well, I already knew *that*. Lenny told me earlier, "The guys think you're using me. Even my partner, Billy Barnes, thinks you're bullshit." Who was surprised? A few years back I met Barnes on a dope matter and we had a shouting match.

So I'm still sitting around the big open area on the fourth floor and another cop walks up and says, "You Barbara?"

"Yeah."

He checks me out and says, "You're pretty old. You make any money?"

"Sure."

"What do you charge for police blow jobs?"

Lenny chased him off, told me he didn't mean nothin'. I just said to myself, "Cops." That said it all.

We drove to G&G and parked across the street. It was broad daylight. A guy came out that looked a little like Mitch. I said, "No, Lenny, that ain't him. If I see this asshole, there's gonna be no mistake, ya know what I'm sayin'? I'll never forget that face."

Four or five hours later Lenny says, "Look, this don't make no sense. I'm gonna go inside and ask."

While I'm waiting, I spot a compact like Mitch's in a used-car lot next door. It's a blue hatchback, four-door, the same windshield wipers on the back, a perfect match. I take a closer look. It's a fucking Dodge Omni! All this time I been telling the cops it was a Chevette.

Lenny came out. "We got the wrong place," he said.

I says, "No we don't. If it's not this fucking G&G, it's another one."

Lenny says he talked to the owner and the foreman and gave them a good description: fifty to fifty-five years old, five-eight to five-ten, stocky build, gray hair, light complexion, name of "Mitch." He said they were cooperative but couldn't place the guy. They were gonna check with some of the other workers and get back.

I came up with a new idea. I says, "Why don't you let me wear a wire? Mitch'll hit on me and you can bust his ass."

"Naw," Lenny says. "That's entrapment."

Back at Physical Crimes, I went through a hundred and eighty mug shots without finding Mitch. Lenny took me to one of the technicians and we made a composite from a kit. Turned out I got everything right but the nose. The composite went to every cop in town. And they *still* couldn't find the guy.

13.

It was a gloomy holiday season around police headquarters on North Plymouth Avenue and a few blocks away in the dark universe known as "Lake and Lyell." Desperate citizens were beginning to criticize the police department and look elsewhere for a solution.

"I understood completely," Chief Gordon Urlacher said later. "The cases were so close together, so similar, and so many were working on it and getting nowhere. People began to ask, Would you be handling this different if these victims were housewives instead of prostitutes? I began to wonder myself. My sleep went all to hell."

The United Church Ministries aggravated the PD with a public plea to the killer to "stop killing the women and come and talk to us," and the press played up the announcement. Print journalists provided suggestions of their own and swarmed into the frozen battle zone in parkas and boots. TV reporters accumulated sound bites, firing questions through luminescent puffs of breath.

Newspaper editors ordered daily stories on the hunt for the killer, and headline followed headline:

"I STILL HAVE HOPE THAT SHE IS ALIVE"
SEARCH FOR ACCEPTANCE AND SEX
"THERE MAY BE MORE BODIES OUT THERE THAN THEY REALIZE"
"I JUST WANT ONE $20 DATE AND THEN I'M GOING HOME"

Urlacher was known for his booming voice and Pepsodent smile, but Deputy Chief Terrence Rickard was the field general in charge of this manhunt, and he was all business. The meticulous DC feared that too much coverage might spook the killer into changing his methods or his theater of operations, derailing the investigation. To the working press, his attitude seemed arbitrary, and a shoving match ensued.

Seasoned investigators like the *Times-Union*'s Corey Williams and the *Democrat and Chronicle*'s Steve Mills and Leslie Sopko began chasing angles of their own. When their articles appeared, Rickard banned the media from the sixth floor nerve center of the Public Safety Building. The newspapers fired back with articles suggesting that Rochester's image was being tarnished by police incompetence:

FUROR OVER KILLINGS HURTS MERCHANTS
NEIGHBORS ASK, "WHY HERE?"

A week before Christmas, the *Times-Union* ran a front-page article that hinted of official misfeasance. Under the black-edged daily logo, "Rochester's Unsolved Murders," the newspaper asked:

DID WARNING TO PROSTITUTES COME TOO LATE?

Readers were reminded that the police had started investigating links between the slayings a year earlier but hadn't informed the public. The newspaper quoted an angry mother: "I think they should have said something. That is my child lying out there in that cemetery." Said one prostitute's close relative, "If they know what they're up against, if they know there's a killer out there, maybe they would have had a chance." Viola Brown, mother of the murdered Frances, was quoted as saying that she'd learned more about the killings from the media than from police. "The girls on the street," she said, "I don't think they really know what is going on."

Policemen were quoted in their own defense, but the article annoyed the top cops. In another video address to the troops, Terrence Rickard warned his men, "Expect more media attention. They will be watching you and how you're investigating. They're looking for a journalism award, we're looking for an arrest. Intercept them if they're interfering. . . ."

He advised that the national media were headed for Rochester. "Treat them respectfully but firmly," the strait-laced DC instructed. "Do not allow them to overwhelm you or to interfere with your work."

Reporters from New York's *Daily News* and the *New York Times* arrived, followed by correspondents from newsmagazines and TV crews from CNN, *Crime Watch Tonight, Inside*

Edition, and other tabloid shows. Lake and Lyell resembled an alfresco convention of newsmen. Prostitutes went hoarse from being interviewed. A TV news director cruised the area nightly, talking to the streetwomen from his car. After he'd been reported to police several times as a suspicious person, a detective scribbled a memo, "I've just about had it with this guy."

Mark's Texas Red Hots resounded with talk about "standing heads" and "lead time," "two-shots," "camera angles" and "follow stories." Reporters and prostitutes sipped coffee and exchanged banter: "This just in. Rickard confessed. . . ." "Our halftime score: Killer 16, Cops 0. . . ."

After a few frantic days, the visitors produced their articles and videotapes and returned home. Lake and Lyell turned quiet again. Half-frozen policemen had no choice but to remain at their posts. Lately the prostitutes were becoming harder to track. Their nocturnal clientele detoured to side streets, where a few enterprising women in long johns and fake-fur jackets turned fifty-dollar tricks. Each night the ratio of customers to women increased. The Cicero disappearance had finally convinced all but a hopeless few that tricking meant death.

With Christmas approaching, money ran low on the street. Pimps sought new scams, a few even taking straight jobs. As usual, the innocent suffered most. Many of the dead or missing prostitutes had supported children or elderly parents and other dependents. The police department's Victims Assistance Unit held group counseling sessions for the survivors and soon picked up on a grim message.

"Prostitutes don't have savings accounts or life insurance," one of the counselors told Terrence Rickard. "These families are really poor. All they can talk about is what kind of Christmas it's gonna be for the kids. Can the department come up with some money?"

"Not officially," the deputy chief replied. With his customary brisk efficiency, he passed the hat and raised several thousand dollars, a sum that was matched by the Gannett

Lend-a-Hand Fund and other charities. Police cars pulled into headquarters with trunks and backseats brimming with toys and other gifts. Newly orphaned children were picked up at the homes of their murdered mothers and taken on picnics. Others were adopted for the holidays.

"It was a problem," Rickard recalled later, "but not our worst. Every expert said that serial killings escalated at Christmas. I wasn't sure we'd be ready. The guys had been going two or three months at top speed, coming in on weekends and their days off. I'd chase 'em home and they'd sneak back. My wife called me about a neighbor's Christmas party, and I said no way we could go. She said, 'How can you tell you're gonna find a body that day?' I said it didn't matter if we found a body, I'd be working. She said, 'This is really gonna be a crappy Christmas.' Her first complaint in eight years of marriage. And she was right: it *was* a crappy Christmas.

"Some of the men were approaching burnout. Lynde Johnston, our CID commander, was up to seventeen cups of coffee a day and wondering why he couldn't sleep. He took the case personally. We *all* did; every time a woman turned up missing, it was an insult.

"I heard that Lynde was going home just long enough to shower and change. A few days before Christmas, I asked if he'd done his shopping. He said his little boy wanted a Teenage Mutant Ninja Turtle and he'd been in a hurry and bought the wrong one. I made an exchange with a Ninja Turtle we'd bought for the prostitutes' kids. Then I told Lynde, 'You're on leave for three days. Take your phone off the hook. Don't respond to scenes. Your car number doesn't exist. *And don't take your goddamn pager!*'

"I got to work the next morning at three. He was sitting there."

14.

Rochester's senior prostitute, Jo Ann Van Nostrand, moved from her shelter to a dopers' hotel and finally holed up with a girlfriend. She kicked cocaine for the twenty-fifth or twenty-sixth time and refused to answer the phone for anyone except Investigator Lenny Borriello.

At his request she agreed to come out of hiding to help find "Mitch." He took her to dinner and discussed strategy. She was touched by the way he introduced her to police friends at another table. She wasn't used to being treated like a lady.

On Christmas Eve they studied passing cars. His girlfriend had picked out an inexpensive makeup kit for her, and Van Nostrand reciprocated with a book, *Jokes of the Johns.*

They looked for the Omni till midnight and then gave up.

At Mark's Texas Hots, a sign near the cash register informed the clientele of a raffle. There was no charge; customers merely filled in their names and addresses.

The killer had been hurting the restaurant's business, and the manager was happy to cooperate in this latest police method of collecting more names. The prize was a thirty-inch TV. Once a day the slips were collected and the information punched into Edicon and other police computer systems. The street people didn't know the raffle was a scam.

Still disobeying orders, Lynde Johnston cruised the icy streets of the prostitution corridor and thought how convenient it would be if he spotted the killer in an on-view Christmas Eve homicide. As he drove, he considered the latest proposal from the enterprising Tac Unit. Jim Bonnell and his men wanted to wire a female officer as bait.

To Johnston, the idea seemed unrealistic. How would other units back her up? This man grabbed his victims off the street, killed without sound or struggle. Some of the detectives theorized that he used a stun gun or Mace or chloroform. How else could he have handled a hard case like Cicero? Or was he using a quick-acting, nondetectable poison?

And how was he luring them into his car? Dropping tin? *Was he a cop?* Johnston shuddered at the possibility.

He wondered if his questions would ever be answered. As he cruised under the dark canopy of trees, he thought, What's the guy up to right now? He's ruined everybody else's Christmas. What's he doing for the holidays?

15. LINDA NEAL

That goddamn Art had the balls to show up at my Christmas dinner in my mom's gray Celebrity. I was thinkin', Why cain't that son of a bitch leave us alone? I thought, Why'd you come out here, you freaky thing? To sit on my boys? Chase me upstairs?

He give me a present of a five-dollar bill and my boys three dollars each, and then he sits there and stares at my breasts. I thought to myself, Is that your Christmas spirit? You could see the meanness in those dark eyes. Green, blue, I never knew what color they were except not brown.

It wasn't tacky enough that he drove my mom's car to my house—he brought his wife Rose! And he had those Pakistan people, the ones that ran the Dunkin' Donuts. My mom had to ride out from town with my brother Robert.

Everybody sat around and talked like old friends while Art stared at the women. Mom was so happy about some steak knives he'd gave her for Christmas—I knew where *they* come from. I could imagine Cock Robin talkin' to hisself—"I'm married to that there one and I'm sleeping with this here one and pretty soon I'll be sleeping with the young bitch, too." That's me, of course. I coultn't stand being looked at like that, so I went in the other room.

Just before everybody cleared out, my mom whispered to me, "You know sumpin'? Art give me more Christmas presents than he give his wife!" I thought, Yeah, along with how many black-and-blue marks? But I ditn't say nothing. I loved my mom. Let her dream.

• • •

The morning after Christmas, my car woultn't start and I called my mom around 4:00 A.M. to ask her to pick me up on her way to our job at the Wedgewood Nursing Home. She says, "I'll be there as soon as Art gets back. He's got the car."

When they pulled up around five-thirty, he's driving. It pissed me off. I thought, Why is that son of a bitch always gotta be in my mom's car?

I got in the backseat and seen marks that looked like blood. I asked what it was and he said he'd kilt a deer. We hatn't hardly pulled away when I feel his hand slipping behind the seat, trying to grab my leg. I moved out of reach.

He began acting all weird, making faces. He'd lick his tongue up and down a candy cane and then give my mom a dirty stare. He turns his head and says, "You coulda sat up front with us."

I says, "No, I'm fine back here. Hurry! We're gonna be late."

On our way on Route 31, he kep' raising the windows up and down with the push buttons. I guess they ditn't have things like that before he went to prison. Then he began passing cars real fast. The road was slushy, sloppy, snow piled up on both sides. I never saw him drive that bad before.

At Salmon Creek, he slowed down. I ditn't know till later about the body hidden there. He pointed toward Colby Road and said, "I was up in there all night long. Seen a big field of deer." I ditn't know there was a dead girl up there, too.

After he let us off at Wedgewood, he says to me, "I'm goin' to your house to sleep. When I come back to pick you up, I'll bring Billy." My son was sick with a high fever and strep throat. I ditn't want him alone with Art at no time, so I said, "Bring Robert and David, too."

He brought my sons back at eleven-thirty and the boys told me he'd been rooting around in my dresser drawers.

Said they never seen him acting so queer. When I got home I was missing my blue Lizwear jeans, size seven, that I'd draped over a chair in the bedroom. Gone! Now what do you make of *that*? After I woultn't let him feel me up, he stole my jeans to feel *them* up? I thought, Why, you squirrelly son of a bitch. You belong in a zoo. But I still ditn't say anything to Mom.

On the last day of 1989 I phoned her up and Art answered. I says, "Where's my mom?"

He says, "She's here. Don't you wanna talk to me?"

"No. I wanna talk to my mom."

"You at home? What're ya doing?"

"Nothing."

"Can I come over?"

"No! I'm going to the Laundromat."

He started making kissy sounds into the phone, and I'm wondering, How can my mom *stand* this asshole?

The two of 'em showed up a while later and I noticed three parallel scratches close to his right eye and three more on the right side of his neck. He said he got 'em chasing a deer.

16.

Just after noon on that same New Year's Eve, a guard at Northampton Park, where Dorothy "Dotsie" Blackburn's body had been found in Salmon Creek twenty-one months before, spotted a dark patch in a snowbank on the park's border. He pulled his car into an opening off Sweden-Walker Road and peeled an ice-encrusted pair of denim jeans from the snow. In a front pocket were a 1970 South Carolina birth registration card in the name of "Felicia Stephens," a Social Security card in the same name, and an ID card bearing the name "Lillian Stephens" and a local address. As the guard was backing out, a state trooper intercepted him, then radioed the information to his headquarters.

To police, the park guard's find was electrifying. The

owner of the jeans appeared to match the victim profile; most young prostitutes carried birth certificates or Social Security cards to prove identity and age. If another body was nearby, it suggested that the killer had returned to his original dumping grounds. It also suggested that he was playing more games with the law.

State Police officials called in reinforcements to search an area of broken woods and fields, farms, orchards, iced-over streams, and scattered houses. The Monroe County sheriff's office provided deputies and a cadaver dog. Rochester police units sped to the scene on their sirens. A helicopter flew grids over the area and checked out a nearby quarry. The flashes from news cameras and floodlights illuminated patches of brush and woods till long after dark.

Back in town, investigators from the Rochester PD called on the woman named Lillian Stephens. She said Felicia was her daughter and she hadn't seen her in two or three weeks.

"I don't have anything to do with her," the woman explained, "'cause she's using drugs and she's prostituting herself. I'm raising her two kids myself." Mrs. Stephens reported that her daughter sometimes stayed with a twenty-four-year-old janitor.

The boyfriend told police that he'd last seen Felicia on the afternoon of December 26, when he'd put her in a taxi at Genesee and Frost. The parting had been strained; they'd spent Christmas Day arguing about her cocaine habit and her prostitution and some names he'd found in her pockets: "Tyrone," "Melvin," "Marshall." Just two months earlier, they'd argued over similar subjects and she'd filed assault charges, later dropped. Asked why he hadn't reported her missing, he explained that Felicia sometimes left for as long as a week or ten days, usually after fights, but always returned.

He described her as a small woman, five-five, about 115 pounds, with black hair, brown skin, and brown-black eyes. Was she wearing dark jeans? "Yeah," he said. "Two pairs." Her usual cold-weather outfit consisted of jeans over jeans, a favorite white sweatshirt proclaiming "Advocate of a Two-

Party System,'' a tan corduroy jacket, sweat socks, a black knitted ski cap, and a gold scarf. She wore silver and gold rings on each hand. And when there was deep snow, she pulled on a pair of pleated gray boots.

A radio report crackled in from the search scene west of Rochester. A jogger had found a pleated gray boot about a hundred feet from the pants. A little farther north, another boot turned up. Everyone was sure that the latest victim lay somewhere under the snow.

17. NEW YORK STATE POLICE REPORT CASES NO. 90-004 THROUGH 90-007

. . . Mr. Shawcross went on to explain that he was driving down Plymouth Avenue to Main Street at about 2:00 A.M., the Wednesday or Thursday after Christmas. He said that he was stopped at the red light at Main and Plymouth with the passenger window about halfway down. He said he was driving the gray Celebrity. He said that a female black ran up to the passenger side of his vehicle, stuck her head into the passenger side window, and he put up the automatic window, catching her throat in the window. He said that he reached over with both hands and choked her while she was screaming rape. He went on to say that he lowered the window, grabbed her by the hair, and dragged her into the car. He then said that he pulled her in through the window, finished choking her, and drove to the expressway. He said he ended up at Northampton Park where he dumped her body. . . .

18. CLARA NEAL

New Year's Eve we was all gonna party in Gramma Irene Kane's apartment on St. Paul. Every time Art went into that building, Gramma's elderly friends came around. He used to run errands for 'em, fix things, give 'em presents. One paraplegic woman, he kept trying to take her fishing, give the poor old thing a day in the sunshine. Said he'd carry her and her wheelchair right down to the water. He would've, too.

The afternoon before the party, he asked me on the phone what did I want to drink. I said, "I want a bottle of Concord grape wine. The good, not that cheap crap."

He said, "You ain't gettin' the cheap."

At midnight, me and Art, Gramma Irene, Rose, and a coupla friends, we watched the fireworks over the Genesee River. You shoulda seen Gramma, ninety-two years old, sittin' there a-drinkin' champagne overhanded. *Yes!*

Art only had a drink or two 'cause one bottle of beer was more'n enough to make him woozy. Rose drank vodka. Me, I swallered that whole bottle of Concord grape wine! I don't know why I needed to drink so much; maybe I had a woman's intuition.

When it come time to leave, Art says, "You're drunk. Let me drive you home and I'll ride my bike back."

I kept saying I'm gonna take myself home, so he says, "Soon as you git in that house, you ring my number! I'm gonna be settin' there with the phone in my hand. I wanna know you got home safe. If not, I'll come looking for ya."

Just to get his goat, I says, "Tell ya hwut, Art, I'm gonna go to some nightclub and finish up the night. I'm gonna get really plastered."

He said, "If you do, I'll turn you across my lap tomorrow."

I says, "You *would*?"

So Art left with Rose and I drove home nice and careful. He picked up the phone on the first ring. He sounded *so* relieved. Now does that sound like lovers or what? I'll be plain about it: in my mind, him and I was together for good.

XII

RENDEZVOUS

1.

At 9:00 A.M. on New Year's Day 1990, lawmen from six jurisdictions converged on the woods and fields of Northampton Park to search for the final remains of Felicia Stephens. It was the season when even the soggiest ground turned hard and hunters walked across swamps in straight lines—"cross-lots," as Arthur Shawcross would have called it. Despite punishing gusts off Lake Ontario, there was an air of camaraderie among state troopers, Rochester police, sheriff's deputies, park guards and officers from surrounding towns and villages. The first priority was to find the body and catch the killer. The second, largely unspoken, was to get credit for helping to solve the worst serial murder case in New York history. In the frantic activity, there was no hint that the order of priorities would soon reverse.

Just before noon, a State Police search dog sniffed at a snowbank on the dirt road that led to the stream where Dorothy Blackburn's body had been found nearly two years earlier. The dog's busy paws sent a shower of snow through the air; soon the flecks turned pink, then red. Bones appeared and a few shreds of flesh. The dog tugged at the dismembered carcass of a deer.

The next morning, Tuesday, January 2, forty-eight hours after the discovery of Felicia Stephens's black jeans, State Police resumed their search by air. With Bureau of Criminal Investigation agents aboard as observers, helicopter pilots flew grids over the suburbs of Hamlin, Clarkson,

Greece, Parma, Sweden, Ogden, Spencerport, and Brockport, all within a short drive of Northampton Park.

Charles Militello, the same BCI investigator who'd warned the Brognia brothers that they were employing a child-killer, realized that he was the wrong man for the airborne assignment. As the small aircraft lurched and yawed in the unsettled winter air, the forty-eight-year-old detective felt sick.

"I can't take all this ba-boom ba-boom ba-*boom*," he informed the pilot as the tan State Police helicopter rattled over Route 104 near the Ridgemont Country Club. He grabbed for a bag, but the seat pocket was empty. "Hey!" he yelled. "Put this thing down or I'm gonna make a mess in here!"

After an emergency landing in a field, the searchers headed north into staccato winds off Lake Ontario and soon found themselves in a whiteout. The pilot was forced to return to Rochester-Monroe County Airport.

By Tuesday night, both ground and air searches had been shut down.

2. CLARA NEAL

Wednesday morning at four I was asleep in my house on Morrill Street when he woken me up with that "shave and a haircut" tap on my front bedroom window. Was I glad to see him! The time was drawing closer for us to leave Rochester for our new life. I let him in after he parked his bike and we just kinda laid there in my bed, me in my nightgown, him in his clothes. My back was still a little sore from the guy rear-ending my little blue-gray Omni.

When it was time to get ready for work, Art said, "I'm gonna use the car today." He was using it a lot lately, and welcome to it. What he always did, he taken me out to my part-time job at the Wedgewood Nursing Home in Spencerport, about ten miles west of town, and then he'd drive back into town to do his errands. My job started at six.

After I helped with the lunchtime cooking and dishes, he'd come and pick me up at one.

This morning he brought three plastic cups of green olive salad from G&G, just the way I liked 'em: olives, celery, onions, pepperoni, oil, a little salt and pepper, MSG. When he dropped me off at work he give me two of the cups and kept one for hisself. We was both dieting, and he knew that every penny counts when you got a bunch of mouths to feed. He was always thoughtful about things like that.

3.

A few hours after Arthur Shawcross dropped his girlfriend at work, BCI Senior Investigator John McCaffrey asked a colleague to prepare for another day in the State Police helicopter.

"Not me, John," said Charles Militello.

"Charlie," McCaffrey said, "the captain wants us to fly till we find the body."

"Hey, you want me to puke on the instruments?"

Everyone in the office had a deep respect for the lanky McCaffrey and usually took his suggestions as orders. Once the youngest trooper in New York, he was in his thirteenth year as a BCI investigator. He was also "connected" and chauffeured Mario Cuomo whenever the governor came to town. As a detective, McCaffrey had a long record of clearing difficult crimes.

Militello rolled a toothpick in his mouth and said, "If I gotta fly, John, I gotta. But why can't you send somebody that *likes* it? Why not Dennis? How about Hoopie?" By the time he was finished, he'd named the whole staff.

McCaffrey smiled. "Never mind, Charlie," he said. "I'll go."

"*You'll* go?"

"Yeah."

"No, no," Militello said. "If you want me to go, I'll go."

The argument continued in reverse until McCaffrey put

on his heavy coat. Militello took a close look at his colleague. He didn't seem annoyed.

4. SENIOR INVESTIGATOR JOHN MCCAFFREY

Truth was, I was dying to get in on this case. The BCI's a proud outfit and we wanted to arrest the serial killer. But the Rochester PD was playing it close. We'd sent an investigator to help out and they told him next to nothing. It was like, Thanks, but this is *our* case.

Our colonel from Albany tried to break the ice and they wouldn't confide in him, either. So at the highest levels there was kind of an unwritten, unacknowledged competition. Funny thing was, I was tight with a lot of the RPD guys, including Jimmy Bonnell and the guys in Crime Analysis, and they were keeping me informed every day. That's the way it is with us hired help. There's so much work to be done, we don't have time for politics.

Just before I left for the airport, a friend of mine showed up, Tom Jamieson, a real-estate man. He was a hunter and knew the area. I said, "Hey, come on along, Tom. You can be an extra pair of eyes."

At 10:30 A.M., four of us took off in chopper 1H11: the pilots, Mark Wadopian and Ken Hundt, with Jamieson and me as observers. The first thing I did was apologize to Mark and Ken for working them so hard. They'd been flying their tails off, a tough job, boring.

En route to Northampton Park, I contacted Trooper John Standing by radio and asked him to be in the area if we needed anything on the ground. He was twenty years on the job and he'd been in the helicopter, so he knew the routine.

Jimmy Bonnell had reminded me that the killer usually left his victims around water, but we could hardly find any, except in Lake Ontario. The streams were low, frozen, hidden under snow. We checked out fields and farms, a couple of orchards, backyards, woods. It was a clear, sunny day, perfect for searching. The trees had shed their leaves by now, and we could see the floor of the woods, but nothing showed except a couple of deer, bedded down in the snow. I had a gut feeling we were in the wrong area.

Around eleven-thirty the pilots started talking about a lunch break. One of 'em said, "Maybe we should come back when it gets a little warmer." What the hell, they were doing all the work; Tom and I were just staring out the windows. But I didn't want to give up. I'm thinking, Let's start where we found the clothes, then follow Route 31 east till it turns into Lyell Avenue, see if the killer dumped anything on his way back to town.

We circled over Northampton Park and headed east, paralleling 31 along the south side of the road, flying between two hundred feet altitude and treetop level. I was on the left side of the chopper, and I had a real good look at the shoulder of the road.

Five minutes after we started the run, something white jumped out at me from the culvert under Salmon Creek. All I could think was that Felicia Stephens had been wearing a white sweattop and it still hadn't been recovered.

I squinted and thought I saw a body, dark, naked from the waist down, wearing a white top.

I tapped the pilot on the shoulder and said, "We got her."

A gray Chevy Celebrity was parked up above on the shoulder. I thought, What the hell's a car doing there?

5.

Dale Pickett didn't know quite how to react. He'd been returning from a morning kaffeeklatsch with friends in Spencerport when he noticed a man standing alongside a parked car on Route 31 above Salmon Creek. The right front door was open, the man's left elbow rested on the roof, and he appeared to be urinating. The scene was a peaceful, secluded area of fields and brushy trees, swales, farmers' fields and graceful old homes, and its natural beauty seemed diminished by the brazen act.

The middle-aged Pickett drove past, then watched in his rearview mirror. The man finished whatever he was doing and reached inside his car. He appeared to throw something over the embankment.

Pickett looked for a cop. There'd been plenty in the area the day before, digging in snowbanks and poking in fields, but now there was no one in sight. He decided to go back and take the offender's license number. As he slowed for a U-turn, he saw the helicopter hovering overhead.

6. SENIOR INVESTIGATOR JOHN MCCAFFREY

The Celebrity's blinkers were off. The front passenger door was open and it looked like a guy was sitting in that seat with one leg sticking out. The pilot put us into a steep bank and as we're coming around, the car door shuts and the guy slides behind the wheel. He heads east toward Rochester, not speeding, just doing the limit or a little below. I'm thinking, Whoever that guy is, whatever he's up to, he's part of a murder scene and he's got to be interviewed. Rule No. 1: *Protect the scene.* But . . . the scene's changing.

I told the pilot, "Stay on the car." I figure the body's not going anywhere.

We banked into another quick turn and followed at normal speed, just above the telephone poles and directly behind the car. We dipped down to read the plate, but the trees kept us from getting close enough.

After a few miles the Celebrity pulled into the municipal parking lot in Spencerport, across the street from the Wedgewood Nursing Home on Church Street. I called Trooper Standing and he said he'd be there in five minutes. We went into a hover and watched the driver get out. He was heavyset, wore a beige jacket, blue jeans, and a ball cap. He walked across the street and into the home.

Trooper Donald Vlack radioed that he'd heard the air traffic and was coming to assist. I asked him to locate the driver so we could interview him. I wasn't thinking the guy was a killer; I just wanted to know what he was doing there.

Standing pulled in behind the Celebrity and radioed the license number, XLT-125. It came back to a Clara Neal.

As soon as Standing and Vlack radioed that they had the guy, we returned to Salmon Creek. I halfway expected to find a bunch of police buffs with scanners, but it had only been a few minutes and we'd used a lot of jargon to camouflage our radio transmissions.

It took three minutes to find a landing spot in a snowy field a couple hundred yards from the culvert. Ken Hunt and I got out and walked as close to the scene as we could without contaminating the evidence. A fresh set of footprints headed down to the creek from the shoulder. You couldn't see the body from the road.

Another BCI investigator arrived, Paul DeCillis of the Brockport Barracks. After he helped us protect the scene with orange pylons and tape, I asked him to drive to Spencerport to interview the guy in the car

I was happy we were finally on the case. I figured, We've found Felicia Stephens and it won't be long before we catch the killer. The BCI has a lot of pride.

7. CLARA NEAL

Around noon Art come into the kitchen at the nursing home. I was putting the lunches on the trays and setting 'em on the portable racks. He held out a plastic Diet Pepsi bottle and he says, "Where can I dump this? I had to weewee in the bottle."

I pointed to the little bathroom. Then he come back and says, "C'mere just a minute."

I asked my daughter Linda, "Do this job, will ya? I gotta see what Art wants."

We went in the break room and sit. He told me, "I stopped over here on the road to eat my salad and take a pee in the bottle. And there was a cop coming over in a helicopter. They follered me over here." Then he said real short, "One of the cops just come in here and wanted to see my ID. *For what?*"

I said, "I don't know for what. Surely they didn't see ya takin' a wet in a Pepsi bottle?"

We was both puzzled, but I knew it'd get straightened out. What're they gonna do, put him in Sing Sing? I had to go back to work, so I left him setting there reading the morning paper. The troopers come in and ask if he'd step out to their car. Art just said, "All this for taking a piss?"

He grabbed the Pepsi bottle out of the wastebasket and asked if they wanted it for evidence. They said, No, just leave it there. Then they all walked outside. I'll put it straight plain: I thought those cops was goddamn crazy. I told Linda and some of the others not to worry. I told 'em all Art done was he used the woods for a bathroom. Then we got busy with feedin' time.

8.

Seated in the back of John Standing's State Police cruiser, the man named Arthur John Shawcross didn't seem reluctant to talk. He said that he'd borrowed the Celebrity from a friend and driven into nearby Brockport to buy a take-out lunch. He was returning to Spencerport on Route 31 when he pulled off the road to eat. He said he threw his empty salad container into Salmon Creek and started to urinate on the shoulder, but when he heard the helicopter he switched to the empty Diet Pepsi bottle. At the end of his recitation, he added, "I guess I really opened up a can of worms when I stopped there."

The BCI's Paul DeCillis elicited more details, including home addresses and work information about Shawcross and his friend Clara. He told the investigator that he dropped her at the nursing home just before 6:00 A.M., drove across the street to the municipal parking lot, parked next to a Dumpster, and napped till ten. He produced a New York State Motor Vehicle nondriver photo ID card and explained that he hadn't held a valid license since 1970. When the investigator asked why so much time had passed, Shawcross hesitated, then said he'd been "in jail."

"What for?" DeCillis asked.
"Manslaughter."

9. CLARA NEAL

I was too busy serving lunch to fret about the cops, but when I got off at one o'clock and went outside for Art to drive me home, here was the whole damn parking lot full of 'em. About *eight* cop cars! They had my Celebrity blocked. I thought, What in the name of God's goin' *on*?

When they seen me coming down the walkway from the nursing home, a cop runs up and says, "We wanna talk to you a minute."

A man in street clothes come over and introduced himself as Investigator DeCillis. I said, "What the hell's goin' on?"

He asked me a million questions, if I seen Mr. Sharcross with any strange women, if I knew of any other women being in my car, that kind of stuff.

Then Mr. DeCillis told me not to be embarrassed but he had to ask me some stuff about our sex life. He was nice and polite. He asked if we was lovers and I was just plain about it, I said we was more lovers than Art ever was with his wife and he always told me I was like a virgin, only firmer.

He asked me some more stuff and I began to see what was going on. Owing as they'd caught Art peeing in public, they thought he was some kind of pervert. Well, I knew he wasn't, so I just said, "Tell ya hwut, mister: You ask any question you want."

He wanted to know what style of lovemaking we used, and I told him right out: perfectly normal, Art on top, me on the bottom, nice and patient and loving. I said we saw each other maybe five times a week and made love once or twice't. Art didn't have no trouble staying big, but his left testicle hurt lately and it made him take longer. The cop wanted to know did Mr. Sharcross ejaculate, and I said yes

Mr. Sharcross did, and I could tell when it happened, too. Neither one of us ever had no trouble in that department.

He wanted to know how we dressed, and I told him we always got nekked. He asked did we always do it the same way? I said, Yeah, but lately Art saw something new in a movie and wanted to try it. It's where I put my ankles up by his neck. I explained that I wouldn't let Art lick me and I wouldn't lick him, not while he's still living with his wife. And I wouldn't let him use my rear end, either. Anyway, Art likes plain sex, himself on top. He's very passionate and works up a sweat. Sometimes he gets playful and bites a little. I showed Mr. DeCillis a few love-bite marks around my shoulders. Don't mean nothing, just Art gettin' a little excited. It doesn't hurt and I don't object. We love each other.

Mr. DeCillis must've interviewed me for an hour, kept saying he had to ask these questions. Nice as he was, I still got a little mad when he asked if Mr. Sharcross ever abused me or hit me hard. I said, "No! I wouldn't stay with no man and let him pound on me." I said, "I'll tell ya this rat now. I got a buncha grown sons that live within six, seven hundred miles of here, and better not *nobody* put bruises on my body in madness or to hurt. 'Cause they'd be a *war.*"

All this time Art's sitting off to one side in a cop car. I figure they're gonna let him out and we'll drive back to town in my car. I figured wrong.

10.

From the moment Arthur Shawcross revealed that he'd been convicted of manslaughter, pulses quickened in the little municipal parking lot. Till then, he was considered a minor witness, a citizen who'd inadvertently parked near a body. But to seasoned investigators like McCaffrey and DeCillis, the new information was galvanizing. More than any other type of criminals, sex killers liked to return to the scene of the crime. They seemed to enjoy fondling their victims, gathering mementos, gloating, exulting, reliving the kill. They also became more daring, contemptuous of their trackers, eager to raise the level of tension according to their own twisted needs. And what could be more daring than urinating over the latest victim in broad daylight?

The BCI men decided to move the questioning indoors, but they had to have the subject's permission. He wasn't under arrest or even being detained. It was the same sticky problem Detective Charles Kubinski had faced seventeen years earlier: how to convince Shawcross to talk even though he had the right to thumb his nose and leave.

"Art," said Investigator Dennis Blythe, a BCI interrogation specialist who'd rushed to the scene on orders of John McCaffrey, "we need to talk to you, but it's kinda embarrassing with all these people around. Would you mind coming back to the State Police Barracks at Brockport? We'd like to talk to Clara, too."

Blythe was thinking, If this guy says no, we're screwed.

"Where's Clara?" Shawcross asked. "Is Clara okay?"

"She's fine," Blythe said. "How about it, Mr. Shawcross? Can we go someplace more private?"

To the investigator's surprise, the man answered, "No problem."

"You're sure you don't mind coming?"

"No *problem*." He sounded almost eager.

Blythe said, "Thanks a lot, Mr. Shawcross. We'll get you home, don't you worry about that."

Before they left the parking lot, Shawcross signed two "voluntary consent" forms, authorizing searches of the gray Celebrity and his apartment on Alexander. He handed over the keys. The detectives couldn't remember a more cooperative subject. That was another characteristic of serial killers: they liked to toy with cops.

On the six-mile drive from Spencerport to the small Brockport Barracks, Shawcross rode with Paul DeCillis, while Clara Neal went with the newcomer Blythe. On the way, Clara mentioned that Art had made some mistakes when he was a young man, but he'd paid his debt to society and become a good citizen, "just so nice to me and my grandkids. I don't see why you all're hasslin' him for peeing in a bottle."

Someone produced a key for the back door of the barracks; the thermostat was turned up, and coffee was prepared. It was just before 3:00 P.M. Clara sat quietly in an adjacent room. Shawcross pulled up a chair. He still seemed relaxed.

11.

In the culvert under Route 31, the frozen body remained untouched. State troopers stood guard to make sure that no one but the medical examiner and evidence technicians would be allowed past John McCaffrey's pylons and tape.

From every direction, Northampton Park began to fill with official searchers. If this was the murderer's dumping ground, how many more bodies lay under the snow, how much valuable evidence? June Cicero, Darlene Trippi, and Maria Welch were still missing, and there might be others. By now it was all too clear that the strangler had matched the profilers' predictions and kept busy over the holidays.

Soon sixty state troopers were either on-scene or on the way, some of them called back from days off or reassigned from other shifts and jurisdictions. In their Day-Glo orange slickers, they stood out against the white drifts and crusts. Park guards and forest rangers offered their expertise on local trails and topography. Two helmeted RPD mounties rode into the deepest brush and soon were followed by three riders from the Monroe County sheriff's office. The BCI's Captain Howard Allen arrived, along with the RPD's Major Lynde Johnston and Lieutenant James Bonnell, plus several detectives from Crime Analysis, two evidence technicians and First Assistant DA Charles Siragusa. They'd been monitoring their radios.

The State Police helicopter was joined by two others, churning up clouds of powdery snow. The RPD's flashy new command van lumbered into position, and evidence technicians gingerly unloaded a phosphorescing Luma-lite and other delicate equipment.

Word went out that the suspect was giving up nothing.

12. LIEUTENANT JAMES BONNELL

Myself and Sergeant Dick Hare, in charge of our evidence technicians, decided to go across the road and peek at Felicia Stephens's body from the other end of the culvert, taking a path that wouldn't disturb the footprints in the snow. She was laying on the ice, nude from the waist down, about fifteen feet away.

I had a funny feeling. "Whoa, Dick," I said. "She ain't no black chick."

He said, "My God, you're right."

We stepped closer. The daylight was fading but I could make out a white jacket with a fur hood. It was pulled up a little and exposed part of her left breast. I thought, *What?* Do these hookers all wear the same clothes when they go out to get killed? It looked like the jacket June Cicero wore the night I talked to her on the street.

I stopped. I could hear my own heartbeat. She was pitched forward and her face was frozen to the ice. Her bare backside was up and her right leg was stretched out, like a sodomy position. I remembered that some of the other bodies were found like that.

I slid a couple steps closer. I said, "Aw, shit. Aw, *shit*! My God, Dick, it's Cicero."

It got to me right away. I was one of the last to see June alive. It shook this old cop, humbled the shit outa me. Not only did this guy kill her, he took her *right out from under my feet!* Not my unit's feet, *my* feet! I got pride after all these years. I knew I was better'n that. I thought, She got herself killed even after I warned her, even after everybody on the street said he'd never get her. It must've happened right after she walked away that night, within a block or two of me and Tim Hickey, maybe while we were still cruising. What the hell are we dealing with here? A fucking *ghost*?

Then I thought, Poor June. What a waste. What a *waste*! Even as nasty as she was.

As usual there wasn't much to find. She was wearing white knee socks and the white jacket and one small pierced earring with a pink stone. We looked around for the mate but couldn't find it. The Luma-lite turned the snow an eerie blue, and bright specks of orange showed up on the ice. Nobody could figure out what they were till the ME turned June over. She was cut deep on both sides of her crotch, right into the bone. Apparently the killer came back and tried to saw out her sex organs, but all he took were the externals, the genital lips. Maybe it was too hard a job to saw a frozen body. The flecks in the snow were human sawdust.

13.

Dennis Blythe, a compactly built football referee and former college linebacker, had narrow green eyes, springy brown hair, a quick tongue, and a serious problem. He knew next to nothing about the case he'd just been assigned. At thirty-eight, Blythe was a BCI transfer from a rural area not far from Delhi and Fleischmanns. After graduating from college, he'd used his training in finance and economics to manage a ten-million-dollar portfolio for several years, then taken the state trooper's test as a lark, and ended up as one of the BCI's experts on narcotics and organized crime.

After three months in Rochester, he was still trying to learn the historic old city's byzantine maze of streets. He'd lost his way two or three times while piloting his red Porsche 924 from the BCI office south of town to this top-priority assignment in the Brockport Barracks. Now he was sitting across a table from a killer and wondering how to get started.

14. INVESTIGATOR DENNIS BLYTHE

Paulie DeCillis and I had used the computer terminal to do a quick history on Arthur J. Shawcross, the name on his ID. It came back in minutes: burglary second, burglary third, arson second, manslaughter, other stuff. It told where he was from, where he did time, everything. Paulie says, "Bingo!"

After I talked to Clara a little more, we invited Shawcross into Paulie's office and introduced him to my partner, Charlie Militello. I needed Charlie's help 'cause he knew the Northampton Park area and he knew Rochester and he's a hell of an interviewer. Being interrogated by Charlie was like talking to your best friend—right up till he pulled out the handcuffs. Believe me, this is an *art.*

We took Shawcross to a conference room and sat him down at the end of a long table. I scootched over so I could be on his right, and Charlie sat on his left. We kept saying, "Art, do you have to go to the bathroom? It's right down the hall. . . . Art, you want a cuppa coffee? . . . Lemme get you some coffee." We're being the nice cop and the *nicer* cop. Getting coffee was a good way for us to go out and brief the others.

One of the first things we wanted to know was where he fished and whether the locations matched up with the bodies. He said he and his wife Rose had taken a one-week fishing vacation at the end of June.

I said, "Where'd ya go, Art?"

He said, "We didn't go anywhere. Didn't have any money."

"Well, what'd you do?"

"Oh, you know. We . . . fished."

"Where?"

"Down to Charlotte." That was where June Stott was found, only I didn't know it at the moment.

He talks about fishing in the warm water from the electric company outflow near Russell Station. He mentioned the Driving Park area and a few places where he went for trout and bass. He said he slipped and broke an ankle and had to wear a cast for a while. I still didn't know if any of this was significant, but Charlie looked like a guy that's just flushed an eight-point buck.

Shawcross mentioned that he'd worked at a fresh produce place in the Public Market. Charlie said, "Brognia Brothers?"

Shawcross said, "Yeah."

Charlie says, "Why'd you leave there?"

"It was too far to ride on my bike, so I got another job."

We took a break, poured him more coffee. In the hall, Charlie says "Holy shit, Denny, this is the asshole that worked for Fred and Tony Brognia!"

The locker room was the only secure place in the barracks, and it was beginning to look like a police convention. There was our troop commander Major Sal Valvo; our BCI boss Captain Allen; John McCaffrey; the Rochester police chief and his deputy Rickard; the Monroe County DA Howard Relin and his first assistant; the CID chief Lynde Johnston; a couple of our profilers; Lieutenant Bonnell of the Tac Unit; and about ten other guys, and *everybody* babbling at once. They circled around us and asked, "What's he saying? What's he saying?" We said he's saying nothing so far.

Johnston and Bonnell asked if we could slide an RPD investigator named Tony Campione into the interview because he'd worked the killings and knew the case backward. It was also a way to show that our two departments could work together and the BCI wasn't trying to steal the case and get the credit, which we weren't, hah-hah. They peppered us with a bunch of questions to throw at Shawcross. Chuck Siragusa stressed that we tell the guy he's not being held, he's not a suspect, he can leave whenever he wants, he can call a lawyer, et cetera. He was insistent: "Make absolutely sure he knows his rights."

I said, "Yeah, okay. We already gave him his rights six times. I think we can handle it."

We went back in with Tony Campione and resumed the questioning. Tony turned out to be great. I had an idea how to conduct this interview and he fit right in. I told him,

"Tony, no talkin'. *No talkin'!*" I had him sit behind Art, out of his line of sight. He fed us all kinds of cues and questions just by his facial expressions. He would nod or shake his head or roll his eyes, and Charlie and I would get the message. If we got too pushy, Tony would frown and we'd back off, 'cause we couldn't challenge this guy, didn't dare irritate him.

After a while we asked him if it was a coincidence that he was parked over a body at Salmon Creek. He says, Yeah, he was just driving around. Bought his lunch at Brockport, sat in his car at Ames Plaza on Route 31, then drove east toward Spencerport before stopping to answer the call.

I'm thinking, Gimme a break, man. You're way out of town on a country road, taking a whiz in a bottle? There had to be another reason. Why'd he park at Ames Plaza? To ogle housewives? I'm thinking maybe he saw a few hot numbers and went back to the body to masturbate.

I asked him if he'd ever been arrested and he said, "Yeah." He said two kids died. That was the way he put it—"Two kids died, a boy ten and a girl eight."

I said, "Were they your kids?" and he said no. Then he clammed up on the subject.

Charlie told him we knew it was tough to talk about these things, and the guy went into a long story about how he'd been on the way to a party and the boy was bugging him and he hit the kid in the forehead. I asked him if sex was involved and he said no.

I asked about the little girl. He said it happened three months after the boy; he strangled and raped her. He said he was having troubles about Vietnam and also with his wife. He said he'd seen a lot of shrinks since then but nobody could figure out why he killed the girl, himself included.

We let him ramble, free-form, no pressure, a rap session. We kept telling him, If you wanna go, you can go; we hope we're not keeping you. We were hoping he'd say no, and he did. He told us that Clara was his girlfriend, and when I asked if Rose knew, he kinda grinned and said, "She probably does. She's not stupid."

He talked about his birth, his family, his early arrests, life in prison. Griped about how a landlord screwed him and Rose out of their deposit money. On and on. He wasn't giving up anything about the serial killings, but we were picking up leads, building our case.

He seemed to take a liking to Charlie. If I'd leave the room to get debriefed, the two of 'em would be giggling and laughing. Charlie said, "You got two women, huh? Clara and Rose? You must be a good man!"

We knew that sooner or later we had to start taking notes, but we didn't want to spook the guy. "Hey, Art," Charlie says, "it's no problem, but I'm just gonna write down a few things. I've got a terrible memory. Just gonna keep track." After that, Charlie basically took down every word, writing like a madman in his beautiful penmanship. I was new to the area, so anytime Art mentioned a locale, Charlie automatically jumped in and pinned it down for me.

We got to talking about my old backyard. I grew up in Binghamton and I'd been stationed in Sidney, thirty-two miles to the northeast. Shawcross says he and Rose lived in Fleischmanns for a while. I say, "Yeah, right between Delhi and Hamden."

You could see he was surprised. He said, "We had an upstairs apartment in Delhi."

I says, "Yeah? Over the bar, or over the department store?"

He blinked. I says, "You got the traffic light here, the grocery store here, the college up on the hill. And you're one street away from the courthouse and jail. Now which apartment were you?"

So we got it straight, where he lived. Then I said, "Now let's talk about Binghamton. Where'd you stay?"

He says, "In the Volunteers."

I said, "Oh, on State Street? Over by Binghamton Plaza?"

He says, "I think there was a shopping center, yeah."

We did a little more detail on Binghamton. Some he remembered, some he didn't. The whole exercise was to convince him we knew all about him—don't lie to us, Art, because *we already know.*

He told us about the parole officers taking him and Rose to the motel in Vestal. I said, "You mean the one down by the Four Corners, on the left there, with the swimming pool?"

He said, "Yeah, yeah."

Then he started talking about the western parts of Rochester, and Charlie jumped in again. He was from Brockport and he did the same number that I'd done on Binghamton. Pretty soon we had the guy thinking we ate New York maps for breakfast.

He told us he'd been a weapons expert in Nam and a lot of bad things happened there but he couldn't remember. Said he'd been wounded twice, once in the shoulder and once in the upper chest. And he said he was Agent Oranged. He told us how to make silencers: put a baby bottle nipple over the muzzle. It's only good for one round. He says, "It works great. All you get is a little *pffff.*"

We found out he could talk all day about fishing and hunting, harmless subjects to him, but when we tried to pin him down on dates and exact places, he no spikka da English, ya know? He was a lot tougher nut than he looked.

We took another break and all the big shots wanted to know what he was saying. I told 'em he's playing a game, he's dancing, he's telling us and *not* telling us. Somebody said we couldn't keep going all night. I said, "I can't get into the murders yet. I don't know enough, and he's gonna *know* I don't know."

We went back in for another round. My goal was just to keep him talking, get some background, and maybe slip in a zinger once in a while. I asked him, "Have you ever been with a prostitute?"

He changed like that! *Snap!* Up to then he'd been happy-go-lucky, looking us straight in the eye. He says, "No!" and he's angry.

I switched subjects quick. But about five minutes later, I said, "Art, I don't know why you don't tell me why you don't like hookers."

Boom! He's angry again. He mutters, "I don't want to get AIDS."

We waltz back to the subject of Watertown. We're trying to get a few details of the killings without making him antsy. I said, "Did you have sex with the little girl?"

"No."

"Did she have her clothes on?"

"Yeah. Shorts or pants, I forget."

You could see him sag when he talked about the kids. His whole body language changed. He was that way whenever we mentioned anything that bothered him. He would frown and put his hands tight in his lap, shoulders hunched, head down. He just closed in on himself, shrank into this posture and tried to change the subject. We would change it back or bring it up again later.

We finally got some details about the little girl. She didn't want sex with him; he forced her; she was crying and bleeding. It took a while to get him to admit penetration.

"Yeah," he said, "I put my dick in her." We asked if it was from behind, and he said, "Yeah." The cold way he said it made me sick, but I didn't dare react. Being a cop, one of the things you have to get used to is hearing the vilest remarks and not changing your expression. I could see Campione and Charlie trying to stay composed. We tried to get details on how or when he choked her to death, but he claimed he didn't remember.

He started rambling about his sister Jean. At first I thought he was changing the subject again, but then I realized it had something to do with the little girl. He said he'd had "a thing" with his little sister, three years younger. He said he'd admitted to his mother that they were "more than brother and sister."

Charlie asked what kind of "thing" he was talking about —touchy-feely, intercourse, or what? He said he touched his sister and "ate" her when she was fourteen to seventeen and he was seventeen to twenty. When he was finished, he went back into his hangdog position, and Charlie thanked him for being honest.

After a while he started talking about his sex life with

Clara, said he had an erection problem and an orgasm problem but he could keep it up longer with her than with Rose. I asked why, and he said, "Clara blows in my ear and puts her tongue in my ear."

At home, he said, sex worked better with Rose on top. He couldn't reach orgasm with either of them and it hurt when he tried; he thought it had something to do with guilt from his past. The doctors had scheduled him for a urological examination but he didn't show up for it.

Late in the afternoon we took a break. John McCaffrey says, "Listen, I want you guys to think about something. You both started at eight this morning and you're gonna get tired long before Shawcross. You're day workers and he's nocturnal and he's coming on. You can only play with a guy like this so long, and then he's gonna figure, Hey, you gonna arrest me or let me go?"

John alerted us that some of the brain trust in the locker room weren't sure we had the right man. A profile expert had looked at Shawcross's record and said a confirmed pedophile would never switch from killing kids to killing women.

John and Charlie and I thought different. So did Campione, and he had a better background on the case than the rest of us put together. Shawcross was the man, all right. Let the shrinks figure out the whys and wherefores later.

15.

Lieutenant James Bonnell, in his usual direct manner, described the scene in the Brockport Barracks as "a fucking mess." Salvatore Valvo, the local State Police troop leader, spent most of his time on an open phone line, updating his headquarters in Albany. Howard Allen, the local BCI commander, used another phone to call Watertown for details on the killings of the two children. After a while, the high-level phone conferences took a political turn, with State Police officials in Albany insisting that Blythe and Militello stay with the suspect till he confessed. Shawcross was their discovery, and they were asserting proprietary rights.

But the Rochester PD had worked the murders for a year and didn't intend to be offstage at the climax. Chief Urlacher warned that the State Police were jeopardizing the case, that Shawcross would never confess unless the knowledge and skills of veteran RPD officers like Investigator Lenny Borriello were added to the mix.

"Our men should be working together," he told the BCI officials. "You're never gonna get a confession if your guys don't know what the hell they're talking about. We've been going to school on serial murder for six months."

His deputy Rickard suggested, "Why don't we cut him loose overnight? I'll put a hundred men on him. We've already got men standing by the phones with duty rosters, ready to call in extras. We'll watch him, we'll work the new leads together, and we'll make a case that'll stick in court."

The local State Police leaders remained bound by their superiors' orders. The room fell quiet as Charles Siragusa started to talk. The prosecutor was a lean, graceful man with an overbalancing shock of dark brown hair and a youthful appearance. He'd won a long string of murder convictions and worked hard on the serial murder investigation. No matter what agency got credit for solving the case, it would be Siragusa's job to put the killer away.

"We all agree," he said. "The BCI did a hell of a job. But legally Shawcross is only a witness, a man sitting in a car over a body. You've got to develop probable cause before you can start a custodial interrogation, and even then he can refuse to talk."

Someone offered the opinion that a suitable degree of probable cause might emerge from the questioning.

"It's too big a risk," the first assistant DA insisted. "He's been questioned off and on for five hours and that's enough. You're gonna blow the whole damned case. My advice is to let him go home and then try to develop more information. That way everything's nice and legal."

The two top police officials on the scene, Chief Urlacher and Major Valvo, adjourned to a side room to thrash out a decision. Urlacher recalled later, "Whatever we decided, it was a gamble. If the guy runs, we're all fools. Can you see the headline: 'Serial killer slips through police hands'? But if we question him for an unreasonable length of time, it can wreck us at trial.

"Sal Valvo and I took five minutes to make our deal. It was a much more courageous decision for him than it was for me, because I was the boss of my own department. If I screwed up, only the mayor would get on my case. But Sal had tremendous pressure from Albany. We went back out and made the announcement together. Some of his guys thought we were nuts. So did some of mine."

16. INVESTIGATOR DENNIS BLYTHE

When they told me to cut Shawcross loose, it didn't bother me as much as it did some of the others. By now we had plenty of leads to work: Brognia, G&G, Dunkin' Donuts, the broken ankle and the cast, Clara's old blue-gray Omni that he'd let slip, the Celebrity, his night work, his sex life, his apartment, et cetera. We needed time to develop the new information. Like the DA said, we can't arrest the guy for illegal parking.

The main problem now was to keep him occupied while the surveillance people took up positions around his apartment building. We figured out an excuse to hold him a while longer. I said, "Art, I'm starving. You getting hungry?"

"No," he says. Sounded like he meant it, too.

Charlie says, "Man, I'm starving."

Shawcross said he'd eaten a salad and that was all he needed.

I left the conference room for a minute, and when I came back, Charlie was saying, "C'mon, Art, let's go get something to eat. Then we'll drive ya home."

Tony Campione says, "Yeah, Art, there's a great place right near here."

Finally Art says okay and the four of us take off for a

restaurant on Main Street in Brockport. We had Dutch apple pie and he had coffee. He acted like he was out with his pals. Tony got involved in the talk, laughing, having a good time.

Somebody mentioned hunting and Art asked if we'd ever killed a deer with a knife.

Campione said, "Get outa here, Art! You can't do that."

So he told us how to use farm salt and black powder to bait Bambi. The deer'll eat the stuff, get thirsty, drink, and eat more. After a while they can't move. They twitch a little and the hair'll stand up on the back of their neck. He says, "Then you just walk up behind 'em and cut their throats."

We're sitting there nodding and smiling and every one of us is thinking, Doesn't this crazy son of a bitch realize what he's saying? He's giving us a seminar on controlled killing, taking it nice and easy, savoring every second. He was like a little kid telling how to tear the legs off frogs.

Then he launches into how to handle eels while they're twisting around on the hook. You just shove a cigarette butt down their throat and the nicotine stiffens 'em up. We all tried to look enlightened.

We got back to the Brockport Barracks a little before six-thirty. Shawcross wanted Clara to drive him home. We didn't want them comparing their stories, so we said, "No, no, Art, Clara's son's gonna drive her. Charlie and I'll take you right to your front door. We gotta go back to town anyway."

Just before we left, it occurred to me that we needed a picture. I said, "Art, you've been so cooperative. You wouldn't mind if I took your picture, would you?"

He says, "No problem."

I don't trust myself with a thirty-five-millimeter, so I shot a couple of Polaroids. The pictures made him look old. I thought, Well, he *does* look old. He's forty-four and looks sixty. Poor guy had a hard life. But not half as hard as the people he killed.

We left the Brockport Barracks at 6:40 P.M. Charlie was driving the BCI car, a blue '86 Buick Century sedan. It was a cool night, very dark. Art rode up front with Charlie and they're still jabbering about fishing.

At the apartment building, I said, "Art, there may be some more questions later. You won't mind if I come back and talk to you tomorrow or the next day?"

"No problem, no problem."

"Art," I says, "thanks for your help."

He says, "Anytime."

I gave him my card with my phone number. We all shook hands and he went inside. Now he's thinking he's come close to the fire but didn't get burnt; he's fooled the poor dumb cops and he's out of the woods again.

We start to drive away and I realize there's something wrong. Where the hell's the RPD surveillance? "I'll put a hundred men on him," all that bullshit. I started to panic. What's to stop the guy from heading for Brazil as soon as we turn the corner?

I told Charlie, "Stop! Lemme out."

I walk up the street toward Monroe Avenue with the BCI car crawling alongside. Then I begin to see 'em. They're in the parking lot behind the building. They're parked on either side of the building, and there's another car across the street in the hospital parking lot and a van a little further down with a couple of mountain bikes in case he goes out for a ride. And not a uniform or a police car to give it away. Beautiful!

I got back in the Buick. The whole operation had been moved from our barracks in Brockport to the fourth floor of RPD headquarters, 'cause they had the records. I was told that both agencies would work together but I would still be the lead interviewer. Somebody took my Polaroid pictures and started preparing photo lineups to take out on the street. Did the hookers know this guy or not? That would tell us a lot.

17. INVESTIGATOR LEONARD BORRIELLO

Billy Barnes and I had a murder on Jefferson Avenue that day and we got back to headquarters after supper. Major Johnston comes rushing in and starts telling us about this guy the BCI stopped—worked for G&G, had a plastic brace, used his girlfriend's blue-gray Omni. A search team found plastic sacks of apples and potatoes in his apartment. I said, "My God, Major, that's the guy we've been looking for!"

When we heard they planned to let him go for the night, I said, "Billy and I'll pick him up."

We were reaching for our coats when Johnston says, "C'mere," and starts explaining the situation. I was so excited I barely heard what he was saying. I said, "Major, *Major*! Billy and I'll break him tonight!"

Johnston says, *"Slow down!* It's not that simple." He said what it came down to was the State Police had the suspect and the RPD had the facts of the case, so neither could do much without the other. The plan was to hit the guy with more questions in the morning. I says, "Me and Billy, right? We're partners, we know the case."

The major explained that it had to be a combined interrogation team, one man from RPD and one from BCI. That was the deal our chief and Sal Valvo had made to divide up the credit. They'd also agreed that the bust would be announced at Troop E headquarters.

Billy says, "Well, if we can only send one man, let it be Lenny."

Johnston said the state wanted most of the interviewing done by its hotshot interrogator, a guy named Blythe. I thought, Oh, shit, why can't it just be Billy and me? We know each other's rhythms; we got signals we can't even explain. You get that way after eleven years. We'll break this Mitch in five minutes. But the deal was set in cement.

The major says, "Lenny, get some rest. You're gonna be our designated hitter."

18.

Detectives from Physical Crimes took a six-photo spread to Lake and Lyell and showed it around. Several prostitutes pointed to the mug shot in the middle of the bottom row and said they'd seen the man. Said one, "That's Mitch." He seemed to be regarded as a harmless old john.

At 10:00 P.M., Lieutenant James Bonnell's Tac Unit reported that Arthur Shawcross was in his apartment with his wife Rose.

An hour later, RPD Investigator Terry Coleman and Detective Gordon Hall knocked on the door of Apartment 107 and were greeted by the suspect. A heavyset woman stood in the shadows behind him.

Hall handed over the apartment keys and apologized for not returning them sooner. When the detectives left, the couple appeared to be preparing for bed.

19. INVESTIGATOR LEONARD BORRIELLO

It was getting late, and I wanted to have a few manhattans with Billy, get his ideas, but I had to find Jo Ann Van Nostrand before the questioning began in the morning. If "Mitch" wouldn't sit still for a voluntary interview, she might give us enough probable cause for an arrest. What the hell, she'd seen Liz Gibson in his car the night she was murdered.

But Jo Ann wasn't at any of the usual places. She'd gone up in smoke! Of all nights! Somebody said her social worker had been trying to put her in a dope rehab center in Buffalo, but we couldn't find the social worker either.

Just before midnight, Billy and I went over to Shields for a pop. He didn't smoke, and my girlfriend and I'd quit two days before. We figured we had a pretty good shot at staying off for good.

So naturally I lit up. Pretty soon I've got a cigarette in my mouth and one on the ashtray and Billy's giving me the usual lecture: "Listen, Lenny, how're you gonna live to enjoy your retirement? Listen, for every cigarette you smoke, be sure to put a dollar in a jar, so you'll be able to buy an oxygen tank to carry around on the golf course."

I'm thinking, Who gives a shit about oxygen? What the hell am I gonna ask this asshole in the morning? *Where the hell's Jo Ann?* I've been looking forward to solving this case for a year and now I'm getting nervous! A few pops did me no harm.

Around 12:30 or 1:00 A.M., the DC, Terry Rickard, dropped in with Chuck Siragusa and Jimmy Bonnell. They said they'd just left the fourth floor but some of the other guys were gonna work all night, set things up for the morning. Then a coupla FBI agents arrived. I'd played ball with 'em, good guys, friends. I said, "We're gonna have a confession to the serial killings in the morning. No doubt about it. I'm 125 percent positive this guy did it. I *guarantee* ya I'm gonna have a confession."

They said, "Yeah, sure."

I knew I'd never sleep, so I didn't try.

20. CLARA NEAL

It was late when I finally got home, waited around in that little side room in Brockport for nine or ten hours and didn't even get to see Art. Those cops didn't offer me refreshments, either, but I wouldn't have eat it if they had.

Around eleven o'clock, I started my laundry, 'cause I only had three outfits of white clothes for my job at the nursing home. I got two loads washed when I heard a knock. I listened for shave and a haircut two bits, but it wasn't Art. It was two cops, wantin' me to show 'em where he took me to fish.

I was about fed up. I said, "What *is* all this crap?"

They hinted that something had gone on in my car; they said that's why they taken it. That made two cars gone: my Omni and my Celebrity. I wondered how was I gonna get to work.

I said, "It's midnight, too dork. I cain't show you no fishing holes in the dork."

But I'm a law-abidin' citizen and I got in their car to help. I showed 'em Turning Point Park, the dam by the nuclear power plant, the road next to the "Y" that led down to the gorge, the Russell Station sewer treatment plant, and out Route 104 to the nuclear power plant. I said, "By the way, he didn't just taken *me* here. He took his wife Rose, and one of my sons. My son's wife, too." I showed 'em where a crick come out of the nuclear plant and the waves from the lake pushed the water back up.

When we left the nuclear plant, they said, "That all?" and I said yeah. By then it was two o'clock in the morning and I thought they were gonna take me home, but they made a couple of turns to confuse me and taken me out Route 31 toward Northampton Park. I laughed and said, "You don't have me fooled. I know where I'm at. This is the Brockport–Spencerport Road." Art and I used to go out in that area to make love.

When we reached the park, I said, "We never fished here. They ain't no water here to fish."

They showed me some standing water near Salmon Creek and I said, "My God, you couldn't catch a minner in that little puddle."

It was quarter after three when I got home. My son Douggie was getting up to go to Brognia's. I barely laid my head down 'fore the daylight come through the curtains and I had the whole day ahead of me—no car, no Art, nothing to do but think. I wondered if we was ever going to Clay County, West Virginia.

21.

Shortly after 7:00 A.M. a man named Richard Thompson parked his pickup truck on an access road just west of Northampton Park and trudged across the crunchy snow toward a patch of woods. The area was closed to hunting, but he had a nuisance permit to shoot deer that wandered onto the runway of a small adjacent airfield. As he passed the brick foundation of a wrecked farmhouse off the heavily traveled Colby Road, Thompson thought he saw a hand protruding from the ruins.

He walked over and found a body frozen in the snow. The woman looked to be about twenty, small-figured, black. She wore a brown corduroy coat, a black jacket, and socks. A pair of black slacks dangled from her left ankle. She was lying facedown, but her bare buttocks were slightly elevated.

The deer hunter rushed to a phone and dialed 911.

22.

An hour later, Dennis Blythe arrived at the fourth floor of the Public Safety Building to meet with top cops and lay plans to induce Arthur Shawcross to confess. He'd spent the night studying at his kitchen table. State Police cruisers had relayed old files from Watertown at top speed; the RPD had prepared synopses of its open murder cases plus other material; the energetic Deputy Chief Rickard had photocopied several chapters from an FBI manual on serial murderers. All night long the documents had poured into Blythe's home.

In the RPD's "war room," Major Lynde Johnston conducted an intense briefing. He reported that the body of Felicia Stephens had just turned up near Northampton Park; he'd learned of the find on his police radio as he drove to work.

"They're dropping like hailstones," he said as everyone paid close attention. The cramped little conference room bulged with top cops: Troop E commander Valvo, BCI boss Allen, RPD chief Urlacher, his deputy Rickard, Lieutenant Bonnell, Charlie Militello, Tony Campione, Blythe, eight or ten investigators from Physical Crimes and the Tac Unit.

The CID commander emphasized that Shawcross could still slip through their fingers. No matter how simple the guy looked, said Johnston, he was no ordinary criminal.

He'd committed twelve or thirteen murders and left almost no clues, no fingerprints or fingernail scrapings, no body secretions that could be analyzed for blood type or DNA. He'd continued to lure his victims at the height of the panic. He'd placed the bodies where they would decompose and maximize the medical examiner's problems. He was an ex-con who knew how to confound lawmen and almost seemed to enjoy it.

"He won't give up anything he doesn't have to," said the young police major. "If we don't get a confession, he walks, or he winds up with too short a sentence. It's already happened once in his life."

Johnston's alerter went off and he grabbed the phone. He repeated the message from the Tac sergeant so that everyone could hear: Shawcross had just left his apartment and was bicycling toward Monroe Avenue.

Dennis Blythe hadn't quite finished memorizing the information on the wall displays. He'd planned to pay quick visits to a few of the closer locations so he could ask more intelligent questions, but with the suspect already on the move there was no time.

Johnston took the BCI investigator aside and said, "You'll do great. We're teaming you up with our best man."

Blythe tried not to show his chagrin when he was introduced to Leonard Borriello. "I was expecting James Bond," Blythe said later, "and I see an underweight guy who looks like me—same silly grin, same hair sticking up, same red eyes. I'm thinking, This isn't gonna work. Who's gonna take the lead? The guy's acting real businesslike, like he'll do the job solo. Lenny told me later that his main concern was, 'Who the fuck is this asshole?' "

Word came in from the surveillance teams that Shawcross was having coffee and doughnuts at the Dunkin' Donuts, conversing with a middle-aged man and two uniformed cops. Then he pedaled up Monroe Avenue toward midtown.

He was watched as he checked in at the Parole Office, then as he entered and left a grocery store. He rode a few more blocks, locked his ladies'-style bike to a rack in front of a high-rise apartment at 125 St. Paul, a five-minute walk from the Public Safety Building, and disappeared inside.

The watchers waited a minute or two before checking the sign-in register. It showed that "Art Shawcross" was visiting "Irene Kane" on the twentieth floor. A maintenance supervisor reported that the woman was a respectable citizen in her nineties and the man was a frequent visitor. A certain nervousness developed about her health and welfare.

23. LIEUTENANT JAMES BONNELL

There was still a lot of political infighting going on at headquarters, and the BCI captain Howie Allen and I were getting fed up. We had a serial murderer in our sights and our bosses were still yammering about who was gonna get the credit and whether Dennis Blythe was gonna do all the questioning or if it was gonna be half him and half Borriello, all sorts of stupid shit like that. Howie and I decided, Fuck this, once we get the guy in an interrogation room nobody's gonna care who does the questioning. Let's just *do* it.

We were worried about the old lady. Was this a friendly visit or did he go up there to do his thing? We had no idea. Maybe he figured he might as well enjoy one last killing before we put him away. It was a risk.

Two of our men put on maintenance outfits and listened outside her door. A backup team pretended to vacuum the rug in the hall. No noise came from inside, but how much noise does it take to strangle a woman in her nineties? We figured we better get him outa there.

We dialed her number and advised her that her friend's bike was parked in a bad spot. Would he come down and remove it? She said he'd be glad to.

24. INVESTIGATOR LEONARD BORRIELLO

Blythe and I had about three minutes together to plan what we were gonna do. The first thing we decided was to forget everything we'd been told; this was *our* responsibility, not the armchair quarterbacks'. Driving to the high-rise, he asked for some insight into the cases, and I said, "Look, Dennis, it'd take all day long to get you to first base. Most of my information is on Elizabeth Gibson, so when we pick him up, let's start with her. If we get a confession on that one, we're in the ballpark. Then we can try for the rest."

We'd borrowed the DC's big Ford LTD 'cause we wanted Art to be comfortable if we had to drive him somewhere. We didn't want some wiseass defense attorney claiming that we stuffed him into one of those cheap little K-cars the department uses to save gas.

We parked about fifty yards from the high-rise and we see the guy heading toward the bike rack. We bailed out and did a speed walk. He looked surprised to see us, a little shocked. Blythe flashes a silly grin and starts talking fast—"Art, how are ya? Remember me? Denny Blythe again. Glad to see ya. Remember I told ya I might have a few more questions? Well, I do. This is my partner, Lenny Borriello. We'd like to talk to ya for a few minutes. You don't mind comin' with us, do ya, Art?"

Shawcross blinks and says, "Well . . . I got my bike."

Blythe slaps him on the back and says, "Hey, we'll have somebody take care of it."

Shawcross says okay and puts it back in the rack. Blythe says, "Jeez, Art, I really appreciate your help in this, ya know? How'd it go last night with that search?"

"No problem."

"Didn't tear your place up, did they?"

"Aw, no."

"Jeez, I'm glad, Art. Sometimes those guys can be assholes. You gotta be careful."

I'm thinking, When is Shawcross gonna ask for a lawyer? If he does, we're outa there. He's not under arrest and we still don't have probable cause. We're working four hundred feet in the air without a net.

Blythe gave him his rights in bits and pieces, not to spook him. As we're getting in the DC's Ford, he's saying, "Art, we're gonna take you to some spots 'cause you said some things yesterday that we're not quite sure of. But I wanna protect you here, Art, okay? You know, of course, that you have the right to remain silent. You understand that, right?"

Shawcross says, "Yeah."

Blythe says, "And Lenny has some questions for ya, too, so he's gonna be talking to ya, right? And Art, ya know, if you need an attorney and you can't afford one, we'll getcha one. You know that, right?"

Shawcross goes, "Yeah, okay."

"And of course if you don't wanna talk to us, you can stop anytime. And anything you say can and will be used against you in a court of law. You know all that, right?"

After Blythe gave him the five warnings from the notification and waiver card, he read off the two waiver questions again. I'm holding my breath, but Shawcross says, "Yeah. Okay. Fine." Then he opens the right rear door of the Ford and jumps in like he's impatient to help us out and why don't we knock off the bullshit.

Blythe piles in next to him and I head for Durand-Eastman Park. Now the trick is to convince the guy we know everything and he might as well confess. But we've gotta do it carefully or he gets out at the first stop sign and all we can do is wave bye-bye.

On Lake Avenue, I looked in the mirror and spotted a couple of police cars backing us up. The way things were going, it wouldn't've surprised me if the mayor was back there, Governor Cuomo, the pope. Nobody wanted to miss out.

We reached the spot where he took Jo Ann Van Nostrand, and I backed the car right up against the tree exactly the way he'd backed up the Omni, two or three feet from the edge of the drop-off.

I said, "Art, do you remember this spot?"

No comment. He's staring out the window.

I says, "You turned a trick with a hooker here, remember? Around Thanksgiving?"

He says, "I don't know why you guys are talking like this. I didn't do nothin'."

Blythe says, "Jesus, Art, it's tough." He sounds like the guy's confessor. "We know how tough it is for ya."

I kept right on: "Remember, Art, she put a knife to your leg? You told her to play dead? Art, we know *all* about it."

Shawcross looked upset but kept quiet. I figured it wouldn't be long now.

25. INVESTIGATOR DENNIS BLYTHE

On the way back to town, Borriello headed for the Bausch Street bridge. He says, "Art, we're gonna show you the route you took with your friend Barbara." That was the name Van Nostrand used the night they tricked.

Art says, "I don't know what you're talking about."

"Just be a good guy and watch, Art."

I say in a soft nonthreatening voice, "We already know, Art." I'm leaning close to him in the backseat. I pat his knee, stare into his eyes. "It's okay, Art," I says. "We already know. It's . . . all over." But I keep my voice low, solicitous.

Borriello starts telling him what we know about him: works at G&G, hurt his leg near Driving Park bridge, wore a plastic brace, drove a blue-gray car with seats that reclined, had a rifle scope between the seats, kept potatoes and apples in plastic bags—all the stuff he'd learned from Van Nostrand.

Shawcross looks straight ahead and says, "I don't know what you guys are talking about."

I said, "Yes, you do, Art. But . . . it's okay. I understand. It's not easy to talk about these things."

We reach the bridge and Borriello says, "You stopped and picked Barbara up right here. Then you went down this street and made a right and went over there."

Art was still quiet. Borriello says, "Ya know, Art, Barbara saw you with Liz Gibson the night she disappeared. She was wearing a pink coat. Barbara knows a *lot* about you."

We asked if he'd mind going to the Public Safety Building for more talk. He said, "No problem."

26. INVESTIGATOR LEONARD BORRIELLO

Major Johnston and the DC and the others stayed inside the war room even though they were dying to get a look at the killer. We got off the elevator and hustled Shawcross toward the Victor Woodhead Conference Room, named for a hero cop. Charlie Militello and Tony Campione were in the anteroom just outside, and Art shook hands, seemed glad to see them.

As soon as Dennis and I took him inside and shut the door, a guard popped into place so we wouldn't be interrupted. The shade had been drawn and the walls stripped; even Victor Woodhead's picture was gone. In an interrogation, you want the guy to look at *you*.

I sat across from Shawcross and Dennis sat next to him at the end of the long conference table. Right from the start, he was tough to talk to, a typical ex-con. You had to draw him out inch by inch. He ad-libbed nothing—no embroidery, no cracks or jacking around. His face was blank. He sat with his head down and his hands in his lap.

The first ten or fifteen minutes, we're dancing the polka. "Art, you did Liz Gibson." "No I didn't." "We know you did." "I know I *didn't*." Et cetera.

Dennis is leaning into him, patting his knee, his shoulder, anything to settle him down. Dennis says, "Come on, Art, it's all over. We *know*. Barbara saw you with Gibson. Didn't we just take you out to the park and show you we're not bullshitting?"

I'm thinking, Is this son of a bitch gonna stonewall us? Is he gonna walk outa here and the whole damn town's gonna say we had the serial killer and let him get away? I wondered if I was doing something wrong. I usually develop a little sympathy, maybe end up liking the guy a tiny bit, but not this time. There was nothing to like about him —a cold killer. I figured maybe my face was showing my feelings, so I tried to look more friendly.

I slid a picture of Liz Gibson across the table. I said, "Art, you were seen with this woman eleven hours before she's found dead. Is that another coincidence?"

Yeah, he said. It was.

I told him the evidence techs had found tire tracks and a blue paint chip where his car bottomed out when he was dumping Liz. I wasn't positive that the chips matched the Omni but I didn't go out of my way to tell him. He says, "How do I know you got a paint chip?"

Dennis says, "We got it, Art. Believe me, we got the evidence." He pats him again and says, "Come on, Art. It's all over. You *know* we're not bullshitting ya. Did we bullshit ya yesterday?"

Art says, "No."

"Did we treat you good?"

Shawcross starts to get up. When he's halfway out of his seat he bangs his fists down on the table so hard that the whole room shook. He yells, *"Why are you fuckin' with me?"*

Dennis and I're leaning into him tight, not moving an inch. We're thinking, He's gonna jump one of us. *Which one?*

Militello and Campione heard the outburst and rushed in. Charlie says, *"Art, are you okay?"* like the most important thing in the world was this goddamn killer's welfare. You have to conduct about a thousand interrogations to learn techniques like that.

Shawcross nodded, calm again. The raging bull turns into a choirboy. How do you figure the guy?

Charlie and Tony went back outside. Dennis and I looked at each other like, What now? What's the book say? We both had the same idea: let him stew. We went for five or six minutes, not a word, no motion. Leaning on our hands and staring at him. Sometimes it works.

He started mumbling about Clara and how concerned

he was about her. I mentioned that he seemed more worried about her than he was about himself.

Dennis acts like a light's just blinked on in his head. He says, "Art, Art, wait a minute!" He touches his arm and says, "Art, we know you drove Clara's car. Oh, Art, I'd hate to think . . ." He hesitates. "Art, I'd hate to think that Clara's involved in this? *Is she?*"

Shawcross says, "No, no. Clara's not involved."

"You sure, Art?"

"I'm sure." He lowers his head in that sheepish look. He says, "Clara is *not* involved."

When he said that, Dennis and I looked at each other. Now we knew we had him dead nuts. "Okay," I said, "why don't you tell us about Liz Gibson?"

He's staring at the floor.

Dennis says, "We know how tough it is, Art. We *know.*"

Shawcross looks up and says, "I killed her."

27.

At the other end of the fourth floor, behind a thick security door that opened to a three-number code, knots of public officials waited for a report from the Victor Woodhead Conference Room. Said Lieutenant James Bonnell, "It was a total stressed mess. All the brass were there—the DA, his assistants, the state, beat cops, deskmen, everybody. Different groups were pocketed together. Some guys stared at the wall. Some paced. It was like a maternity waiting room. Everybody was a fucking wreck."

At eight minutes after 1:00 P.M., Charles Militello and Tony Campione rushed through the door. Militello said, "He's going for it."

Campione said, "We got Gibson."

Dennis Blythe, his collar open and his shock of brown hair bouncing, asked two narcotics plainclothesmen to get him a typewriter. When they hesitated, he said, "Get me a fucking typewriter and a statement form. *Right now!*"

A helpful detective carried the CID secretary's IBM

Selectric down the long hall and placed it at the end of the conference table. Someone else set cups of coffee in front of Shawcross and his confessors. Blythe rolled in the paper and began to hunt and peck.

When the typing chore was finished at 2:00 P.M., Blythe asked Shawcross to read the statement for accuracy and apply his signature.

"Is there anything else we can do for ya?" the BCI man asked.

"Yeah," the killer said. "I want my wife."

In the war room, hardcase lawmen tried to conceal their emotions. "In our own way, we were all crying," Bonnell recalled. "We'd been living this thing for a long time. Chuck Siragusa went into a corner by himself, and when he turned back, his eyes were wet. Lynde Johnston, too. I kept punching my hand and saying, All right. *All right!* Borriello looked like a zombie. For three months, he'd been on double shifts. He was one of the guys who did their shopping on Christmas Eve."

Billy Barnes grabbed his partner in a bear hug and said, "Well, Lenny, I'm a true believer now. I'm sorry I broke your balls about Jo Ann."

Borriello informed him there would be plenty of opportunity to make amends later at Shields.

When Dennis Blythe's two-finger typing job was completed, the questioning resumed with relief help from Militello, Campione, and Barnes. As soon as Borriello said, "Art, we got some other things to clear up," Shawcross reverted to his withdrawn state: eyes glazed, head down, mumbling or mute. The RPD investigators were relieved about the Gibson confession but still frustrated; they'd solved a murder case in an adjacent jurisdiction but still had a dozen open cases of their own.

Barnes pulled three- by five-inch photos of Darlene Trippi and Maria Welch from a portfolio of unsolved murder victims, laid them on the shiny maple table, and said, "Won't you help us find these girls? They're entitled to a Christian burial, aren't they, Art?"

Shawcross glanced at the pictures, then stared past his questioner's shoulder. Barnes went on, "This girl here, she's got a five-year-old son."

Shawcross muttered, "I don't know nothin' about her."

Barnes displayed one picture after another. At each showing, Shawcross said, "No" or shook his head. Once he said, "I don't know what you're talking about," and later he complained, "Pick pick pick *pick*!"

Barnes responded, "You sound like my girlfriend." The killer didn't laugh.

Word arrived that the mate to June Cicero's small pierced earring had been found in Clara's rented Chevy Celebrity. When Shawcross was informed, he said, "How do I know you're telling the truth? How do I know you got 'em outa the car?" He repeated that he knew nothing about the other killings and didn't understand why he was being bothered.

"Where's my wife?" he asked. "I want to talk to Rose. Get my wife in here, will ya?" It was as though he'd never confessed to strangling Liz Gibson and dumping her body. Now he was just a poor misunderstood citizen who missed his wife.

Militello informed him that a police car had picked up Rose and was on its way.

At 4:00 P.M. Clara Neal appeared at headquarters and the investigators decided to let her inside. Blythe briefed her in the anteroom: "Art's being good, but you gotta tell him to be completely honest. Tell him to get it off his chest."

"Get *hwut* off his chest?" the woman asked. She looked puzzled.

Blythe said, "Just . . . whatever."

The perplexed woman promised to cooperate and was led into the conference room. The official police report quoted her as saying, "Why are you doing this to me?" But

Clara insisted later that she said, "Hon, why did you do this?"

Shawcross muttered, "I don't know."

Borriello held up two plastic Baggies holding the matching pierced earrings and said, "Mrs. Neal, are these yours?"

"No," she said.

"See, Art?" Borriello said. "She has nothing to do with this. Why get her involved? Why don't you tell us the truth?"

Clara pointed at the earrings. "These could belong to anybody," she snapped. The interrogators were dismayed. Instead of sticking by her promise to help, she was backing up the killer. They'd made a mistake.

She plopped into the seat next to Shawcross and reached for his hand. "Oh, honey," she said, "what happened? Don't worry. Whatever you did, I love you, I'm behind you. Wherever you go, I'll foller."

She was hustled out the door. Shawcross seemed indifferent.

28. CLARA NEAL

I grabbed the first cop I seen in the hallway and I said, "Now what'n hell's goin' on here?"

He said, "All's I know, this is a murder investigation."

I said, "Murder investigation? Of *who*?"

He said, "Arthur Shawcross."

I was froze. I said, "Where? When? *How?*"

He didn't say.

29.

A few minutes after Clara was shown the door, Charlie Militello gave Rose Shawcross a few terse instructions and escorted her into the room. She hugged and kissed her husband.

"I love you, darlin'," the stocky woman said. "No matter

what happened, I'll be behind ya all the way." Then she added the words Militello had requested: "Just tell these fellas the truth. Do you know anything about the girls?"

Shawcross mumbled, "It's over, it's over."

"What's over?" Rose asked.

"You and me."

"No, no, it's not over! Never will be. I'll never leave you. There's no divorce from me." When he didn't respond, she added, "Art, you should tell what you know about the girls."

Militello said, "See, Art? What a fine lady you have here. Just tell the truth for this beautiful woman here."

Rose sniffled. "What happened, Art?" she asked.

Shawcross looked straight at Rose and spoke haltingly. "Remember the night I came home and—my, uh, my eyes were scratched?"

She nodded.

"I—I hurt a girl. A—a—hooker." Then he added, "I *had* to hurt her."

He lowered his head and fell silent as Rose kneaded his hand. She said, "Art, you're the only one I have." She started to cry. "Even my own children don't care for me."

Militello said, "Look, Art, we did what you wanted. You wanted your wife and here she is. This beautiful woman here, she loves you so much. You've been a man so far and told us about Gibson. Now tell the rest, the whole truth. You don't want to put this beautiful woman through any more."

Shawcross nodded slowly but remained silent. It looked as though he didn't want to confess in front of his wife. That was one reason why suspects were kept away from their loved ones.

Militello said, "Rose, maybe you should sit outside in the waiting room to compose yourself." He promised that she could return.

"I love you, darlin'," Rose said as she left. "I'm with you all the way."

The door closed behind her and Borriello said, "Art, why put your women through this? The earrings were found in your girlfriend's car. People are gonna put a stigma on her. Why don't you help her, your wife, your loved ones? They're staying behind ya. Now do the right thing for 'em."

As Shawcross sat in silence, Billy Barnes remembered the killer's complaints about the swarms of reporters bothering Rose in Delhi and Fleischmanns. It suggested an area of vulnerability.

"Why don't you let it happen one time, Art?" he asked. "Get all the bad shit outa the way, *the bad press,* give your wife a little peace. Because if you don't, we're gonna find out anyway, and each time we charge you with a different murder, the more shit she's gonna get. The *press, publicity,* the heartache, the anguish. Art, the *reporters* are gonna worry the poor woman to death."

Shawcross raised his dark green eyes and said, "Show me them pictures."

Barnes set the stack of three- by five-inch photos on the table, fifteen or sixteen open cases that met the profile of the serial killer's victims. "And get me a map," Shawcross added.

He went through the shots like a card player, dividing them into two stacks. He showed no uncertainty about which women he'd killed and which he hadn't. He seemed affronted when shown pictures of other killers' victims—Rosalie Oppel, Nicola Gurskey, Jacqueline Dicker, Linda Lee Hymes. It was as though he had pride of authorship and didn't want credit for others' handiwork. A map was placed on the table in front of him, and he marked the spots where he'd dumped the bodies of Darlene Trippi and Maria Welch. Several times he commented that as far as he was concerned, the murders were a simple matter of "business as usual."

A grand jury stenographer recorded formal questions and answers that later became a seventy-nine-page typed confession. By the time the killer had described two or three of his crimes, a pattern of self-justification began to emerge. Gibson, he said, tried to scratch out his eyes. Blackburn bit his penis. Keeler threatened to tell Rose about their affair. Steffen shoved him in the river. Ives wouldn't shut up when children wandered near. Brown broke the gearshift of Clara's car. Stott "wasn't no virgin" and started to scream. Welch stole his wallet. Trippi questioned his manhood. Cicero called him a "faggot" and threatened to expose him as the serial killer.

Most of his formal admissions were suspiciously nonsexual, especially in light of his record as a sadistic pederast and his tendency to leave his victims in a facedown buttocks-up position. Any suggestion that he'd attempted postmortem sodomy was briskly turned aside, sometimes angrily. But there were occasional confirmations of deviant sexual behavior. He had a clear recollection of the tattoo on Frances Brown's buttocks—"KISS OFF"—despite never having seen her in daylight. He admitted cutting June Stott from breastbone to groin, claiming that it wasn't a sexual act but an attempt to help her body decompose "because I liked her." He stubbornly refused to acknowledge the inept postmortem surgery on June Cicero and denied stripping or killing Felicia Stephens—"I don't touch black girls," he explained with righteous annoyance.

30.

At 6:30 P.M., some six hours after the interrogation began, Rose Shawcross was allowed in the conference room for another visit. A report noted:

> Mr. Shawcross talked to his wife about a VCR that they had just purchased through a mail-order house, because they no longer needed it and didn't want to make the payments. Mrs. Shawcross told her husband that she loved him and that she would stand by him throughout the entire matter, and if he went to prison, she would move to be near him. She said that it wasn't his fault. She talked about Viet Nam and Agent Orange. Mr. Shawcross asked his wife not to let his mother find out

because she hadn't talked to him for 17 years, since his arrest in Watertown.

It was after dark before the paperwork was completed and a search party was formed to locate the long-missing bodies of Trippi and Welch. Shawcross was handcuffed in front of his body, taken downstairs to the shadowy street-level parking area of the Public Safety Building, and put into Deputy Chief Rickard's Ford LTD with Borriello, Barnes, and Blythe. As the car pulled out, it was trailed by four backup units: Campione and Militello in the first car, Lieutenant James Bonnell and BCI Captain Howard Allen next, and uniformed troopers and RPD officers bringing up the rear of the caravan in case they were needed to secure crime scenes.

The January air was bitter cold, the streets glazed with ice and snow, the temperature dropping fast—"typical disgusting Rochester weather," as Bonnell complained.

Driving past the corner of Lake and Lyell, Borriello felt punch-drunk with success and fatigue. He suppressed an urge to open the window and shout at a prostitute: "Hey, look at the john I got for ya!" The sign "Mark's Texas Red Hots" reminded him of the phony raffle for the new TV, aimed at developing a roster of street people. He was willing to bet that one of the slips was signed "Art Shawcross." It was probably sitting at the bottom of an unread stack of FIFs and Crimewatcher tips and leads.

As they headed north toward Lake Ontario, the prisoner pointed out where he'd met some of his victims. At the Maplewood "Y," he said, "That's where I did Patty Ives."

Borriello said, "Yeah. We already found her." He forced himself to sound warm and friendly. Even though Shawcross was officially in custody, he'd been informed several times that he retained the right to terminate the proceedings. If he did, the detectives feared, the bodies of the two women might never be found.

Alongside a wooded area just past Charlotte, not far from the reed-filled swamp where June Stott had been mutilated, the killer said, "Welch is back in there." He pointed into the woods with his manacled hands. "By the two tall trees."

"Why don't you show us the way, Art?" Blythe suggested.

Shawcross accepted a flashlight and walked past some bare-limbed saplings, the lawmen crunching along behind on the new snow.

"Don't get too close," Bonnell's voice called from the rear. "Lenny, you and Dennis go in. The rest of us'll hang back. We don't want to trample evidence."

They walked for three or four minutes before Shawcross stopped and pointed. Blythe whisked away an inch of snow and found the bent-over body of a woman. She looked as though she'd been in a sitting position and her head had been shoved sharply forward till her face nearly touched her knees. She was wearing sneakers, pink silk underpants, jeans, and two cheap necklaces.

"That's Maria?" Borriello asked.

The prisoner nodded.

Bonnell's voice boomed out again: "This is a crime scene. Let's get outa here."

It was 7:25 P.M. The temperature was fifteen above zero. Bonnell ordered a uniformed team to secure the body and remain on guard.

The caravan headed west on Route 104 at Shawcross's direction. En route, Barnes asked how he selected his dump sites. "I just drove around," he answered.

"Where'd you keep the bodies while you were driving around, Art? In the trunk?"

"Right in the front seat," he said nonchalantly. "Next to me."

"Nobody ever noticed?"

"They just looked like girls sitting there."

Barnes asked, "Once you decided what you were gonna do, did you go after 'em? Take a strong hold?"

"Oh, yeah," Shawcross answered. It seemed to answer the question of how he'd been able to dispatch so many women without attracting attention. He certainly looked strong enough to kill quickly and silently.

Barnes idly asked if he ever talked to his victims while driving them around.

"How do you talk to a dead person?" Shawcross responded.

After a twenty-minute drive on back-country roads, they came to a small bridge and the killer said, "Stop!"

The detectives were surprised. There were several houses nearby and the road was heavily traveled. They'd expected to be directed to a secluded place like Northampton Park.

"Over there," Shawcross said, pointing to a small concrete headwall above a culvert.

Bonnell and Captain Allen walked up. Bonnell asked, "Why'd ya stop here?"

"He says Darlene Trippi is here, Lieutenant," Borriello said.

"Here?" Bonnell said. "Right off Redman Road?"

"Yeah."

He aimed the yellow cone of light six feet down and saw what looked like a body in aspic. The naked woman appeared to be floating spread-eagled, face up, arms stretched backward over her head, brown hair flowing as if it had just been brushed. A closer inspection revealed that the body was locked in clear ice.

31. LIEUTENANT JAMES BONNELL

After we got back downtown and Borriello parked the DC's car in the garage, I asked him to leave Shawcross in the backseat for a minute. I climbed in next to him and took a good look, just to see his face.

He glanced and looked away, like "Who the fuck is this idiot?" I studied him for a minute or two. It's one of the main things I get out of doing my job, staring into the bad guy's face after we catch him. And thinking, Well, we got you, you son of a bitch!

A cop would understand.

32. INVESTIGATOR CHARLES MILITELLO

It was nine at night when we took the cuffs off and made the guy comfortable again in the conference room. I'm beat, but the high-monkeymonks are still saying, He won't admit Felicia Stephens; he won't go for a black girl. He likes you, Charlie; you gotta turn him around.

I says to my lieutenant, "Jeez, I'm whipped."

He says, "Give it another half hour, Charlie."

I go into the room and pull up a chair. "Art, are you okay? You want some coffee, something to eat? You wanna go to the bathroom?" He'd been saying no all day and he said it again. Cast-iron kidneys.

We talk for five or ten minutes. I'm telling him he did the right thing, I'm proud of him. Blah blah blah. Then I start on Stephens. "Art," I says, "it's exactly like the others. You admitted the others, didn't ya?"

He nods. He looks like he's just slept ten hours.

I says, "We found her right near Cicero and Blackburn. You admitted them, didn't you?"

He says, "Yeah. But I don't do colored girls."

He must've repeated that same line fifteen times. It didn't matter what I said, *he didn't do black women.* He was pleasant enough, but he wasn't gonna change.

Tony Campione came in and took his shot—"Lookit, Art, we won't tell nobody. If you're worried about Rose finding out, I promise ya—she won't." That didn't work either.

So after twenty-five more minutes of dancing I decide the personal card is all I got left. The guy liked me; you could see that. What the hell, I'd been his buddy for two whole days.

I put my hand on his shoulder. I says, "Art, I'm gonna stop beatin' around the bush. I gotta tell ya my bosses are pissed at me because they do *not* understand why you won't go for Stephens."

He says, "I'd like to help ya, Charlie, but I—"

"I know. You don't do black girls."

"Never."

I sighed. I acted like my career was over. "Art," I says, "I'm tired and so're you." He didn't look tired at all; he looked like he could go fifteen more rounds. I said, "It doesn't matter anymore. Don't get me wrong: I'm not mad at you. You did good. But I gotta go tell my boss that . . . I blew it."

Borriello's waiting outside the door. He looks like his eyes should be propped up with toothpicks. I took him aside and said, "I need you to tell Art I'm getting my fucking ass chewed out. Tell him they're yellin' and screamin' at me."

Lenny waits a few minutes and then goes inside. "Tony," he says, "what the fuck's going on? Charlie's in the chief's office. They're goin' up one side of his ass and down the other. *What happened?*"

Campione turns to Shawcross. "See, Art? Charlie's been good to you and now he's in trouble. Look, tell us about Stephens. We won't even get the stenographer."

"Nothing'll go on paper," Lenny promises. "Charlie's ass is in a crack. We gotta help him out."

Shawcross looks up and says, "What'd you guys ever do for me?"

Lenny pretends to be hurt. "What'd we ever do for *you*? We been good to you all day. We brought your girlfriend, we brought your wife. We got you coffee, food. Come on, Art. We won't tell Rose. Do it for Charlie."

Shawcross thinks it over. Then he says, "Well, okay. But . . . I didn't have sex with her!"

He tells how he caught Stephens's head in the automatic window a block from police headquarters, pulled her inside, and strangled her. Tony asked him how come she was found naked, and he said he just wanted to look at her body. So parts of his statement were obviously bullshit, but what the hell—it was a confession.

Imagine, here's an asshole that killed two little kids and eleven women, and he gives up a homicide to keep me from getting hollered at! How do you figure a guy like that?

33. JO ANN VAN NOSTRAND

I was hiding out at a friend's when the TV reported that the cops caught the strangler. I called Physical Crimes and the guy said, "Where the fuck are you? We been looking for you for two days."

Well, that was the first I knew. I gave 'em my address and he said they'd be there in ten minutes.

Investigator Terry Coleman showed up with his partner. They said they wanted me to look at six pictures and see if I saw Mitch. I picked the first one. Terry said, "No, no, look at 'em all!"

I said, "I don't have to look at 'em all. That's him."

He said, "Well, you're right on the button, Jo Ann. None of us believed you except Lenny. And you had the guy the whole time."

They drove me out to the State Police Barracks to identify the car. It was dented in back, but it was Mitch's, all right. On the way back to headquarters, Terry said, "How ya been getting by lately? Need anything?" He gave me twenty dollars. Some guys got class even if they're cops.

When we went to the fourth floor, I heard that the pimps and prostitutes were lined up fifteen deep at Lake and Lyell. They were all yelling "It's over, *it's over*!" A preacher was arranging a prayer meeting of thanks and every ho in town intended to go. A ho's Mass!

The other detectives crowded around and I asked one of 'em, "Did Mitch tell ya why he didn't kill me?"

He said, "Yeah. He said you were the best sex he ever had, baby."

I said, "Fuck you." I thought he was jiving me. But Lenny said, "It's the truth, Jo Ann! That's what the guy said. 'Barbara was the best.' "

I went into shock. Ya hear what I'm sayin'? A fucking strangler thought *I* was the best? What is that, a business recommendation or a message from God or what? The son of a bitch was half an inch away from killing me and rolling me down the bank. I decided never to trick again.

34.

At midnight, after Arthur Shawcross had been handcuffed and booked on multiple charges of murder, the lawmen decided to celebrate. Just across the freeway at Shields, the burly Chief Urlacher squeezed into his New York Yankees jacket and told a reporter, "Get your interview now. I won't be in any shape to talk later." He announced that the drinks were on him. It was a typically broad stroke; he'd always been quick to pick up tabs, especially for his fellow cops.*

At 12:15 A.M., Terrence Rickard arrived and ordered coffee. He'd slept two hours of the last forty-eight, more than some of the others, and as he stood at the oak bar his eyes kept falling shut. After a while he gave up and drove home in his LTD. As soon as he climbed into bed, his eyes popped wide open and he couldn't sleep.

Lenny Borriello decided to award himself a party in honor of the biggest bust of his career. "The first thing I did," he said later, "was pick out two guys to take me home —one to drive me and one to drive my car. A good cop *never* drives when he drinks. Then I ordered a beer and an ouzo."

He clinked glasses with Charles "Chuck" Siragusa, the first assistant DA, and said, "Thank God I didn't retire in June and take that investigator's job you offered me. It woulda killed me to miss this." Then he ordered another beer and another ouzo.

"My partner matched me drink for drink," Borriello recalled later, "but Billy can put away a distillery and never feel it. The next thing I remember, I'm home asleep and the phone rings. It's the crack of dawn and somebody says we gotta go to a press conference with the state. I phoned

* And later lost his job after being charged in a federal indictment with stealing some two hundred thousand dollars in department funds. (Ultimately he was convicted.) His protégé and friend Terrence Rickard was cleared of any involvement, but his position became untenable and he took early retirement.

Billy and said, 'Make me a manhattan and we're on our way!' He said his fiancée would drive us. That was a break."

35. HELENE HILL

At 6:00 A.M. I was at home in Rochester making my bed. My little TV was up on the dresser and I was halfway listening. The announcer said something about a serial killer. My back was to the TV, I'm pulling up sheets, fluffing pillows. The voice said, "His name is Arthur Shaw——."

I spun around and almost fainted. I'd seen him eighteen years before, in court. He'd aged and put on weight, but it was the same face.

I slipped to my hands and knees, staring at the picture. I couldn't believe it. He looked ten years older than I expected. I had an urge to touch the screen, make sure it was real. Then they mentioned Karen.

I called my son Tom. I mumbled into the phone, hysterical, and he couldn't tell what the heck I was saying. I kept screaming, "He's here. *He's here!*"

Tom said, "Who?"

I said, "Arthur Shawcross. Turn on your TV!"

He said, "Mom, I can't understand you."

I wanted to yell, You silly kid, don't you hear your mother? I wanted to grab him and pull him right through the phone. Why couldn't he understand? They caught the guy that killed his sister! The guy that was supposed to be put away!

Tom said, "Mom, I'll be there as quick as I can."

He lived forty miles away at the other end of the parkway in Waterport. After he showed up, my mom and my other kids began to arrive. My place was packed.

I couldn't calm down. Here I'd thought Shawcross was gone away forever, and all this time he was living in my hometown. He could've killed another one of my kids!

I freaked out. I couldn't stop shaking. They put me to bed and I broke out in hives. The doctor said it was from shock. Then I got chills and fever and everything swelled up. I couldn't move. It was a nightmare come true. Arthur Shawcross!

Then we heard that the press contacted my ex-husband Bob, Karen's father, and he blew up and said, "Shoot the sucker. Hang him!" It was all just too much. My mother was so upset she had a stroke.

36.

Reporters tracked Mary Agnes Blake to her run-down apartment above a pizza restaurant on the Black River in Watertown. Speaking in her North Country accent, she told them that the news of the arrest made her feel numb, "unreal." She said she'd overheard neighbors talking about her dead son Jack—"How strange it was after all this time. Nothin' was ever settled over Jack. Art Shawcross never gat a day in prison for what he did to Jack."

She characterized the killer as "a walking time bomb" and expressed surprise that he'd been freed. Now fifty-five, the bereaved mother and widow said that the law hadn't listened to her at the time of Jack's disappearance "and they're not listening now. There's something wrong with the system. My son had a chance to grow up and be somebody. Karen Ann Hill, she wanted to be a movie star. But he took all those hopes and dreams away. I don't think he has a right to be on this earth. . . . I don't think Gad would even accept him in heaven."

37.

At a formal press conference, tall, erect Major Salvatore Valvo took pains to emphasize the role of his State Police colleagues in capturing the killer. While cameramen duck-walked around his feet and reporters scribbled notes, the Troop E commander told the assembled press, "A major breakthrough occurred on January 3, 1990, when a *New York State Police* helicopter manned with *troopers* observed a body. . . . A car was observed in the vicinity by a *State Police* helicopter. Surveillance of the car was coordinated from the air using *State Police* patrols. . . ." He thanked the RPD for its assistance.

The BCI boss, Captain Howard Allen, waved an olive branch by describing the Rochester Police Department as "one of the finest organizations I've ever dealt with, a bunch of class people."

Terrence Rickard spoke last. "A lot of time and a lot of effort has gone into this case by the *Rochester police people* who are here today," the DC said, gesturing toward the sixty RPD members assembled in Troop E headquarters in Canandaigua. "We refer to them as the Victory Team, these people who have spent hours, days, weeks, months. They didn't see a Thanksgiving, they didn't see a Christmas, they didn't see their families for days on end. But they brought a killer to justice. . . ."

His voice quavering, the deeply religious Rickard concluded, "It's to their credit that we're here today, and the assistance of the State Police. I know the pilots and the investigator who were in that aircraft may have been flying the plane, but I think the hand of God was on the controls."

Lenny Borriello was uncertain about God's credentials as a pilot, but he was too tired to take issue. As soon as he got home, he planned to emulate a mythical Catskills resident and sleep till his beard reached his knees. It had been months since he'd experienced untroubled sleep. What a thrill it would be to wake up, realize that the killer was behind bars—and flop back in bed. He'd been a cop for twenty-three years. He decided to go for twenty-three more.

38.

On the advice of his court-appointed attorney, Arthur Shawcross pleaded innocent. He was held in the Monroe County jail without bail. Word went out that he intended to employ an insanity defense.

XIII

PUZZLE PARTS

1.

From the first day of his latest incarceration, the serial killer was a puzzle to his jailers. Most of the time he acted like a tired old con, preinstitutionalized, a cipher in scuffs and coveralls. But sometimes his motions would quicken and his manner turn sharp and menacing. He seemed more active when the sun went down and was often awake at 2:00 and 3:00 A.M., reading science fiction and war books, mostly about Vietnam, or playing solitaire and working crossword puzzles. He griped about the noise level and slept with wet toilet paper in his ears. In his fitful sleep he assumed odd shapes, often the fetal position, and clawed at his arms and legs.

He was slow to awaken and seemed disinterested in his breakfast tray, usually settling for coffee and a few sips of juice, then going back to sleep till 10:00 or 11:00 A.M. He put away mounds of food at lunch and supper. He seemed concerned about his ballooning girth but unable to do anything about it. One minute he would talk about dieting and the next he would complain about the unavailability of fast food. He said he missed the coin machines that dispensed soft drinks, sandwiches, cocoa, candy, cookies, and pizza in state penitentiaries.

Sometimes he appeared in an almost euphoric state, leaning back on his bunk with his eyes closed and his head tilted upward, as though listening. For hours he sat in front of his Bible, usually opened to Acts, without turning a page. He leered at the female stars of TV soap operas and game shows. He got along well with his fellow inmates. He copied poems and claimed they were his own creations, fooling all but an erudite few who noticed that the grammar and spelling were perfect.

In occasional conversations, he spoke animatedly about his Vietnam experiences. He seemed to savor stories about hurting or killing fellow human beings and animals. Other inmates listened to his tales but began shying away after second and third recountings of how to silence an M-16 with a baby-bottle nipple or cut a deer's throat or rip a weighted treble hook into a salmon's guts.

A *Times-Union* op-ed piece was headlined "TURN THEM INTO LAB RATS: Don't demand death for serial killers; we know far too little about them." The text asked, "Who knows what goes on in the minds of such people? The only way to find out is to turn them into laboratory rats for a long time—in fact, forever."

Shawcross predicted that he would die in the electric chair, even though New York had abolished the death penalty years before. Jailhouse lawyers wondered why a man who'd spent most of his adult years on the wrong side of the law knew so little about the Penal Code. Brooding over his imminent electrocution, he went into periods of despondency so profound that he barely moved, as though stealing a march on death.

A suicide watch was put on his cell. But just when his mood seemed to bottom out, he snapped back with no apparent stimulus. Certain code expressions seemed to elevate his spirits. Whenever he was asked if he was "all right," he held up his left arm and cracked that he was "half left." He seemed amused by homosexuality and made snide remarks on the subject. Transvestite inmates seemed to produce a special delight.

He made his bed with military corners, kept his cell spotless, washed his face when he awoke in the morning and several times during the day. Before visiting hours, he scrubbed his face and hands again and combed his thinning gray hair. He complained about the jail's dandruff remover shampoo and asked for another brand. He was frequently seen leaning over his washbasin, scrubbing socks, shorts, and T-shirts. He argued that he wasn't issued clean jail clothes often enough. Eighteen years after Penny Sherbino had stamped the "neat freak" label on her difficult husband, he hadn't changed.

Behaviorists regarded such fastidiousness as an external attempt to control inner chaos. For the experts who were working the case, it was a relief to isolate one predictable trait. Psychologists and psychiatrists began running tests and conducting in-depth interviews that lasted as long as five or six hours. For the most part, Shawcross was patient, especially considering the repetitiveness of the process. But once in a while he bristled, especially when he was asked about certain subjects.

2. ARTHUR SHAWCROSS (PSYOHIATRIC INTERVIEW)

Q. If I go back to Karen Hill while we are on it, back to September the second 1972 and somewhere near Watertown, when they found her body they found sperm in the vagina and in the rectum?

A. Possibly.

Q. So, had you had her both in the rectum—up the ass—and in the vagina?

A. I don't know.

Q. You mean you've forgotten?

A. Right.

Q. Art, I feel you are not telling me about what really happens.

A. You want me to get up and walk out of here?

Q. No, I want you to stay where you are and tell me what goes on in your mind.

A. I'm telling you, I'm answering the questions. If you don't like the answers, I'll get the fuck outa here.

Q. I won't get the fuck—

A. No, *I'll* get the fuck outa here.

Q. No, you must stay and you must try to answer the questions and stop being quite so childish and angry, because you *can* do it, you *can* control it. . . . Going back to Karen Ann Hill, when that happened, you say you've forgotten a lot, but did you think anyone was telling you to kill her, telling you to rape her?

A. No.

Q. Why did you kill her?

A. I was sitting under that bridge fishing and I just leaned back on—there was a concrete bunker just below the bridge itself. I was sitting up on there and the fishing poles were sitting with the bobbers on. Karen Ann Hill came down along the creekbed. She was upstream somewhere and she came up there and I looked at her and the first thing that came to my mind was my sister Jeannie. And I just grabbed ahold of her and that is when I started to sweat, and the sounds and the lights got brighter, and I just lost control of everything around me. And I just went back in the past with my sister Jeannie.

Q. But you never killed your sister Jeannie, did you?

A. Not yet.

Q. You have that in mind, you're telling me? You never thought of that, have you, with your Jeannie?

A. Sometimes . . . I wanted to kill my mother and my sister Jeannie just to get all that past out of my head.

3.

Visiting lawmen who peeked at the prisoner came away surprised at his ordinary appearance. Why had he been so hard to catch? How had he managed to leave so few clues? Could there be a touch of criminal genius behind that potato face?

The medical examiner's office filled in part of the puzzle by confirming that Shawcross killed his Rochester victims by a process known as "soft strangulation." He didn't squeeze hard enough to shatter the hyoid bone, which might have been detectable in remains. Instead he administered a controlled squeeze that was just tight enough to close his victim's windpipe, killing more like a cheetah than a lion.

"It went fast, a soft choke," Deputy Chief Terrence Rickard explained. "Not a lot of trauma. Then he used the body for sex."

In the decomposition process, maggots and other larvae recycled such evidence as marks, bruises, and body fluids. Shawcross admitted that he'd taken pains to hide the bodies to give them time to decompose, thus making it harder for police to connect him with the victim. It was a technique that he'd used on Jack Blake and perhaps on unknown others.

After the killer's name and face were publicized, it developed that dozens of Rochesterians had known him or dealt with him. Some thought he was normal, some peculiar, but none had found reason to communicate with police. June Stott's boyfriend Joe Tibbetts told about seeing him with June. Maria Welch's roommate, who'd fled south to Scranton during the homicide scare, said he'd tricked with her and the murdered Maria. Barbara Dotson recalled him as an ordinary john with rough hands. He'd paid her fifty dollars for a "half-and-half." She said, "He wasn't weird. He wasn't rude. He meant nothing to me." A resident of the prostitution neighborhood reported that "every night since June he's been parked down there sitting in his car."

Jim Bonnell and his colleagues began to realize why Shawcross had been so hard to catch. "He was invisible," the Tac Unit boss explained. "He hung around the side streets, a fat old guy on a bike, inconspicuous. He did a lot of favors, gave away venison and salmon, talked nice to people. Everybody thought of him as good old 'Mitch' or

'Joe.' When he showed up in Clara's car, the hookers jumped in. He was a regular, one of the safe ones. And he wasn't stupid. Toward the end, he started approaching the area by a back street, wouldn't drive Lyell, wouldn't drive Lake. He parked on side streets and sat there till he saw what he wanted."

Along with Bonnell and others, Major Lynde Johnston tried to discern a motivation for the murders. "Almost every woman Shawcross killed was small, around five foot, with brown or dirty-blond hair," the thoughtful CID boss noted. "There are hookers of every size and description, but this guy picked out eleven short women with brownish hair. Can that be an accident? Maybe it's because a pedophile's always a pedophile. He knew he'd go back to prison if he went near kids, so he stalked little women. Or maybe it was because he hated another short woman with brown hair. Say . . . his mother? Who the hell knows? I doubt that he knows himself."

George Ehle of the Crime Analysis Unit leaned toward the pedophilic hypothesis. "I think he wanted to kill kids but didn't dare," said the amiable sergeant. "If he'd killed a child in this city, ten parole officers would've called my office and identified him in an hour. That's how Parole had him tagged: 'homicidal pedophile.' But nobody was looking for that. We were out looking for a guy who killed whores."

Now that the killer was in custody, Ehle admitted finding a few good clues buried in the stacks of FIFs and other paperwork. "We had a report on the ten-speed bike with the fishing poles. And an oddball named Mitch. A citizen saw a potbellied guy go into the bushes with Patty Ives. Somebody noticed a suspicious man with a limp. The blue-gray compact was reported a few times. Maybe we should've put it all together, but these were just four or five items out of thousands. It would've taken one man reading and remembering every word of every report to make any connection."

Investigator Lenny Borriello, back at work after his brief celebration, was bemused by some of the ex post facto theorizing. "You know what it came down to in the end?" he said. "A basic homicide investigation—following leads, developing witnesses, snooping, interviewing, and finally getting a break. Plain old-fashioned detective work. We might've got him earlier, but we spent so much time on computers, stopping johns, checking game licenses, generating paper. We got hundreds of names from that damned TV raffle, but would you believe whose name we *didn't* get? Shawcross hung out in Mark's Texas Red Hots and he loved getting something for nothing, raffles, radio giveaways, things like that. But he was too smart to sign a raffle slip. And anyway, who the hell was gonna check out all the raffle names when we still had FIFs we hadn't read?"

With the killer awaiting trial, the raffle was brought to a quiet end. The murder investigation had already cost the police department $575,000 over budget; the unnecessary award of a $2,000 TV, possibly to a pimp or other street person, was too painful to consider. A slit was razored into the inner wall of the Styrofoam box and a fake entry inserted. At the public drawing, an undercover cop was the winner. It was as if the raffle had never happened.

4.

Circuit riders returned from Syracuse, Scranton, Binghamton and points south, and veteran prostitutes like Jo Ann Van Nostrand took to the street, drug lust overriding good intentions. Teenyboppers milled around Lake and Lyell, encouraged by fast-talking pimps who explained that the Lilac City was a tolerant place where friendly cops teamed up with working girls to catch criminals.

The daily communicant Terrence Rickard drove through the prostitution corridor and was shocked. "It's wall-to-wall action," he commented to Chief Urlacher. "It's Mardi Gras out there."

A two-day sweep was ordered, and extra bunks were set up in the Monroe County jail. Fifty prostitutes, pimps, and johns were booked in the first twenty-four hours, thirty-two more on the second day.

"Prostitution is *not* a victimless crime that should be tolerated," Rickard emphasized to reporters. "The events of the last few months show that. It ruins too many lives and it spawns too many spin-off crimes."

He said he wasn't so naive as to think that his officers could put an end to streetwalking, but it could certainly be kept under control. He suggested that newspapers do their part by giving the johns some personal publicity.

"If I were these men," said the straitlaced deputy chief, "I'd be much more embarrassed to tell my wife than tell a judge." The media declined his request but otherwise supported his position.

In his cage, the killer seemed titillated by the activity. Three of the arrested working girls turned out to be working boys, and one was assigned the next cell. Clara Neal described her lover's reaction: "Art laughed till he cried! The guy come in there and what did he have on but a lady's silk underwear with a big picture of a vagina drawed on the front of it. This big guard tore the underwear off him and threw him in the cell. Art thought that was a riot."

The killer's superior stance kept him from mentioning his own predilection toward homosexual acts, beginning in childhood. Presumably his sordid life story would come out in trial, along with some idea about what on earth made him tick. Everyone wondered.

5.

A media tempest began over why such a dangerous offender had been released after serving less than fifteen years, and why such an evil shadow had been allowed to fall across Rochester. The *Democrat and Chronicle* headlined a page one article "SHAWCROSS PAROLE RIPPED," and quoted a state senator as saying that the Parole Board shouldn't have released such a "psychosexual maniac."

Once again, the former Jefferson County district attorney was called upon to defend his handling of the original case upstate. "Obviously he didn't serve enough time," William McClusky admitted. "But I have no control over that. That's entirely up to the Parole Board." He repeated that his case against Shawcross had lacked many essential elements and the public was lucky that he'd arranged a plea bargain that resulted in a twenty-five-year sentence.

Mary Blake and retired detective Charles Kubinski were among others who criticized both McClusky and the Parole Board. The highly respected Commissioner Thomas Coughlin III of the Department of Correctional Services, a North Country resident himself, weighed in with a clarification: "Mr. Shawcross was not released eight years early, as has been repeatedly suggested. Under New York law, his release would have been mandatory after he served two thirds of his maximum sentence, less time off for good behavior. The Parole Board saw fit to release him about a year early. If it was an error, it certainly wasn't a major one."

Added Edward Elwin, executive director of the Division of Parole, "We have fifty thousand inmates in New York prisons, and every year we turn out sixteen to eighteen thousand. That's a lot of opportunities for misjudgment—and the state doesn't issue the Parole Board a Ouija board. As for sending Mr. Shawcross to Rochester, a parolee has to ensconce himself in one New York community or another. Are we supposed to conduct a referendum every time? What if *no* community accepts him? What do we do then?"

When no answer was forthcoming, the tempest died.

6.

While waiting for the trial, neither Clara Neal nor Rose Walley Shawcross appeared willing to let go of her man. At the suggestion of lawyers, Rose avoided media attention by moving in with a daughter in another town, but she kept in touch with her husband by phone. The lovesick Clara arrived at the jail in Mata Hari shades that were certain to draw the attention of reporters and cameramen. The *Times-Union* memorialized the first jailhouse meeting of the lovers under a new logo, "TRAIL OF DEATH," and the headlines: "SHAWCROSS TO SEEK HELP. Tells girlfriend he wants to see a psychiatrist."

A lengthy page-one story quoted Clara as saying, "When I first walked in he was down. He looked like the whole world was sitting on his shoulders. It was like the whole world had forsaken him." But when he saw her, she said, "Heaven lit up in his eyes."

She announced that he intended to seek psychiatric help even though he was a "gentle, loving, kind, caring and freehearted" man. Personally, she doubted that he'd killed more than two prostitutes, and certainly not the eleven claimed by the cops.

Clara was quoted by reporter Linda Kanamine: "I told him I still love him and he said, 'I know you do. I'm sorry.' He said, 'I love you.' "

The article closed on a poignant note. Clara said she would never use the steak knives he'd given her for Christmas; she didn't even keep them in her kitchen. "He bought them to use with me," she explained. She still had no idea they were stolen from G&G.

For the TV cameras, she raised her pudgy fingers and showed the ring that her lover had yanked from the finger of Patty Ives. Clara said, "I've got his ring on. I love him and I always will. . . . I knew one side of the man that supposably did it. . . . He's not a monster. He's a loving human. Please believe me."

7. CLARA NEAL

The dark glasses wasn't to make me look like a movie star. It was because my eyes was swelled near shut from crying. I'll say it plain: I thought about driving my car into a brick wall, driving off a bridge, a clift. Me and Art was gonna spend the rest of our life together and all of a sudden I didn't have nobody. The worst thing in the world: alone.

I was taken to Rochester General Hospital for nervous exhaustion and the doctor gave me some sleeping pills. There was a part of me wanted to take 'em all and be done with it, but it wouldn't been fair to my man. The only thing that helped get me through the first few weeks, I read Matthew, Luke, Acts.

That first visit to the jail was awful. We sat in a big room with tables, a contact visit like the ones I have with my son. The inmate sits on one side and you sit on the other, and you can hold hands and kiss across the table.

Art looked like he just lost four hundred dollars in a poker game. The only thing he did was cry. I ask him, "Why, Art? Why?"

He kept saying he didn't know. He said every one of his friends dropped him cold turkey since he went to jail. Not a single visit from all those people that he used to mow their lawns and shovel their snow and give 'em fish and things.

We held each other's hand the whole time. He said, "I didn't think you would come to see me after this."

I said, "I'll come to see ya anytime I can. You didn't do nothin' to me. You never hormed me, never treated me nasty. You always treated me with kind, loving respect."

He said, "Why do things have to be like this, Clara? *Why me?*" I told him I wish I knew.

He said the only whore he remembered hurting was the one that kicked my gearshift rod and broke it, 'cause it made him mad that she did a thing like that to my car. Said she asked for it and he give it to her. A West Virginia woman could understand *that.*

I came back two days later and all he could talk about was the 'lectric chair. He said, "I'll commit suicide first." That night he called me at home and said the lawyer told him he couldn't be 'lectrocuted, said some politicians wanted to bring back the death penalty in his case but it couldn't be done. He sounded a little relieved, but I could tell he still wasn't sure. It bothered him that people were so mad at him.

Next time I visited, I brought some clean underwear and a sweat outfit and a Bible. Made me proud his Bible come from me and not from Rose. He asked me to try to get in touch with his son Michael, said he lived up around Watertown or Pulaski someplace, but I knew I'm never gonna find him. They hadn't seen each other in twenty years. He asked me how Gramma Irene Kane was doing and I told him her mind was so far gone she didn't even know he was in trouble. I called her one day and she said, "Where's Art? How is he?" I just said he was sick.

I went to the jail one more time after Rose came back to town. She moved in with some friends of Art's and I asked was it okay with her if I kep' on viztin'. She said I could have a little bit of each hour. I went to the jail and after the first ten minutes she was buggin' the guard to throw me out and let her through the door.

I taken her aside and said, "Rose, if I could just get fifteen minutes with him onc't a week I'd be happy. And it would make him feel better. You got nothing to worry about. What can we do sitting there looking at each other?"

She said, "I don't see why not." So I went there a couple more times with her—and she used up every minute! Art cried and threw me kisses through the glass. I wrote on the side of a newspaper, "I love you," and held it up when she wasn't looking.

He started phoning me every night. I told him I wasn't gonna put up with Rose's crap no more and I was gonna wait till she got in there with him and stand outside the glass so he could see me and get his spirits lifted. I told him be sure'n look at me while you're talking to her. He said what if she turns around and sees you, and I said if she did, I would give her the finger. I told him to wait till he seen the new blond perm my daughter Linda give me.

The next day Art's lawyer called and told me I couldn't viz't at all, not even just stand there. Rose was behind it. *Bitch!* If Art hurt any women, it was because Rose and his mother aggravated him so much. I wanted to meet her in some dark alley and fight her for Art. He was worth goin' head, teeth, and toenails over. That was just the way I felt.

Next thing, Art asked me help her. He said, "Hon, she's living with folks that're ripping her off. She got no place to turn and I don't want her out in the street. Cain't you give her a home?" He said, "Us three gotta stick together."

Course, I would do anything for Arthur Sharcross. Rose paid ten dollars a week and helped with the dishes, laundry, and cleaning. Me and my sons, we shared what we had, but I wouldn't let nobody touch those last two olive salads I still kep' in the refrigerator. Art made them for me with his own hands and it hurt me we couldn't eat 'em together. I had a lot of frozen salmon he caught—I swore I'd keep 'em forty years if the 'lectricity didn't give out.

Rose and I got to know each other better. After a while I even felt a little sorry for her. This whole deal, it was no bed of roses for her either. She'd never had no life. She married when she was only a kid, some old fart twic't her age. Her kids hated her for running off with Art. Then he gets arrested and she's left with nobody.

One night she pulled out her and Art's wedding pictures. I wanted a good shot of him and I asked if she'd make a copy off'n the wedding shots. She said no. I cried and begged, but she wouldn't give in.

What I wanted to do, there's one picture of him and her together. I would cut out her face and paste my face over the top of hers and get it rephotographed so it looks like a wedding picture of me and Art. Then I was gonna send him a copy.

When Rose wouldn't lend me the picture, things kinda soured between her and me. I started wearing a T-shirt that said, "Made for loving him." I guess she got the message. She moved into some church shelter.

8. ROSE SHAWCROSS

When the police drove me back to Rochester from my daughter's, they put me in a home where I left $165 in my room and somebody stole it. I complained, but nobody did nothing. That money was for Art and my's bills. It was my severance pay from when I got fired from the visiting nurses after the arrest. So Art fixed it up for me to move in with Clara.

I was talking to him on the phone every night and visiting every Tuesday and Thursday. First time I went, one of the guards said, "He's never gonna see the outside again. You oughta leave him."

I said, "Well, I got news for you. I'm *never* leaving him. I'll follow him to the penitentiary walls and I'll go inside if they'll let me."

Each time I visited, Art seemed more down. Said he had nightmares, woke at night in a deep sweat. In his dreams he was either in Vietnam or the electric chair.

We had two prayer rugs that his Pakistani friends gave him. He asked me to send 'em to his mother. He was still mixed up about her. We didn't talk much about the dead girls, but he said, "Every time I killed, I saw my mother's face."

On one visit he says, "Rose, do you regret you lost your home, your family, your job?"

I says, "I don't regret nothin'. I got you and that's all I care."

He says, "I wouldn't last two days if you didn't love me. How could I hurt you so bad?"

I said, "You didn't hurt me, darlin'."

He started to cry. He said, "Look at you. You're my heart of gold girl."

My family kept asking, How can you deal with this? What're you gonna do when he gets sent away? Aren't you gonna change your name? You'll never get a job, can't do this, can't do that. . . .

I said I'm gonna stay just the way I am. Wherever Art goes, I go. I'm his wife. I'm all he's got and he's all I got. I talked to my friends at the Church of Jesus Christ and they said I was following a good example. Jesus didn't turn his back.

9. ARTHUR SHAWCROSS (EXCERPTS FROM LETTERS TO CLARA NEAL)

Love comes in many forms, and the love I have for you is differant then the love I have for Rose. My love for two women; differant in so many many ways! I love you Clara for who you are, as to being a warm, considerate, kind, loving woman! I'll not write anything about Rose, it's too soon to do so. . . .

Honey, what have I left to deserve such a wonderful woman like you? I cry about the situation I am in and can't for the life of me see much into the future. . . . I am repeatly asked if I intend to hurt my self in any way. I keep telling then no, "But."

If I thought I'de die in the electric chair, I most deaffinetly would. But enough said on this!!

. . . My lawyer had called and talked to my Mom on the phone. Sometimes I wonder if I have been living two different lives. Mom does not remember some of the things that have happed to me when I was a youngster. . . .

Clara, I have not been totally truthful to you in our love making; you see I have not had one orgasium except one that I know of in almost three years. I have learned to fake it most times. At other times I am overtired. I had thought that by going to see some other girls I could cure myself!! That did not work either! I am truly sorry about this. I did use a rubber though!

My memory will always hold what we have for each other. Please beleave me Clara that I care for you very much and at this time I can not truly say what is in my heart. . . .

Be good now my lady and keep in touch with me. A kiss I give you apon this paper right

down
here
Love, kisses, want and need you near,
Good day my dear,
Love always
Art
xoxoxoxoxoxoxoxoxoxoxoxoxoxoxoxoxoxoxoxoxoxoxoxo . . .

I am caught between two women who love me very very much. What ever you do or decide, please don't do what you have in mind to do when you get behind the wheel of a car. . . . Please stop thinking of dieing. I couldn't live with that on my mind too much after if you did. . . .

. . . I do laugh when I think of that morning in the cemetary when that truck came up on us. We were just a rockin' and a rollin' and a swingin'. That was funny when you trying to fix up and that truck was following us. Gee doing it in a cemetary. Morbid to say the least. It was nice down in those bushes on that small little road or path with the skeeters. . . . Blowing in your ears melted you. Even when I made a wish bone out of you. Pleasant memories I'll have to override all this bull shit.

Clara, Viet Nam is the cause of this. Over 20 years went by and it came back to haunt me. I break out with nerve blisters and shake in my bed at the night or even in the day time. It's a bitch to even rest.

What should be or shouldn't be can not be changed now. Two things will happen, either I'll go to prison or to a Mental Hospital some where. I'de prefer a Mental Hospital. I may be able to get back out from there. . . .

Went out this morning for that E.E.G. test. Went to St. Mary's Hospital. This afternoon I had the Brain Scan there also. . . . We will see in a few days what this machine shows if anything. There better be something there! otherwise my ass is cook, fried and roasted!! Don't forget to add salt:

If I got out today, I'de head south! All the way south to Brizil, SouthAmerica.

I'de have to give up family to do it too so by now I am quite used to my own family rejecting me.

. . . If the Lawyers can prove I was Mentaly ill when these things happened then I'de go to a Hospital for awhile. I sure hope so! . . .

The psychatrist stated that the Cat-Scan came back with no abnormal spots on my brain. *Not* good news to me though I fear! David Murante [Shawcross's lawyer] stated I'll not go too the Electric Chair! I wanted to be sent to a Mental Hospital to get the evil out of me. There must be some way someone can do it! In fact I know there is!

. . . Clara, there is something wrong with me now! I can not very well write anymore. I can't seem to get my right hand to form the words right. If I take it real slow I can get it down on paper OK.

. . . You know your self that my own folks don't give a shit. Someday they will know what it feels like. My Mother and Dad could have come out to visit me but no! they didn't want me around. Didn't even want me to come home ever again. What does that make a person feel? No matter what I did in the past, I am still their child or AM I? I wonder at times. I just got a sharp pain across my head. Head aches, chest pains and bad nerves plus my emotions. What can it be. Maybe my time is near. The Second Coming of Christ is coming soon. I feel this. Hope I can ask for forgiveness in time to go to Heaven.

I am very down in my soul. . . . Rose's test came out clean. Now I am told that the Gibson girl had aides. I want you to get a test done OK!?

. . . Clara, I know you love me very very much. You know of my feelings toward you. I wished I had come to

Rochester alone. But I did not and can't change the fact with Rose. Clara, you are my one and dear friend. . . .

Maybe one day when the weather gets warmer you'll go up to Watertown to visit my folks. Where ever I go from here I will only ask all of them for 1 photo each for they will never see me again, alive that is or dead.

You and I have become World Famous!! Hell of a way to do it though! One of the psychatrist said I was a Mister Jekly and Mister Hide two people in one body. . . . Maybe one day I can volunteer to have an operation on my head in the area of they brain of reason! . . .

I am one worn out man who is helpless in thoughts, feelings and emotions! I am numb inside. totally devestated!

. . . Clara, at this time you can not come into see me. Rose has that option. Even sometimes she can't see me. . . .

I've put in a slip to get my toe nails cut. I even have long finger nails. I've stopped biting them. One thing is bad though, I dig and scratch myself when sleeping. I wake up all bloody and sore. I have to keep my socks on or I'de do damage to my feet and legs too.

. . . I never knew a person to love his mother and hate her all at the same time. Why is this? Dear, my child life was all being alone. The woods near home I knew very well, for I had makebelieve friends and animals to play with. At times it got to the point where I could hear voices of kids my age playing with me. But I cryed a lot growing up, still do. Not a man yet!

. . . I'll always carry you in my heart. . . . Fix your garden and plant some marigolds for me. Good night, honey. . . .

10. CLARA NEAL

I wanted to go to the jail on visitors' day, but—I'll just say it plain—that bitch wouldn't let me see him. He asked for my daughter Loretta to come in to show her new baby, but Rose refused. I sent him a pretty Easter card with a tracing of the baby's hand. He didn't acknowledge. It was Rose ordering him around. I wanted to tell her to jump off the deep end of the pier.

Imagine him asking me to visit his parents in Watertown. I didn't wanna see his mom. If Art was my boy, I'd be on my knees a-beggin' to viz't him. He's got a right to a mom. *My son!*

When my boy was in prison, I sent packages, letters, cigarettes, candy bars, fruit, nuts. Every two weeks when I got paid, I fixed him a big box. I said, He might be in prison, but he's still my son, I brought him into this world. I guess some folks don't think that way. Those Watertown people, they're screwier than a buncha goddamn asses. There's people down there that I would like to get 'em by the hair of their head and pound their heads agin' the wall!

Art phoned so upset he couldn't hardly talk. A guard told him his mom had a heart attack. How it happened, the Rochester papers was fixin' to write a bunch of articles about him, and a reporter went to Richmond, Virginia, to interview his sister Donna. When the mother found out they was snoopin' around, it give her a heart attack.

Art couldn't stop crying over the phone. He kept saying, "Pray for me, girl. Oh, please, pray for me." He said if anything happened to his mom, he'd kill hisself the same night. I begged him not to. I told him I'd try and find out how she was doing and he give me her phone number.

I called and said, "Miz Sharcross, this is Clara Neal? In Rochester? I heard you wasn't feelin' so good."

She got all excited and said, "I don't know who you are. Who *are* you?"

"Art's friend. *Clara.* He just phoned me."

She says, "No you're not! No no no no *no*! He couldn't call you. He can't make outside calls." And she hung up.

I wrote her a big letter, said what kind of a goddamn mother are you? Didn't you have Art? Ain't you got a bit of sympathy for yourself, even if you don't have none for him?

She didn't answer. His parents won't even correspond with anyone who tries to help their son.

Well, Art didn't kill his self. He wrote me a poem instead. Listen: "The shards of broken covenants lie sharp against my soul. The wraiths of long-lost ecstasy still keep us two apart. The sullen winds of bitterness still keen from turn to pole. . . ."

I won't read the rest. It's too deep; it makes me cry.

After he sent the poem, he phoned and ordered me to burn his letters. Then he cut me off. Just like that! I heard it was on his lawyers' order, but I knew better. It was Rose again.

Next thing I knew, that TV show *A Current Affair* called Art a "lousy lover." It made me so mad. How in the hell did they know? *Did they ever go to bed with him?*

I'll just be plain about what a lousy lover he was. After he was arrested, I had to change my bed around twice to keep from hearing that peck on my window. That was the most exciting sound I ever heard in all my years.

11.

For those who were busily engaged in pretrial analysis of the serial killer's behavior, a perplexing set of reports arrived in the offices of the Monroe County district attorney. Numerous studies had shown that pedophilic murderers were brutalized as children, and Arthur Shawcross was presumed to fit the pattern. But the earliest information from Watertown strongly indicated otherwise.

In handwritten affidavits, Arthur Roy Shawcross and his wife Betty Yerakes Shawcross recalled that their son Artie ran away from home twice and "slapped his sister several times," but insisted that his childhood was "as normal as any child's." Corporal punishment was infrequent and reasonable: a few licks with a belt, usually administered by the reluctant father.

According to the parents, Artie did well through most of his school years, attended church regularly, displayed a pleasant disposition except for the odd temper tantrum, got along with other children, and didn't become a loner till after he'd been left back several times and found himself attending class with students three years his junior. He was kind to animals and set no fires until he was an adult. As a child, the parents said, he showed none of the classical signs of maladjustment: head-banging, thumb-sucking, nail-chewing. And he neither drank nor smoked.

The youngest sibling, brother James, confirmed the upbeat assessment in an interview with a BCI investigator. He described "a happy childhood filled with many jubilant occasions." Artie "lived among other clan members in harmony," displaying no problems with alcohol, drugs, or sex. "He did get angry fast sometimes," the brother remembered, but his school attendance record was excellent and he'd never been cruel to animals. He "loved to fish and ride his bike and loved his mother and father."

Sister Jean told the BCI that she hadn't seen her brother in twenty years but had spoken to him on the phone. As a child, she said, he was "like all the other kids." He hung out with friends, went to school regularly, and "didn't lie any more than any other child."

The killer's uncle, Fred Shawcross, had slightly darker recollections. He admitted that the residents of Shawcross Corners had been embarrassed about Artie ever since the high school years. He was "strange when growing up," the uncle reported, "but we couldn't pinpoint why. He was mentally slow and had a bad temper."

Fred's son David said that his older cousin Artie "exaggerated things and ran away."

After calling on neighbors and other relatives, investigators described Betty Shawcross as a forceful and sometimes profane parent, but never abusive, and the father as a straight arrow who worked hard and stayed in the background. No verifiable instance of parental cruelty was found.

While the new reports were confounding the experts in Rochester, Betty Shawcross was tearfully discussing her son with a reporter. "Arthuh would nevuh do anything to anybody," the New Hampshire native said in her Down East accent. "He would do anything you asked. *Anything.*" She added, "I won't get over this for the rest of my life. That won't be much longuh."

She insisted that she loved her son and he loved her in return. His talk about family friction was false. But she didn't condone his crimes. "I can't imagine why he did these things," she said. "It's hahd on my husband and I. You don't know how empty I feel inside for the people he hurt."

The upset woman offered several theories about her first-born child's misbehavior; none related to parenting skills. She said that Arthur had been an eight-month baby and spent twenty days in an incubator; "maybe his brain didn't develop." At ten, she said, he'd been hospitalized with a mysterious malady that crippled his legs. He'd been knocked unconscious several times. But after each of those childhood mishaps, he remained a good-hearted, generous person—"a decent boy who loved othuhs."

To another journalist, Betty blamed Vietnam. She described his letters home as "descriptions of hell," reeking of "blood and horror."

"I think he saw things that he shouldn't have seen," she confided to a reporter from the *Syracuse Post-Standard*. It seemed as good a theory as any.

12. ARTHUR SHAWCROSS (PSYCHIATRIC INTERVIEW)

Yeah, I go out there and came across a woman—a girl. She was putting an AK-47 on the side of a coop and I shot her, tied and gagged her, took her up where I had a clear view of the area and tied her to a tree. . . .

I didn't have nothing to eat that day, and I took a big chunk off the hip of the girl. . . . I took off all the skin and took a piece of green bamboo and I ran it up inside the bone and I roasted it on the fire. . . . After it cooked down, it was almost like eating charcoal-broiled pork, the consistency of a dry roast beef. . . .

I was just in the mood, that's all. After I was eating it—it didn't taste that bad—I took the body and carried it down through the jungle area where I knew there was a big anthill and laid it beside the anthill, went back to the tree, and was sitting there sharpening the machete and eating that meat. The other girl had the sweat running off of her. I untied her hands and tied her on the ground and raped her. . . . And I cut her throat, took her head up there where the house was and put that head on a stick right in front of the house. . . .

13.

Rochesterians demanded a full flow of information about the man who'd kept their town in fear, and the *Democrat and Chronicle*'s Steve Mills and J. Leslie Sopko began to research a major series. They wrote to the National Personnel Records Center in Overland, Missouri, and asked for the service record of Arthur John Shawcross.

A skimpy fax response indicated that SP4 Shawcross, 52967041, earned the National Defense Medal, Vietnam Service Medal, Republic of Vietnam Campaign Medal, two overseas bars, and an expert rifle badge. He received no Purple Heart or awards for bravery. He served two six-month tours as a supply and parts specialist at Camp Enari, headquarters of the U.S. Army's 4th Infantry Division, and was discharged honorably in April 1969, at twenty-three.

The reporters learned that Camp Enari was a military complex in Pleiku with first-run movies, service clubs, a post exchange, chapel, and swimming pool—a small, secure military city. Although it was shelled sporadically, the camp itself was removed from the action, and the only combat seen by a parts storekeeper would have consisted of ducking under a table after an infrequent cry of "incoming."

Mills and Sopko dug for more on SP4 Shawcross, but their job was made difficult by the fact that the killer, in thousands of written and spoken words about his wartime experiences, had referred to only a single comrade by name: William Westmoreland, commanding general of U.S. forces in Vietnam.

The reporters learned the names and addresses of members of Shawcross's unit and began telephoning places as far away as Los Alamitos, California, and Tacoma, Washington. None of the ex-GIs remembered the self-styled "one-man army" by name or description.

In a prizewinning three-part series, "SHAWCROSS: THE RAGE WITHIN," Mills and Sopko wrote that the Vietnam tales "almost certainly were fabricated" and "two dozen soldiers who served in his unit said that it is unlikely he would have seen much fighting. . . . What is more likely is that he could have witnessed other men in combat, said soldiers in his unit. Still, those experiences would not have approached the drama of the stories he told his family."

More specific information emerged slowly. Toward the end of his overseas tour, the supply and parts specialist had been chastised for repeated mistakes and reassigned to weapons repair at Fort Sill. His disability pension, seventy-three dollars per month, was based on a Stateside arm injury of cloudy origin, and a claim of Agent Orange damage was denied as spurious. The Army also confirmed that Shawcross saw no combat and never made a jungle patrol.

14. ARTHUR SHAWCROSS (PSYCHIATRIC INTERVIEW)

Q. . . . It's just that so many things don't jibe that I get worried, Art, that you might be telling me a few tall stories.

A. I'm going to get up out of this fucking chair and I'm going to leave and I'm going to go out and kill myself. I don't give a shit no more. You people are getting on my nerves. I tell you this is what happened to me in Vietnam. You believe me, you believe me. You don't believe me, that's it. That's—the hell with it.

Q. Yes, but I want to find out what did happen.

A. I told you what happened.

Q. You want to have a rest then?

A. When I go out the door, I'm not coming back.

Q. If you want to have a rest for a minute because I've riled you up, that's up to you. . . .

A. Did I ask for a rest?

Q. You didn't ask for a rest, but you got riled or angry and hostile because the questions, I suppose, are a little difficult.

A. No, you keep saying I'm lying, I'm lying, I'm lying. I'm telling you as I know it.

XIV

THE KRAUS DIAGNOSIS

Misbegotten *adj* 1: unlawfully conceived
2: of improper origin.

—Webster's Seventh New Collegiate Dictionary

1.

Richard Theodore Kraus, M.D., F.A.P.A., was interviewing Arthur Shawcross and trying not to show his befuddlement. The fifty-nine-year-old psychiatrist had spent a quarter century in the trenches of psychotherapy, treating neurotics, psychotics, multiple personalities, coprophiliacs, sleepwalkers, schizophrenics, sex offenders trying to go straight, convicts enduring court-ordered therapy, pedophiles, kleptomaniacs, suicidal housewives, and patients with physical diseases and disorders, and he considered himself an adept analyst of human behavior.

The moral delinquents known as psychopaths, for example, were easy to spot. Three days after Shawcross's arrest, a fat black headline in the *Democrat and Chronicle* had announced:

DOCTORS LABEL SUSPECT A "PSYCHOPATH"

From long experience, professionals like Kraus knew that psychopaths (or "sociopaths" or "antisocial personalities," as they were also called) lied, manipulated, denied, and deceived to avoid taking responsibility for their misdeeds. Their robotic cruelty reflected dehumanization, stunted consciences, and inability to empathize. They were usually smooth, verbose, glossy, neat, artificial—both controlled and controlling. Behind a "mask of sanity," they lived superficial and often destructive lives. From everything that Kraus had heard about Arthur Shawcross, he seemed to fit the syndrome.

But in this first nose-to-nose encounter, three weeks after

the arrest, the psychiatrist found himself as bewildered as the other experts whose files he'd perused in preparation. There were dozens of diagnoses, going back to the second grade, and the only common theme was that Shawcross was disturbed. After ten or fifteen minutes of listening to the killer's rumbly voice, Kraus shared his predecessors' confusion.

"When I met him," he explained later, "I expected to find a pure sociopath—sinister, perverted, sly, evil, satanic. I expected another Ted Bundy, another Son of Sam. Instead, the deputy led in a large-bellied, big-proportioned man with sloping shoulders, glasses pushed down his nose, curly gray hair and an alert expression. He looked prematurely aged, somebody's nice old uncle, patting his Santa Claus stomach and joking with a guard. I couldn't imagine a multiple murderer being so at ease in jail. It was as though he were welcoming you to his home. And almost the first words out of his mouth were that he was guilty as hell, a *very* unsociopathic thing to say."

Kraus had been retained by the chief public defender of Wayne County, his friend Ronald Valentine, to determine the plausibility of a psychiatric defense in the Elizabeth Gibson murder case. (The other ten killings would be tried in Monroe County Court in Rochester.) Kraus had often testified as a forensic psychiatrist, interpreting a defendant's state of mind for a judge or jury.

"Defense lawyers like Ron always hope you'll agree that their clients have mental problems," Kraus explained. "The last diagnosis they want is sociopathy. Antisocials may be a huge problem for society, but they're not legally insane. The first time this matter came up between me and Ron, I told him, 'If you want a different opinion, get a different psychiatrist. I can't call sociopathic behavior something it isn't.' Well, Ron is a reasonable man, and he's accepted my approach for fifteen years.

"In the Shawcross case, he was very specific. He said, 'Dick, I don't want you to jump to a diagnosis. Don't just tell me he's an antisocial—we know that already. Keep an open mind. Hang back and listen. Sociopathic or not, tell me why this guy became a serial killer.' That was my assignment from the beginning."

2.

Richard Kraus's choice of profession wasn't immediately apparent from his speech or attire. An unpretentious man with an explosive *opéra bouffe* laugh, he eschewed the jargon of his profession, using such words as "hebephrenic" and "neurasthenic" only when they were unavoidable. He admired patience and thoroughness and was possessed of an overdeveloped curiosity that sometimes sent him off on time-consuming tangents.

The psychiatrist was a medium-sized man with thinning dark hair, vivid dark brown eyes, a hawkish nose, a striking black mustache, a softly controlled basso voice, and a tendency to clear his throat with short, rasping sounds. He was usually viewed through silver-gray ribbons of smoke ascending from a Silva Thins Menthol. He wore the dark suits and conservative ties of his profession but preferred well-worn clothes that looked selected from out-of-date Orvis or L. L. Bean catalogs. When he wasn't working, he engaged in comfortably predictable activities: on summer days, he dug in the garden of his rural home, swam laps in his indoor pool, or romped with his chunky golden Lab, General Beauregard. In winter he chopped wood and performed virtuoso feats with his snowblower. Divorced and the father of six, he relaxed by playing Joplin and Chopin on his old grand piano, the centerpiece of a large baroque living room presided over by his eighty-seven-year-old mother, who tried to protect her overbooked son by telling late-night callers in her Black Forest accent, "I'm sorry. Doctor iss not in."

The psychiatrist's parents were intellectual German émigrés who'd arrived in New York in the late twenties and were quickly drawn to the cultural center of Rochester. His mother, Maria, was a skilled painter. For thirty-five years his late father, Alfons, a linguist, chemist, and church organist, translated foreign patents and documents for Kodak. At fourteen, their only child practiced piano three hours a day and imagined himself appearing before thousands as an artist of the stature of Horowitz or Paderewski. Richard auditioned at Eastman School of Music but balked at his teacher's selection of the Rachmaninoff Prelude in C Sharp Minor, "because every damn pianist in town was playing it." He was denied permission to play a favorite Schubert scherzo.

"To my surprise," Kraus recalled, "I played the Rachmaninoff quite acceptably—that old war-horse, *Bom, bom, BOM*. But then they decided that my father's small salary was too high to justify a scholarship."

The disappointed young musician placed himself under the tutelage of the Vincentian Fathers at Niagara University, earning a B.S. in 1953, then hauled his portable phonograph to Georgetown University Medical School in Washington, D.C., where repeated playings of Beethoven's Fifth Symphony helped inspire him to a medical degree. After a stint as a naval officer, he completed his residency in psychiatry at Seton Psychiatric Institute in Baltimore, eventually becoming chief psychiatrist at the prestigious DePaul Mental Health Services in Rochester. In addition to his administrative duties, he treated about a hundred patients.

Now Kraus sat across a small table from a different kind of prodigy, Arthur John Shawcross, and heard about the serial killer's ambivalence toward his family, the strained relationship between his parents ("My mother says, ya know, she'd kill him if she caught him looking at another woman. . . . I'm ashamed of my father"), his disinterest in education ("I'd go to school and sleep and then I'd look up and stare out the window"), the numerous traumas to his head, his "thirty-nine confirmed kills" in Vietnam, his wounds ("This is shrapnel here and here and I had a bullet right here"), his affair with Clara Neal, his love for his wife, his impaired sexuality, his detached accounts of the ten women he'd strangled in Rochester and the one in Wayne County ("You just push it away and just forget about it"), on and on without any obvious signs of reluctance, deception, or deceit. Whatever the killer's problems, he wasn't tongue-tied.

3. RICHARD KRAUS

For that first interview session, I'd driven to the jail with Ron Valentine in his rackety red sports car. It had "DEFENDER" on the license plate, but it should have had "CHITTY-CHITTY-BANG-BANG." The reception area was a gloomy place with one-way windows. A spooky voice comes out of nowhere and you walk into a world of steel, tile, bars, and noise.

They assigned us a storage room, maybe four by eight. A long time ago I learned that when you're working on the defense side, you don't get the perks. Forensic psychiatrists who evaluated Shawcross for the district attorney's office were provided with a nice quiet office with coffee and comfortable chairs and plenty of room. Ron and I worked in a box. But Shawcross didn't seem to mind. I guess he was habituated. The din was unbelievable up on the tier and it made interviewing tough.

He'd barely started answering my questions before I was thinking, Holy smokes, where are we *going* here? He seemed honest, but very little of the life material matched established behavioral patterns. I'm saying to myself, What the hell's the matter with this guy?

When I'm doing a forensic eval, I usually get a sense of the person pretty quick, sort of a feeling sense. I had no such reaction with Shawcross. He listed a bunch of silly excuses for killing: one woman bit him, one grabbed his wallet, one called him "faggot," one talked too loud, one claimed she was a virgin. . . .

I thought, Jesus Christ, you're offering these as justifications for *murder*? He presented so differently from what I expected, made no secret about his crimes, talked a lot of nonsense. I thought, Well, he's got antisocial tendencies, sure, but what else? He wasn't like any sociopath I've ever seen.

4.

It didn't take long for the psychiatrist to realize that Shawcross showed almost no symptoms of that old familiar hobgoblin, posttraumatic stress disorder. Kraus had been chief of psychiatry at the VA Hospital in nearby Canandaigua and was familiar with the syndrome—nightmares, trembling, palpitations, substance abuse, flashbacks, panic attacks, adjustment difficulties. Unlike victims of PTSD, Shawcross seemed relaxed about his wartime experiences, happy to spin his gory stories by the hour.

To be sure, some of his narratives sounded inflated. Kraus wondered, Why does he need to cast himself in the role of jungle avenger? To shore up a weak ego? To convince himself he's a person of value, of substance, someone who deserves to live? Who deserves to *kill*? A hint of a less egocentric motivation popped up toward the end of the interview:

Q. When was the first time you had that feeling that you really wanted to kill somebody?

A. Uh, I was probably, when I started going on patrols going out in the jungle by myself I kept thinking about my sister, my younger sister, Jeannie.

Q. Why were you thinking about her?

A. Her boyfriend got killed in Vietnam while I was in basic training. Half his face was gone. And I had orders to go to Germany and I went home on AWOL to see my sister and I told her I was going to put in for Vietnam. I told my company commander I'm going to Vietnam—or Canada. So they cut my orders for Vietnam. At that time I didn't think about it. Probably about seven months later, when I was in Vietnam, I started thinking about things.

Q. What kind of things?

A. Getting my revenge, for my sister.

In the final minutes of the first interview session, Kraus asked Shawcross if he thought he could kill again. A garden-variety sociopath would have entered an impassioned denial that he'd killed in the first place, or shed crocodile tears and promised to mend his ways. Instead, Shawcross said straightforwardly, "I'd be lying if I said no and I'd probably be lying again if I said yes."

Kraus thought, What this guy is really telling me is that he doesn't know his own mind. The question is still . . . why? What the hell is wrong with him?

In the parking lot under the Public Safety Building, Public Defender Valentine asked if there was a shot at a psychiatric defense.

"I don't know," the doctor answered. "I have more questions now than when we started."

After he arrived at his home in the rural exurb of Honeoye Falls, Kraus pondered another anomaly about the killer. What mature forty-four-year-old man would choose a woman's bike as his primary means of transportation, routinely pedaling eight or ten miles through slushy, icy, congested streets? Both Shawcrosses worked, and every month he cashed a seventy-three-dollar disability check from the government; they could certainly afford a used car. Was he phobic about driving? Apparently not; he frequently borrowed his girlfriend Clara's car. The bike just seemed a voluntary choice—quirky, unusual, like so many of his other choices. Like stuffing grass down a little boy's pants. Like serial murder . . .

5.

In an unusually candid interview a week later, Kraus and Valentine were surprised when Shawcross began to describe steps he'd taken to fool police. If he was trying to appear mentally ill to avoid the penitentiary, these were highly unstrategic admissions. He'd already confessed that one of his reasons for killing Felicia Stephens was to throw police off by changing to a black victim. Now he provided details on how he'd concealed evidence and covered his tracks in other cases. And he admitted that at least one of his postarrest explanations had been false. He said a detective had planted the idea that a victim tried to steal his wallet—"I just played on that," he explained.

Kraus thought, Well, there's no shortage of pathology here, but I doubt if any court would find him legally insane. Legally *odd*, perhaps, or legally eccentric, if such classifications existed . . .

In this second interview, the psychiatrist learned that Shawcross had spared at least one Rochester prostitute's life out of a sense of compassion, again marking him as no ordinary sociopath. He said the woman was about twenty-nine, a welfare mother of two. She was acting "a little weird," he recalled, and when they were having intercourse he felt an impulse to strangle her.

"You know, I had her by the throat," he said, "and you know I mean she was fighting me and she was telling me, 'Please, I'm on medication.' She says, 'I know *you're* on medication.' And when she said that, I come out of what I was doing . . . and I sat down in the driver's seat and I just hold my hands like this, trembling, and started crying. 'What the hell am I doing?' . . . It just shocked me. I just pulled away and said, 'What the fuck am I doing?' You know? Then we talked for a while. Then she asked me could I take her home. I said all right."

He claimed that his homicidal urges emerged only after he started to perspire heavily—"like you know, I'm in like a daze and I'll start sweating and my whole shirt is wet, my face and hair is completely wet, but it's just like something closes in on me."

As usual, the conversation turned to Vietnam, and Kraus scribbled a note about inappropriately flat affect as Shawcross launched into one more horror story—how he helped destroy a village, to the last chicken and pig, and "did things to the women that were there but didn't die outright." He sounded as though he were relating a warm memory.

The narrative ended with a U.S. Army lieutenant shooting one of his own soldiers in the head to put him out of his misery.

Ronald Valentine, sitting in on the interview, asked, "Do you know who the lieutenant was?"

Shawcross quickly answered, "No."

"Do you remember the names of anyone that was with you?"

"I don't remember nobody down there. I tried to remember people that were over there and I can't remember."

Kraus and Valentine exchanged glances. Earlier they'd discussed his peculiar inability to recall comrades-in-arms. No names or nicknames were ever mentioned—no buddies, no noncoms, no company officers. His place-names were slightly more precise: "north of Kontum . . ."; "in an airstrip right in the middle of the valley . . ."; "a mountain range called Mile High . . ."; "a firebase next to Ho Chi Minh Trail. . . ." The two men had also noticed that his narratives varied with each telling.

But the killer didn't sound deceptive as he continued his recollections. He seemed calm, comfortable, sure of his facts, like a Legionnaire reminiscing at a convention. It flashed through Kraus's mind that the man might be his own truest believer. Genuine delusions would suggest schizophrenia, of course, but where were the other benchmarks of that common mental illness?

Now Shawcross was saying that he once reached the point "where I just wanted to do this by myself . . . be a one-man army."

"You wanted to kill 'em all?" Kraus asked.

"Yeah . . . my way. . . . They'd have never known I was coming. . . . I'd set traps, shot them with my little make-believe silencer."

"You thought you wanted to be a one-man exterminator?"

"Yeah."

He told about joining a Civil Affairs team and ended up with a fifteen-hundred-dollar bounty on his head after capturing a North Vietnamese lieutenant. "These little guys, they carried these little crossbows, got these little bamboo things and they got poison on 'em. Wouldn't take much to shoot me."

Kraus thought, *Little guys with poison arrows?* Where will this scenario end? Will he award himself the Congressional Medal of Honor?

"We had the 155s and APCs there and different units and the helicopter pad," Shawcross went on, "and I used to walk by myself with all my gear. I used to carry it like a Boy Scout pack. What I had was a regular file cabinet with all these little tiny drawers in it for cleaning and fixing weapons. I had it inside of my knapsack, you know, the big rack on my back? The M-16 usually carried seven or eight bandoliers of ammunition, twenty rounds, nineteen rounds with a clip, seven clips to a bandolier. Sometimes carried a grenade or C-4 plastic explosives, and I'd just go out by myself . . . see what I could find."

Kraus asked, "Were you kind of a loner?"

"Yep," Shawcross said agreeably.

"No buddies?"

"No."

He spoke of the tension and anxiety that he felt when he returned home from the war. "If I see a car coming with lights on, I'd duck in the woods, I'd think, Damn, what's this car coming down the road for? There aren't supposed to be no cars on the road. I was getting paranoid."

"I take it you didn't have nightmares or dreams about your experiences?"

"I didn't have nightmares on the killing aspect. I only had nightmares on being overrun."

Kraus was dubious about such selective dreams. He asked if the nightmares were still a problem. "Not really," the killer asserted. "I know that the sessions I was taking at Green Haven for about eighteen months, they helped."

The doctor remembered reading reports that Shawcross had seemed bored with the veterans' group therapy program, failing to attend a third of the sessions and taking little part in the others. As though he realized that an explanation was in order, Shawcross added, "I was the only person in that classroom with the felony of the little girl and the little boy. The other guys in there done a lot of talking and I just sat mute, more or less."

Kraus thought, If you sat mute, how in the world were you "helped"? Another contradiction. There was no doubt the man was reworking his life material. And yet . . . there were elements of sincerity in his affect and style.

Throughout the long interview, the psychiatrist saw occasional signs of the warmth and likability mentioned in earlier reports. Shawcross was soft-voiced and unthreatening as he leaned back in his chair with his arms folded across his paunch. Now and then he displayed a sense of drollery:

Q. Do Clara and Rose know each other?
A. Well . . .
Q. They both knew you were sleeping with both of them?
A. I wasn't sleeping with Clara. I didn't get no sleep. Ha-ha . . .

But his easy manner disappeared when he wasn't creating the agenda. If he was questioned too closely, his eyes narrowed, his facial muscles began to pulse, his language turned coarse. Sometimes he flattened his feet on the floor and leaned forward as though preparing to spring. When he was asked to explain a conflict in his version of the

Gibson murder, he snapped, "Apparently you forget wha[t] the fuck I just said."

After a few tense seconds, he regained his poise. "Whe[n] I got bantered by a cop here, a cop here, a cop there," h[e] explained, "I get paranoid. . . . I can't take somebod[y] pounding me on both sides."

Yes, Kraus said to himself, and sometimes it makes yo[u] kill. The catch-all term was "poor impulse control." Clearly, the man couldn't handle his emotions. Again, th[e] question was why. What caused such a spring-loaded temper? After four hours of interviews, the psychiatrist still ha[d] no idea.

There were occasional indications that the kille[r] matched the classical sociopathic profile in terms of general lack of remorse or guilt, if not in other ways. He tol[d] about driving to Dunkin' Donuts after killing Elizabeth Gibson—"went in, got a cup of coffee and two doughnuts."

"And what were you talking about?" Kraus asked.

"Nothing special."

"Nothing special? How did you feel?"

"I just put it out of my mind."

"You can do that, can't you? And you were okay?"

"Yep," Shawcross said. He sounded as though he were discussing a traffic ticket.

At another point in the interview, Kraus asked, "You can shut feelings off?"

"I can open and close the door," Shawcross replied. "I mean anything that hurts me or gets me mad, I put it on the side." To the psychiatrist, it sounded like a textbook description of certain types of disturbed thinking. But it still didn't sound like legal insanity.

6.

Kraus and Ron Valentine held a strategy session with David Murante and Thomas Cocuzzi, law partners who had been court-appointed to defend the confessed serial killer n Monroe County. One forensic psychiatrist had already nformed the blue-ribbon defense team that their client was sociopathic but sane. Now the defense lawyers were discussing whether they should try for a manslaughter conviction, something on the order of guilty with mitigating emotional disturbance, perhaps leading to a shorter sentence, or whether they should tailor their case toward a verdict of not guilty by reason of insanity, which would mean confinement to a mental institution.

Kraus shot down the insanity idea, at least in terms of his own participation. "So far," he told the defense team, "I can't give you *any* kind of a psychiatric defense. This is a very disturbed guy, aberrant, definitely abnormal. But he hasn't told me anything that would absolve him of these crimes. As you know, our New York rule is cognitive, a rule of knowledge: Did he know what he was doing? Did he know the consequences of his act? Did he know it was wrong? The answer is yes, yes, and absolutely."

After Murante and Cocuzzi agreed that Kraus's testimony wouldn't be helpful in the ten Rochester killings, the meeting broke up. On the drive back to Honeoye Falls, Valentine asked Kraus to continue with his investigation nonetheless.

"Maybe you're right that the guy's legally sane, Dick," said the public defender. "But you're still nowheres near a diagnosis, are you?"

Kraus hated to admit it, but he had to agree.

7.

For the third time in two weeks, the psychiatrist sat across from Arthur Shawcross. This time the two were alone. After some opening chatter, the killer began to discuss Karen Ann Hill, and once again he seemed to be sabotaging his own desire to be committed to a mental hospital instead of a penitentiary.

"I kept thinking about it off and on," he said, "and I can, just like you said—photographic memory—I can just stare and just think and I can see her just plain as day, and she reminds me so much of my sister."

"Oh, really?" Kraus said. "Which sister?"

"Younger sister. Jean."

"The one that you were kind of involved with sexually as you were growing up?"

Kraus waited for Shawcross to correct him, to explain that the affair with his sister had been fantasy, as reported in several earlier interviews, but all the killer said was "Yeah."

Q. When you were with Karen—now I'm really going back in memory with you—but first you had the sexual attraction to Karen. You had sex—

A. That's when she slid down the embankment. She fell into the river, feet first. I grabbed her and pulled her out of the river and I set her up on a stone where I was sitting. And we're talking. . . . Then I started getting aroused. All noise around me ceased, the general area where we were on the bridge got brighter, just like her and I were the only ones in that area. I just picked her up, set her on my lap. She didn't say a word. I kissed her, she kissed me back. Then I just started, ya know?

Q. Fondling her, and so on?

A. Fondling her, and she didn't say a word. Then we got on the ground and I had her pants off and gave her intercourse. She didn't scream, didn't cry.

Q. Was it bloody at all?

A. Afterwards. The only thing she did was get tears in her eyes. She didn't scream or cry. . . .

Q. But you were having intercourse, or you had intercourse. And then what happened?

A. . . . The sweat, the instant sweat, all the water, perspiration. Then it's just like the light was closing into that one spot. A tunnel going dark and I just had the urge to—I was scared, why I did what I was doing. And I just grabbed her and choked her.

Q. And killed her?

A. No. She wasn't dead. . . . She was unconscious, and I laid her down and caved the bank down partially onto her. It didn't dawn on me why I didn't cover her up all the way, cover her legs and part of her face. Then I find out later, she died in the hospital.

Kraus realized that this latest version of the incident was at least partially inaccurate and blatantly self-serving. It was also typically sociopathic. Sex offenders often had problems of cognition and managed to convince themselves that their victims led them on or were otherwise blameworthy. The classical rationalization for rape was, "I only gave her what she wanted." The psychiatrist didn't believe that eight-year-old Karen Ann Hill had kissed a perfect stranger or allowed him to fondle her. The original police reports showed that she'd been penetrated vaginally and anally and died of suffocation when her face was shoved into the silt. Of course the poor child "didn't scream, didn't cry," as Shawcross claimed. She was probably dead before the rape began.

His expression bland, Kraus listened as Shawcross jumped back to his favorite topic: Vietnam. The killer suggested that his pedophilia might have started with an eleven-year-old Vietnamese prostitute and other camp followers—"That's probably where a lot of that shit came from."

After repeating a few of his well-worn horror stories, he provided another farfetched explanation of his failure to recall names: "I can't remember one person I went to Vietnam with, not one person over there. I didn't associate with anybody. I just did my job, went about my business. Sometimes I went into the jungle by myself."

He admitted that he hadn't wanted to come home from Vietnam. "You wanted to kill more people?" the psychiatrist asked.

"Yeah. . . ."

He claimed that when he returned home "I'd wake up in a sweat or I'd scream out at night and then when I finally got down where my wife was—her and I were living in a cottage that belonged to her mother and dad—I'd be having nightmares and screaming and hollering in my sleep and she'd grab me, and I'd pound the piss out of her. . . . She was a blonde. She looked like a raccoon, two black eyes. Her mother wanted me arrested and everything. The city, town cop, he says, 'Fourth of July's comin'. Go somewhere. Get out in the woods somewhere. Just get away from here.' "

Shawcross admitted that he enjoyed the challenge of hunting humans in Vietnam. "You ever find anybody?" Kraus asked.

"Oh, yeah."

"Kill some people?"

"Nope."

Kraus thought he'd misheard. Since the day of his arrest, Shawcross had bragged incessantly about his wartime atrocities. "Why not?" the psychiatrist asked.

The killer appeared thoughtful, then said, "I just wanted to scare them more than I wanted to kill anybody. I searched a lot of people. I'd step out from behind some trees or something and I'd have the M-16 pointing right at them. . . . *But I never killed them.*"

Kraus asked himself, Doesn't the guy remember from one minute to the next? Is his brain function *that* impaired?

Shawcross was already rambling on about how he would put nipples on his M-16 and "just shoot into their fire." He spoke of the efficacy of the improvised silencers and explained that he bought them by the case at the PX—"I used to take those and I'd lay there with an infrared scope next to the M-16 and I'd shoot monkeys out of the trees at night."

Kraus thought, Don't you remember calling them "my little *make-believe* silencers" last week? The Rochester PD had made tests at its firing range and found the nipples useless. But why would a killer confess the most horrifying crimes and then lie about something so insignificant? Kraus wondered if he was lying or just confused or if there was an X factor, something as yet undiagnosed. Brain damage, perhaps.

The conversation circled back to the homicides. Kraus asked, "Did the girls that you killed in any way remind you of Karen Hill?"

"Uh, most of them, if you look at their photos," Shawcross replied, "they all look basically alike."

Q. Do they look like somebody else?

A. Uh, a few of them look like Karen.

Q. And others?

A. A few of them look like my sister [Jean]. I can't say Karen exactly looked like my sister.

Q. Okay, let me ask you the obvious question at this point. Did you ever think about killing your sister?

A. No.

Q. Never?

A. I was in love with her.

Q. You still in love with her?

A. Um-hmm.

Q. Is it a sexual love that you have for her?

A. Both.

Q. If you could be with her today—your sister, that is—

A. If I was with my sister today, I'd talk it all over. . . .

For a moment, the sociopathic "mask of sanity" seemed to slip. Shawcross sniffled and turned his head.

Kraus said, "So . . . your sister is very important to you. This is the first time I've seen you have some other emotion on your face as we're talking about it." He asked what else the killer remembered about his victims' appearances.

"Some look like my mother, too," he admitted in a shaky voice.

Q. Have you ever felt like you want to kill your mother?

A. Sometimes. . . .

Q. Every try to imagine it, that you killed her? How would you kill her?

A. Strangle her, I guess. . . .

Q. Why would you kill her?

A. For what she's doing to my father.

Q. What did she do to your father?

A. The way she went after him after the letter came—Australia.

Q. Are you angry right now? You're crying. Are you angry?

A. No.

Q. What do you feel?

A. Emotion.

Q. I know. What's the emotion?

A. Getting it out.

Q. Do you think you've wanted to kill your mother for a long time?

A. Yeah.

Q. You've been aware of that for a long time?

A. Um-hmm. Every time she refused to come and see me it got stronger.

Q. Why has she refused?

A. I don't know.

Q. Do you think she hates you because of what you did? And you hate her because of what she did to your father?

A. I hate and love my mother, but I don't know. Hate takes control too much.

Q. Were you thinking of your mother when you were strangling some of these prostitutes?

A. I don't know what I was thinking. I was, you know, in a fog. . . .

Q. I kind of get a sense that you had these feelings about your mother inside of you for a long time, that you've sort of been aware of it inside of you for some time, I think. Is that right?

A. Yes.

Q. So that if you are with a woman who reminds you of your mother, that woman would be in danger, wouldn't she?

A. Kind of, yeah. . . .

Q. How would [your mother] carry herself? How would she behave toward you?

A. She was a bitch.

After a few minutes, Shawcross asked for something "to keep my nerves down."

The doctor responded, "Are you saying that going over all these things is kind of upsetting you?"

"Yeah . . . very. I thought about suicide. . . . The pressure's getting too hard."

"The pressure of being in here?"

"The whole thing. Not just being here. Why I did it."

"Tell me," Kraus said gently, "just let your thoughts go for a minute. Tell me what's running through your mind."

Shawcross lowered his head again. "I'm ashamed of all this," he said in a soft voice. "I can't believe it. One side of me, I've got this cloud inside of me and I can't understand." His voice was low, his speech pressured. "It gets too—emotional."

Once again the psychiatrist wondered what manner of man this was. Sociopathic, certainly, but with variations. Sadness, shame, guilt—such emotions were alien to most antisocials. When they exhibited feelings, it was usually an act, an attempt to influence a judge or a parole board, to fool potential victims, to gain unfair advantage, deceive, manipulate. But this hen-shaped killer with the curly wisps of gray hair wasn't faking—a first-year resident could have seen that. Slumped in the hard chair, he didn't seem to be suffering from any of the specific mental disorders set forth in *Diagnostic and Statistical Manual DSM-3R*, the clinician's field manual. He just seemed like a tired, depressed, discouraged old guy who wished he knew what the hell was going on. It wasn't easy for Kraus to empathize with a man who'd slaughtered two children and eleven adults, but if serial murderers were to be understood and explained and properly processed by the legal system, they had to be studied as human beings and not as monsters.

Still obviously distressed, Shawcross mumbled about "bad things coming out too fast."

"Coming out here?" Kraus asked.

"Yeah."

Kraus asked, "Can you bear with me while we go through this process? It's not easy. I have to tell you that what I'm trying to do with you is find out a lot about you, okay? I'm trying to answer the question why, and who you are. And doing it this way, it's going to upset you at times."

He slid a new tape into his recorder and continued. "I've wondered at times if there was some connection to all the gals that died and Karen Hill and others earlier in your life. I think obviously there is."

Shawcross told how he'd felt stigmatized in prison because of the Hill killing, and the doctor recalled reading an early report that suggested he'd seemed bored about the dead Jack O. Blake ("It was just an accident") but remorseful about the little girl.

"Well," Kraus said, as he tried to pull some of the threads together, "I think what we've got is a connection between Karen and the women who died. They remind you of your sister and they remind you of your mother. And tonight when we talked about your mother, how you feel about her . . . a lot of emotions really came to the surface. That's the first time I've seen this much emotion."

He turned to a series of questions about phobias. No, Shawcross answered, he didn't feel uncomfortable in crowds or elevators or airplanes. Nor did he ever feel threatened by his fellow man—"People talk about going to rough neighborhoods in the city. I'd be riding my bicycle through there, no problem. I make it a point of saying hi to people."

But he admitted that he had a strong need to be in control. "When I was with Rose, like, Rose, you know, she says, 'Let's go here. . . .' I said, 'We're going *here*.' "

Kraus brought up his mother again, and Shawcross said, "I think that's basically where all my problems are."

Q. In the sense that she controlled everything?

A. Yeah.

Q. She controlled your father, she controlled you?

A. She's always telling me, Don't do this. I'd do it just to spite her.

Q. Are you saying that you think your anger, your hatred over what she did to your father, has a lot to do with what's happened to you and your problems?

A. I think so.

Q. How do you see the connection?

A. Well . . . Mom's always in control of her husband, my father, the kids.

Kraus recalled earlier reminiscences about talking to imaginary friends—"I wished I had a friend." Even though Shawcross had loved his younger sister Jean and entered into a fantasy sexual relationship with her, he kept insisting that he hadn't been close to his siblings. Kraus asked, "Are you saying that you were really different than they?"

"I was kind of different from my sisters and brother," he answered. "I kept after my mother, 'Are you sure I wasn't a doorstep baby?' "

". . . Did you wonder if you were adopted and dropped off?"

"Yeah, I kept thinking about it. . . ."

Kraus probed deeper:

Q. Have you ever wondered if you were illegitimate?

A. Well, Mom was pregnant. They weren't married yet.

Q. And you were the oldest?

A. Yep. I was born June 6, '45, and they weren't marrie until November 23, '44.

Q. A little close. Have you ever wondered if your fathe was really your father?

A. Yeah. . . . Because I looked more like my mothe than I do my father. Sometimes if I was thinner I' look like my father.

Q. Okay. So as you grow up, you're wondering if you'r really, if your father's really your father, if you're reall part of the family and may have been adopted?

A. I ain't like the rest of the kids.

8.

Richard Kraus didn't consider himself a doctrinaire disciple of Sigmund Freud (although a pencil sketch of the Viennese master hung in his cramped little study, along with drawings of Carl Jung, Adolf Meyer, and Harry Stack Sullivan), nor was he a slavish follower of a particular school of psychiatry. "I'm an eclectic," he liked to tell his patients. "Whatever works, works. I use a realistic approach."

One of his earliest successes was a severely depressed woman who complained that her husband, a former U.S. Marine drill instructor, treated her like a recruit. Kraus interviewed the husband and suggested that he "stop acting like a DI."

"I didn't see my patient for about a year," Kraus recalled. "I figured she was annoyed that I'd sounded like Ann Landers. But it just seemed like the right approach."

Then he bumped into the woman at a lunch counter. "Thanks," she said. "You saved my marriage. He's been a pussycat ever since."

9. RICHARD KRAUS

Some cases can be simple. Sometimes if you intervene early and decisively, you don't have to wait years for a cure. And sometimes you can work on a case till you're blue in the face and get nowhere. Of course, it helps to know what the hell you're dealing with. The most frustrating situation is when all sorts of data jumps up and hits you in the face, but it never comes together into a cohesive diagnosis. All you need is a couple of pieces of the puzzle—and you can't find them and don't even know where to look. That was the Shawcross case.

I was going home after that third interview, February 8, 1990—a dark night, patches of black ice on 390S. I'm driving along in my old blue T-bird and thinking, The guy says over and over that he's different. He says he's always felt different. Well, he sure as hell is. But . . . what made him that way?

I stuck the tape of our interview on my car radio and listened to that sad, heavy tone. No doubt about it, his early life added up to a hell of a lot of alienation—imaginary friends, playing alone in the woods, running away, friction with the neighbors and his classmates, being tagged as "Oddie," bored with school. . . .

As I listened, I noticed his tendency to go silent, to ignore questions he didn't feel like answering. Somewhere I'd read that other interviewers thought he might be mentally ill or dissociative because he shut them out. To me, it just seemed like a lack of social graces. If he didn't feel like talking, he didn't talk. If he didn't feel like answering, he didn't answer, especially if it wasn't in his self-interest. I found nothing odd about that, nothing pathological. It couldn't even be called a neurotic symptom. Most of us would be better off if we kept quiet when we had nothing to say. On a primitive level, the silences seemed reasonable.

I kept wondering how to get a handle on the guy. He presented so differently, said so many things about his life that were contradictory, confusing, vague, misleading. And yet he seemed open with me. He wanted to talk about his

mother and oral sex and Vietnam and sexual fantasizing a
a child and fending off sodomists in prison and everythin
under the sun, and it didn't hang together. In the leg
sense, he kept digging his hole deeper. Other antisocial
constantly rationalize their behavior, and so did he, bu
only to a degree. Or they deny—"You got the wrong mar
officer." Or they blame society, relatives, teachers, cops—
and he did some of that, too, especially about his mothe
But he didn't do it in the way you'd expect. He seeme
genuinely upset about her, genuinely disturbed. He didn'
seem to be using her as a cop-out or an alibi, at least in th
early stages of our interviewing.

By now I'd spent seven or eight hours with him, and stil
. . . no diagnosis. He continued to show no evidence o
multiple personality, dissociation, epilepsy, schizophrenia
PTSD, or any specific mental disorder. We CAT-scanned hi
brain and found no gross abnormalities, certainly nothin
to explain his behavior. X rays for shrapnel were negative
He seemed to be a normal physical specimen.

As I listened to his droning voice on my car radio, I had a
nagging feeling that there was something else about th
guy, something that no CAT scan or interviewing coul
uncover. I remembered some of the stuff I'd read abou
him: school report cards, psychological tests, prisor
records, interviews with his relatives. What unusual thing
he'd done! Screwy arsons, bungled burglaries, igniting gun
powder on his desk, dumping a child in a barrel, carrying a
tire iron on the school bus, busting through a front doo
like a cartoon character. Odd, eccentric, inexplicable.

I couldn't see a pattern beyond the obvious one that he
was polymorphous perverse, in Freud's phrase, with a
child's emotional mentality and an adult's hormones, complicated by a terrible shortage of impulse control. But those
are *symptoms,* not causes. I couldn't think of anyone to compare him with. He'd had behavioral problems since he was
six years old, and yet there was no indication anywhere tha
his sisters or his brother or his parents were anything other
than upstanding members of society. My God, he'd had his

first mental-health eval at seven! He was *very* different *very* early.

I fast-forwarded the tape and heard him say, "I ain't like the rest of the kids." It didn't sound contrived and it didn't sound phony. It sounded like a sincere statement of fact based on forty years of bewilderment about his own behavior. "I'm just *different*"—he'd made that point in five or six different ways.

I was pulling into my driveway when it occurred to me that there might be a clinical significance in his repetitive use of the word "different." Maybe he was intuitively correct; maybe he was manifesting a visceral wisdom that went beyond my years of psychiatric training. I thought, Does something about his *biology* make him act so odd? Or is it a mix—biological, mental, environmental, maybe other causes?

I thought about the man who supervised my psychiatric training in Baltimore—Leo Bartemeier, a distinguished psychiatrist, past president of the American Psychiatric Association, a teacher and scholar of great influence. He'd been an internist before he was analyzed, and he always emphasized that it was important to learn everything you could about your patient, including the complete medical background. Assume nothing! Overlook nothing! Not even an oddly shaped toenail or a childhood case of mumps.

Toward the end of my training in Baltimore, I'd been having a hell of a time trying to diagnose a young woman—very manic, excited, delusional, hallucinated. Just plain wild. She was hypersexual and wanted to have intercourse, but Dr. Bartemeier had already provided some sage advice about *that* problem: "Tell your patients it may be fun, but it's bad therapy."

A couple of days after the woman was admitted, I was presenting her history and mentioned that she'd recently had an upper respiratory infection. Dr. Bartemeier took a long puff on his cigar and said, "Dick, make sure she doesn't have meningitis."

She did, and it explained her symptoms. She died in three months. If it hadn't been for Dr. Bartemeier's advice,

I'd have wasted that time looking for the psychological origins of her illness while she was slowly dying of organic brain disease. I always remembered that case.

Later I was influenced by George Engel, another fine psychiatrist, a professor at the University of Rochester. In 1963 he published a book on the psychological correlates of disease, a timeless contribution to medicine. He called his concept the "bio-psycho-social approach." With Engel, it wasn't a matter of nature versus nurture; it was nature *plus* nurture plus anything else of significance. It was another way of saying what Bartemeier had said: Look for *everything*.

I thought about taking Engel's bio-psycho-social approach to Shawcross. What choice did I have? Nothing else was working.

I decided to start at the beginning, with genetics. I wish I could say that I used a very sophisticated, polished set of academic criteria to arrive at that conclusion, but I didn't. It was a feeling, a hunch. Something crucial was missing from the mass of data we already had; maybe it would show up in the genes and chromosomes. I'd never taken the genetic approach with a criminal, but I'd never confronted a diagnostic problem like Shawcross.

I called a friend at St. Mary's Hospital and learned that the University of Rochester Hospital had a cytogenics lab that did genetic testing. I got in touch, but they refused to get involved on the excuse that there was no guarantee they could protect the chain of evidence; i.e., that the samples they tested were indeed from Shawcross. It sounded like double-talk, public relations. In Rochester, Shawcross was Godzilla and the case was just too hot to handle.

I checked around and couldn't find anybody else in Rochester who did chromosome analysis. I felt no urgency. The first murder trials were six or eight months away, even without the usual legal stalling, and I needed to draw together a lot of anecdotal and statistical material and other data. I jotted down "chromosome studies" in my appointment book and headed back to the Monroe County jail.

10.

Once again, Shawcross seemed eager to talk. By the time of this fourth visit, on February 15, 1990, six weeks after the arrest, he'd confided his mental-illness strategy to his wife Rose and his girlfriend Clara Neal. He hinted that he would practice his act on visitors.

But in this late-afternoon session, he seemed to be making an exception of the psychiatrist and providing fairly straight answers, although there were a few hints of outlandish claims to come. His main interest still seemed to be to figure himself out, a goal shared by Kraus.

Asked how he was disciplined as a child, he said simply, "Mom would hit me with a broom. My father would chase me with a belt and I'd be running like hell and he'd be laughing and I'd trip and that would be it."

To the question of whether he was punished more than his siblings, he answered, "Probably," and then, after a thoughtful pause, "I think I was punished equally." To Kraus, the responses sounded honest, reasonable. They were also another sign that he wasn't a mere psychopath; most classical antisocials wallowed in the role of victims and enjoyed blaming their parents.

The killer still seemed preoccupied with his mother; his childhood memories made it sound as though the two of them had been the only residents of Shawcross Corners. Kraus had already taken note that his dramatizations of childhood seldom offered more than walk-on roles to friends or other members of the family.

He asked, "Your mother, would she yell at you a lot?"

"Oh, yeah," Shawcross answered. "All the time . . . She'd scream and holler. Call me dummy, stupid. . . . Dumb bastard, son of a bitch. Whatever else, she would say in Greek."

"Would she talk the same way with your sisters or your brother?"

"Sometimes she'd be screaming at them, too."

"Did she ever call them a bastard?"

"No. Usually a son of a bitch."

"They were son of a bitches?"

"Yes."

"You were both a son of a bitch *and* a bastard?"

"Yeah . . . Then I kept thinking I was a doorstep baby. I didn't act like the rest of the kids."

There it is again, Kraus said to himself. That same feeling of separation from the others, of being different. He asked, "Did you resemble each other at all?"

"Sometimes," Shawcross said. "Like now, I might look like my father. Growing up, I'm taller than anybody. . . . I think everybody in my family is type O blood and I got type A blood. . . . I remember Mom and Dad got married and she was eighteen and he was twenty-three or something like that. . . ."

Kraus asked, "Did you get the feeling that she cared about you?"

Shawcross hesitated. "She always said she did. She'd love me one minute and beat me up the next minute. She'd go around telling me, 'Don't do this' and I'd do it. . . . She'd tell me, 'Don't go down in the field' and I'd go down in the field. 'Don't go out in the woods' and I'd go out in the woods. 'Don't go down to the swamp' and I'd go down to the swamp—and almost drowned."

He confessed to wetting his bed till he was thirteen or fourteen, thus providing the third component of the "homicidal triad"—arson, cruelty to animals, and enuresis—that was believed by many criminologists to presage criminal behavior. Kraus was less certain about the magic formula, although the indicators seemed to apply to Shawcross.

He claimed that his mother's sister "Tina" had introduced him to oral sex when he was nine or ten.* He talked about cunnilingus with his sister Jeannie and once again reported it as reality, not fantasy. And he said that he still loved his first wife, Sarah.

Kraus asked if he was a proud man. Shawcross answered,

* It developed later that his mother had no sister Tina, whereupon Shawcross claimed he was thinking of a cousin or another relative.

"Yeah. . . . I'm proud of the achievements I've made on the outside, but I'm very ashamed of what happened to me."

My God, the psychiatrist said to himself, you're talking about *achievements*? It seemed another confirmation that the Shawcross brain didn't function the same as others. Could there be a less appropriate word than "achievements" to characterize a lifetime of crime and misbehavior?

The two men turned to the specifics of the murders:

Q. Which two did you cut now? Stott was one . . . ?

A. Yeah, I know, and Cicero was another one.

Q. How did you cut Cicero?

A. I cut her with like a saber saw.

Kraus had read the police reports and knew that Cicero had been strangled; days later, her frozen body had been slightly mutilated, but apparently no body parts were missing. He asked, "Where did you cut her?"

"Between here and down to here," Shawcross said, drawing an imaginary line from his abdomen to his crotch.

Q. Belly button to vagina?

A. Cut her open.

Q. Opened her up?

A. I just cut—she was froze—I cut this way and this way.

Q. Why did you cut her?

A. Ate it.

Q. *I'm sorry?*

A. Ate it.

Q. What do you mean?

A. Ate it. Women! Ate it.

Q. Ate what?

A. The vagina.

Q. After she was dead?

A. Yeah. She was there four days.

Q. You went back? You cut her down to the vagina, and then you ate her vagina? Like oral sex, or you actually ate it and swallowed it?

A. Ate it.

Q. Chewed it up? Swallowed it? Cannibalized it? The sexual part of her?

A. Yeah.

Q. . . . Did you roast it?

A. Naw. Ate it raw, cold, frozen, driving down the road.

After the interview, Kraus felt sick. Even for a professional who'd dissected cadavers in medical school, the revelation was hard on the stomach. He phoned Ron Valentine and recounted the details.

As usual, the lawyer asked, "What do you think, Dick?"

"I don't know what to think," the psychiatrist answered. "It sounds like he's trying to convince me he's insane. I need to see the autopsy reports."

"You still don't think he's nuts?" Valentine sounded a little incredulous.

"No," Kraus said. "It's still too early to tell."

11.

In a fifth session a week later, Shawcross once again cast himself as a jungle avenger. "I had an interpreter tell me one day," he recalled with gusto, " 'There's a ghost out there in the jungle, and he's raising hell.' And I chuckled, 'That's me!' "

Kraus realized that the killer was repeating himself, with minor variations. The female hip that he'd roasted and eaten had now become a breast. His techniques of warfare varied, and his descriptions of time and place were different from earlier versions. He told about inserting a fire hose into a Vietnamese prostitute's vagina and blowing off her head, an anatomical impossibility. And once again he related the implausible story of the Vietcong spy who was tied to two trees and split down the middle with a machete, trying to hold herself together and spitting at her captors till she died.

The doctor scribbled on his notepad, "As talks, sense he presents with a mix of lies, distortions, memory lapses and deliberate unwillingness to talk about certain events."

There'd always been a fanciful tone to the Vietnam memories, but now they were beginning to sound like plain old-fashioned ravings. Kraus thought, Is it possible that he believes this bullshit? There was a phenomenon known as retrospective falsification in which a person revised his life experiences and came to believe the new version. In this case, it seemed possible but unlikely. Once again the psychiatrist asked himself if there might be something seriously wrong with the man's brain.

As the interviewing continued, the possibility of a psychiatric defense faded. Whatever was wrong with the killer, it was obvious that he'd been aware of what he was doing. He was asked how long it took to strangle his victims, and he said he always took five minutes.

"Why five minutes?" said Kraus.

"Because people can hold their breath for four."

Such thought processes effectively ruled out an insanity defense under New York law.

Ron Valentine accepted the latest evaluation with reluctance. The highly competitive public defender had a strong sense of justice, but he preferred to win his cases on facts rather than tactics.

"Are you sure there's no posttraumatic stress?" he pressed. Since the Vietnam War, PTSD had been a popular defense in criminal trials.

"Ron," the psychiatrist answered, "he has none of the symptoms."

12.

In a sixth interview two weeks later, Shawcross spoke intimately about his overactive sex life. If he was telling the truth, he'd spent nearly three years in a frantic attempt to ejaculate, and he'd achieved one success, during anal intercourse with a prostitute behind Tent City—"I don't know if it was a tighter fit or what, but I did have an orgasm. And I gave her twenty-five dollars and I went and bought her groceries." It was typical of his discursive answers.

Toward the end of the two-hour session, Kraus asked again about his bad temper. With unusual intensity, Shawcross answered, "What I'm saying is, you look at me now, right? This is me. I'm easy to get along with, make friends with, happy. If something ticks me off, I'd be mean."

Q. Just like that?

A. Instant.

Q. No buildup?

A. You haven't talked to my wife yet? She could tell you. Instant mad! It's little stuff, right? And I'd let it just build and build, and sometimes I'd get in the house and I'd be so mad I'd just take a plant and smash it on the floor and I would back off, just like that. Sweep it up like it never even happened.

Q. That happened a lot?

A. Yeah. . . . I didn't want to beat up Rose. . . . The times I got angry, what did I get angry over? *Bullshit!* . . . Rose would come home and complain about her job.

The psychiatrist couldn't resist a leading question: "Were those the nights you killed a hooker?"

Shawcross said softly, "Those were the nights."

It seemed like another stunning admission. The homicidal rages hadn't begun with a prostitute reaching for his wallet or threatening to expose him or annoying him in some other petty way, as he'd claimed again and again. They'd begun with irrational anger at an important female in his life, just as earlier felonious rages had begun after arguments with his mother or his ex-wives.

Kraus noted that the killer never mentioned any such blowups with males. He voiced hardly any memories of his father and brother, and he'd made no attempt to see his own son in twenty years. Women seemed to define his life. Who but Shawcross could describe a year of wartime service almost entirely in terms of females—spies, thieves, preteen sluts, camp followers? And who could relate in loving detail how those evil creatures got their comeuppance from fire hoses, machetes, Claymore mines, and other cruel devices? It appeared that Shawcross had spent a lifetime overreacting to women.

But did this simple observation explain his repeated homicidal rages? Had his mother and other females rubbed him so raw that the most innocuous remark set him off?

Only in the movies, said the psychiatrist to himself. Only in cheap novels. He'd treated patients with far more torturous histories, men who'd been locked in closets, battered, whipped, tortured, sexually abused from the cradle to the mental ward, and not one had become a serial killer. Something crucial was still missing from the Shawcross etiology.

When he got home from this sixth interview, Kraus placed a call to Watertown. It took him ten minutes to calm Betty Shawcross, but then she spoke for nearly an hour about her troubled son. After initial hysteria, she came across as cooperative, if somewhat defensive about her family. She admitted that little Artie had engaged in petty thievery and caused a few problems, but he'd also been a loving boy in a loving home. "We loved him then, love him now," the mother insisted. It sounded as though she were starting to cry. "He knows it, too. All those things he says about me and Jeannie and the family, he's lying. I wish I knew why."

She discounted most of the tales about eccentric childhood behavior and confirmed Shawcross's own appraisal that he'd been disciplined reasonably. "My son was treated good," she said in a pronounced New England accent. "He was *nevuh* abused."

Kraus finished the conversation with the feeling that he'd heard the essential truth, give or take a shading of denial and pride.

He phoned Ron Valentine at home. "I don't know if his mother was the best parent in the world," the psychiatrist reported, "but what are the criteria? To me, she sounded credible. She had to raise a problem child and she did the best she could. Her other kids turned out fine." Then he told the lawyer about Shawcross's admission that arguments with Rose drove him to murder.

At the end of the update, the public defender said, "So he was a nice little boy and everybody loved him. And now he's got an uncontrollable temper and hates women. Where's that leave us, Dick? What the hell's *wrong* with the guy? You're telling me what he's like, but you're not telling me what made him that way."

The psychiatrist was stymied. "Ron," he said, "I still don't know."

The two old friends agreed that the most promising approach was to analyze Shawcross's outbursts of temper. Were they the result of psychological problems? Or were there organic causes? What about nutrition? Chemicals?

They discussed a landmark case: a San Francisco politician had won a light sentence after a psychiatrist attributed his killing of a colleague to hypoglycemia caused by overindulgence in junk food—the "Twinkie Defense."

"If I'm gonna help this guy, I need something better than Twinkies," Valentine said. "Something tangible, something a jury can understand. Otherwise he just looks like a mad dog and gets warehoused for the rest of his life and nobody learns a goddamned thing."

Kraus reminded his friend of their attempts to find a lab to analyze the Shawcross genes. "I've about given up on that angle," he told the lawyer. "The way our New York law's written, I don't think it would help you anyway." He said it might be useful if a skilled psychologist tested the killer for baseline data on intelligence and personality, supplanting the mishmash in the files from school and prison. Valentine replied that the testing had already been ordered by the Rochester defense lawyers.

In March 1990, a copy of the psychologist's report turned up on Kraus's desk. Among his findings, James R. Clark, Ph.D., had taken note of the killer's "truly amazing failure to look at what he is doing," and certain repeated themes of sexuality, "evil" women, and mixed emotions about his mother. The psychologist's conclusions seemed to verify earlier insights about Shawcross and his attitudes toward women. Kraus was grateful. At last, he told himself, we're making a little progress.

He was eager to continue his talks with the killer, but he temporarily sidelined himself while other court-approved experts conducted their own interviews. Courteous and retiring by nature, Kraus sat in on a few of the sessions and was briefed on others. One of the new interrogators, a self-appointed "expert" on serial murder with two potboiler books to his credit, demonstrated his concern for professional ethics by attempting to peddle tape recordings of Shawcross interviews to a TV station. Kraus was appalled.

13.

By midsummer the killer had been examined by five or six behaviorists, "hypnotized" and "age-regressed," peppered with hints, questions, and ideas. His slight hold on reality seemed to grow even weaker as he jumped through the hoops of one interviewer after another. Neuropsychiatrist Eric Caine summed up later: "The more Shawcross was interviewed, the more bizarre his stories became."

Kraus wondered how to separate fact from propaganda—and if he would ever have the chance. The killer was giving the impression of being a bathetic, muddled mess who'd been so abused as a child and so traumatized in Vietnam that he couldn't be held responsible for his actions. In hypnotic sessions, he slipped with suspicious ease into trances in which he seemed to be faking the voice of his mother, usually portraying her as tyrant and torturer. In his own squeaky childhood voice, he told a defense psychiatrist that "Mom" practiced unspeakable cruelties, including sodomizing him with a toilet brush and making him perform oral sex.*

Ronald Valentine, who audited most of the interviews, described some of the sessions as "pseudo-psychiatry at its worst," "a goddamn forensic circus."

From his temporary position on the sidelines, Kraus tried not to become disheartened. In fifteen hours of head-to-head meetings with the worst killer in New York history, he'd found it difficult enough to develop a few insights, a few legitimate avenues of study. He felt that Shawcross had provided somewhat more truth than fiction in their talks. Now it seemed that the pattern was being reversed.

14. RICHARD KRAUS

It took me the whole spring and summer of 1990 to go through the boxes of material from the district attorney's office. The stuff was coming into Ron Valentine's office under courtroom discovery rules, and some of it went all the way back to the Watertown cases.

Unfortunately, it wasn't much help. There were lots of psychiatric evals and diagnoses, some contradictory, some perfunctory and useless. Stacks of interview transcripts and police files and prison reports and official documents confirmed a pattern that I'd already noticed: every time Shawcross discussed a killing, he altered the details a little.

* The friendly interrogator failed to press him on why he'd failed to make such allegations earlier, nor was he asked to explain dozens of obvious contradictions, including the fact that the Shawcross family used an outhouse at the time of the supposed toilet brush incident.

Among sociopaths, this tendency isn't uncommon—they're always upgrading their stories and fine-tuning their images —but Shawcross didn't seem to be improving things, just *changing* them. Several of his coworkers were on record that he was a "bullshitter." At the moment, it seemed as apt a scientific description as any.

I kept asking myself, Does the guy have a bad memory or is he lying? If his memory is defective, why? I thought it might have something to do with the blows he'd taken to the head, and I went back and took a look at all the tests that had been made through the years. Essentially, they showed that his brain had sustained minor damage but functioned within normal limits. There were no signs of tumors or other pressures.

I kept wondering about his genetics, but I still couldn't find a lab that did chromosome analysis. I spent a lot of time familiarizing myself with the literature on serial killers, attending strategy sessions with Ron and the other lawyers, listening to my own tapes, and trying to make sense out of the interviewing that was going on. As it happened, I didn't see Shawcross for months, and it was probably just as well. It gave me strength for what was to come.

Late in June, Ron Valentine heard about a biochemist named William Walsh and a place called the Carl Pfeiffer Treatment Center in Wheaton, Illinois. They'd been having success in treating people with poor impulse control and other behavioral disorders. Dr. Walsh suggested that Ron have Shawcross's blood analyzed for liver and kidney function, serum copper, serum zinc, whole blood lead, blood count differentials, histamine, urinalysis, thyroid panel, hair composition, and urine kryptopyrrole.

Ron asked me to write the prescriptions, and when he finished dictating his grocery list, I said, "Urine *what*?"

"Urine kryptopyrrole," Ron said.

"How do you spell it?"

"Who the hell knows? Just write the scrips so I can get a court order."

I asked the local SmithKline Bio-Science Labs to collect specimens of Shawcross's blood and urine and send them to Norsom Medical Laboratories in Harwood Heights, Illinois, as Walsh had instructed. In the process I was surprised to learn that SmithKline Beecham had a chromosome analysis lab in Van Nuys, California, so I wrote an extra scrip marked "chromosome analysis" and sent it off. I didn't know what the hell I was looking for, but I figured it wouldn't hurt to follow Leo Bartemeier's principles and check out *everything.*

That was on June 26, 1990, five months after I'd been retained on the case. Two weeks later Ron called and said that Shawcross had been put on a suicide watch. I hadn't seen him since March and had no idea how much he'd deteriorated. Ron asked me to go to the jail.

The guy looked awful, depressed. As soon as he started talking, I could see he was agitated. His arms were covered with excoriated lesions from his elbows to his wrists; he'd been picking at himself in his sleep. He was being treated with a vitamin A and D cream that didn't seem to be helping.

He said he'd been clawing at himself for months, but everything seemed to get worse on the Fourth of July. The city had put on a fireworks display alongside the Genesee River, and there were explosions above the jail. He said the noise made him tremble and shake; his head got "messed up" and he curled between the bed and the toilet in terror.

He seemed anguished as he talked, and also a little defensive: arms tightly crossed on his chest, a frown, evasive eyes. I hadn't seen that attitude before. He'd always had a tendency to look down, which is sometimes interpreted as a sign of deception, but now it seemed more pronounced. He told me that the fireworks made him remember having sex with the women he'd killed in Vietnam, but then he corrected himself and said he was referring to "the ones here." Then he corrected himself again and said he was referring to "those two girls . . . just where I butchered that one girl. I don't know why I butchered her. I cut her. . . ."

He sounded more confused than ever. Either he was in a fog or he was running a scam. He said, "Then I started thinking about the questions everyone's been asking about, Did I have sex with the bodies here? And I'm not sure." In earlier talks with me and others, he'd been sure that he hadn't.

He switched to the subject of Jack Blake. "I remember I did hit him and I think I hit him twice," he said. "Then I strangled him." He said he left the boy face up in water and leaves and returned the next day. "Like with Stott, it just happened. I wasn't sure. Then I know I cut off his penis and balls."

I tried not to show my surprise. He'd always described the Blake killing as a one-punch outburst, almost an accident. And of course the Jefferson County prosecutor had handled the case as a postscript to the Karen Ann Hill killing, as though it had no importance or weight of its own.

So I'm sitting there wondering, *Why now, Art?* Why didn't you tell me these things six months ago, when you presented so frankly? It didn't make sense.

I asked what he'd done with the severed genitalia, and he said, "Ate 'em."

I was shocked. "You think you *ate* them?"

"And I did the same thing to him I did to Stott."

"You cut him open? Did you take any organ out?"

"His heart."

I looked deep into his eyes, and for the first time I saw a trace of guile, a slyness.

I asked, "What did you do with his heart?"

"Ate some of it."

"And the rest of it?"

"Just laid it on the ground."

"Left it there? How were you feeling when you were doing this?" The psychiatrist's stock question.

He began the same old litany—how he was overwhelmed by the bright lights and the sweating and the silence. To me, it was another self-serving claim, another attempt to avoid responsibility for his acts, but at least it was consistent with what he'd said earlier. I wondered if he'd read somewhere about the auras that sometimes accompanied genuine psychotic outbursts. It seemed a rather sophisticated alibi, but I had to admit he'd been using it from the beginning.

He added a few touches to his Jack Blake story, said he'd lost touch with reality till he left the killing ground in the swamp—"I was all covered with all kinds of shit and stuff. Tried to figure what happened to me."

I asked when he'd dredged up this memory.

He said, "This all came out July Fourth, in the morning hours."

He claimed that he'd been feeling frightened and suicidal ever since. He confessed that he'd attempted to kill himself as a boy and when he was in the Army. He acknowledged that he was having problems with his fellow inmates and had been moved to a different cell. He said he'd been in a fight with an inmate named Tyrone and battled so ferociously that his opponent had screamed, "Get him offa me. *Get him offa me!*" There'd also been a few less violent encounters. He talked about being "wound up" and avoiding human contact. All this was markedly different from his earlier jailhouse demeanor. I wondered what was going on. Was he losing control or was he faking insanity? Or was it a combination of both?

I turned the conversation to the claims of childhood incest that he'd been making to other psychiatrists. In our earlier sessions, he'd described his mother as a bossy, jealous woman, a martinet, but he'd never mentioned sexual abuse. Now I said, "We talked a little bit about some of the things you claimed your mother did to you—the beatings, the threats. Do you remember anything else?"

He said, "She hit me over the head with a broom once—broke the broom."

"Did she ever do anything else with the broom handle to punish you?"

He seemed to tense up. "Don't remember," he said.

"Did she ever try to spank your behind or in any way injure your behind with the broom handle?"

Instead of answering directly, he began a little divertimento: "She cut a switch out behind the house. That hurt like hell. She had a long paddle with a handle like this, long narrow board like this, Ping-Pong paddles. She hit me with a toilet brush."

I thought, Yeah, Art, but that isn't the half of what you've been telling the others. He'd claimed that his mother rammed a broom handle and a toilet brush into his rectum. Why the two different versions?

I put the question directly: "Did she ever try to stick it up your rear end as a form of punishment?"

He hesitated, then said, "I don't remember."

"Is it possible that could have happened?"

"Possible." He was answering jerkily, impatiently, as though he wanted to change the subject, his customary technique when he was dissembling. I said, "Was she that kind of person?"

He thought for a few seconds, then said, "I can remember her giving me enemas."

I thought, Another evasion! What the hell does that have to do with my question? Every kid gets enemas, but how many are violated anally by their mothers? I figured he was lying to me or he'd lied to others, and I had a pretty good idea which. No point in pushing him any further.

He talked again about his "strange feelings" when his father and mother argued. He said his father was "so ashamed he couldn't keep his head up anymore," and added, "Many times I wanted to get rid of my mother."

He lowered his voice. "Most of the time when I think of my mother," he said, "I hate her with a passion. Only one moment in her whole damn life that she ever told me she loved me. She says, 'I love you only because you're my first-born.' "

He seemed chastened by the memory, and I was reminded that he'd cried in an earlier interview. But this time he maintained control. There was a finality and firmness in his voice: "That was the only time I had any feelings toward her. But after that, well—I just didn't want her around. Then when I got out of prison in '87 and I couldn't convince her in no way, shape, or form to come visit me—I just needed her at that moment. And she wouldn't come. . . ."

I said, "That hurt you pretty badly, didn't it?"

"Yeah. I talked to her in Delhi, New York, and cried for about three hours. I wouldn't let Rose in the bedroom. . . ."

"Did you get the feeling that nobody really cared about you?"

"Yeah. The only one that cared about me was Rose. And I still loved my family. And now—*I don't want them at all.*"

We talked some more about his short fuse and his dark moods and I asked if he understood what caused them. "I don't know," he said. "I'd fly off the handle. Two minutes later I'd be back to normal. But there were some days that I wouldn't be feeling right. I'd just get a funny feeling inside."

I asked him to describe the feeling. He said, "I knew I was getting agitated. I knew that something was coming over me that I couldn't control. And I knew at times when I was home or at a neighbor's apartment, physically I would get stronger. Why, I don't know. I just felt like I got bigger. . . . Sometimes I even got nauseated. I'd feel clammy, feel numbness in my lips and hands, fingers going numb, usually three fingertips on each hand."

I asked if he connected these feelings with the killings, and he said, "No." Sometimes, he said, he would leave the house when the strangeness overtook him. "I'd get withdrawn into myself and would walk out the door and just go up and down the streets, and [Rose] would follow me. It didn't mean nothing to me."

And when he wasn't having these odd feelings?

"I was a happy-go-lucky guy," he said.

When we returned to the subject of his sexuality, he showed a flash of his old good humor: "I haven't had a hard-on in so long, I've forgotten what it's like. I might need a string next time I pee to hold it up there."

A few minutes later his head dropped to his chest and he sounded ashamed. "The only thing that's keeping me alive right now is Rose. There are times, even when I know that she loves me, there are times when my feelings go beyond her."

"Beyond her love?" I asked. "In what sense?"

"I want to end it all."

I guess I should've been sympathetic, but even psychiatrists dislike being conned. I was becoming very skeptical about Mr. Arthur Shawcross.

Before the interview ended, I picked up a hint of one more physical symptom. The interview room wasn't brightly lit, but he kept blinking. I'd already noticed that he was more alert in shadow and shade, a typical night person. Now he said, "I'm just trying to keep my eyes open, so they don't squint." I jotted down: "photophobic." I figured it was probably meaningless, like the rest of the interview.

As usual, I briefed Ron Valentine. I'd always admired Ron for his honesty and integrity, but never more than lately. If there was one thing I'd kept hammering home, it was that the more I looked into the Shawcross case, the more I was convinced that a psychiatric defense wouldn't fly, and the Wayne County public defender's office was wasting a hundred dollars an hour keeping me on the case. Ron would always say something like, "I don't give a shit. I want to know what's going on in his brain." He also kept reminding me that I hadn't provided an answer.

We talked on the phone for almost an hour. In sum, I said, Look, we've got a guy whose behavior is influenced by something we can't understand. That's a hell of a problem right there. But on top of that, he's faking his symptoms and malingering. I don't know why. Maybe he's become contaminated by so much professional attention; maybe his head's been pulled in too many different directions. I said, "I'm beginning to think we'll never figure him out. It was hard enough when he seemed cooperative. Now that he's deliberately obfuscating, it looks impossible."

Ron said, "Look, Dick, this is the only serial murderer we'll ever meet. Let's learn everything we can about him. If it doesn't help Shawcross, maybe it'll help some other poor bastard. You don't really want to give up, do you?"

"Well, uh—no," I said. Of course I didn't.

I hung up the phone and lit another cigarette. Dr. Freud stared from the wall of my study and made me wonder how he'd have handled this case. General Beauregard wagged his tail for attention. I said to myself, What am I missing here? Where am I going wrong? In so many years of listening to troubled people, I'd never confronted such a diagnostic puzzle. I gave myself a simple quiz:

Is Shawcross a deliberate liar? *Yes.*

Is he also confused, muddled, vague? *Sure. And that makes him sound like an even bigger liar.*

Is he sociopathic? *Absolutely.*

A victim of PTSD? *Not even close.*

A victim of child abuse? *Doubtful.*

The "bad seed" of a degenerate family? *By all accounts, the Shawcrosses are painfully average.*

Brain-damaged? *Not significantly.*

By now I knew a hell of a lot about the man, but I seemed to be establishing a reciprocal corollary to the cliché that "less is more." With Shawcross, the more data you collected, the less certain you became about *anything,* including your own capabilities.

I went back to the boxes of evidence that the DA had turned over to Ron and tried to see what I'd missed. I reread Shawcross's school records plus voluminous data from his childhood. I still found it interesting that he'd maintained an "A" average through the second grade and that his family insisted that he'd been a normal, loving child who lived "a happy childhood with many jubilant occasions," in the words of his brother James. I couldn't find anything to refute the mother's claim that Arthur was loved to the point of being spoiled, at least as a small boy.

The old files also reconfirmed that he'd had major behavioral problems. After his successful year in the second grade, he'd never again achieved eighties and nineties. What the hell caused such a profound change?

I tried to form a working hypothesis. It seemed clear enough that Shawcross had been learning-disabled from the beginning, despite those early "A's." Borderline learning problems are often masked in the first few years, when school is less demanding and teachers are tolerant. By the second and third grades, the studies become more complicated; the student has to begin integrating information instead of just accumulating it, and the learning-disabled and cognitively impaired child falls behind. He might also begin acting out because of poor impulse control and poor judgment, leading in turn to more classroom problems and more maladjustment. It seemed a good bet with Shawcross.

I also suspected that by the time he was seven, his classmates were well aware of the same "differentness" that he felt about himself. He didn't even cry like the other children! He made a bleating sound that only emphasized how different he was. That would explain why they were already provoking him. He fought back, usually unsuccessfully, which led to more tension and rage. The situation deteriorated to the point where he became stigmatized as "Oddie," further distancing him from his peers.

It seemed to me that his life at home must have been equally demoralizing. Correctly or otherwise, he saw his mother as stern and rejecting, his father as an empty figure who denied him support and allowed the mother to dominate. The situation must have created a frightening sense of masculine inadequacy.

So he retreated to a fantasy world: daydreaming, cutting class, hiding in the woods, conversing with imaginary playmates, running away, creating "a new person with respect and dignity," as he put it in our talks. Thirty-five years and thirteen murders later, he was still involved in the same fantasies, denying his sense of failure and masculine inadequacy by convincing himself that he'd been a "one-man army" in Vietnam.

With these ideas, I thought I was on the right track. But the biggest puzzle remained: what made him so different in the first place? To me, that question wasn't merely central to the mystery; it *was* the mystery. All his misbehaviors seemed to follow from unknown forces that twisted and stigmatized him from his earliest years of school.

In most of our talks, he'd seemed sincere in wanting my

help, but few of his life events shed any light. Clearly he'd been "different" long before the family blowup over the Australian woman, long before the incestual occurrences (which he later recanted anyway), long before the mysterious paralysis when he was ten, long before he was first hit on the head, and long before he'd begun to wonder if he was adopted or a "doorstep baby" and wasn't really his father's son. I wondered where to turn.

On a Wednesday morning, July 18, 1990, in my sixth month on the case, I finally received the blood tests and urinalysis report from the Norsom lab. As I checked the numbers I felt a letdown. Copper, zinc, iron, histamines—one by one the results were within the normal range. Then I came to "urine kryptopyrrole: H 200.66 mcg/100 cc. Expected value 0–20."

The "H" was lab shorthand for "high," already evident from the numbers. Arthur Shawcross was carrying around a minimum of ten times the normal amount of kryptopyrrole, whatever *that* was.

My medical textbooks and dictionaries were blank on the subject. I knew that "crypto" was from the Greek word for "hidden," and "pyro" was a prefix for "fire." Could it mean "hidden fire"? (I learned later that the derivation was both Greek and Latin: "crypto" meant "hidden," all right, but "pyrrole" was a combination word meaning "fiery oil." So "kryptopyrrole" could be decoded as "hidden fiery oil.")

I phoned the Pfeiffer Treatment Center in Illinois to speak to William Walsh, the scientist who'd suggested the tests in the first place, but he was out of town. So I called my friend Jim Wesley, director of the lab at St. Mary's Hospital in Rochester, and asked for a briefing on kryptopyrrole.

He asked, "How do you spell it?" I remembered asking Ron Valentine the same question. I thought, What *is* this stuff and why hasn't anybody heard about it?

Jim did some research and called me back. "Dick," he

said, "nobody knows that word. Are you sure you didn't make it up?"

At his suggestion, I called Tai Kwong of the biochemistry lab at the U. of Rochester. After I repeated the spelling twice, Dr. Kwong said, "Nope. Never heard of it."

I asked myself, When did I pass into the Twilight Zone? Can the Shawcross mystery be explained in terms of a substance that doesn't exist?

On Monday, five days after I'd received the data from the Norsom lab, I still hadn't reached Dr. Walsh, but I found an envelope in my mailbox from the SmithKline lab in California. Their tests had shown that Arthur Shawcross's genetic constitution was abnormal; specifically, he had an extra Y or male chromosome in each cell. The scientific designation was "47,XYY."

I wasn't quite as ignorant about this syndrome as I was about kryptopyrrole. Every psychiatrist had heard about the 1961 discovery of the 47,XYY disorder and the brouhahas that followed. I didn't remember specifics, but there'd been a hell of a fight among the experts. I was pretty sure that the XYY theories had never been accepted by the American Psychiatric Association, of which I was proud to be a Fellow. As for kryptopyrrole, I still wasn't sure that it existed, except as a notation on a single sheet of test results from Arthur Shawcross's urine.

That evening I leafed through my old copy of John M. MacDonald's *Psychiatry and the Criminal*, a forensic psychiatrist's handbook. I wasn't surprised when nothing showed up under "kryptopyrrole," but there was a short passage about the other disorder. I read, "It has been suggested that males with an XYY sex chromosome complement are genetically predisposed to behavior disorders."

I thought, Behavior disorders? Gee, that's interesting.

I read on: "In 1965 Jacobs and her colleagues reported that the incidence of XYY males in a Scottish maximum-security hospital for mentally abnormal criminal offenders was higher than could reasonably be attributed to chance.

A 1968 report showed that 4.7 percent of these patients were XYY males. Almost one in three of the patients were six feet or taller. . . . The title of the first report, 'Aggressive Behavior, Mental Subnormality and the XYY Male,' might suggest that aggression and mental retardation characterize the XYY male."

I made a mental note to follow up this material, especially after I read that the percentage of XYY males in one prison hospital was twenty times higher than in the general population. Then I read, "Yet cases of socially well-adjusted men with XYY constitution have been reported, and one man had an IQ as high as 139." And there was "no evidence that the XYY male is inexorably bound to develop antisocial and criminal traits."

I thought, Who's this Jacobs? I needed to see her report. Then I learned that the 47,XYY abnormality was first discovered by a scientist named Avery S. Sandberg and reported in the British medical journal *Lancet.* I had to read that one, too.

I phoned an old friend, Dr. Rene Linares, at the VA Medical Center in Canandaigua. Rene had been my assistant and had taken over my old job of chief of psychiatry. After we talked a little about the XYY syndrome, I mentioned kryptopyrrole and drew the usual blank response.

I said, "Nobody knows about this damned stuff. Can you go down to your library and run a computer search?" I'd used that computer myself; it accessed a mass of scientific data from a whole bunch of banks. That system could *inundate* you with information.

A few days later Rene came up with some facts. Kryptopyrrole had been discovered in the late 1950s during a study of LSD-induced model psychosis. In the early '60s, Irvine and Osmond found elevated levels in the urine of schizophrenics and wondered if there was a connection. After extensive research, they concluded that the compound was toxic but not a schizophrenia marker. There didn't seem to be a hell of a lot of research after that.

Rene's computer made me feel better. Kryptopyrrole existed. At least I was out of the Twilight Zone.

• • •

I finally reached Dr. Bill Walsh on August 2. He told me that he'd heard about Shawcross's elevated kryptopyrrole from his friends at the Norsom lab but hadn't heard about the XYY finding. He asked, "Is this Shawcross a criminal?"

I was a little surprised. I said, "How'd you know?"

"Because both those conditions are associated with violent behavior."

I gulped.

He explained that kryptopyrrole was related to bile and resulted from an error in metabolism. Excessive amounts produced a condition called "pyroluria," which occurred when kryptopyrrole bound up vitamin B_6 and zinc and caused serious deficiencies. Pyrolurics functioned well in controlled settings of low stress, proper diet, and predictability, but fared poorly on their own. The condition appeared to be inherited. Walsh mentioned that one of the original kryptopyrrole researchers was the founder of the treatment center, the late Dr. Carl Pfeiffer himself. The facility treated dozens of victims of pyroluria on a daily basis. According to Walsh, most of the patients led normal lives.

I was so fascinated that I forgot to take notes. I grabbed my ballpoint pen and started scribbling. Walsh was one of those individuals whose minds work so fast it's hard to keep up. Also, he seemed to have total command of his subject. When I went over my notes later, they streamed across the page:

"Pyroluria, major symptoms—terrible behavioral problems. Such individuals unable to control anger once provoked. . . . Have mood swings, can't tolerate sudden loud noises, sensitive to bright lights, tend to be night people. . . . Usually skip breakfast. . . . Have trouble recalling normal dreams and poor short-term memory. . . . Level of kryptopyrrole in blood varies at time of day and no way of determining a pattern. . . . Any reading above 20 mcg/ 100 cc cause for concern (Shawcross 200!). . . . Sometimes lack pigment in skin and are pale. . . . Hair prematurely gray. . . . Have severely diminished ability to handle stress. . . . 'Dangerous' . . . 'The public must be protected.' . . ."

I thanked Walsh and hung up. I thought, Jesus Christ, what am I running into here? I remembered Shawcross's reaction to the loud noises on the Fourth of July, how upset he was, anguished, agitated, at odds with his jailmates, trying to suppress a feeling of violence. I remembered the way he'd reacted to the light and noise and huddled on the floor of his cell in the fetal position. Less than forty-eight hours later, we'd collected a urine specimen that was saturated with kryptopyrrole. I wondered if there was a connection.

At first it seemed a hell of a stretch. My medical instincts were classical and conservative. Like most physicians, I was skeptical about vitamin therapy and I viewed most of the claims of orthomolecular medicine as speculative and unscientific.

On the other hand, I had to admit that the symptomology was an uncanny fit for Arthur Shawcross, at least as Walsh had described it. He'd sounded reliable, but I knew next to nothing about the Carl Pfeiffer Treatment Center, and I didn't want to be suckered into accepting inflated claims. There was already enough misinformation circulating about serial killers.

I put in a call to the Norsom lab and asked for the man in charge, David Sommerfeld. He assured me that pyroluria was a real ailment and that the Pfeiffer Center was salvaging human lives by treating it successfully. He had nothing but praise for Bill Walsh and the program.

I took a long hard look at the test results. It's tempting to grab at dazzling new concepts, but it seldom produces good medicine. Besides, the lab reading was so high that I wondered if it was spurious. It wouldn't be the first time that blood and urine specimens had produced false values.

I decided to double-check. At my request, Ron Valentine went back to the judge for more test authorizations. We sent another specimen of Shawcross's urine to Norsom lab and this time they reported a kryptopyrrole level of 87.2

mcg/100 cc, lower than the first reading but still four and a half times higher than the high end of the normal range. We sent another specimen to Monroe Medical Laboratories in Southfields, New York, and they came up with an elevated value of 25.17. The Princeton Bio Center recorded a very high reading of 122. It looked as though Walsh was right, that the level varied without apparent reason. But in Shawcross's case, every reading was high. It was clear that he was walking around with an oversupply of "hidden fiery oils," plus genetic deficits as well. Walsh told me later he'd never heard of both disorders occurring in the same individual.

When all the recheck results were in, I called Ron and found him in his usual state of lawyerly impatience. The Monroe County cases were scheduled to be tried in Rochester in mid-September, a month away, and Ron's Wayne County case would follow. He was coordinating with the other defense lawyers and they were still hoping against hope for a diagnosis that would support an insanity defense.

When I filled him in on XYY and pyroluria, he asked how useful the material might be in court. I had to tell him that all my data were secondhand and I could draw no conclusions. For all I knew, I was dealing with snake oil.

He asked where that left us and I wasn't quite sure how to answer. So many things were going on. I had a full-time job as chief psychiatrist at DePaul Mental Health Services and I'd been spending a hell of a lot of time looking into the genetic and biochemical possibilities on Shawcross and also lining up additional medical tests: more CAT scans, an MRI scan, a Spect scan to measure brain metabolism, neurological exams, etc. I was hopelessly behind on my personal schedule, including the laps I tried to swim twice a day to help make up for my smoking. I repeated what I'd told Ron more than once: when I came up with something conclusive, something that met reasonable scientific standards, I'd let him know. As usual, he accepted my position with good grace.

Under courtroom discovery rules, our lab findings had to be made available to the prosecution, and First Assistant District Attorney Charles Siragusa responded by ordering his own tests at the U. of Rochester Cytogenics Laboratory. These were the same folks who'd refused to do the tests earlier; obviously they'd changed their minds about being able to protect the chain of evidence. Or maybe they felt more comfortable working on behalf of a prosecutor.

The cytogenics lab analyzed twenty spreads by G-banding and Q-banding, an exacting process. An extra Y chromosome was identified in every spread. By a count of 20–0, it appeared that Arthur Shawcross was indeed genetically different. I began to wonder if there was something to this after all.

Then I heard about a respected geneticist, Dr. Arthur Robinson, who'd once screened 40,000 newborns for the extra Y chromosome and was now following an unselected group of 39 XYY males aged ten to twenty-two. I phoned him at his office in Denver.

Dr. Robinson told me that 2,000 XYY males were born each year and there were about 120,000 in the United States. Two thirds were tall, thin, awkward, with an IQ range of 80 to 140. They were excitable, easily distractable, hyperactive, and intolerant of frustration. Fifty percent were learning-disabled (compared to 2 to 8 percent in the general population), and most suffered delays in speech development. To my surprise, he told me that in his personal experience with XYYs, violent behavior was unusual. I wondered if that might be due to the relative youth of his test subjects. Arthur Shawcross hadn't killed till he was nearly twenty-seven.

When I put down the phone, I knew I wouldn't rest till I figured out whether the extra Y chromosome and the elevated kryptopyrrole had something to do with Shawcross's behavior. But another part of me wondered if I wasn't wasting my time on nonscientific nonsense. I thought about a famous Frenchman's comment that judging men's inner motivations was an arduous undertaking and fewer people should try. And Montaigne never came up against Arthur Shawcross!

By this time there was strong pressure to put the guy away for life, even to bring back the electric chair in his honor. I'd always opposed capital punishment, but I could understand the frustration. As a physician, I viewed Shawcross as a suffering human being, and as a psychiatrist I believed that even the most distasteful human behavior could be understood and explicated. But only a totally screwed-up system of justice would have given a man like him a third chance to kill.

It wasn't long before I encountered another problem in my research: the most recent material on kryptopyrrole and pyroluria dated back thirty years. I was puzzled. Had the subject flared into prominence and then dropped out of style, like other orthomolecular fads? Had it been exposed as fakery? There were moments when I felt like an ancient scholar studying the flatness of the earth. Over and over, librarians informed me that certain reference works were out of print. I spent days in the stacks of the Miner Medical Library in Rochester, picking up yellowed old articles and trying not to sneeze. I wrote Dr. Abram Hoffer in Canada—he'd done some excellent early research—and he told me that no psychiatrist had mentioned kryptopyrrole to him in fifteen years. He referred me to a book called *Orthomolecular Psychiatry*.

Surprise!—it was out of print. I hired Book Bear in Massachusetts to run it down. They did a good job of finding that book and others, but it took months.

I was still researching when the Monroe County Circuit Court trial opened in mid-September. It would be another few months before Shawcross could be tried for the Elizabeth Gibson killing in Wayne County. I figured I still had time to get the answers that Ron Valentine and I wanted, and as usual he backed me all the way.

In the Rundel library in Rochester, I picked up some

data about pyrroles in general. An old edition of *Encyclopaedia Britannica* described them as "any of a class of organic compounds of heterocyclic series characterized by a ring structure composed of four carbon atoms and one nitrogen atom." The simplest formula was C_4H_5N. They were first isolated by a Scottish chemist, Thomas Anderson, in 1857. Pyrroles imparted a fiery red color to wood and were used in ancient dyes, which helped explain why the derivative word "kryptopyrrole" broke down to "hidden fiery oil." Pyrroles were a moderately toxic neurogenic poison and were present in some amino acids, in chlorophyll, in alkaloids like cocaine and nicotine, and in certain biopigments. In the body, they were breakdown products of hemoglobin, coming out through the liver and gallbladder.

Now that I was getting a handle on kryptopyrrole, I turned to the XYY syndrome. There was much more material, and I soon found myself suffering from information overload. I neglected my family, my practice, my dog, my lawn, my swimming pool, and my woodpile. If I'd been my own patient, I'd have said I was suffering from obsessive-compulsive disorder.

Early in my research, my eye was caught by a paragraph in the *New York Law Forum* quoting a comprehensive study of XYY criminals by Price and Whatmore in England (I've added some underlining):

> The subjects' personality problems were categorized as: extreme instability and irresponsibility, and in their criminal behavior these men do not appear to have considered any but the most immediate consequences of their acts. They have few constructive aims for the future and the plans they make are generally unrealistic. In their emotional responses, they show little depth of affection for others, and their capacity for understanding is more limited than would be expected from their level of intelligence. They display an impaired awareness of their environment, which appears at least partly to account for their inability to respond appropriately to the ordinary requirements of life. Their greatest difficulty in

social adjustment, however, resulted from emotional instability, combined with an incapacity to tolerate the mildest frustration.

I remembered the very first observation that the school principal had passed along to the Jefferson County mental health department when Shawcross was seven years old: "The problem seems to be *unreliability*." I thought, Isn't that a variant of "irresponsibility"? There were many similarities between the Price and Whatmore findings and the Shawcross symptomology.

I uncovered a lot of other material on XYY and also some references that were hedged with disclaimers and doubts. Detractors referred to "the crime gene" and acted as though the very idea was a threat to society. In 1963, a child psychiatrist named Stanley Walzer and a pediatrics professor named Park Gerald, both of Harvard, developed an inexpensive two-cell technique for kerotyping and began chromosome tests on a randomly selected group of Boston infants. Walzer enlisted the support of the Center for Studies of Crime and Delinquency and began to screen consecutive male newborns at Boston Hospital for Women. A similar study in Maryland was stopped by a lawsuit, but Walzer plowed ahead. The resistance turned hysterical: screening for XYY was "racist," "political," "unfair"; it would cause preventive detention, exploitation and manipulation of the genetically impaired and finally to social control and communism, etc. The opponents formed an organization called Science for the People (some said it was misnamed) and applied pressure. As far as I could tell, that was the end of the trail for the 47,XYY theorists, just as the study of kryptopyrrole seemed to have hit a brick wall years earlier.

The Rochester trial was in progress, and one day I read that the state's star witness against Shawcross, forensic psychiatrist Park Dietz, testified that the 47,XYY syndrome wasn't relevant to the case. Dr. Dorothy Otnow Lewis, of

New York University and Yale, the defense's sole witness, didn't seem to disagree.

The news was dispiriting. I thought, Holy smokes, did they do their own research, or are they just basing their statements on old information? It was hard for me to imagine that a psychiatrist who'd studied Ted Bundy and a nationally known behaviorist like Park Dietz could come to similar conclusions about XYY from opposite sides of the case. Was it snake oil after all? I reminded myself not to let their attitudes influence my judgment, but it wasn't easy.

At Ron Valentine's urging, I began looking into legal aspects of the syndrome, and once again the available material was skimpy. It took me months to learn that in 1968, three years after Patricia Jacobs had reported the details of the Scottish prison study, the XYY abnormality popped up for the first time as a legal defense. A Frenchman was charged with the murder of a sixty-five-year-old prostitute and claimed that his criminal behavior was influenced by the extra Y chromosome. A committee of psychiatrists found him sane, but the French jury took his genetic defect into consideration and gave him a reduced sentence.

The first American to use the defense, a twenty-six-year-old killer from New York City, didn't fare as well. His lawyers produced evidence of a connection between XYY and violence, but the prosecutor argued that he'd killed in a drunken rage and, in any case, the disorder didn't mandate criminal behavior. He was found guilty and sentenced to twenty-five years to life.

The New York case reinforced my feeling that no matter how impaired Shawcross might be, genetically or otherwise, he lacked a psychiatric defense under our law. But that bulldog Ron Valentine wasn't ready to give up, and neither was I. The next day I was back on the chase, and the next day, and the next six months after that.

Lying in bed one night, too preoccupied to sleep, I said to myself, Who the hell do you think you are? You're not an endocrinologist, geneticist, cytologist, biochemist, or orthomolecular physician. You're a clinical psychiatrist from Honeoye Falls, New York. Why the hell are you poking around in those other specialties? Then I remembered the British alpinist who'd been asked if it wasn't an affectation to spend his life climbing mountains. He answered that if someone accused him of eating olives out of affectation, his reply would simply be to go on eating olives. It made sense to me.

By now a bunch of tests had been run on Shawcross's brain, with more or less negative results. Ron and I suspected that there was more brain damage than had been documented; no one with normal brain function would distort, forget, confabulate and contradict himself the way Shawcross did from minute to minute. But his EEG readings had been in the normal range. A CAT scan showed a slight asymmetry, "normal variant." MRI scans revealed a small subarachnoid cyst, an old healed right frontal skull fracture (apparently from the discus), and a slightly atrophied and foreshortened right temporal lobe. A nasopharyngeal EEG produced "normal record, no indication of epilepsy." Other tests showed "slight loss brain substance," bilateral scars in the left hemisphere, and "reduced cerebral perfusion."

None of these separate findings showed us much, but Ron and I wondered if they might mean something in the aggregate. It took us months to arrange a computerized EEG, a relatively new tool in the study of the brain. Six nights before Christmas 1990, almost a year after Shawcross's arrest, a high-powered team arrived from the Brain Function Monitoring Laboratory in Tarrytown, New York, 230 miles downstate.

When Ron and I went to the jail to observe, Shawcross was sitting upright in a chair while two technicians attached so many leads to his head that he looked like a woman getting a permanent. Off to one side a neurologist fiddled with knobs in front of a computer screen.

I hadn't seen Shawcross in several months. "Art," I said, "do you remember me?"

He frowned. "Never saw you before in my life," he said.

I took a close look and saw the smile.

The test took an hour and Shawcross didn't budge. Once again I realized what an enigma he was. There was no question that he fell within the general parameters of the antisocial personality syndrome; no question he was a liar, an embellisher, a faker, a manipulator, and, of course, a killer. There was also no question that I would be the last person on earth to recommend his freedom; to do so would have been a monstrous act of professional irresponsibility.

But he was different from other antisocials in significant ways. He freely admitted that something was wrong with him, and he was willing to endure just about any discomfort to help us find out what it was. He'd gone through fifty or sixty hours of intense videotaped interviewing, sometimes threatening to walk out but controlling his temper in the end. He'd been subjected to one intrusive medical procedure after another—dyes squirted into his veins, radioactive tracers directed to his brain, wires threaded up his nose, his body palpated and X-rayed, his blood drawn eight or ten times, all without complaint. This was one serial murderer who desperately wanted to know what made himself tick and apparently wanted to change. Typical sociopaths are narcissistic; they're happy with themselves and haven't the least desire to alter such godlike perfection. Their attitude is that *you* must change to satisfy *them.* Shawcross wasn't that way at all.

The results of the computerized EEG arrived in mid-January 1991, a few days after the first anniversary of Shawcross's arrest. When I read them, I realized that I probably had enough data to start preparing my final report. The taxpayers of Wayne County had anted up nineteen thousand dollars for my year of work and I figured I owed Ron Valentine a diagnosis even if it was one he didn't especially want.

I stacked my research material on the desk in my study—twenty-two three-ring binders stuffed with material, twenty-four reference books, a two-and-a-half-foot pile of files and reports, and about ten pounds of pamphlets and medical journals and other material. I wondered where the hell to start. Here you had a guy who was impaired in five or six different ways, a case of behavioral beriberi. And even after I wrote everything I knew, there were bound to be aspects I'd missed.

I had a ton of work to do.

15.

Arthur John Shawcross, the psychiatrist wrote, was "an emotionally unstable, learning disabled, genetically impaired, biochemically disordered, neurologically damaged individual, psychologically alienated from significant others throughout his entire life, venting his frustration and rage, mixed with fear and defiance ('I will not do what they tell me. . . . I will do the opposite. . . .') in a lifetime of ever more violent and destructive aggression, which ultimately turned to overpowering murderous fury."

Kraus reported that Shawcross "is not normal, extremely dangerous, impulsive, unpredictable, emotionally unstable, and subject to overpowering outbursts of murderous rage and temper in those situations he perceives as personally threatening, demeaning and humiliating."

But despite the conglomeration of behavioral deficits, he was not legally insane. Nor, the report continued, did he suffer from posttraumatic stress disorder or temporal lobe seizure disorder or "a psychological dissociative disorder associated with altered mental states of awareness or consciousness."

Then what was wrong? What had turned a lonely little boy into a remorseless killer?

Kraus broke the answer into five sections. The first was titled "Psychological Findings" and drew on the examination conducted by James Clark. The psychologist had found Shawcross to have a verbal IQ of 88 (low-average intelligence); a performance IQ of 107 (average range) and a full-scale IQ of 95 (average range). The 19-point difference between verbal and performance ability, Kraus pointed out, indicated "learning disability, acting out, and likely organic brain impairment. . . . In Mr. Shawcross's case, these impairments are relevant. The learning disabled and cognitively impaired frequently 'act out' because of poor judgment, poor impulse control and limited intelligence. These tests also indicated that he has poor memory and difficulty with 'abstract' (higher level) thinking."

Kraus quoted Dr. Clark's illustrative example of how the killer's explosive temper and low frustration tolerance had caused him to lose control during the examination. "He made an angry sweeping gesture across the work surface," the psychologist had reported, "indicating he would like to . . . 'wipe it all away' . . . 'just blow it away. . . .' His anger grew rapidly and he appeared to lack the verbal skills to explain his feelings. . . . His anger was reduced to physical activity and gesturing. . . . The rapid development of this sequence of behaviors when faced with frustration, perhaps, offers a model for his behavior in other frustrating and *angry* circumstances. . . . [Shawcross] can only express his anger through physical acting out. . . ."

Kraus underscored the psychologist's observation that the killer strongly resented his mother but also felt affection and esteem. "This ambivalent hate-love feeling towards his mother, with its origins in early childhood, was first described in 1953 in the Jefferson County Mental Health Clinic records," wrote Kraus. "I believe Mr. Shawcross ultimately came to view women as either 'good,' i.e. loving, caring, reassuring, accepting, as were his wives; or 'bad' or 'evil,' i.e. rejecting, hostile and not caring (as he describes his victims). He never came to terms with this mental conflict and, as his history shows, always reacted to real or imaginary feelings of rejection, humiliation, and reactive fears of his own personal (sexual) inadequacy—'She doesn't really care'—with outbursts of incredible murderous rage, a displacement from his mother to his victims. Such a finding is not unique to Mr. Shawcross. . . ."

Under "Genetics," Dr. Kraus noted, "A finding, never previously suspected, was the discovery that Mr. Shawcross has an abnormal genetic constitution. Chromosome study revealed that he is a 47,XYY individual, a condition where psychiatric diagnoses such as antisocial personality disorder, schizoid personality and emotionally unstable personality are frequently made."

Kraus took issue with the findings of other experts in the case, noting that some had dismissed the genetic data as incidental or spurious.

"My review of the literature," the psychiatrist observed, "simply does not support such a view. . . . Mr. Shawcross's history of deviant or maladaptive conduct/behavior is consistent with the many reports linking chromosome abnormality with a predisposition to crime and violence."

He explained that the XYY disorder arises at the moment of conception. "Normally, human beings have a total of 46 chromosomes and gender is determined by the sex chromosomes called X and Y. Females have two X chromosomes and males have one X chromosome and one Y chromosome. Females are genetically described as 46,XX and males as 46,XY. These packages of chromosomes are located in every cell nucleus of the body and brain and function as 'biological computer chips' in determining growth, development and interaction with the environment.

"For reasons not yet determined (perhaps a virus, according to some authors), at the moment of conception an extra Y or male chromosome fertilizes the X-carrying egg resulting in the chromosomally abnormal genetic condition known as the 47,XYY syndrome." In other words, Arthur Shawcross was misbegotten, doomed to be different from the beginning.

The psychiatrist noted that XYY males were heavily overrepresented in prison populations and quoted an early report by Pitcher: "Studies have confirmed that the risk of maladjustment, including a propensity for crime and violence, increases when there is chromosome abnormality." Kraus added:

> An XYY vulnerability or pre-disposition to anti-social disorder is a frequently reported finding. Other studies report that the XYY male has a 10 to 20 fold increase in his lifetime risk as compared to their incidence in the population of being institutionalized in a mental hospital or prison—a risk that is not trivial.
>
> XYY males have a much higher than average rate of learning disability and are described as problem children who cause serious behavioral and management difficulties at home and school. Studies describe how "at least some XYY boys show behavioral disability that makes them not only a great problem in family management, but also *quite disparate from other family members in their behavior together* . . . ," a finding consistent with Mr. Shawcross's early life history and his own frequently reported belief that he was "different" from all of the other family members. Personality characteristics associated with these children also describe them as drifters, loners with running away behaviors who as they grow up are frequently agitated, experiencing pedophilic urges; setting fires, threatening to kill others; molesting children; stealing and exhibiting moments of sudden violence and aggression. These are all personality traits well documented in Mr. Shawcross's early and more recent life. . . .

Kraus observed that there are a hundred billion brain cells in the average human being, and "the presence of one extra chromosome in each brain cell in an individual equates to the presence of an additional one hundred billion chromosomes in the XYY male, not normally present in the XY male."

His section on genetics ended with a quotation from an article titled "Human Behavior Cytogenetics" by Dr. John Money, published in the *Journal of Sex Research:* ". . . It seems perfectly obvious that an extra chromosome in the nucleus of every cell of the brain somehow or other makes the individual more vulnerable to the risk of developing mental behavioral disability or abnormalities."

Then the Kraus report turned to the even more arcane

subject of kryptopyrrole. Since the elusive "hidden fiery oil" was all but unknown, even to professionals in medicine and pharmacology, he started with basic information:

> Kryptopyrrole is a biochemical metabolite (5 Hydroxy-kryptopyrrole Lactam) normally present in humans in either very low amounts or not at all. . . . It was first described in 1958 by Dr. A. N. Payza and in 1961 called the "mauve factor" because of the color it can impart to urine. (Ref.: Irvine et al., *Nature* 224, November 1969). Research has shown that the presence of this substance in the human body is not an artifact, nor related to diet, drugs or other substances such as coffee or tobacco (Ref.: Hawkins, *Orthomolecular Psychiatry,* 1973).
>
> The chemical structure of kryptopyrrole resembles other known chemicals that are toxic to brain function, such as LSD, but the presence of kryptopyrrole in the body in elevated amounts is not considered a sign of a particular or specific disease entity. Rather, its presence in abnormal amounts is considered a biochemical marker of psychiatric dysfunction much like the reading of an elevated clinical thermometer (Ref.: Hawkins et al., *Orthomolecular Psychiatry,* 1973). David Sommerfeld from the Norsom Laboratory says that kryptopyrroles are an indicator in very aggressive people.
>
> The source of endogenous kryptopyrrole is thought to arise from either bile pigment or an abnormality in the body's biological pathways involved in the biosynthesis of hemoglobin.
>
> The presence of abnormally elevated kryptopyrroles in humans is described as similar to another medical condition called porphyria, a well known but also uncommon disorder associated with psychiatric disturbance (emotional instability, long histories of vague nervousness and in some cases severe psychosis which looks like a schizophrenic disorder).
>
> The clinical correlates of abnormally elevated kryptopyrroles in humans are partial disorientation, abnormal EEG's, general "nervousness," depression, episodes of dizziness, chest and abdominal pains, progres-

> sive loss of ambition, poor school performance and decreased sexual potencies, all of which are found in the history of Arthur Shawcross.
>
> Abnormal levels of kryptopyrroles also correlate with marked irritability, rages, terrible problems with stress control, diminished ability to control stress, inability to control anger once provoked, mood swings, poor memory, a preference for night time, violence and anti-social behavior. . . .
>
> As a biochemical marker, elevated kryptopyrroles can identify individuals at high risk for becoming violent.
>
> Mr. Shawcross's medical and psychiatric history well document all the clinical correlates found associated with a kryptopyrrole disorder. . . .

Under "Neurological Findings," Kraus outlined Shawcross's "history of head trauma and complaints of headache, dizziness, 'blackouts,' fainting spells and violence," and cited the various abnormalities and deficiencies that showed up in scans and other brain testing. But he put most of his emphasis on the final test, the computerized EEG. He quoted neurologist Turan M. Itil, M.D., that the tests showed "paroxysmal irritative patterns in bifrontotemporal areas more in the right side," a pattern similar to that of patients with seizure disorders but something short of temporal lobe epilepsy. According to the neurologist, the CEEG testing showed that Shawcross's brain function was "abnormal."

"In other words," Kraus summed up, "a psychological test finding of 'modest organicity' is supported by these findings. Mr. Shawcross does have a neurologic impairment in his ability to reason and exercise sound judgment."

Under "Psychiatric Findings," the psychiatrist noted that Shawcross's eccentric behavior dated back almost forty years, when he "began exhibiting conduct-disordered behavior that predicted his risk for eventually becoming antisocial." At seven, "his behavior was clearly different from all the other family members . . . exhibiting the features found in genetically disordered XYY male children."

Kraus wrote that it was understandable that the immature boy "came to believe that his 'difference' from everyone else was due to either being adopted ('a doorstep baby') or the illegitimate son of his mother, with his 'real' father elsewhere and not the father he had at home. This belief was reinforced by the knowledge that he had a half sibling in Australia."

The report went on:

> Although his school record for grades 1 and 2 was good, his subsequent poor school performance from grade 3 onwards indicates problems with learning disability which is found more often than expected in XYY boys. As a result, Mr. Shawcross was less intellectually endowed to cope with his growing hostility towards his mother from whom he felt only disapproval and rejection, possibly the only basis for identification with his father. As he said, "I hate and love my mother . . . hate takes control too much. . . ."
>
> At the same time, he felt no support from his father, believed he really wasn't his father and felt no physical resemblance to him. He only felt shame and later rage at seeing his father humiliated by his mother. As Mr. Shawcross once said, "I always made the statement that I would never let a woman do that to me."
>
> In saying this, Mr. Shawcross provided some insight into the multiple murders. In each instance, "the girls" (as he calls his victims) all reminded him of his mother when they "didn't care." In contrast, prostitutes who handled him with reassurance were in no danger.
>
> Mr. Shawcross took refuge in fantasy as a means of defending himself against his feelings of masculine inadequacy, in which, even as a child, he ". . . perceived himself as a new person with respect and dignity. . . ." I believe this is the origin of the storyteller in later years in which his sense of personal failure and inadequacy were denied and replaced by such imaginary figures as the Vietnam "warrior" who committed atrocities. At the

same time, these fantasies reveal the deep hostility and anger that had come to preoccupy his inner mental life.

His biochemical abnormality (the kryptopyrrole disorder) further correlates with his diminished ability to always control his rage, once provoked, and in his case it takes very little to provoke it.

His violent behavior and fantasies to which he is biologically predisposed are also compensatory mental defense mechanisms . . . a means of maintaining control of his fears and anxieties about his own personal (sexual, social, interpersonal) inadequacies, especially when confronted by the stress of having these exposed to others. Associated with this are his alienation and "difference" from others; pervasive anxieties about his own masculine and sexual abilities; a constant desire/search for reassurance that others "cared for" him, i.e. a reassurance that he was adequate; rage when this was denied, rage as acting out to stress situations he perceived as threatening to reveal his "impotence" to others; a failed life of which he is acutely aware, and an absence of internalized standards of social norms and socially accepted behaviors as commonly understood.

A pattern that emerges is that whenever Mr. Shawcross left the relative security of a structured environment (first seen when he quit school), he was soon out of control. The structure of military life contained him, but not long after discharge from the Army, he was again out of control. The same pattern occurred when he left Green Haven. . . .

Mr. Shawcross could never live very long in the unstructured setting of community life, and I believe he feels more secure in a prison setting. I also believe he knew he was completely out of control as the homicides increased and, without conscious awareness, desired to be apprehended and returned to prison. I do not believe his presence at the Salmon Creek Bridge was "accidental."

These clinical findings, together with the observations of many others who knew Mr. Shawcross as a child and adolescent, depict a seriously emotionally disturbed individual who, contrary to usual expectations, became more violent as he grew older.

Under "Recommendations," the psychiatrist wrote:

Arthur Shawcross will adjust to the structure and control of prison life in much the same way he did at Green Haven. Prison provides external controls for individuals who lack internal controls. In this sense, prison can be seen as therapeutic. However, he is still a violence-prone individual. Such violence, when it occurs, will happen suddenly and without warning. Stress situations that may seem trivial or insignificant to others but have personal significance for him will quite likely result in outbursts of intense rage. This happened at Green Haven and will surely happen again at some future time. . . .

His problems with violence and emotional instability can be treated with one or a combination of a broad range of medications with which psychiatrists are familiar (neuroleptics, anticonvulsants, beta-blockers, antidepressants, lithium and others). . . .

Counseling, combined with a medication regimen, is superior to treatment with medication alone. . . . In addition, the Carl Pfeiffer Treatment Center in Wheaton, Illinois, recommends high doses of vitamin B_6 and zinc for the treatment of kryptopyrrole disorder. Such nutritional treatment should be provided to help him with stress control. These recommended interventions should also include periodic monitoring of urine kryptopyrrole and reevaluation of his neurologic status. . . .

My own experience in this case demonstrated the value of genetic, biochemical and neurological studies. The findings that resulted from these studies were unexpected and of considerable value in identifying previously unsuspected correlates to his violent behavior. If some or all of the various indicators referred to in this report are present in an individual, a serious warning alert for future dangerous behavior exists. . . .

Arthur Shawcross was not "born bad," but the influences which shaped his life and behaviors were beyond his awareness and control. He was born with an unusual combination of predispositions to violence. . . .

In this case, law and punishment were insufficient remedies for his violence. Mr. Shawcross's "latent projected homicidal intent" was recognized and documented before Jack Blake and Karen Hill died. That he is "a real danger to the welfare and safety of society" was also recognized and documented before the serial homicides. The very earliest warning signs of future antisocial conduct and violence occurred in his childhood. . . .

The recommendation I am attempting to make is that early recognition of future dangerousness by itself is obviously not a sufficient safeguard. But early recognition combined with a careful diagnostic evaluation of all risk factors for future dangerous behaviors and a realistic plan of corrective action/intervention offers, in my view, the best opportunity for protecting both the individuals at risk and the community.

16.

The Kraus report, submitted on April 20, 1991, went largely unnoticed, even though Ronald Valentine distributed copies to the media. A squib in the *Democrat and Chronicle* mentioned "Buffalo psychiatrist Richard T. Kraus." The Monroe County proceedings had ended four months earlier, and the public seemed sated with Arthur Shawcross and his silly claims about eating human flesh and blowing up babies.

For all the local hoopla over the trial, including daily front-page headlines and gavel-to-gavel TV coverage, it had been a laborious affair, lacking in tension or suspense, perhaps because the only real issue was whether Shawcross would spend the rest of his days in a maximum-security mental ward or in a penitentiary. At times the proceedings sounded almost scripted, a droning, passionless morality play in which the actors' roles were predefined and the outcome never in doubt.

In a bravura attempt to convince jurors that he was insane, the defendant cast himself in the role of a zombie, hands folded on his Buddha belly, chin lowered almost to his chest, green eyes narrowed to slits. Through eleven weeks of trial he remained in the same position, never speaking or moving as long as court was in session.

The state's star witness, Park Dietz, M.D., testified that the killer had "a condition currently known as antisocial personality disorder" as well as "unusual sexual desires." The California forensic psychiatrist noted that the defendant "pretends to have some kind of illness or exaggerates what he is experiencing." As a court-approved expert, Dietz collected ninety-seven thousand dollars in public funds.

The only defense witness, Dorothy Otnow Lewis, M.D., testified that Shawcross had been "hideously traumatized" as a child and suggested that he was a multiple personality. She cited "psychomotor seizures" and "brain damage to the temporal lobe [which] causes the limbic system to fire abnormally." She also diagnosed "posttraumatic stress disorder" caused by "early brutal abuse and subsequent war experiences." She was paid forty-eight thousand dollars by Monroe County taxpayers.

Richard Kraus wasn't called to testify.

The jury took six and a half hours to return verdicts of guilty on all counts. Shawcross was sentenced to 250 years. There was no trial in Wayne County.

On Kraus's recommendation, medics at the Sullivan Correctional Facility in Fallsburg ordered extra vitamin B_6 and zinc for their newest lifer, and after a few months Shawcross claimed that the therapy was helping to "calm me down in temper." But in the hurly-burly of the crowded prison, the supplementation was soon cut back, then eliminated. The killer wrote that he was feeling angry again.

17. RICHARD KRAUS

Friends asked me how I felt about the guy after it was all over. Well, I liked a lot of things about him, but I didn't like what he did. He could be quite engaging—wry, humorous, alert. He loved to bullshit with the boys, drink coffee, fish and hunt, flirt with waitresses. With all his physical and mental problems, he tried to be a regular fella, not unpleasant at all.

I also remember him as a pathetic creature—never had a future, lived in the here and now and in his fantasies. He had a deep inner need to be Rambo, killing the enemy, barbecuing their women. I'm not sure he could have survived without that belief. It was his "accomplishment," as he put it.

After I wrote my report, I was drawn into conversations with a few of my colleagues in psychiatry. I told them it took me fifteen months to *begin* to understand Shawcross and a twenty thousand–word report to explain what I'd learned, and I still wasn't completely sure of my conclusions. I emphasized all the things we still didn't know about him and probably never would. I stressed that he didn't become a serial killer only because of kryptopyrrole or his extra Y chromosome or only because of certain specific psychological or neurological deficits or only because he'd formed a sociopathic carapace as an outcast kid. He killed because of a matrix in which all those factors existed, and maybe more. It was the *package* that turned him into a killer, starting with a quirk of conception.

Well, who can fathom every detail of our behavior? Tennessee Williams wrote in a stage direction, "Some mystery should be left." He needn't have worried. In any study of human beings, there's bound to be some mystery left.

I'll always be troubled by the Shawcross case—the loss of life, the suffering of the victims and their loved ones, and every bit of it avoidable. From childhood on, so much was known about him. There were bells and whistles all the way back to the second grade, maybe earlier. In prison, experts repeatedly warned that he was dangerous. A few tests would have shown why.

My biggest hope is that people will learn from this case. What if you had a six- or seven-year-old kid who was acting like "Oddie"—compulsive, violent, unresponsive, a wild thing in your living room? Wouldn't it be worthwhile to run some tests? And if the tests showed the same general profile, wouldn't it be worthwhile to follow that child closely and provide some extra guidance and counseling? Wouldn't that make a difference? *Couldn't it save lives?*

I keep thinking, What a *pathetic* story. Jack Blake and the cinders in the soles of his feet. Karen Ann Hill and her rabbit. So many victims brought together by illness: the prostitutes, some with mental problems, some with AIDS, working the street for pimps and habits. And they all converged in a gray little plexus of misery and unhappiness, illness, poverty, addiction, despair.

So it's a story of many things, but isn't it mostly just sad?

EPILOGUE

1.

Helene Hill lost most of her pictures of her murdered daughter Karen in a fire. The few that survived were blackened around the edges and kept in a sealed Baggie, along with a charred funeral notice. The packet gave off a faint odor of burned flowers.

"I can smell every petal," the mother said, "especially the roses and carnations." She acted relieved when a visitor registered the sweet dusty odor and nodded.

"Oh," she said anxiously, "you smell it, too? It's not just me?"

2. HELENE HILL

Karen would be in her late twenties if she'd lived, but to me she'll always be eight years old. Her murder is still real, still frightening. I've been fearful ever since the night Father Doste told me she was dead. I rush home from work and slam my door. When I'm inside, nobody can hurt me, nobody can touch me.

I don't believe in heaven and hell, but I have the notion that Karen's waiting for me. I don't know where. I don't know if we're gonna be able to look at each other or I'll be able to hold her on my lap and tell her that I love her. Maybe we'll just be two souls together. But I *will* see my baby again.

Yes, I wish Arthur Shawcross was dead. I wish he'd never brought me this agony. I feel so sorry for the families he hurt. When I saw a newspaper article about the cruel things the North Country people were doing to his parents, I couldn't get the mother off my mind. I was thinking, She's another victim, just like Karen. So I got the phone number from Information and called.

As soon as she answered I heard the hurt in her voice. She said, "Are you another reporter? I have nothing to say. You've got to leave me alone." She was crying. I thought, That must be all she does these days—sit around and cry. My heart was beating so hard.

"Mrs. Shawcross," I said, "I'm not a reporter. I'm Helene Hill."

"Who?"

"I'm the mother of Karen Ann Hill."

She sobbed and sobbed and sobbed, and so did I.

I said, "I did *not* call to give you any more pain. I've been thinking about you all day."

She said, "Oh, my dear, how terrible this must have been for you." We both cried some more.

Then her voice stiffened and she said, "I've had reporters call me and try and fool me. Is this really you, Mrs. Hill? *Is this really you?*" She was breathing so hard she could barely talk. I found out later she had heart trouble.

I said, "Yes, it's me, Mrs. Shawcross. I probably should've called you years ago, but I couldn't."

She said, "Oh, no, my dear. I should've called *you.*"

I said, "I wouldn't have been ready. I was numb all those years. But don't think I haven't thought about you and your family. I know the torment you've gone through."

She said, "I know what it is to lose a child."

She sounded wiped out. She said she saw Art's victims in her dreams and it kept her from sleeping. She and her husband had to keep their shades pulled down. People played dirty jokes and pranks, even made midnight phone calls—"Raised any killers lately?" Nasty remarks were passed in stores, and they had to do their shopping twenty miles away, where they weren't known. Relatives and friends cashed checks for them. Mr. Shawcross waited till no one was in sight before collecting their mail. Whenever he worked on the car, he hid behind a blanket.

As she's telling me all this, I'm thinking, These people

have served a longer sentence than their son. I couldn't understand why Watertown didn't show more compassion toward them, why they didn't just come together in love. My family and friends in Rochester were what kept me alive all those years. I'm *so* lucky I'm from here. Rochester holds a lot of love in its heart.

She started to cry again and I told her, "I want you to know that never for a second did I have any bad feelings toward your husband, your other children, any of you."

I gave her my address and phone number. I said, "If anytime you want to talk to me, just call. We don't have to talk about the . . . incident. We don't have to talk about your son or my daughter. Whenever you feel like talking, I'm here."

She sounded so grateful. I'll bet she thanked me five times.

She wanted to know if I'd seen her son's girlfriend, Clara. I told her, "Only on television."

Her voice turned sharp. "Well," she said, "I don't know why that woman was calling my home. I wouldn't talk to her." Then she asked, "Did you see Arthur on TV?"

"Yes."

She moaned and said, "You saw him? He looked terrible. My son looks like an old man. I was shocked. Look what prison did to him." She sounded so tired, so hurt, but still concerned about her son! He'd told all those terrible lies about her and the family in the newspaper—incest, beatings—and yet she still loved him so much that she couldn't stop crying.

I worried about her. I said, "Mrs. Shawcross, are you alone?"

"No," she said, "my husband's here."

She was crying so hard, I thought she might have convulsions. So I just said good night and told her I hoped she felt better.

A month or two later somebody who knew Mary Blake thought it might be a good idea for the two of us to meet.

They drove her from Watertown to Rochester, and the minute I was introduced, I knew something wasn't right. We hugged each other and she said, "I've been trying to find you for years."

I told her I would've been in touch but I couldn't handle it.

She sits next to me, grabs my hand and says, "Arthur Shawcross never murdered your daughter." She had this glint in her eye.

I said, "What?"

I made her repeat three times. Then I said, "Mrs. Blake, who told you this?"

She just said, "Never mind, I *know*. It was a teenaged boy that murdered your daughter."

I was shaking. My insides were coming loose. I wondered if she could possibly be right.

She asked if Karen had been mature for her age. She said, "Were her titties in bloom? Did she have hair on her pelvis?" I thought I was gonna be sick.

I decided to get to the bottom of this fast. I stood up and said, "Would you come with me, Mrs. Blake?"

I drove her to the nearest police station so she could tell her story. I still wasn't sure what she knew.

A nice officer took her in a room and interviewed her. After he made a telephone call, he took me aside and said, "Get rid of this woman, ma'am. The Watertown PD knows the Blakes. They're always in trouble."

I got away as fast as I could. I was shaking. It revived all my memories, all my fears. I didn't go to work for two days.

3.

Not long after the meeting with Helene Hill, two of Mary Blake's daughters were caught shoplifting meat from the P&C Market in Watertown. Mary was charged with receiving stolen property. An article appeared in the *Watertown Daily Times:*

SLAIN BOY'S MOTHER, SISTERS
CITED IN SHOPLIFTING SCHEME

The matriarch explained that they'd run out of food at home and hadn't eaten in two days. It was a frequent problem. The insurance check from her husband's death came to $375 a month, and even with food stamps and welfare she was hard-pressed to feed three generations of Blakes.

4. MARY BLAKE

Those damn police bust in here and I asked 'em who the hell do you think you are? They twisted my arm and handcuffed me. Mary Agnes Blake, Public Enemy No. 1!

My lawyer told me the shaplifting charge was really because of Shawcross. The local police wanted to get in on the publicity, roit? The prosecutor asked me to plead guilty to possession of stolen property, but I woultn't do it 'cause I din't know about no stolen property. Meat's meat, ain't it? How could anybody prove what parts were stolen and what weren't?

We were held all night and released on bail. The caps warned me I could get a year in jail. What's my family gonna do while I'm gone? How would they eat? We paid fifty-dallar fines for disorderly conduct. I'm still waiting for an apology.

After that set-up, I went a little easier on my kids. If murder wasn't a crime in Watertown, how could it be a crime to steal? How could it be a crime to take food when you din't have no other way to eat? I turned against the law; I just din't have no use for 'em.

I use to lecture my kids against stealing. Nat no more.

5.

Like Helene Hill, Mary Blake planned a reconciliation with her murdered child. "I know Jack's not dead," she explained. "But if he is—well, I'll join him when I die. I *know* I will. Whatever happened, I don't believe Jack felt any pain. I think your spirit leaves your body in a gentle, *loving* way."

Despite her difficulties, Mary maintained her steadfast belief in the healing powers of love. She could recite every kindness ever done for her and her family since the days when she'd picked trash with her mother on the sulfurous slag heap.

"You shoulda been here in the blizzart of '77," she said, clapping her hands. "Folks showed such love. Snowmobiles brought us food, the stores airlifted groceries. It was *great.* I woultn't mind having another blizzart like that one, bring out so much love between people. And nobody lyin' to each other about little boy human beings."

She recalled the love affair with her dead son's wealthy father and recited his phone number.

"I haven't called him in eighteen years," she said, her fingers drifting over her phone dial. "I just want to ask him, 'Bob, are you *sure* you don't know what happened to our little boy?' " She lowered her voice. "What happened was, I think Bob took Jack somewhere and din't want his wife to know."

Since Mary was no longer convinced that the bones and hair delivered to her by the authorities had been her son's, she stopped visiting his grave. It was on an outer edge of the North Watertown Cemetery, squeezed between "Leland B. Parker" and "William L. Howard" and marked by a bare metal rod that stuck up a few inches.

"There use to be a little nameplate," Mary explained. " 'Jack O. Blake, 1961–1971.' Somebody stoled it for a souvenir. To me it's another sign Jack was never buried there in the first place."

• • •

Early in 1992, Mary presided over a series of unexpected events in her drafty flat above the Italian restaurant. Despite the long hours she spent staring out the front window, her murdered son failed to reappear. But in one of those inexplicable sea changes that make family life so unpredictable, her alcoholic male companion kicked his habit and made it stick; her son, Little Pete, followed suit and looked for work; other family members swore off drugs and shoplifting, and Mary's youngest child, twenty-five-year-old Pam, enrolled in a school of cosmetology. The Blakes looked forward to something refreshing and new in their history: a cash flow.

The years had taught the matriarch to take a balanced view of unfolding events and expect no miracles. "You never know what's gonna happen tomarrow," she philosophized. Her brood might become law-abiding or return to stealing; she was prepared for either eventuality. But for the first time since little Jack had left for good, she felt encouraged. There was promise. There was hope.

Coming
October 6, 1993
KEN
FOLLETT
A DANGEROUS
FORTUNE
The new hardcover
from Delacorte Press
Delacorte
Press